P9-DWA-259

JACL
IN
QUEST OF JUSTICE

Best wishes,
Bill Hosokawa

Other Books by Bill Hosokawa

EAST TO AMERICA
(with Robert A. Wilson)

THIRTY-FIVE YEARS IN THE FRYING PAN

THUNDER IN THE ROCKIES

THE TWO WORLDS OF JIM YOSHIDA

NISEI

THE URANIUM AGE

JACL

IN

QUEST OF JUSTICE

BILL HOSOKAWA

WILLIAM MORROW AND COMPANY, INC.

New York *1982*

Library of Congress Cataloging in Publication Data

Hosokawa, Bill.
JACL in quest of justice.

Includes bibliographical references and index.
1. Japanese American Citizens' League—History.
2. Japanese Americans—Social conditions. 3. Japanese Americans—Politics and government. 4. Japanese Americans—Economic conditions. I. Title. II. Title: J.A.C.L. in quest of justice.
E184.J3H6 973'.04956'006 81–22576
ISBN 0–688–00994–8 AACR2

Printed in the United States of America

First Edition

1 2 3 4 5 6 7 8 9 10

BOOK DESIGN BY MICHAEL MAUCERI

Dedicated to Mas and Chiz Satow and others of like spirit who gave so unstintingly of themselves to the Japanese American Citizens League. Many, unfortunately, could not be recognized within the limitations of this volume.

Preface

For twenty-five years Masao W. Satow served as national director of the Japanese American Citizens League. He died March 3, 1976. Those who had been beneficiaries of his dedication to JACL felt a need to honor his memory in some lasting way.

A year after Satow's death, on March 5, 1977, JACL headquarters in San Francisco was renamed the Masao W. Satow Building. On that same day a committee to find a way of honoring Satow, headed by his friend and longtime colleague Mike Masaoka of Washington, D.C., met for the first time. Others present were George Inagaki and Harry Honda of Los Angeles, Bill Matsumoto and Jerry Enomoto of Sacramento, Charles Kubokawa of Palo Alto, Hi Akagi of Alameda, Tad Hirota of Berkeley, Yone Satoda, Don Hayashi and George Kondo of San Francisco, Tom Shimasaki of Lindsay, Akiji Yoshimura of Colusa and Jim Murakami of Santa Rosa, all in California.

They discussed a number of ways in which Satow might be memorialized but finally decided to commission a history of the organization he had served. The minutes of that meeting contain this paragraph:

> It was Mas's conviction that only by telling and retelling the JACL story could new generations of Americans, including the Japanese Americans themselves, know and understand not only how JACL was organized, developed and functioned during World War II and thereafter, but also how, in a democracy, citizens' organizations like JACL could render vital and viable public services to their own membership and constituencies and also to the public and nation at large. At the same time, Mas knew that the "real" story of JACL and the Evacuation and its immediate aftermath have never been told, thereby resulting in misunder-

standings and even distortions in history, let alone bitterness among many who ought to know better. Thus it was felt by the committee that the basic tribute should be "The JACL Story," which would be a living memorial to Mas Satow in this generation and for generations yet to come, for readable histories are deathless and ever challenging.

JACL as a national organization was then forty-seven years old. Those years had sped by quickly and there was no comprehensive account of the momentous events of which JACL had been a part. The loss of JACL leaders who had helped to shape the organization underscored the need to record its history. Saburo Kido, one of the founders and JACL's wartime president, had been incapacitated for years and died April 4, 1977. Dr. Tom Yatabe, whose concerns had led to formation of JACL shortly after World War I, died November 14, 1977. George Inagaki died June 14, 1978.

With a rising sense of urgency the committee set about raising funds among JACL members to implement the project. Late in 1977 Mike Masaoka approached me about undertaking the assignment, and I accepted. In outlining my concept of the book, I wrote to the committee:

> The JACL story would be an account of the Japanese American Citizens League—its origins, its not inconsiderable trials and accomplishments, its failures as well as its triumphs, the great causes that united it as well as the internecine quarrels that threatened but failed to destroy it, and the dreams and ideals that motivated the various individuals who made JACL what it is.
>
> The JACL story would be set in the peculiar social and historical milieu which made such an organization necessary. It would treat the problems the Japanese Americans faced and recount their efforts to solve them. Above all, it would be a human story—a story of people in action, their fears and frustrations, their courage, sacrifice, ingenuity and the good intentions that ultimately overcame whatever shortcomings they suffered as young and inexperienced individuals.
>
> The JACL story will not be a Who's Who of JACL leaders and personalities. In relating the broad sweep of JACL history, it is inevitable that many deserving individuals will be overlooked because not everyone can be recognized. While this project is being undertaken by the JACL Masao W. Satow Memorial Committee, the book should not be considered the Mas Satow story. An objective reporting of JACL history will inevitably recognize his very

substantial role. I feel the most fitting tribute to Mas will not be a biography, but the story of the organization which meant so much to him and to which he contributed so greatly.

An earlier writing commitment, of which the executive committee was aware, delayed start of work on this book, but it is to be completed in time for the 1982 national JACL convention in Gardena, California, where the Mas Satow Library has been established. The committee has been patient and supportive. After suffering health problems, Mike Masaoka yielded the chairmanship to Pat Okura in 1980 at the San Francisco convention but continued his deep commitment to the project. Other members of the committee have been Yone Satoda, Tad Hirota, Tom Shimasaki, Harry Honda, Hi Akagi, Yas Abiko, Judge Raymond Uno, Jerry Enomoto, Bill Matsumoto, Shig Wakamatsu, Charles Kubokawa, Eddie Moriguchi, Jim Murakami, Dr. Jim Tsujimura, Dr. Clifford Uyeda, Harry Takagi, Mary Toda, Frank Iwama, Karl Nobuyuki, who served in his capacity as JACL's national director, and his successor, Ron Wakabayashi. To each of them I owe a debt of gratitude for the opportunity to write the story of an organization which had such a large part in helping Japanese Americans to win recognition as valued, respected Americans.

Special thanks go to Mike Masaoka for all his help; Harry Takagi, who at my request interviewed many national leaders on the East Coast about their roles in JACL's wartime activities; Harry Honda, who located and provided information from *Pacific Citizen* files and contributed his own recollections; Howard Cady, senior editor at William Morrow and Company, Inc., who encouraged the writing of this and other books dealing with the Japanese American experience; and Mary Masunaga for generously and uncomplainingly taking on the tedious work of typing and retyping the manuscript. Literally hundreds of persons provided information for this book, but the errors (of which inevitably there will be more than a few), and the interpretation of the facts, are mine alone.

—BILL HOSOKAWA
Denver, Colorado

Contents

JACL
IN
QUEST OF JUSTICE

I

Like *Rashomon*

A few years after the end of World War II, a Japanese movie set in medieval times was brought to the United States and won critical acclaim in art theaters across the country. It was titled *Rashomon.* It has an indirect but peculiar relevance to the subject of this book, which is the organization known as the Japanese American Citizens League (JACL).

To understand this statement it is necessary to know *Rashomon*'s story line. A Japanese noble and his lady are traveling through a forest when they are stopped by a bandit. He rapes the woman. A short time later a woodcutter finds the nobleman's body. These are the undisputed portions of the story. But as the movie unfolds, substantial disagreement about the details is revealed.

When the bandit is captured he readily admits he tied up the nobleman and raped his wife. Then he says that as he turned to go, the woman stopped him. She said her honor demanded that the bandit and her husband fight. So they dueled, the bandit says, and he killed the nobleman.

The wife tells a different story. She says that her husband scorned her after the rape. Angered, she killed him.

The dead nobleman, speaking through a medium, relates still another version. After the rape, the bandit asked the woman to go away with him. She agreed, but insisted that first he kill her husband. But the bandit refused to do this and fled alone. Mortified by the entire experience, the nobleman says, he killed himself with a dagger.

The woodcutter, who at first said only that he had discovered the nobleman's body, now changes his story. He says he witnessed the rape and heard the bandit urging the woman to go with him. The woman said she could not decide what to do, and insisted the men fight a duel over her. The bandit killed the noble, the woodcutter says, but the woman ran off alone.

Why would the woodcutter change his story? Because he had stolen a valuable dagger found at the scene and feared punishment. Thus, while the woodcutter corroborates a portion of each of the three versions, his veracity too becomes suspect.

Oddly enough, all three of the main characters, including the victim, admit responsibility for the death. But they disagree on the circumstances that led to the killing.

Who, then, is telling the truth, the whole truth, and nothing but the truth? Akira Kurosawa, who made the film, doesn't provide an answer. He leaves the viewer to ponder the meaning of truth. He implies that no one, with the exception of the woodcutter, lied. The other principals all told the story the way they believed it to be, or perhaps wanted to believe it to be. Kurosawa's point is that man cannot always tell the whole truth because he is incapable of judging reality. Man's views are colored by his need to deceive himself to conform to his evaluation of circumstances and of himself. The world is an illusion and each person makes his own reality; what is truth for one is not necessarily truth for another.

Thus, it would seem, it is with JACL. Depending on one's perceptions, which may be colored by fulfillment or frustration, baseness or idealism, bias, common rumor or honest disagreement, the Japanese American Citizens League is many things. At the extremes of its image, JACL is either an organization chiefly responsible for the spectacular socio-economic-political success of Japanese Americans, or it is simply a clique made up of pompous, conventioneering elitists. It is an organization with an extraordinary record of accomplishment despite limited membership and resources, or a group of questionable value perennially milking the community for donations to support causes of dubious merit. It is an organization that wisely charted a course of cooperation with the federal government in the tragic Evacuation of World War II, or a group that betrayed American principles and its own constituents by abjectly urging them to cooperate in their own incarceration.

What, then, is the real JACL?

During its fifty-year history it may have had a bit of all the characteristics attributed to it by friends and foes. This writer, with an assignment to paint a word-portrait of JACL, must thus adopt a *Rashomon*-like procedure, telling the story from several viewpoints—that of a reporter trained in objectivity over a professional lifetime, that of an observer and commentator and, finally, that of one who at times was a participant in the events and movements under examination.

Today, JACL is regarded by some as the organization of the Japanese American "Establishment," its members the fat-cat conservatives of an ethnic minority that has "made it." This is not true. Its membership of some thirty thousand cuts through a cross section of the Japanese American community. As a matter of fact, its membership is so diverse that many members are not of Oriental extraction. The membership embraces blue collar and white, Republicans and Democrats, rural and urban dwellers, angry social activists and *status quo* conservatives. In fact, some of those who work most diligently on JACL programs are change seekers who by their energy and the strength of their convictions have pushed the organization into supporting their own goals, a situation disturbing at times for those who are troubled when boats are rocked.

In this respect, JACL is being true to its origins. Those who laid the groundwork for its ultimate founding were dissatisfied young Nisei—the "second generation," the American-born offspring of Japanese immigrant parents—searching for something better for themselves and their peers. They were rebels motivated to improve their lot and that of other Japanese Americans. They were angry about social and economic discrimination based on race, frustrated by their inability to overcome injustice and share in the American dream. Particularly, they were outraged by the legal discrimination that doomed their parents to permanent second-class status.

In a later time these Nisei might have taken to the streets to demonstrate and agitate. But from the beginning they chose to seek their objectives by working through the system. For one thing, abrasiveness ran counter to their cultural upbringing; their values were strongly influenced by their elders, who preferred accommodation to confrontation. In the early decades of this century demonstrations were uncommon. The standards of propriety and permissible protest were different, even among those most entitled to complain. Moreover, these Nisei had profound faith in the American democratic system. They believed the way to change injustice was through the ballot box, by evolution rather than revolution. Thus the message of unhyphenated good citizenship runs like a golden thread through JACL history. Ironically, JACL still must go out of its way to explain that it is an American organization, that its members are United States citizens and that the "Japanese" in the name is an adjective describing the organization's ethnic origins.

The beginnings go back to San Francisco, chief port of entry for Japanese immigrants—the Issei, or "first generation"—who began to arrive through the Golden Gate in the last decade of the nineteenth century. It was only natural that most of them should remain close to the Bay area. They moved inland to labor on farms or railroad maintenance crews, but usually returned to tidewater ethnic settlements for companionship and cultural sustenance when the work was done. The year with which we are concerned is 1919. The war to make the world safe for democracy had been over for some months and the nation was caught up in the boom that followed the Armistice. But little of this touched a tiny handful of Nisei professionals freshly launched in their practices. These were the first of the Nisei, the lonely handful born before 1900 when there were fewer than twenty-five thousand Japanese in the entire United States and, statistically, only one woman to twenty men.

Despite their college educations and brand-new professional licenses, life was not easy for these Nisei. It took time to build a clientele—the Japanese communities were small and far from affluent, and whites were unlikely to come seeking the services of Oriental professionals. With plenty of leisure, these Nisei frequently lunched together and lingered over coffee for long, earnest talks. Dr. Thomas T. Yatabe, then twenty-two years old, a year out of the University of California dental school, articulate, persuasive, was the one the others looked up to. Among his friends were Tom Okawara, an attorney; Dr. Terry Tokutaro Hayashi, the first Nisei dentist; Dr. Hideki Hayashi; Kay Tsukamoto; Harry Suze. George Kiyoshi Togasaki, whose studies at the University of California had been interrupted by Army service in Europe, joined the lunch sessions when he returned to San Francisco. Their conversations took many directions, but would always return to the future in America of the Nisei—of themselves and those who would come later.

Their concern was well founded. All had grown up amid a virulent anti-Orientalism. Most citizens of the frontier West had regarded Chinese immigrant laborers—whose tireless efforts had helped to build the railroads and conquer the wilderness—as less than human. Except that they were not bought and sold as chattels, the position of the Chinese in the West was somewhat analogous to that of black slaves in the Deep South. Like the blacks, the Chinese were tolerated only when they remained in their place. Thus, during each of the frequent economic downturns, the Chinese were convenient scapegoats to be victimized by white politicians who, in many cases, were themselves immigrants or the offspring of immigrants. The hostility crystallized in 1882 when further immigration of Chinese laborers was banned; Congress had singled out the Chinese by statute as undesirable. Soon Japanese laborers were being recruited in place of the Chinese. But in inheriting their jobs the Japanese also fell heir to the discrimination that had been directed against the Chinese. (Ironically, the peace conference ending World War I was also convened in 1919 with Japan seeking a statement endorsing the principle of racial equality. The request was denied.)

Yatabe, Togasaki and his sister Kazue and some of the other participants in the lunchtime discussions had been among some fifty Nisei consigned by San Francisco Board of Education decree, in the fall of 1906, to the segregated Oriental school in Chinatown. The earthquake and fire earlier that year provided the school board with a convenient pretext. Some schools had been damaged, causing overcrowding in those that remained intact. To ease the congestion, the board announced, Oriental children from all over the city would be reassigned to Chinatown. Had Yatabe, then eight years old, obeyed the order, he would have had to ride clear across town each day in horse-drawn streetcars. Fortunately for history the Issei parents refused to accept the school board's order, although it would have been the easier course to agree to it. Togasaki's father, Kikumatsu, was among leaders of the resistance. He reminded the educators that all American-born persons were citizens and asked: "How can our children become good Americans if they are not allowed to associate with other American children, to become familiar with their customs, to meet and play with the children of the many peoples who make up America?"

While the order was being fought, the Japanese boycotted the Oriental school and held classes of their own to tutor the Nisei. Eventually Theodore Roosevelt's White House entered the controversy and the school board rescinded its decision after five months. Meanwhile, Yatabe's father, a shoe repairman, had moved his family to another part of the city. Long after he reached adulthood, Yatabe could recall reporting for enrollment at the new school. In Tom's presence the principal telephoned the superintendent's office to ask: "We have a Jap child here. Can we let him in?" George and Kazue Togasaki also had vivid recollections of the humiliation if not the pain they shared with their father when he was assaulted by hoodlums for no reason other than that he was Japanese. When he bought a horse and wagon to make deliveries from his provisions store, teamsters crowded him into an alley and whipped him. The author's book *Nisei* carries this passage:

> These *Nisei* knew they were American citizens, but few others seemed to know or care. They were accustomed to having well-intentioned strangers ask: "When did you come to the United States? What is Japan like?" In their bull sessions the *Nisei* asked themselves: "What good is our citizenship? Are we going to live with the same discrimination that our parents experienced? What should we, as *Nisei,* do?" Many admitted there had been times when they resented their Japanese blood because they felt it was a handicap in their efforts to become good Americans. Although the members of the group were in their early twenties themselves, they were deeply concerned about the future of *Nisei* boys and girls who were still in school, those who were just being born, those who were yet to be born.
>
> Out of their discussions came a determination to claim their rights as Americans, to let others know they were Americans.

In the fall of 1919 the informal lunch sessions gave way to a better-organized night meeting at the Japanese YMCA, to which other San Francisco Nisei were invited. Only a handful showed up, but with more hope than confidence they did three things. Realizing the Nisei and their problems were virtually unknown to the greater American public, they agreed to set up a speakers' bureau. (As it turned out, there wasn't much demand, except from a few small church groups, for lectures about Japanese Americans.) Second, they reviewed the qualifications and platforms of candidates in an upcoming election and launched a drive to get Nisei to register as voters. (When Yatabe first went to register a clerk asked his race. "I'm Japanese," Yatabe said. The clerk said there was no listing for Japanese, only for white, black and Mongolian. "I'm not Mongolian," Yatabe insisted. "And I'm not white and I'm not black. I am an American of Japanese parentage." The clerk and her supervisor conferred, then agreed to let Yatabe register his race as Japanese.) And finally, after lengthy discussion, they decided to call their organization the American Loyalty League, after rejecting the name American Loyalty Club. Considerable debate had developed over use of the word "Japanese." Some felt "Japanese American" ought to be part of the name, but in the end the majority agreed it was wiser to leave out any reference to Japan, as a way of emphasizing loyalty to the United States.

People of a later time, when the loyalty of Japanese Americans is seldom questioned, may wonder about the defensiveness of these early Nisei. It must be remembered that Asians were set apart from the Caucasian majority in the United States by race and culture and, historically, were considered unassimilable even to the point of being denied citizenship through naturalization. It was citizenship by birth that entitled the Nisei to strive for a full share of what we now call the American dream. And so they took an extraordinary pride in that citizenship, underscored their citizenship at every opportunity and in their zeal often ignored or even rejected their Japanese heritage. It was to be many years before they were secure enough to take pride in that heritage.

There is no record as to the number of meetings held by the American Loyalty League of San Francisco, but there weren't many. Despite their laudable intentions the members realized they were seeking answers to problems that were beyond their capacity to solve. The demands of making a livelihood began to make inroads on time and energy. Even before bylaws could be drawn up, Yatabe moved in 1923 to Fresno to open a practice. Without his drive the League drifted briefly before becoming inactive.

Meanwhile, a somewhat parallel organization was getting under way nine hundred miles to the north in Seattle. That development is reported in *Nisei:*

About the time the American Loyalty League was going into its decline, *Nisei* in Seattle, with no knowledge about what was going on in San Francisco, organized what they grandly called the Seattle Progressive Citizens League. This was partly at the instigation of two long-time *Issei* community leaders, Henry H. Okuda and Chusaburo Ito who were concerned about legalized discrimination against "aliens ineligible to citizenship." Proponents of an anti-alien land law were threatening to make it a reality in Washington. Business licenses were being denied *Issei* on the ground that they were aliens. Okuda and Ito considered an organization of *Nisei* voters as an arm with which to fight discrimination, but Seattle *Nisei* of legal age also saw the advantages of banding together even though there were only about a dozen of them. The League was founded in 1921 with Shigeru Ozawa as president, George Ishihara secretary, and Miss Yuki Higashi treasurer. Okuda and Ito were two of three *Issei* advisers. However, they apparently did little advising, for the League held only three meetings between 1921 and 1928.

Despite these two faltering starts, a civic organization to provide Japanese Americans with a vehicle for exercising their obligations and defending their rights as citizens was an idea whose time clearly was approaching. Other than Yatabe, the two men who saw this most vividly were Tamezo Takimoto, a San Francisco Issei, and a charismatic youngster from Seattle, Clarence Takeya Arai. Takimoto was secretary of the Japanese Association of North America, a loose-knit confederation of groups set up anywhere there were a substantial number of Issei. The Japanese Association had five areas of concern—finance, social welfare, commerce, education and young people's welfare. It served as an informal arm of the Japanese consular offices, which weren't equipped to handle the relations of widely scattered Japanese nationals with their home country, but it functioned primarily as a social welfare organization and not as a spearhead of Japanese nationalism as some jingoists contended.

Arai was born in Seattle in 1901 and received his law degree from the University of Washington in 1924. Long before graduation, however, he was deeply concerned about the future of the Nisei. A boyhood friend, Toshio Hoshide, now of Washington, D.C., recalls how impressed he was with Arai's vision when they were tentmates at a church summer camp. "Even then," Hoshide says, "Clarence—we called him General because he was enrolled in the Reserve Officers Training Corps at the University and talked about making the Army his career—would talk late into the night about the need to band Nisei together in a political organization so they could make their votes more effective." Though Arai was not one of the nineteen charter members of the Seattle Progressive Citizens League, he joined it soon after its founding and quickly became a leader.

Takimoto also understood only too well that an organization of Nisei citizens could do far more to improve the lot of all Japanese Americans than his Japanese Association. In 1923 he invited older Nisei from various parts of Northern California to a meeting in San Francisco. Takimoto had been impressed by Yatabe's ideas and energy and invited him to address the meeting. Most of those who attended were teenagers and Yatabe's earnest message—take an interest in civic affairs, register and vote, lay the groundwork for the upcoming Nisei generation—went over their heads.

Small wonder. Census records show that in 1900 there were only 269 Nisei in the entire United States; most of these people would have been in their mid-twenties by the time Takimoto called his meeting. The 1910 census figures show 4,502 Nisei, most of whom would have been teenagers at the time of the San Francisco gathering. The number of Nisei rose to 29,672 in 1920, and then to 68,356 in 1930. Even in 1930 the American-born were less than 50 percent of the Japanese in the continental United States, and their average age was ten years.

Long afterward, Yatabe wrote: "With the exception of a few, the majority at this first conference were not too enthused, nor could they fathom or imagine the potentialities of a citizens league movement." Nor did Yatabe have more than vague suggestions for fighting discrimination. In the absence of specific ideas, he made what appeared to be a sensible suggestion: "You fellows go home and think about it. We'll have another meeting next year. Meanwhile, remember you are Americans, that you must be recognized as Americans. Go out and tell everybody who will listen."

One of Takimoto's hopes was that the American Loyalty League in San Francisco would be revived and affiliated chapters established in various other communities. Fresno was the first to respond. The American Loyalty League of Fresno was founded May 5, 1923, with Yatabe as president. In time some fifteen chapters were formed in California—as far away as Brawley in the Imperial Valley, where chunky, forceful Lyle Kurisaki was a leader, and as close as San Jose, where scholarly Kay Nishida took the presidency. But their total membership was less than three hundred—an average of twenty members each. Some chapters were stillborn. Others quickly faded away from lack of interest or leadership, leaving only vague memories of their brief existence. Yatabe wrote: "If we could not make the Nisei conscious of the organization, we were determined that the city of Fresno would recognize us, so we took every opportunity that came about to actively participate in every affair which, by so doing, gave us a great deal of publicity, making the average Nisei conscious of our League. . . . It gives me a great sense of pride to know that the Fresno American Loyalty League weathered these years."

There were enough survivors to call another conference in San Francisco over the Labor Day weekend in 1924, a year when the fears of Takimoto and others were fully realized. In 1913 California, as a consequence of growing anti-Oriental feeling, had adopted laws prohibiting "aliens ineligible to citizenship"—meaning the Japanese—from owning land. Repeated efforts by the Japanese immigrants to gain citizenship through naturalization had been blocked by the courts. California's anti-alien land laws were tightened in 1920 following a bitter campaign of villifying Japanese immigrants. That same year some of California's leading citizens—including members of the Native Sons of the Golden West, the American Legion, labor and farm leaders, the California Federation of Women's Clubs and numerous others—formed the Japanese Exclusion League. Not satisfied with denying Japanese land ownership, the Exclusion League sought to halt all immigration from Japan. The Exclusion League's efforts led to passage in Congress of a sweeping new immigration law, one provision of which in effect categorized Japanese as inferior and undesirable, and totally barred their entry. Congress ignored Secretary of State Charles Evans Hughes' plea that Japan be granted a token quota—which would have amounted to a mere 146 immigrants per year—a gesture that might have placated Japan and possibly headed off war in the Pacific. President Coolidge criticized the exclusion provision. Expressing regret that the exclusion feature could not be severed from the overall immigration bill, he signed it into law on May 26, 1924. It was in the shadow of this blatantly racially discriminatory action that the

American Loyalty League meeting was held.

Among those attending were two Seattleites, Shigeru Ozawa and Arai. They had been invited to sit in as observers, but Arai found himself pressed into service as the banquet speaker. Arai was given to florid oratory of the old school, and he did a stirring job of pointing with alarm, waving the flag, expounding on the need to organize a patriotic Nisei organization. The delegates went away inspired, but once again the inspiration could not be projected to young Nisei who were more preoccupied with baseball and church socials than with their political obligations.

Except in Fresno, where Yatabe and his bride, Mary, made the American Loyalty League a potent community force through their ingenuity, persistence and boundless energy, the other chapters remained dormant. But a change was coming. Other Nisei, fresh out of college, were beginning to take an interest. One was Saburo Kido, born in Hilo, Hawaii, in 1902, who had come to the mainland at age nineteen to study law. He received his degree from Hastings Law College in San Francisco in 1926 and set up a practice on the fringes of Japantown. A graduate of the University of California school of optometry that same year was Henry Takahashi who opened a practice on Post Street across from the present Miyako Hotel. Another was Walter Tsukamoto, born in Reno, Nevada, in 1904 but reared in Sacramento. Tsukamoto was a brilliant, hard-driving youngster. While still a high school student he had helped organize an American Loyalty League chapter in Sacramento in 1922, but it withered away when he went to study law at the University of California. He received his degree in 1927. Still another was Tamotsu Murayama, born in the United States but educated in Japan, with aspirations for a newspaper career. He spoke a fractured brand of English but was a spellbinder in Japanese, and invaluable in contacts with the Issei, many of whom regarded the Nisei as potential rivals for community leadership.

George Togasaki's brother, Susumu, better known as Sim, was graduated from DePauw University in Indiana in 1927 and came back to join both the family import business and the small circle of Nisei leaders. Unlike Yatabe, Kido, Tsukamoto and Murayama, who had the common ability to stand before an audience and speak smoothly and convincingly, Sim was not particularly articulate. But he had a talent the others did not possess; he knew how to raise and handle money. It was a skill that would be badly needed before long. Few people owned automobiles in those days and George Togasaki remembers that when his friends had to go out into rural areas on Loyalty League business, they would borrow the Chandler touring car his father had bought for company use.

Meanwhile, in a distant part of the country, fate stepped in. In New York City a young Nisei prizefighter, James Yoshinori (Jimmie) Sakamoto, born in Seattle in 1903, found his eyesight failing. Doctors diagnosed his trouble as detachment of the retina, an irreversible condition in those days, caused by blows in the ring. Unlike his contemporaries in California, Sakamoto was not a college graduate. He made no pretense to being an intellectual. But he fit the prototype of the restless rebel, having drifted on the fringes of serious delinquency after several seasons as an outstanding high school football and basketball player. Dissatisfied with his prospects in Seattle, he headed east to, as he once put it, "study and loaf." He did little of either. While boxing professionally he learned the rudiments of journalism at the *Japanese American News.* Jolted by the knowledge of his impending blindness, he went back to Seattle in 1927. By then he was twenty-four years old, more thoughtful and mature. Sakamoto was distressed to find the Nisei community split by a bitter rivalry between two athletic clubs. Before he knew it he was cast in the role of mediator because of his not inconsiderable status. He quickly envisioned the defunct Seattle Progressive Citizens League as a logical common rallying point for the warring factions. He also realized the need for a newspaper to give the Nisei a voice. His father, Osamu, offered Jimmie his meager savings and the weekly *Japanese American Courier* was founded on January 1, 1928. Sakamoto's sight was practically gone by that time.

An editorial in the first issue dedicated the *Courier* to Nisei public service "as a medium in expression of their opinions and to guide them in the most commendable fashion in their political actions as well as their social activities." It went on to say:

> The time has also arrived when the American born Japanese must take his rightful place in the life of the community and discharge his obligations and duties that were inherited by him as a natural born American citizen. Identification with the political life and the institutions of the national, state and municipal gov-

ernments has become a paramount obligation with him and that obligation must not be looked upon otherwise than the privilege that came to him by right of birth in this country.

The Courier is given to understand that there has already been established in this community a citizens' league to stimulate greater political action among the voting American-born Japanese. It is commendable that such an organization has already been formed in this community and it can well rest assured that it will receive the heartiest cooperation from The Courier on any measure or action that she deems will serve justly and genuinely the best interests of the American born Japanese and the community at large. . . .

Sakamoto's offer of the *Courier*'s "cooperation" was something of an understatment. Rather than simply cooperating, the *Courier* provided vigorous leadership, with Sakamoto himself coming up with ideas and suggestions when movement seemed to lag and making sure they were carried out. By its second issue the *Courier* was no longer "given to understand" that there was a citizens' organization; it sounded a somewhat confused, verbose clarion call to the League:

AWAKE! CITIZEN'S LEAGUE

There is in this community today an organization which by virtue of its importance and political prestige, should be the outstanding association. Probably no mention need be made as to its entity, but it might just as well be said that the Citizen's League is deep in slumber and needs a thorough awakening. The Presidential election year is already upon us and it would serve the voting members of the community well to have a few meetings that they might be advised as to the political platform of the candidates or parties and vote according to their best judgment. Furthermore, upon this the League should be kept active and people well advised on the political situations of the country. Experts on the national, state and city politics should be invited and induced to speak so that ignorance, at least, with the paramount issues of the day will not handicap the voters at the polls. With the oncoming years, people of voting age are becoming numerous and the League has its greatest duties to perform ahead of it. This is no time to slumber in indifferent peace. Political identification as good American citizens is a necessity and a privilege that should not be lightly cast aside through any lethargic reasons. Too much is at stake. It is time that the Citizen's League should rise majestically to the occasion.

And in his third issue Sakamoto editorialized again on the importance of Niseis registering as voters, declaring there were two primary reasons why they should:

> The first is that political identification is necessary for the American-born Japanese if he is to assume his rightful place in the life of the city. Secondly, the American-born must vote to put down any measure of political aspirant that will work against the best interests of Japanese Americans. The Exclusion Law is already in force and today there is virtually no Japanese problem on the Coast, but still there is a strong line of demarcation between Americans and Japanese, even though born here. This may of course be from racial differences and may never be really overcome, but the endeavor to attain to a better degree of association in politics and society should never be discouraged. . . .

Not content with editorials alone, Jimmie Sakamoto wrote opinion pieces "By Jay Esse" and published them on page 1. In one of them he said:

> The League was an active organization several years back but today it lies in a dormant stage. Still, there are thinkers among the younger people today who wish to arouse this organization to its duties. Probably the man who would like to see the League awakened to greater possibilities is Clarence T. Arai, the first Japanese lawyer in this city.
>
> The fact that this element in the voting constituency of this city needs a thorough awakening probably needs no questioning. The unpaved muddy streets and poorly lighted sections susceptible to hold-ups not to say the harboring of houses of ill-fame, denotes the small voice the voters in the Japanese community have in the administration of city affairs. . . .

Interestingly enough, Dr. Yatabe in Fresno a few years earlier had stirred up the dissatisfaction of Japanese Americans, Armenian Americans, German Americans and other minorities over the lack of paving and street lighting in their part of town, and led a delegation to city hall to seek action. The mayor was amazed. No one from that area had complained previously about these matters. Improvements were quickly made. There weren't enough votes among Japanese Americans to influence many politicians even on a local level, but Yatabe had discovered the secret of successful political action. A united front with other small groups with similar concerns improved one group's clout immeasurably. But because of their desire to retain their identity, the Japanese Americans didn't absorb this lesson until many years later.

Under Sakamoto's determined pounding the Seattle Progressive Citizens League was reorganized early in 1928. Arai was elected president, George Ishihara vice-president, Kimi Takayoshi (who was soon to marry Ishihara) secretary and Yuki Higashi treasurer. Not all Issei were hostile toward the movement. Kenkō Nogaki, one of the early members, recalls that her father encouraged her to join the League because he saw it as a medium through which Japanese aliens could win citizenship.

From the beginning the Seattle group sought support in other communities. Arai made it one of his first orders of business to visit Portland, Oregon, two hundred miles by winding highway to the south, to help the Nisei there organize. As in Seattle, Portland Nisei had met to discuss mutual problems, the first time in 1922. Nothing concrete came of sporadic talks over the next six years, but Arai's enthusiasm proved contagious. Local leaders vowed to get something done and Arai promised to come back again.

In the summer of 1928 Dr. Yatabe made one more effort to organize an association of loyalty leagues. He scheduled a convention in Fresno for September 1. By then the Seattle group was strong enough to delegate Arai and Ishihara to attend as observers. They were en route when the convention was postponed to September 14, then canceled due to lack of support. Sakamoto was dismayed when he received a telegram from Ishihara saying the "convention just blew up." After hurried consultations Arai and Ishihara decided to tour California in an effort to drum up interest in a coastwide federation of Japanese Americans. From San Francisco they traveled to Stockton, down the San Joaquin Valley to Fresno, to Los Angeles, up to Santa Barbara, San Jose, Alameda and Oakland and then back to San Francisco. They made an effective pair, Ishihara selling the citizens' movement with a quiet combination of humor and logic, Arai doing the same with oratory.

In the Los Angeles audience was a petite and unusually pretty young woman named Yone Utsunomiya. She lived in Santa Barbara where, as one of the older Nisei, she and Takazumi Asakura had organized what they called the ABC Club. The letters stood for American Born Citizens. Yone's family had been associated with Arai's parents in a brief, unprofitable abalone-harvesting venture off the Santa Barbara Islands when Clarence was a toddler. When Yone's mother read about Clarence's tour in a Japanese-language newspaper, she urged her daughter to go to Los Angeles to meet him and hear what he had to say about Nisei organizations. Arai accompanied Yone back to Santa Barbara for a week's visit. A year later they became engaged, and in April of 1930 they were married. It may have been the first of many interregional marriages brought about by JACL contacts.

From San Francisco, Arai and Ishihara headed north to Portland, where they reported on developments in California. Dr. Frederick Kayama, a dentist, then appointed Roy Yokota to draft a constitution for the projected Portland Progressive Citizens League.

In San Francisco, the need had been for moral support rather than help with organization. Kido had the situation well in hand, and on October 19, 1928, the New American Citizens League was founded with Kido as president. Vice-presidents were Dr. Henry Takahashi, Kay Tsukamoto, Toshi Takao, Shizu Sakai, Dr. Terry T. Hayashi, Mrs. Charles Yonezu and Kay Nishida. Secretaries were Hide Sasaki and Eiko Enomoto, and Henry Uyeda was elected treasurer. Nine days later, on October 27, some fifty Nisei gathered at the Clift Hotel for the inaugural banquet. Kido, whose modest office at 1623 Webster Street doubled as organizational headquarters, set the keynote. A contemporary account reports: "Mr. Kido emphasized the fact that the citizens of Japanese ancestry had many difficult problems confronting them which must be solved sooner or later, and that to rely on the first generation was inevitable to a certain degree, but ultimately, the real solution would have to be made by the second generation members and this could be done only by cooperation."

The organization's first major project was a convention to make another try at forming the federation that had been advocated for so long by Yatabe, Takimoto, Arai and Kido. It was held April 5 and 6, 1929, in San Francisco. Kido was the principal organizer and he made sure that Arai came down from Seattle with some concrete proposals. A photograph appearing in the *Nikkei Shimin,* the San Francisco League's publication, identifies the following as attending: J. W. Aoki, Clarence Arai, Hisashi Arie, K. Doi, George Hiura, G. Isonaka, Saburo Kido, T. Koga, Lyle K. Kurisaki, M. Kuwada, Yone Kuwahara, Saiki Muneno,

Tamotsu Murayama, T. Namba, Kay Nishida, T. Ogata, H. R. Okamoto, T. Okamoto, L. Oki, Miya Sannomiya, Henry Takahashi, Tamezo Takimoto, George Togasaki, Kay Tsukamoto, Tom Yego, Charles Yonezu and Mrs. Charles Yonezu.

No doubt there were a few more attending the convention than the twenty-seven photographed, but in any event the turnout was hardly likely to impress politicians with the voting power of Japanese Americans.

Two of the principal speakers were Chinese Americans who, as it turned out, showed more maturity and vision than their Japanese American hosts. Kenneth Fung, secretary of the Chinese American Citizens Alliance, congratulated the Nisei and urged closer relations between them and his group. "The success of this convention means our success because we have so much in common," he said. Then Victor Kwong, a San Francisco newspaperman, told of his dream of Sino-Japanese friendship and cooperation in Asia which could become the foundation for world peace, and in the United States where the two peoples faced mutual problems. These messages were applauded politely but they failed to create much of a stir. Perhaps there was an element of ethnocentrism in the Nisei lack of enthusiasm for joining hands with Chinese Americans; after all, the Nisei had plenty of problems of their own. In any event, they were not aware of the lesson Dr. Yatabe had learned about cooperation among minorities in Fresno. It was to be many years before Japanese Americans felt secure enough to take an active interest in the concerns of other minorities. At this point the important thing was to listen to what Arai had to say.

Arai's proposal, which had been shaped by Seattle leaders in Jimmie Sakamoto's office, was to set up a federation to be called the National Council of Japanese-American Citizens Leagues. It would be a loose organization of chapters to be established in any community with a substantial number of Americans of Japanese ancestry. Citizenship would be a requirement for membership. Chapters in various areas would be affiliated in semi-autonomous district councils to cope with local matters, but each chapter would be considered equal under the national banner.

The only point to stir discussion was the proposed name of the organization. Some delegates, particularly from areas where American Loyalty League sentiment was strong, objected to the word "Japanese" in the name, contending it carried a connotation of split loyalty. Others argued that "Japanese" was an adjective describing the ethnic origin of the members of an American organization. Finally, it was agreed to let individual chapters pick their own names, such as the Fresno American Loyalty League, but the national organization would be known as the Japanese-American Citizens League, with a hyphen between the first two words to emphasize the adjective.

As the final part of his proposal, Arai suggested a second meeting the following year at which such details as a program and a constitution could be hammered out. Then he extended an invitation from the Seattle Progressive Citizens League to host a convention of the National Council of JACL. Aside from San Francisco and Fresno, the localities represented at the first meeting were totally unprepared to stage a convention. Many had only good intentions to form a chapter, and much hard work lay ahead before an active organization could be set up. And Seattle in the distant Northwest seemed like such an exciting place to visit. The invitation was quickly accepted.

Almost as an afterthought, Clarence Arai was elected president of the National Council. It seemed only appropriate that if his chapter was going to host the next convention, he should be president.

II

The First Convention

After a decade of struggle and apathy among the Nisei, the momentum and enthusiasm leading to and generated by the San Francisco convention resulted in formation of several new Citizens League chapters. In each case the impetus came from strong local personalities with the ability to rally their friends to action.

Perhaps the most prominent of the new groups was the one that took shape in Los Angeles. It called itself the Japanese American Citizens Association. The older Nisei in the community had been seeking a way to draw the attention of municipal officials to the needs of a community which had been largely ignored even though it lay in the shadow of city hall. But lack of a leader frustrated their efforts. They finally found one in Masao Igasaki, a Hawaii-born graduate of the University of Southern California who had just passed the bar examination. Igasaki, whose immigrant father operated a horse-drawn stagecoach line from Hilo to the other side of the Big Island, had known Saburo Kido in boyhood. Like Kido, he felt a mainland education was important to his ambition of becoming an attorney. He had paid for his schooling at the University of Southern California by working nights as a bookkeeper in a wholesale produce house. ("Fortunately," he recalled not long before his recent death, "I had a photographic memory. I could sleep through class and still pass my courses." A friend says that no one wanted to play poker with Igasaki because he could remember all the cards that had appeared on the table.)

In addition to his sense of community service, Igasaki had a practical motive for agreeing to take the presidency. He was just beginning his law practice in a community where he was a relative newcomer and had to become known in a hurry. Under his leadership the Los Angeles group came into being a month after the San Francisco meeting. Igasaki's cabinet included James Suyenaga, vice-president; Elmer Yamamoto, secretary; Dr. Edward Tanaka, sergeant at arms; and Thomas Takayama, treasurer.

At about the same time the Placer County and Portland chapters were organized. Placer County, in the lovely Sierra foothills orchard country east of Sacramento, was led by Tom Yego, a husky young farmer. Portland's first president was Charles Yoshii, who a few years later, frustrated by inability to get a decent job, went to Japan. He became well known as an English-language radio announcer.

Some months before the San Francisco meeting a remarkable Nisei woman, Miya Sannomiya, had launched a chapter in Stockton, California. Born in Hawaii in 1902, she had moved with her family to San Francisco, Oakland, Alameda and Klamath Falls, Oregon, before her father settled down to farm sixteen hundred acres near Stockton. She was a premed student at the University of California when her father died in 1927, leaving $160,000 in debts. Miya, then twenty-five years old, took over operation of the farm to try to liquidate the debts. As she tells it, the first year was bad, the second season a bit better and the third year very profitable. But there wasn't enough to pay all the creditors in full. They agreed that Miya had done more than anyone could expect and wrote off the rest of the debt. There was a place still waiting for Miya in medical school, but she had to forget about becoming a doctor; there just wasn't enough money. While working as editor of the English section of *Nichi Bei,* a San Francisco newspaper, she met a Japanese nobleman who urged her to visit Japan and study that nation's culture. She went there in 1933 and a few years later joined the staff of Kokusai Bunka Shinkokai, an organization chartered to introduce Japanese culture around the world. Miya's particular beat was the United States, where she gave lectures and demonstrations at schools, churches and women's groups. She opened the Kokusai Bunka Shinkokai office in New

York's Rockefeller Center, but she was becoming progressively more disturbed by the way the militarists were interfering with civilian government in Japan. Eventually she became one of the Japanese Army's targets. The men in uniform didn't believe that a Nisei, and a woman at that, ought to be representing Japan abroad, even though she refused to talk politics, sticking strictly to cultural matters. Finally fed up, she resigned in 1938, married a dentist, Dr. Yoriyuki Kikuchi, and settled in Los Angeles.

Meanwhile, Seattle busily prepared for the most ambitious meeting in Nisei history. Clarence Arai, as president of the National Council, and George Ishihara, as secretary, set up a budget of fourteen hundred dollars and went about soliciting contributions, mostly from not entirely sympathetic Issei merchants and businessmen. The concept of a coastwide convention was strange to the Issei. The Issei community was accustomed to looking to the Japanese consulates for leadership and the idea of Nisei going off on their own was disquieting. Still, some individual Issei like Henry H. Okuda, who had encouraged the founding of the Seattle Progressive Citizens League, urged the Nisei to strike out on their own. Arai and Ishihara were assisted by a local committee made up of Jimmie Sakamoto, who handled publicity; Tomeo Takayoshi, entertainment; Toshio Hoshide, transportation; Ishihara, housing and banquet; Shiro Hashiguchi, convention finances. Officers of the Seattle chapter at the time were Arai, president; Ishihara, first vice-president; Tsurue Nakamura, second vice-president; Kimiko Takayoshi, secretary; Kenko Nogaki, treasurer.

They received plenty of assistance from JACL nonmembers. For example, there was Bob Okazaki, a blithe spirit who later was to become a Hollywood bit player and dialogue coach. Okazaki had been born in Japan and brought to the United States as an infant. He had been reared as a Nisei, but on account of the technicality of being Japanese-born, was an alien. That made him ineligible for membership in the Citizens League. Little matter. Okazaki saw no reason why he shouldn't help his friends prepare for the convention. He felt that the male delegates from California should be given every opportunity to meet the local belles so he went to Pete Yorita's printing shop and put together some datebooks for listing names and addresses. Son of a Baptist minister, Okazaki had the prescience to understand that attendance at a JACL convention could serve as a matrimonial scouting trip as well as an experience in political leadership.

Even the choice of a meeting site reveals the extent of Nisei dependence on the Issei at this stage of their development. In the absence of a more suitable place they selected the Japanese Chamber of Commerce Hall on the second floor of the Rainier Heat and Power Building. Despite the building's imposing name, it was far from prepossessing. It was a two-story structure set into a hillside on the corner of Jackson Street and Maynard Avenue, close to the center of a less than elegant Japantown. The ground floor, facing bustling Jackson, was occupied by several Japanese retail establishments including a shoe store and a fish market. Maynard was a sharply pitched, unpaved side street. The entrance to the second floor was on Maynard. The official convention photograph taken just outside the entrance by Ralph Ochi shows the people on the uphill side several feet higher than those on the downhill side, and those in the front row perched on precariously tilting chairs. The two convention hotels were the Bush and the NP, both only a block from the meeting hall, both somewhat the worse for wear but the most elegant Japantown could offer.

The convention was opened on the morning of Friday, August 29, 1930, by Arai with presentation of the colors, and group singing of "America" and recital of the Pledge of Allegiance. Registered delegates, representing five states and the Territory of Hawaii, totaled 102. There were 18 from seven chapters in California, 5 from the lone chapter in Oregon and 76 from Washington, including 40 from the only chapter there, Seattle. Tasuke Yamagata, who worked in a bank and impressed mainlanders with a Phi Beta Kappa key, was the sole delegate from Hawaii. Tokutaro Nishimura (Tokie) Slocum came from New York, where he had known Jimmie Sakamoto. And Seichi (Bud) Konzo of Tacoma, who was home for the summer from studies as a graduate student in engineering at the University of Illinois, registered from Urbana.

All the other pioneer delegates listed in the first convention program deserve to be named here. Californians in attendance were, from Brawley–Imperial Valley: Charles M. Akita, Ernest Fujimoto; Fresno: Thomas Kanase, Yoshio Honda, Fred Hirasuna; Los Angeles: Miss Suma Sugi, Charles Kamayatsu; San Francisco: Saburo Kido, Miss Toshi Takao, Lloyd Enomoto, Ryuzo Maeyama, Akira Horikoshi, Saiki Muneno, Jerry Isonaka;

Newcastle: Tom Yego; Stockton: Norman Ouye, W. Y. Nishimoto; San Jose: Miss Carol Tokunaga.

From Portland, Oregon, came Miss Ruth Nomura, Miss Frances Maeda, George Sumida, Paul Nomura, and Charles Yoshii.

The Washingtonians were, from Bellevue: Nanoomi Tominaga, T. Sakaguchi, K. Mukumoto, M. Tominaga; Foster: Miss Teru Uno, Miss Mary Uno, Masaru Uno, Kiyoshi Uno; Yakima: Miss Merry Masuda, Kiyoshi Matsumura, Roy Nishimura; Wapato: Tatsumi Uno, Johnson Shimizu, George Honda; Auburn: H. K. Fukuhara, John Arima, Minoru Terada, Minoru Okura, T. Naito; Spokane: Miss Yuki Kuwahara, Welly Shibata; Vashon Island: Miss Hatsue Tanaka, Miss Miriam Takatsuka, Kenzo Yorioka, Miss Margaret Takatsuka, Miss Yuri Hoshi, Miss Dorothy Hoshi, Miss Helen Yoshimura; Fife: Juro Yoshioka, Tadao Yoshida, John T. Fujita, Kiyo Higashi; Tacoma: C. S. Miyazaki, Miss Aiko Konzo, K. Hayashi; Winslow: Masaki Nakata; Seattle: Clarence Arai, Mrs. Yone Arai, Miss Mitsu Fukano, Shiro Hashiguchi, Toshio Hoshide, Miss Masako Hotta, Frank Ishida, George Ishihara, Miss Ruth Ite, Sanny Kaneko, Miss Sato Kawaguchi, F. Kimura, Akira Kumasaka, Thomas Masuda, Miss Kiku Mihara, Mrs. W. L. McGahon, Miss Shizuko Nakagawa, Miss Mary Nakamura, Tsurue Nakamura, Victor Nakashima, Miss Tomi Nakayama, Sab Nishimura, James Nobuyama, Miss Kenko Nogaki, Miss Rae Ota, James Y. Sakamoto, Shosuke Sasaki, Miss Sada Seki, Miss Josie Shinowara, Miss Kay Suzuki, Miss Kimiko Takayoshi, Tomeo Takayoshi, Miss Yurino Takayoshi, Miss Billee Tashiro, Miss Edith Tsuruda, Teruji Umino, Miss Teru Watanabe, Miss Yuki Watanabe, Miss Fusako Yoshioka, Thomas Yoshimura.

While the above were named in the report published after the convention, a number of others appear in the official convention photograph. Among them are Miss Kiyo Ariizumi, Mrs. Misao Sakamoto (Jimmie's wife), Miss Masako Takayoshi and Miss Nobuko Yanagimachi of Seattle, and Miss Ayako Ohashi of Fife. (More than fifty years after the event, Kamayatsu remembered Nobuko Yanagimachi as one of the few Seattle girls who had a car and could drive it. However, he married another girl he met at the convention. She was Yuki Kuwahara of Turlock in Central California who had gone to Spokane as a social worker after graduation from the San Francisco Bible Training School. She registered from Spokane.) It seems likely that a significant number of other Seattle Nisei took part in at least some of the convention functions without formally registering. Not all the delegates were old enough to vote, and several were aliens. Welly Shibata of Spokane, like Bob Okazaki, had been born in Japan and was ineligible for naturalization. But he was a popular and extremely personable journalism student at the University of Washington, a deft amateur magician who entertained at one of the convention functions and a jazz piano player, and it seemed only right to include him. In addition a number of teenagers were recruited to sing, dance and play musical instruments (including a harp) for the conventioneers.

The impressive number of Washington communities represented is misleading. Seattle was the only active JACL chapter in the state, although several others were in the process of organizing. Five of the eleven areas represented were small farming settlements on Seattle's outskirts. In fact, the four Unos from Foster, plus their brother registered from Wapato where he was working, composed the entire Nisei population of Foster except for a couple of siblings left at home because they were too young to take part.

Some delegates from more distant areas had gone to considerable effort to reach Seattle. Kido, who had married Mine Harada of Riverside, California, just two years earlier, was still a struggling barrister and had no idea how he could afford to make the trip. Kido's practice was bringing in about forty dollars a month. The young couple lived on the hundred dollars a month Mine was making as a sales clerk in a Grant Avenue souvenir and Oriental art goods shop. Most of Kido's colleagues were in similar straits. Their plight was eased somewhat when the San Francisco chapter netted seventy-five dollars at a benefit dance and divided it among the delegates. (The *Japanese American News* in San Francisco commented somewhat snidely that not much could be expected from JACL if convention delegates couldn't pay their own way.) Five of the six men in the San Francisco contingent arranged to hitch a ride with Tom Yego, who was driving to Seattle in his Dodge. They took the train to Sacramento, stayed overnight in a cheap hotel and met Yego the next morning. Toshi Takao went to Seattle by train, as did Akira Horikoshi who, as an employee of Nippon Yusen Kaisha, a shipping line, could get a pass.

The Los Angeles chapter had only about fifty members and the dues were fifty cents a year. They wanted Charles Kamayatsu and Suma Sugi to represent them in Seattle, but could offer only half the cost of transportation. Kamayatsu had just bought a new Model A Ford coupe with a rumble seat. He took a vacation from his job in a fruit market and he and Suma Sugi and another friend drove to San Francisco in the Ford. After staying with friends to save expenses, Kamayatsu parked his car and he and Suma Sugi took a bus the rest of the way. Charles Akita and Ernest Fujimoto from Brawley also drove to San Francisco. There they boarded one of the liners then shuttling along the coast and sailed to Seattle. Tasuke Yamagata also took a steamer; air service between Honolulu and the mainland was still years in the future.

Many of the pioneer leaders in California, like George and Sim Togasaki, Walter Tsukamoto, Miya Sannomiya and others, did not attend the convention for a variety of reasons. Dr. Yatabe would have liked nothing better than to be present at the birth of his brainchild, but he had to remain in Fresno to await the arrival of his own first baby.

The convention program was a mix of fun and earnest business. It is not likely that many of the delegates realized the significance of their precedent-setting meeting. It is more probable that they were simply awed by the Nisei giants, like Jimmie Sakamoto who edited a newspaper in spite of his blindness, and Tokie Slocum who was a spellbinding orator when he spoke about loyalty to America. In recollections written some twenty years later, Kido observed about Slocum's speech at the convention: "It was the first time that I heard such an eloquent, high-powered speech in English from a person of Japanese ancestry. Clarence Arai was fluent but Slocum was a firebrand orator. No better person could instill enthusiasm in the hearts of delegates. I was deeply impressed with his oratory despite the fact that I had been raised in an environment in Hawaii where there was constant talk of Americanism."

(Welly Shibata, who wrote a puckish humor column for Sakamoto's *Courier,* was impressed in another fashion. He wrote: "Those who missed the convention missed Slocum and those who missed Slocum missed a million-dollar sideshow. It is rumored that Yakima is seeking his services as midway barker for the Washington State Fair, Sept. 9 to 13. It is also rumored that Cecil

B. de Mille will use Slocum to play the part of Angel Gabriel who wakes up the dead, in the talkie version of *The Last Judgment Day.*")

To get the delegates to unbend, Kamayatsu and Slocum led college-type yells and pep songs. Yone Arai, who could whistle like an aviary full of songbirds, presented whistling solos. At a "mass meeting" one evening for the local community, the delegates opened the program with "The Star Spangled Banner" and the Japanese national anthem, "Kimigayo," in deference to the Issei guests. Arai as chairman wanted a roll call to impress the home folks with the number of visitors from distant places. Kido, however, quickly realized that many delegates had made good use of Bob Okazaki's datebooks and had ducked out in the company of some of the local girls. Arai decided it was wiser simply to ask the guests to stand.

Tasuke Yamagata was chairman of the political round table with Dr. Charles E. Martin of the University of Washington political science department as discussion leader. Martin pointed out that only about one sixth of the eligible voters went to the polls regularly and the Nisei, by registering and turning out to vote, could have an influence beyond their numbers. Charles Akita reported that the Brawley chapter, by fining those who failed to vote, had got every member to the polls in the last election. He hurried to add that bloc voting was not encouraged.

Charles Yoshii chaired the social contacts round table with Ashley E. Holden, secretary of the Japan Society, leading the discussion. Holden declared racial prejudice resulted from ignorance and the Nisei owed it to themselves to get out into the larger community and help eliminate that ignorance. The teaching of the Japanese language, history and culture in American schools would help create understanding between the two Pacific nations, he said.

The economics and vocational round table was chaired by Kamayatsu with Arai leading the discussion. Their conclusions: just as the Japanese had previously replaced the Chinese in the most menial jobs, the Japanese were now being replaced by Filipinos; individual Nisei were distinguishing themselves in various professions but most doors of economic opportunity were difficult to open; college-educated Nisei were expanding farming operations begun by their parents and doing very well; and the vocational problem was shared by young people everywhere.

Kido was chairman and discussion leader of the legal round table, assisted by Jack Yasutake, Issei interpreter for the U.S. Immigration and Naturalization Service, and Jimmie Sakamoto headed the international round table. The political and legal groups waded into two issues, which will be discussed later in this chapter, that established JACL as a credible organization. On Sunday, August 31, everyone took the day off for a sight-seeing trip to Mount Rainier National Park aboard chartered buses. The convention ended with a dance at the Seattle Yacht Club, a striking contrast with the spartan decor of the Japanese Chamber of Commerce Hall.

The organization business was covered in a series of reports and resolutions. Slocum conducted a virtually single-handed campaign against "hyphenated Americanism," and the hyphen was removed from the name of the organization. A JACL membership pin was adopted. It had been designed at Toshio Hoshide's request by his father, Sokichi Hoshide, an Issei jeweler. Kido proposed a mutual-benefit insurance plan, but it was tabled for further study. He felt that fraternal insurance would give members a financial stake in the organization and sustain their interest, but the proposal was too ambitious for JACL at that stage of its development. And Kamayatsu, who had been instructed by his chapter to bring the next convention back to Los Angeles, praised the beauty of Portland's roses and Seattle's girls but declared no one had really lived until he'd been to Los Angeles and become acquainted with Southern California's blushing peaches. As an added attraction, he reminded delegates that Los Angeles would be the site of the 1932 Summer Olympic Games. This speech caused Brawley to withdraw its bid and the convention went to Los Angeles.

The most significant business of the convention was contained in two resolutions having to do with citizenship. Both were the products of Kido's restless mind, although credit for planting one of the ideas there must go to an illustrious Issei, Kikumatsu Togasaki, father of George and Sim and numerous other notable offspring. Some weeks before leaving for Seattle, Kido had happened to visit the Togasakis' Mutual Supply trading company. Kikumatsu invited Kido into his office and they chatted about the convention. In the course of the conversation the older man urged Kido to bring up the injustice that had been done to Japanese citizens who had served in the United States Army in World War I.

Kido was aware of the situation. Recruiters had told young Issei that by joining the Army they could become American citizens. It was true that the law provided that any alien serving in the United States armed forces would be eligible to petition for citizenship, and largely on the strength of this promise hundreds of Japanese aliens joined up. After the war, however, the courts ruled that "any alien" did not apply to aliens like the Japanese who, under other laws, were ineligible for citizenship. In 1922, in the landmark case brought by Takao Ozawa, who was born in Japan but educated in America, the U.S. Supreme Court appeared to settle the matter once and for all. It ruled that since the law limited naturalization to "free white persons and persons of African nativity," the Japanese, who fell in neither of these categories, could not be naturalized.

Kido had assumed it would take a constitutional amendment to change that situation. But Kikumatsu Togasaki, who was a graduate of a school of jurisprudence in Japan and had made American law a hobby, argued that the naturalization law could be changed by an act of Congress. Kido checked this out and, to his astonishment, found Togasaki was right. He went to Seattle prepared to urge JACL to press for congressional action.

Before the war veterans' situation was brought to his attention Kido had been interested in the Cable Act, passed in 1922, which discriminated against Nisei women because of both race and sex. This law provided that American women—but not men—who married aliens lost their United States citizenship. If the marriage were terminated—by divorce, annulment or death—the women could regain their citizenship through naturalization. However, Nisei women, being of a race ineligible to naturalization, were denied that right. The problem for Nisei was intensified by the Japanese custom that the bride should be three to five years younger than her husband. Since Nisei men in this age group were scarce, many Nisei women faced the unpalatable choice of remaining single and a citizen, or marrying an alien and giving up United States citizenship for life.

The veterans' issue that Kido brought up in the legal round table was of intense personal interest to Tokie Slocum, who was so thoroughly American that it was difficult to believe that he, too, was an alien. He had been born in Japan in 1895 and brought to the United States in early childhood. His father was a railroad worker who took his family to Minot, North Dakota. When the elder Nishimura realized the laws prevented him from becoming a citizen, he moved to Canada. Tokie decided to remain in the United States and was reared by Ansel Perry Slocum, whose name he took. Tokie Slocum volunteered for the Army in World War I, reached the rank of sergeant major, saw combat with the same division as the fabled Sergeant Alvin York and was so severely gassed that he was frequently hospitalized in later life. Slocum believed rightly that he had earned the right to become a citizen and was delighted when the convention passed the following resolution:

> Whereas a large number of Japanese residents of the United States of America were induced to join the Army and Navy of the United States of America during the World War by promises made that those who received their honorable discharges would be granted citizenship,
>
> And whereas these World War veterans were denied American citizenship, contrary to the promises and inducements offered them,
>
> And whereas such action is both unfair and unjust,
>
> Be it now resolved that the Japanese American Citizens' League, meeting in Seattle, Washington, requests the attention of Congress to this injustice which has been done to these World War veterans who gave up their positions and careers and offered their lives in defense of our country.

Slocum vowed to carry the issue right into the halls of Congress, and no one who heard his oratory doubted him.

Kido had opened discussion of the Cable Act's inequities in the legal round table and urged an intense lobbying campaign through JACL chapters because "it is a question of demanding equality for ourselves." The Cable Act came up again in the political round table when Suma Sugi told of the concern felt by Nisei women in Southern California. The convention approved the following resolution:

> Whereas, the present naturalization law commonly known and understood as the Cable Act Amendment, discriminates against American women citizens of Oriental ancestry, on the following grounds:

First, it violates the fundamental principles of the United States Constitution by denying equality.

Second, such a discriminatory measure is creating an acute social problem by restricting the American women citizens of Oriental ancestry from the opportunity of entering married life, because there are not sufficient men of eligible age among the male citizens of Japanese descent.

And, whereas we American citizens of Japanese ancestry believe that Congress is unaware of the conditions now existing, and believe that the wrong will be remedied once this matter is called to the attention of Congress, in whose sense of justice and fair play we have absolute confidence.

Be it now resolved, that the National Convention of the Japanese American Citizens League now meeting in Seattle, Washington, hereby appeal and petition Congress to place women citizens of Oriental ancestry on equal basis as other women citizens of the United States.

Aside from its awkward language, the resolution was faulty on at least two counts. The Cable Act was not the naturalization law, but involved only a portion of it. And it was the Cable Act itself that was discriminatory; the amendment was designed to eliminate the act's racially discriminatory features. Nonetheless, Suma Sugi soon was to have an unusual role in getting the amendment passed.

The convention also adopted a constitution drafted by a committee headed by Kido. It was made up of thirteen articles, the highlights of which were:

Article I—The name of the organization was specified as the Japanese American Citizens League.

Article II—All members had to be a member of one of the chapters of the organization.

Article III—The main office of the organization was to be in the city where the next convention would be held.

Article IV—Officers would be a president, vice-presidents, a recording secretary, a corresponding secretary and a treasurer.

Article V—Duties of officers were outlined.

Article VI—The executive body of JACL was to be called the National Council, which would be made up of all the officers and two representatives from each chapter.

Article VII—District councils would be subordinate to the National Council. The Northwest District Council would include

Seattle, Winslow, Portland and other chapters to be formed in Washington and Oregon. The Bay Region District Council would include San Francisco and Sonoma, Alameda, San Mateo, Santa Clara and Monterey counties. The San Joaquin Valley Council would include San Joaquin, Sacramento, Stanislaus and Placer counties. The Central California District would include Fresno, Madera, Tulare and Kern counties. The Southern California District Council would include Los Angeles, Riverside, Imperial, San Diego and other Southern California counties. "When Los Angeles organizes its own league, Brawley may organize the Imperial Valley District Council," the constitution specified. Any new council might be formed by four local chapters petitioning the National Council.

Article VIII—Chapters might choose their own names and adopt their own constitutions and bylaws provided they were not contrary to the policies of the national organization.

Article IX—Conventions were to be held every two years at a place to be designated by the chapters represented at the convention when such action was taken.

Article X—Each chapter would pay ten dollars annually to cover stationery, postage and miscellaneous expenses.

Article XI—A majority of the chapters constituted a quorum.

Article XII—In case of emergency, telegraphic votes would be taken. A majority vote was necessary for passage except when constitutional amendments were involved.

Article XIII—Constitutional amendments would be considered only at national conventions, with a two-thirds vote of the chapters represented necessary for passage.

Three deficiencies in the constitution are immediately visible. Nothing was said about the purpose of the organization, qualifications for membership or the manner in which national officers were to be elected.

Why an attorney like Kido did not address these matters is a mystery. Was it due to inexperience and oversight? Or were they issues that defied easy agreement and were better left for a later time? There is no record to clarify these points and no survivor of the inner councils to provide insight.

Toshio Hoshide, who was an active member of the convention committee although not of the inner circle, has a theory. The constitution was purposely kept vague, he says, because JACL's future was so uncertain. Despite high hopes, Hoshide asserts, there was no assurance there would be a second convention. The organization was without funds and its members were young and mostly impoverished. An economic depression was beginning to cast its long shadow across the country and the Nisei were realistic enough to know that as marginal citizens they would be affected cruelly. And so it seemed wiser not to be locked into a rigid constitution.

It was generally understood, however, that the JACL was a civic and patriotic organization concerned with the well-being and political and economic progress of American citizens of Japanese ancestry. Naturally members had to be American citizens but it was presumed that no one but Japanese Americans would be interested in joining. The election of national officers was solved by an understanding that, as in Arai's case, the chairman of the upcoming convention would be considered the national president. Presumably he would name his own cabinet. A national president and cabinet were not elected until the 1934 convention. As for the purposes, the initiation oath taken by members of the Seattle chapter seems quite adequate: "I pledge my allegiance to the United States of America and my fidelity to the Seattle Progressive Citizens' League, to labor for the best welfare of our Republic and to uphold the principles of liberty and justice for which our organization stands."

Despite its many shortcomings the first national convention of the Japanese American Citizens League had been an encouraging success. Sakamoto's *Courier* editorialized earnestly if not entirely clearly:

> ". . . Ten years ago it would have been difficult to find a Saburo Kido, Charles M. Akita, Thomas Yego, Suma Sugi, Clarence T. Arai, Norman Ouye, Fred Hirasuna and many others. These people were undoubtedly the leaders of the convention, from which sprang this laudable movement for the progress and advancement of Americans of Japanese ancestry. The root of unity at the convention was Mr. Kido himself, a second generation member of San Francisco and a leader of the Bay Region district. To him much of the credit goes for the success of the convention through his diligent work in the committee rooms which accomplished a great deal of the actual work of the big meet.
>
> With these leaders in whose hands will repose the responsibility of the future course of the second generation, the citizens move-

ment cannot but reap the results of progress and the recognized establishment of the Americans of Japanese ancestry in the life of the country.

It can be clearly perceivable that the citizens movement is not an idle psychological trend. It is plain that a great march has been started for the proper recognition and identification of the second generation in American life. It is emphatically certain that the second generation will not be a forgotten race and will persistently and diligently contribute their efforts toward nourishing and strengthening the fabric and ideals of democratic government.

To this end has the citizens movement been started and to this end will it assure and pledge the loyalty and devotion of the Americans of Japanese ancestry.

Overall, the significance of the convention was that the Nisei had proved they were mature enough to take an interest in civic affairs—that they could work together well enough to run a national organization and had dedicated leaders to show the way. None of this had been true just ten years earlier when Doc Yatabe and his friends were trying to give their vision shape and substance.

III

The First Lobbyists

Aside from launching a "national" organization—which in reality meant a half dozen chapters in California and one each in Oregon and Washington—the first JACL convention's most significant efforts were addressed to citizenship matters. As we have seen in the previous chapter, resolutions were passed in support of altering the Cable Act to enable Nisei women to regain citizenship lost by marriage to aliens, and in favor of naturalization for Issei who had served in the United States armed forces in World War I.

That anything came of these gestures is due less to JACL as an organization than, in the first case, to fortunate timing, and in the second to the incredible persistence of Tokie Slocum. Despite the euphoria that marked the founding convention JACL was still small, inexperienced, disorganized and without funds. If it did anything more than simply pass the resolutions—like forwarding them to appropriate members of Congress, for instance—there is no record of it. Without elected officers there was no one to follow through, much less plan strategy for carrying out the organization's goals. In the absence of such leadership, the Cable Act amendment early in 1931 became the special project of the Los Angeles chapter, which by then was headed by Clarence Yamagata. Recognizing Suma Sugi's special interest, he named her to look into the problem.

Suma Sugi (later Mrs. Harry Yokotake) was no stranger to discrimination. Born near San Jose, in 1906, she had moved to Los Angeles with her family as a teenager and was graduated in 1924 from the old UCLA Teachers College. The Los Angeles Board of Education told her she couldn't be hired to teach except at a school with 100 percent Nisei enrollment. She had to settle for a clerical job in the school system at seventy-five dollars a month. To gain experience as a student teacher, she took time off for six months to commute daily to Terminal Island—where most of the pupils were Japanese—for one third of her clerical salary. Still she was denied a teaching job.

The Cable Act, sponsored by Congressman John Levi Cable of Ohio, was passed in 1922. As noted earlier, it provided that an American woman would lose her citizenship by marriage to an alien. At the termination of the marriage she could regain United States citizenship by going through the naturalization process. However, since a Nisei woman was of a race ineligible to citizenship, naturalization was denied her. The Cable Act had been under attack for some time by the League of Women Voters, the YWCA and other women's groups as sexually discriminatory since it had no effect on men.

In response to this charge, an amendment depriving men as well as women of citizenship was proposed. However, Congressman Cable himself introduced an amendment providing "that a woman citizen of the United States shall not cease to be a citizen of the United States by reason of her marriage after this section, as amended, takes effect." The amendment also provided that "if any woman was a citizen of the United States at birth, her race shall not preclude the resumption of citizenship. . . ."

Neither JACL nor Japanese Americans as a group had any part in shaping Cable's amendment. It was a national issue that happened to have an incidental pertinence to Nisei women. So far as could be determined, there was no great opposition to the amendment and it appeared ready to be approved routinely. However, the Japanese American community in Los Angeles felt it was important to have a representative in Washington to help nudge the bill along. Money was raised, primarily among the Issei, and the Los Angeles JACL chapter decided to send three Nisei women to lobby Congress. The mission almost failed to materialize. An attorney who had been keeping an eye on the measure in Washington wrote: "As no hearings are scheduled on either bill, sending a delegation would be useless and I recommend against such an action. There will be time enough to do that later if such bills are taken up for hearing by the committee, which I regard very improbable during the present session." But once a movement gets under way, it is difficult to stop. When two of the women decided against the trip—one pleaded she didn't have a proper wardrobe, the other said she couldn't get away because her husband was scheduled to visit Japan on business—Suma Sugi went alone.

She reached Washington late in February, 1931, armed with a sheaf of introductions to various legislators and business cards identifying her as a representative of the national JACL with headquarters at 115½ South San Pedro Street, Los Angeles. A strong coalition of women's groups had marshaled support for the Cable amendment before her arrival, and her primary role was as a charming example of the kind of American woman who could be injured unless the bill were passed. She met Congressman Cable as well as Representative Florence Kahn from the San Francisco area, visited the White House and viewed a House session from the visitors' gallery.

Of this episode, Kido thirty years later wrote: "Frankly speaking, we were babes in the woods then as far as legislative movements were concerned. JACL was not able to be included in the council groups pushing the amendment to bring equality to women citizens. The appeal for this amendment was based upon equal rights for women. The fact that the chief beneficiaries of this amendment would be of Japanese ancestry was injected by JACL to present one facet of the picture."

The Senate and House quickly passed the bill and President Herbert Hoover signed it on March 3, 1931. (Japanese-language newspapers noted that the traditional Girls' Day festival is March 3.) There may be argument over just how effective Suma Sugi had been as a lobbyist, but there is no denying the fact that a representative of JACL had gone to Washington and pleaded successfully for a bill of special interest to the organization. And she had set a precedent of sorts by working on a minimal budget, letting the merits of her cause do the talking. Decades later, limited funds made it necessary for Mike Masaoka to employ a similar strategy in pushing for JACL bills in Congress. Of course, merit based on justice is the best argument for legal redress, but unfortunately it is not always the most effective. In contrast to Suma Sugi's mission, which cost little more than travel expenses, the Chinese American Citizens Alliance about the same time spent some ninety thousand dollars to secure passage of the Bingham Act, which permitted Chinese Americans to bring in alien wives from China as immigrants.

Fortunate timing had made Suma Sugi's assignment relatively easy. Slocum had a much more difficult job, and he tackled his problem from a different angle. What he accomplished, virtually single-handed, constituted a milestone in American immigration and naturalization history. A deep personal hurt, which he revealed to almost no one, enabled him to pursue his goal of citizenship with single-minded determination.

We have seen that Slocum was born in Japan and grew up in Minot, North Dakota. Although the Selective Service Act exempted aliens from military service, Slocum volunteered and was sent to France. On December 10, 1918, just a month after the Armistice and while he was still overseas, Slocum filed a petition for naturalization. The claim was made under the Congressional Act of May 9, 1918, which specified that "any alien serving in the military or naval service of the United States during the present war may file for a petition for naturalization. . . ." (In the act of July 19, 1919, the language was clarified to extend naturalization to "any person of foreign birth who served in the military or naval forces of the United States during the present war" provided he was honorably discharged.)

Nothing was done about Slocum's petition for seven months. Then Slocum received a letter from Robert S. Coleman, chief naturalization examiner in St. Paul, Minnesota, which was like a slap in the face. It said in part: "You are advised furthermore that as the matter stands at present, it will be necessary for the government to object to your naturalization on the ground that you are inadmissible to citizenship because of the fact that you are not a white person."

Slocum met with Coleman on his return from Europe, got no satisfaction whatever, then went to New York and enrolled at Columbia University. After further correspondence, Slocum received a letter on April 6, 1921, from Judge John C. Lowe of the federal district court in Minot inviting him to appear when he returned for summer vacation. "I am willing to issue the papers to you now," Judge Lowe said, indicating Slocum would not have to make a special trip for a hearing. A few days later Coleman wrote to Slocum:

> Now you already know, from what I have heretofore said to you, that the splendid record that you had in our army during the recent war appealed to me very strongly in your case and yet, notwithstanding my personal feelings in the matter, it becomes necessary and it is my duty, when presenting this matter to the court, to say that the opinion of the Bureau of Naturalization is that the law does not permit the admission to citizenship of a Japanese even though he has a record of honorable and faithful service in our army, and it will also be necessary for me to call to the attention of the court said opinions of the courts that I have referred to. [Earlier in the letter Coleman had cited California court rulings denying naturalization to Issei veterans.] When I have done this, I will have performed my duty under the law, and it will be for the court at Minot to decide the matter.

The citizenship hearing was held late in June, 1921. Coleman entered an objection as he had warned he would do. Judge Lowe promptly overruled the examiner, citing Slocum's brilliant record as a noncommissioned officer in the U.S. Army, and declared him a naturalized citizen. Slocum was elated. But his joy, and his tenure as a citizen, were short-lived. The U.S. Supreme Court ruled soon afterward that the words "any alien" in the act of 1918 and "any person of foreign birth" in the act of 1919 did not include Orientals. The high court decided that the wartime laws failed to override the basic law of 1906 which restricted naturalization to "free white persons and to aliens of African nativity and to persons of African descent."

For Tokie Slocum, America was a beautiful woman who had first encouraged him, then scorned him. But he never lost hope that someday she would accept him. He loved this country with an uncomplicated, unquestioning patriotism perhaps beyond the comprehension of citizens of a later era when dissent and complaint could be applauded as the hallmarks of militant Americanism. His love of country inspired him to make the fervid speeches that moved JACLers in Seattle to endorse his plea for citizenship. A half century later Bud Konzo would write: "The one incident that remains in my memory [of the 1930 convention] is the flag-waving, bellicose pep-talk given by Tokie Slocum who strode up and down the platform to shout that 'if war comes tomorrow between Japan and the United States, I would be fighting for the Stars and Stripes.' This was at a time when there was no hint of impending crisis. I recall that the incident, when reported in the local Japanese newspapers, was received unfavorably by Issei groups." Some convention delegates, frankly, were amused by Slocum's rhetoric; he seemed to be so totally dedicated to such an impossible mission that it was difficult to take him seriously. They passed the resolution but offered him no more than moral support—no funds, no direction, no guidance.

Slocum required little of these. It was enough that he had the moral backing of the JACL. He had his own strategy, worked out in his mind over many years of earnest planning. First, he began a letter-writing campaign. He wrote to a wide circle of friends in veterans organizations—the American Legion, the Veterans of Foreign Wars, the Forty and Eight—in which the men he had known had climbed to positions of influence. He told them of his fight for justice, asked for support and an opportunity to address local and state conventions. His objective was to stir up a ground swell of backing that would give a mandate to the national organizations, which in turn would instruct their high-powered Washington lobbyists to work for the cause. One of the first to respond was the Disabled American Veterans of Arizona, which approved a resolution noting that some seven hundred vets of Oriental birth "because of the present interpretation of the Act [of Congress] are unable to enjoy the right to become citizens." It went on to say: "We, as comrades, honestly and sincerely believe that these Oriental veterans of the American forces, who waived their right to alien exemption from military service and chose to serve and defend the United States of America, their adopted country, in time of war, are entitled to the right to become citizens. . . ."

The backing of the American Legion was particularly important. The Legion was a key member of the Japanese Exclusion League as well as the California Joint Immigration Committee, the latter a powerful coalition spearheading anti-Oriental legislation under the motto: Keep California white. If the Legion would endorse citizenship for veterans of Japanese birth—which it ultimately did—the forces of the opposition would be weakened greatly.

Slocum had no expense account, no office, no secretary. He set up residence in Washington, D.C., painstakingly writing his letters in longhand. He made a little money by teaching English to members of the Japanese embassy staff. Sometimes he washed dishes for meals. The years dragged on, and JACL leaders, recognizing the difficulty of Slocum's task, sent him what little cash they could spare. Kido has written of those times: "Sim Togasaki and I had to find some source which we could tap. It was obvious that the ones who would benefit most should be asked to start the ball rolling. We tried to contact the World War I veterans."

But this was more than fifteen years after the end of the war, and many had given up hope of gaining citizenship. Kido wrote to Japanese veterans in Hawaii and received almost no response. Some of them had contributed to unsuccessful previous campaigns, the Depression had brought hard times, and a new effort appeared to be a waste of money. A few dollars dribbled in from veterans in Los Angeles and San Francisco. Most of the support came from Wallace Alexander, philanthropist and then president of the Japan Society of San Francisco, who was deeply interested in repealing the Oriental Exclusion Act passed in 1924. In all, Alexander contributed about eight hundred dollars to Slocum's cause, and this relatively modest sum kept him going.

It was 1935 before Slocum's efforts bore fruit. Congressman Clarence F. Lea of California introduced a bill, H.R. 7170, which said in effect that it was the will of Congress to grant citizenship to Oriental veterans. (The thrust had been changed from citizenship for Japanese veterans to citizenship for all Oriental veterans in an effort to broaden the base of support.) Senator Gerald Nye of North Dakota introduced a similar bill, S. 2508, in the upper house. Congressman Samuel Dickstein of New York, chairman of the Committee on Immigration and Naturalization, scheduled hearings. Slocum testified eloquently. The committee approved the measure unanimously, calling it "simply a measure of justice." However, reflecting the feeling against Oriental immigration, the committee felt obliged to state:

> There is no immigration question involved within the provisions of this bill as reported from the committee since no one who is not within the United States or not within the Territories of the United States on the date this bill becomes law in its present form will be able to claim any benefits under this legislative measure. Your committee feels sure this measure, as reported to the House, will not result in any immigration of persons from Oriental coun-

> tries who are now excluded under the immigration laws from admission to the United States or Territories thereof.

The Nye-Lea bill sailed through Congress and President Franklin Delano Roosevelt signed the measure June 25, 1935. The individuals who benefited were relatively few—the number of veterans still living and in the United States had dwindled from about seven hundred to perhaps five hundred. But as a legal precedent, granting naturalization privileges to Orientals, it was a milestone. A people who had been "ineligible to citizenship" had now, in this particular case, been made eligible.

Oddly enough, JACL gave Slocum relatively little credit. The April, 1935, issue of *Pacific Citizen,* by then JACL's monthly organ, stated the Nye-Lea bill had been reported favorably out of committee and called it "a real victory for the Japanese American Citizens' League in its fight to win justice for the Oriental veterans." The story continued:

> Both the American Legion and the Veterans of Foreign Wars in their national conventions last year went on record in support of the measure, and recently the California Joint Immigration Committee recommended its passage. Backed by the resolutions and making what is regarded as a valiant fight, Tokutaro N. Slocum, an ex-doughboy himself, took the battle to Washington as the JACL representative.
>
> Behind the scenes however, there was the national JACL lending its effort for introduction and final passage of the bill. Among those taking the lead in the fight were such men as Dr. T. T. Yatabe, national president; Saburo Kido, national secretary; Sim Togasaki, national treasurer; Dr. T. Hayashi, past president of the San Francisco JACL; Thomas Yego, Northern California JACL Council chairman; John Ando, Southern California Council chairman; Tom Iseri, Northwest Council chairman. . . . The fight for the Oriental veterans citizenship was first started when the first convention of the Japanese American Citizens' League held in Seattle in 1930 sent a resolution to Congress. . . .

In the same issue of *Pacific Citizen* an editorial said:

> It was the JACL that really organized the fight for the veterans. Before the League actively jumped into the fray at their first biennial national convention in Seattle in 1930, there had been sporadic attempts to win citizenship for these veterans. But it was really the League that gave direction to all the individual efforts that were being made on behalf of the veterans.

> The League's work on this bill was really two-fold. In the first place, it carried on active campaigns in behalf of the veterans by raising funds, arousing support and by other methods. And in the second place, it served as an invaluable clearing house through which the efforts of individuals could be coordinated. . . .

The editorial failed to mention Slocum by name.

In Kido's reminiscences, published by *Pacific Citizen* in 1961, he tried to make up for this slight. Kido wrote:

> . . . The campaign that Tokutaro N. Slocum waged in Washington, D. C., by himself did not have full press coverage. . . . It may have been my fault since I was the national secretary during the campaign. There may be many reasons for this. In the first place, publicity was an unknown art as far as persons of Japanese ancestry were concerned. The skepticism as to the success of the campaign may have been another reason, causing indifference. . . . However, Slocum must be accorded a place in the history of the Japanese in America for the opening wedge pertaining to naturalization privileges.

IV

Los Angeles, 1932

The 1930–32 biennium was a period of rapid growth for JACL as increasing numbers of Nisei reached adulthood. Many of the earlier members pushed the movement with missionary zeal, giving unstintingly of their time to visit concentrations of Japanese Americans and urge them to organize. Whereas only eight chapters were represented in Seattle, invitations went to twenty-two (including short-lived unorganized groups in Hawaii and New York City) for the Los Angeles convention in 1932.

But it would be inaccurate to suggest that the JACL movement was off and running. With inexperienced leadership most of the chapters had difficult births and even after they were formally organized few became viable units overnight. In many areas JACL faced hostility from Issei who controlled the purse strings and saw it as a challenge to their community leadership. The Japanese-language press was not always supportive. Ordered to write an editorial he considered derogatory toward JACL, Tamotsu Murayama in San Francisco once got into a table-pounding argument with his publisher. Murayama made his point and the editorial was not written.

Sociology Professor S. Frank Miyamoto of the University of Washington, who was a member of the Seattle chapter, described JACL this way: "If the JACL was an opportunistic, unstable organization, the fault lay not merely with its leadership, but the bulk of the Nisei population in Seattle were confused concerning their national and social identity, and they extended these characteristics into their major organization. One might say that almost all the characteristics of the JACL, good or bad, derived more or less directly from the characteristic mental state of the Nisei."

If the veteran Seattle chapter impressed one of its members in this fashion, one can imagine the sorry state that existed elsewhere. All this added up to the impression among some Issei that JACL demonstrated the irresponsibility if not the frivolity of the young. Kido explains that a difference of perception did not add to understanding. "We were thinking of JACL more as a fraternal-civic body to promote the unity and welfare of persons of Japanese ancestry," he has written. "The Issei were looking at this movement from a different angle. They wanted JACL to be more of a political action group. They wanted the Nisei to help fight against the strong anti-Japanese sentiment." That was to come much later.

The dues structure of the Los Angeles chapter would seem to carry out the impression of frivolity. Membership dues were only one dollar per year for regular members and fifty cents for those between the ages of eighteen and twenty-one who were considered associate members. New members paid a fifty-cent initiation fee. Such a modest schedule of levies could hardly enhance the chapter's capabilities.

By 1931 John S. Ando, a law student at the University of Southern California, was chapter president. But before long he had to resign because of ill health. Three were nominated to fill the unexpired term—Suma Sugi, who had represented JACL in Washington, Masao Igasaki, who had been the chapter's first president, and Elmer S. Yamamoto, who had been active in building up the membership. The membership responded by rejecting all of them and electing Karl Iwanaga, the city's first Nisei attorney.

(Los Angeles was one of the few chapters to have contests for the presidency. In 1936 Kay Sugahara, a hard-driving customs broker, campaigned vigorously for a third term. His challenger was Dr. Mike M. Horii. Suddenly Sugahara withdrew and threw his support behind John Maeno, an attorney. Maeno won easily but some thirty-two members signed a protest charging irregularities. A second election was scheduled. Elmer Yamamoto threw his hat in the ring to make it a three-way race. The candidates distributed leaflets in Li'l Tokyo and bought political ads in the Japanese newspapers, stirring up an unprecedented amount of public interest. Maeno won again with 89 votes, followed by Yamamoto with 60 and Horii with 6. In contrast with this spirited race, Hito Okada, later to become a national president, was elected president of the Portland chapter at the very first meeting he attended.)

Because of the limited time he could devote to preparing for the 1932 convention, Iwanaga wisely named Dr. George Y. Takeyama to head the arrangements committee. As convention chairman Dr. Takeyama automatically became JACL's second national president. Born in Sacramento in 1896, Takeyama was the seventh of the eight children of Dr. and Mrs. Suketsugu Takeyama. The older Takeyama came to the United States in 1880 and is believed to have been the first Issei physician. George Takeyama received his medical degree from Stanford University in 1923. The convention was scheduled for three days starting July 27, just before the opening of the Olympic Games. A budget of fifteen hundred dollars was set up with the members turning to the Issei community for contributions. Among the fund-raising functions was an unabashedly arm-twisting benefit dinner suggested by Katsuma Mukaeda, president of the Japanese Chamber of Commerce, and Gongoro Nakamura, both masters at the art of collecting contributions from the community. (After World War II both Mukaeda and Nakamura were naturalized and served terms as president of Downtown L.A. JACL, as the chapter came to be known.) Tickets at ten dollars per person or fifteen dollars per couple were sent out to leaders of the Japanese Chamber of Commerce, the Central Japanese Association, the prefectural associations, the fruit market operators association, businessmen, prominent members of the professional community and others. JACL members, however, were charged only two dollars. A benefit show with plays and skits in English and Japanese, and a benefit dance also helped raise funds.

For some reason Dr. Takeyama's committee was not named until about three weeks prior to the convention. Masao Igasaki and Suma Sugi were assigned to get the speakers. Kay Sugahara arranged the banquets. Suma Sugi had charge of registration and George Nakamoto took care of the publicity. Toyo Arai and Tomi Saito arranged for the dance that would wind up the convention. The Seattle delegation arrived a few days before the convention was to open. Toshio Hoshide remembers that he, Jimmie Sakamoto, Takeo Nogaki and several others drove into Li'l Tokyo and happened to see Goro Murata, one of the more active members of the host chapter.

As Hoshide recalls it, Murata said: "Jimmie, I don't know if we're going to have a convention."

"Why?" Sakamoto demanded. "What do you mean?"

"We just aren't ready," Murata explained. "We haven't got all the details settled."

Sakamoto quickly launched into an eloquent pep talk, at which he was a master. Eventually Murata trotted off with renewed enthusiasm and assurances of support from the Seattleites. Finding a convention hall had been a major problem. Takeyama consulted Councilman George Baker, whose district included Li'l Tokyo, and received permission to use one of the larger chambers at city hall. This was a coup that impressed local residents and visitors alike.

Since most of the leading members of the Li'l Tokyo community were members of JACL, the convention was a major event. The *Rafu Shimpo* English section published an editorial welcoming the delegates and, perhaps in veiled reference to factionalism in the Los Angeles chapter, had this to say: ". . . At this opportune time all petty prejudices must be buried and forgotten, forever, if possible. The time has come when all American citizens of Japanese ancestry must pull together for a common cause—the cause of the second generation and the untold generations yet to come. All our thought and action must be guided with the future in mind. To do the best work everyone must work together in unity, harmony and cooperation. The dead weights of faction and partisanship must be dropped."

A parade headed by Nisei Boy Scouts led the delegates from Li'l Tokyo to city hall just a few blocks away. Mayor John C. Porter opened the sessions with a welcome for the approximately 150 delegates, and Goro Murata offered a moving eulogy on the immigrant generation.

Perhaps the convention's most significant message was delivered by Joseph Scott, a member of the Republican National Committee, who had nominated Herbert Hoover for the presidency only a short time earlier. He asserted that Americans of Japanese ancestry could be, and must be, sterling citizens and take an active part in American political and social life. But this did not mean they should reject their Japanese heritage, he said. Scott declared that the sight of Japanese cherry blossoms should stir emotion in Nisei but this sentiment should in no way detract from their patriotism as Americans. In a way, Scott put into perspective what many Nisei had been feeling about JACL and their status as Americans of Japanese descent, but hadn't been able to articulate to their satisfaction. Issei, in particular, were gratified by Scott's words. They understood Nisei loyalty to the United States and approved of it, but many interpreted that to mean JACL also was advocating abandonment of Japanese culture and values. This they found distressing. Scott's admoniton to the Nisei to respect the land of their ancestry was reassuring. Jimmie Sakamoto was moved to editorialize in his *Courier:* "The impressive speech by Hon. Joseph Scott may indeed be called the keynote address of the Los Angeles convention in that the very ideals of the citizens' movement were strongly emphasized in that speech. Active participation in the political life of this nation will inevitably bring about the recognition with which the Americans of Japanese ancestry may achieve lasting contributions toward Japanese-American friendship and harmony."

Gongoro Nakamura, well known as a Japanese orator, picked up on Scott's theme. He told the delegates: "You are citizens of the United States. Be proud of it. You are part of one of the world's greatest nations; be proud of it just as I am a citizen of Japan and proud of that fact." Nakamura urged the Nisei to retain the tradition of respect for and obedience to their elders. "Keep your politeness," he said. "It has made many, many friends for you. You must keep and develop these good qualities which will make you fit, fit and prepared to take your full place in American society."

The round-table format for discussions initiated at the Seattle convention was continued in Los Angeles with many of the Nisei overcoming their reluctance to speak up and wading boldly into political and legal issues as well as social, economic and vocational problems. The liveliest sessions were in the social round table. One recommendation: Nisei should learn the Japanese language so they could communicate with their parents. Nisei also were urged to widen their contacts in the greater American community, as one published report put it, "to create a better understanding among the diversified races under an American entity which would help to introduce the ability of the second generation in leading toward a proper recognition of their status."

The problem of racial discrimination came in for vigorous discussion, particularly when it was pointed out that under U.S. Immigration Service practice some Oriental Americans were less equal than other Oriental Americans, and both groups suffered from discrimination not applied to Caucasians. Passports for travel abroad were readily issued on presentation of proof of citizenship, but frequently those passports were not recognized when the bearer returned to the United States. Oriental Americans were detained at immigration stations until they produced witnesses who could testify that the person named in the passport was indeed the person carrying it, and that he had been born in the United States. Chinese Americans were able to get around this bureaucratic harassment by obtaining, before going abroad, a certificate of identity which said that they were indeed who they said they were. Some Nisei wanted the certificate-of-identity system extended to them. Others argued that such certificates were discriminatory, that a passport should be identity enough, and demanded that the Immigration Service be ordered to recognize their validity.

The convention's decision was to look into the problem and seek a solution. But the problem was not resolved until four years later when Tamotsu Murayama, on his way to Berlin to cover the Olympic Games, stopped in Washington and discussed the difficulty with Mrs. Ruth Shipley, who headed the State Department's passport division. She apparently had been unaware of the discriminatory practice. She assured Murayama that all American citizens were entitled to the same treatment, and in time persuaded the Immigration Service to end its harassment.

Among its other actions, the convention adopted *Pacific Citizen,* a monthly newspaper published by the San Francisco chapter, as its national organ; approved an oratorical contest for the next convention; authorized regional conventions to be called district council meetings; ordered a study of fraternal and old-age insurance; endorsed Tokie Slocum's efforts to win citizenship for Issei veterans of World War I; and called for a vote by all chapters on a revised constitution. The five members of the committee named to revise the constitution were Clarence Arima of Los Angeles, Fred Hirasuna of Fresno, Kido of San Francisco, Lyle Kurisaki of Brawley and Sakamoto of Seattle. Perhaps the most important change they made was to provide for election of national officers instead of simply accepting the chairman of the upcoming national convention as the League's chief executive.

It was at the Los Angeles convention that Masao W. Satow, a personable, outgoing young Nisei, first surfaced as a JACLer. Satow was graduated from the University of California at Los Angeles in 1929, then attended Princeton Theological Seminary for three years. He returned to Los Angeles in 1932 and was appointed general secretary of the Japanese YMCA in Li'l Tokyo. His office was a single room in the Tomio Building, now the Taul Building, at 312 East First Street. Satow joined JACL and was named the convention's deputy registrar, assisting Suma Sugi. He was soon to take a key role in JACL, and much will be heard of him in the rest of this volume.

V

A Voice for JACL

Jimmie Sakamoto's weekly *Courier,* founded in Seattle on New Year's Day, 1928, was the first journal for Japanese Americans entirely in English. Because of Sakamoto's personal dedication to JACL, his paper almost invariably blew up JACL-related stories beyond their news value. Whether this sort of press agentry helped JACL is a matter for conjecture. In any event, anyone who read the *Courier* could not help but become aware of JACL, its activities and its goals, and it is indisputable that the League was strong in the Pacific Northwest where the paper was circulated. However, the *Courier* was a private enterprise albeit an unprofitable one, and it published other community news.

Nearly two years after the *Courier* began publication the first strictly JACL newspaper appeared. It was a semimonthly called *Nikkei Shimin,* which means "Japanese American Citizen." Its publisher was the New American Citizens League of San Francisco, one of JACL's founding members at the Seattle convention. The first issue was dated October 13, 1929, nearly a year before the Seattle gathering.

Kido and Sim Togasaki had been trying for many months to launch the paper. Sim estimated it would cost fifty dollars an issue to publish *Nikkei Shimin* and he wanted enough cash on hand to keep the paper going for a year. Finally he had nine hundred dollars in contributions and prepayments on advertising and decided to go ahead.

Nikkei Shimin's editorial and business offices were at 1623 Webster Street, Saburo Kido's combination home and law office. The masthead of Volume 1, Number 1, listed Iwao Kawakami as editor; Kido, Miya Sannomiya and Henry Takahashi, associate editors; Asayo Kuraya, literary editor; Fumi Yonezu, society editor; Kaoru Miura, club editor; Togasaki, business manager; Jhosey Aoki, advertising manager; Tomiye Tsushi and Nao Zaiman, circulation managers. All, of course, were volunteers.

Editor Kawakami was an earnest young Nisei with aspirations to serious writing. He wore heavy glasses, read voraciously and for many years kept body and soul together as both an editor and a linotype operator on the English section of the San Francisco *Japanese American News.* Some of his idealism shows through in a rambling, free-wheeling, sometimes disjointed signed editorial titled "Our Purpose," which he published in the first issue of *Nikkei Shimin.*

"One of the purposes of this publication is to give the new Japanese-American citizens an appropriate medium through which they can express themselves," he began. Then he digressed into a philosophical discussion of "creative expression," going back to the golden ages of Greece and Rome, England and France to make his point. Finally, getting back to the Nisei, he wrote: "We, the Japanese-Americans, are in a position where we represent the blending of two races or, in another sense, we are an entirely new group of young people in America. It would not be amiss, therefore, to believe that new forms of creative expression will rise from our group."

Kawakami went on to discuss opportunities for Nisei in agriculture, industry and social and intellectual pursuits. He wrote:

> The social and intellectual aspects are, by far, the least developed by the Japanese-Americans. There are, to be sure, individual examples of social and artistic leadership; yet they cannot begin to compare in quantity or quality with those of other races in America. The Japanese-American, in most cases, confronts the pitfall of imitation or unoriginality; and those are precisely the things that one must learn to avoid.
>
> It is in order to help the new American citizens avoid these pitfalls and in order to encourage the development of healthy sincerity in the matter of expression that we wish to introduce this publication to the Japanese and American people.

Apologizing for his forwardness, Kawakami concluded his editorial with two verses from a "poem" he had written:

From America's oft-quoted "melting pot"
Have bubbled out thousands of newspapers
With their editorial fire or rot
Catering to—or cutting up capers.
Some may be fit to be read, others not—
Though all, at times, indulge in hot vapors.
We rejoice at the power of the press
For good, but not its abuse in a mess.

At first, all our papers were in English
(Though even that speech has undergone change.)
But when the aliens came (by our wish
To clear away the wilderness and range),
They settled and then started to publish
Needed news in their own tongues—some quite strange.
If we promise no transient example
Before you cast your ancient eggs—sample!

Such efforts make it understandable that circulation was a major concern of the staff even though the subscription rate was only one dollar a year. The first issue announced a contest with a prize of two tickets to the Stanford-Army football game or eight dollars in cash to the person selling the most subscriptions. The second prize was three dollars, and third prize a two-year subscription to *Nikkei Shimin.* Unfortunately only a few copies of the newspaper remain and there is no record of who won the prizes or how many subscriptions were sold. The staff apparently was not comfortable with their paper's name and the first issue also announced a contest to provide it with a new one. Early in 1930 it was renamed *Pacific Citizen* but no one recalls who submitted the name. As we have seen, *Pacific Citizen* was designated the official publication of JACL at the Los Angeles convention in 1932.

Kido, who through most of his adult life was connected in one way or another with newspapers, had his own goals for *Nikkei Shimin.* Writing as president of the sponsoring group, he said:

Ever since the organization of the League, the Board of Governors have recognized the necessity of a newspaper or magazine which would serve as a mouthpiece. Though the English section of the *Japanese-American News* gave us wonderful support by

> giving all our undertakings full publicity, still we felt something lacking.
>
> Oftentimes we have read in the Japanese section of local papers articles pertaining to us, second generation members, and we have had the desire to express our ideas and thoughts as a reply because we thought our elders misunderstood us. Inability to write in Japanese, however, has been the chief handicap. Also the Board of Governors have done their utmost to stimulate interest in the League and build up a strong, unified body; but they have fallen short of the goal they have set up. A publication such as we now have will be of great aid.
>
> The publication can be the connecting link between the first and second generation Japanese by trying to dissolve any misunderstanding which may be existing at the present time. It can portray to the American public what we, American citizens of Japanese ancestry, are thinking in regards to our duties as citizens as well as our diverse problems. It can give expression to what is considered true American ideals and guide the growing generation to become American citizens we can all be proud of.
>
> Considering the potential power of the publication to do good, I cannot help but impress on the members of the staff the grave responsibility that lies on their shoulders. In their hands lies the power to help mold the second generation members for good or bad.
>
> The public is expecting great things. I am confident that the members of the staff will do their utmost so as not to disappoint these supporters. Of course, we cannot expect perfect models of journalism from the beginning, but we hope that improvements will be made gradually as time goes on. . . .

This was indeed a weighty charge for a volunteer staff that handled all the production chores except for the actual typesetting and printing. That was done at the Tokai Printing Company, 1824 Post Street, a half block from Kido's office. The papers came out flat from the press and the staff folded them by hand, then wrapped and mailed them. Even though there were only about a thousand copies, some days the work continued past midnight. Kido and Togasaki spent many afternoons soliciting advertising from Japantown merchants, restaurants and professionals. The first issue also carried a single item that might be classified as legitimate news. It was about a young Los Angeles Nisei who had come to San Francisco in an unsuccessful search for work, got the idea of trying a stickup from a movie and tried to rob a Japanese pedestrian. A police officer apprehended the young bandit and turned him over to the Japanese Salvation Army. No names were mentioned.

When Kawakami moved to San Diego several years after the paper was founded, Earl Tanbara and Asayo Kuraya became joint editors. But the burden of publishing a semimonthly with a volunteer staff soon proved too much. Rather than let *Pacific Citizen* die, Jimmie Sakamoto in 1933 agreed reluctantly to produce it as a four-page tabloid monthly in his shop. The understanding was that JACL would pay Sakamoto for the actual printing, which was done in a job shop, and mailing costs. Sakamoto would contribute the services of his editorial and typesetting staff. In return, Sim Togasaki promised to solicit holiday-issue advertisements among San Francisco merchants for the *Courier.*

PC was an onerous extra chore for Sakamoto's tiny staff which, like all Japanese American newsmen of the time, was being paid very modestly. News gathering consisted mostly of rewriting correspondence from JACL chapter secretaries, or going through the English sections of Japanese dailies in California and picking up items about chapter meetings and social events. Kido sometimes supplied editorials or front-page policy stories, and when he failed to do so, Sakamoto would outline an idea and Jack McGilvray Maki of his own staff would rattle off an editorial. Maki was working on his master's degree in English at the University of Washington during a part of this period and reading numerous books. When a large hole had to be filled, Maki would produce a book review, confounding his colleagues by writing it as fast as he could type. The books Maki reviewed had nothing to do with Japanese Americans, but that was a small matter when copy was needed. The type was set on the *Courier*'s clanking old linotype machine by John Funai, and the pages were usually made up by Sakamoto's wife, Misao, and sent out to be printed.

During this time *Pacific Citizen* was beset by a problem that cripples many small newspapers. With limited finances, JACL could not produce an adequate publication. Because the paper provided little that was new or interesting, its circulation was extremely limited. And with limited circulation there wasn't much prospect of increasing the advertising linage that would bring in income. It was a vicious circle without an escape. The JACL convention in 1938 sought to improve the newspaper by combining a subscription with membership. The head of each

JACL family was required to pay an additional twenty-five cents a year in dues, in return for which he received the paper. And each chapter was assessed twelve dollars a year, which could be paid as a cash contribution or by selling advertising, to support *Pacific Citizen.* Such heroic measures raised *PC*'s circulation to three thousand but did little to solve its basic problems.

Sakamoto finally gave up *Pacific Citizen* in 1939. It was returned to San Francisco where Evelyn Kirimura took over as editor and Vernon Ichisaka as business manager. They produced the first *Pacific Citizen* holiday issue, an eighteen-page ad-filled year-end effort which has become a *PC* tradition for producing income. Most issues, however, were no more than four tabloid pages. JACL news of national or regional concern appeared on page 1. The second page carried editorials, occasional columns, essays and literary efforts. Kay Nishida, English editor of the *Japanese-American News* in San Francisco and then the dean of Nisei writers, contributed frequent commentaries. And when there was space, features on job opportunities, farming and even homemaking were published. Chapter news was used on page 3 and the back page was given over to general Nisei activities.

Still, a monthly in newspaper rather than magazine format, carrying material that had appeared weeks earlier in other Japanese American journals, had meager appeal. In 1940 it appeared that *Pacific Citizen* was nearing its end. After the May issue, no paper appeared for four months. Behind the scenes, Kido was taking time he could ill afford to spare from his law practice to try to revive the paper. He persuaded Walter Tsukamoto, a past national president, to write a column on legal problems of interest to Nisei and helped put together a paper in time for October distribution. Five thousand copies were printed and used to push a JACL membership drive. For the holiday issue—at a time when war was raging in Europe—*Pacific Citizen* solicited greetings from a number of national figures. The response from Frank Knox, then Secretary of the Navy, is particularly interesting in view of his actions only a little more than a year later. Knox's message to JACL, published on the front page of *Pacific Citizen,* read:

> Through the courtesy of the Pacific Citizen, I am happy to extend Christmas greetings to the members of the Japanese American Citizens League. At this time of crisis in world affairs

we can all be thankful we are citizens of a free country, living in peace and relative plenty while wars of aggression, with their attendant sufferings and misfortunes to all who are involved, rage all around us.

The National Defense effort, so necessary to our well-being, both as individuals and as a nation, demands the enthusiastic support of all our people. In unity of purpose we can continue along the road of spiritual and material progress. It is satisfying indeed for the well-being of our country to know that its citizens of Japanese descent are enrolled in the struggle to maintain the onward march of liberty.

In December, 1941, just days after the Japanese attack on Pearl Harbor, Knox flew to Hawaii to inspect the damage and assess the situation. Back in Los Angeles on December 15, Knox told a press conference "the most effective fifth column work of the entire war was done in Hawaii, with the possible exception of Norway."

The book *East to America* by Robert A. Wilson and Bill Hosokawa says of Knox's statement: "This was a ridiculous lie, and the most charitable explanation for it is the possibility he was misled in Hawaii by military personnel trying to explain away their shortcomings. Another view, which cannot be substantiated, is that Knox deliberately misinformed the American public in a calculated effort to stir up war fever. In any event, this charge of treachery by the Japanese population of Hawaii was never refuted in the weeks that preceded the Japanese evacuation from the West Coast."

Knox's official report made no mention of fifth-column activity. This reinforces the suspicion that the press conference statement was an intentional falsehood, made the more deplorable by his acknowledgment of the patriotic Nisei role in his message to *Pacific Citizen.*

When war came federal officials quickly closed down all the West Coast's Japanese-language papers, which also meant their English sections were out of business. This made it impossible for the authorities to communicate in any detail with the Japanese Americans, particularly the Issei, either to notify them of rapidly changing regulations or to calm their fears. *Pacific Citizen,* while not affected directly by the shutdown, was not geared for the task of keeping the Japanese American community informed. National JACL headquarters in San Francisco moved into the breech with mimeographed bulletins in English and Japanese which were airmailed to chapter presidents, and they in turn were reproduced for local distribution.

After the first flurry of excitement, Nisei-managed community newspapers were permitted to resume publication. Yas Abiko recalls that his *Nichi Bei* was closed down the day after Pearl Harbor but was allowed back in business following Christmas. The *Nichi Bei* published regularly until a few days before San Franciscans were evacuated to the Tanforan Race Track in May.

Pacific Citizen was one of the subjects brought up at the emergency JACL National Council meeting in March of 1942 where the organization's response to the Army's Evacuation order was shaped. After only brief discussion the delegates voted to move the newspaper to Salt Lake City together with JACL headquarters, recognizing *PC*'s new importance to the Japanese American community as a source of news and a public-relations vehicle. Larry Tajiri, a professional newspaperman, was named editor.

PC's performance during the war years makes stirring reading. It became an articulate, hard-hitting, often inspiring advocate of the Nisei and an evenhanded reporter of the news. Only when Tajiri took over did *Pacific Citizen* begin to live up to the noble role Kido had envisioned for the paper when he wrote for its first issue a dozen years earlier.

But that is getting ahead of the story, and for now we must return to the organization itself.

VI

San Francisco, 1934

Tamotsu Murayama, who had a genuine flair for the spectacular, clinched the 1934 convention for San Francisco by flying to Los Angeles with a formal invitation from the mayor and board of supervisors. Los Angeles had gained use of a room in city hall for its convention, a vast improvement over the facilities Seattle had been able to offer, but then San Francisco was able to persuade its elected officials to extend a welcome. In the subtle game of one-upsmanship played by the Nisei of the two California cities, Murayama's stroke had scored points for the San Franciscans. But the glow from that triumph was short-lived. Ahead lay substantial difficulties.

The third national JACL convention came at a time of growing Nisei maturity, an economic depression that was punishing both urban and rural Japanese Americans, and not inconsiderable Issei hostility. The older Nisei leaders were now in their early thirties. Many were burdened by family and financial responsibilities. Up and down the Pacific Coast other Nisei were being graduated from high schools and colleges, only to face blank walls in their search for economic opportunity. The West's deeply ingrained prejudices against Orientals effectively kept them from finding meaningful work outside their ethnic communities, no matter how impressive their credentials. Inside the ghettos, there were few other than dead-end jobs—the fruit markets in Los Angeles, clerking in a San Francisco Chinatown art or souvenir store, helping in a family-operated grocery or skid row hotel in Seattle.

The Great Depression, which wiped out the livelihoods of millions of able-bodied Americans and sent thousands of Okies and Arkies heading west in their jalopies to the California promised land, caused the Nisei to consider themselves fortunate to have any kind of menial work in their communities. But their problems had to be addressed, somehow, by JACL if it were to serve them.

Friction between Issei and Nisei was inevitable. On the one hand there were the young American-born, American-educated, American-oriented Nisei seeking to assert themselves. On the other hand there were the community elders who were upset by many of the strange American customs embraced by their sons and daughters, and who feared the traditional Japanese virtues were being abandoned. They also saw the rise of JACL as a challenge to their leadership. The Issei viewed the Nisei as frivolous, excessively fun seeking, irresponsible in a difficult time. While these are familiar complaints between generations, the problem in Japanese American communities was intensified by a large age gap. Due to late marriage among Issei because of certain economic and sociological conditions, many of them were old enough to be the grandparents of their own children. The cultural gap between the elderly foreign-born generation and the young American-born generation was particularly difficult to bridge because of the language barrier. Few Nisei could express themselves well in Japanese; few Issei were fluent in English. Their differences were intensified by a historical episode beyond their control, thousands of miles away. In 1931, Japan, in the grip of militarists, invaded the Asian mainland and carved the puppet state of Manchukuo out of China. Many Issei saw nothing wrong with this; hadn't European nations and the United States built empires with just such tactics? Rather than condemn their homeland, many Issei applauded the new Japanese aggressiveness. And most Nisei, at least in the privacy of their homes, condemned Japan and even dared to espouse the Chinese side. There were many heated, if not entirely understood, bilingual arguments over family dinner tables.

Something of the temper of those days can be perceived in an editorial published by the English section of the San Francisco *Hokubei Asahi* after JACL played a role in defeating the Kramer Bill in Congress. (The bill was a gratuitous blow aimed specifically at Orientals, providing that if the wife of an American was an alien ineligible to citizenship, their children born abroad would be regarded as aliens and would not acquire the father's citizenship.) T. John Fujii, who like Bob Okazaki and many others had been born in Japan but educated in the United States, was English-section editor when *Hokubei Asahi* observed:

> Our elders have continually questioned the value and importance of the Japanese American Citizens' League. We have fought and struggled to explain our case and accomplishments; they have considered the Leagues as organizations which were only interested in social gatherings.
>
> It is true that the Leagues have given dances and benefit shows, but they have been sponsored for two main purposes: to attract more citizens to the Leagues through social means, and to raise funds.
>
> But bigger things have been accomplished already by the Leagues. In 1931 the Cable Act amendment was passed through Congress by the united efforts of the League members, and restored American citizenship to many second generation wives of Japanese ineligible to citizenship. . . .
>
> Then again, the Seawell Bill, in which an alien was prohibited to possess any firearms or to fish in California, was withdrawn through the concerted efforts of the Leagues.
>
> Now, in the latest case, the Leagues have been instrumental in quashing the Kramer Bill in Congress, which would have been highly detrimental to the children of citizens with alien wives.
>
> We believe these instances are sufficient to show the power and influence of the Citizens League and that these organizations are ready to protect and advance the welfare of both first and second generation Japanese in America. In view of this constructive work, it is regrettable to find some writers among the first generation who express opinions publicly, to discourage the second generation.
>
> We believe that such critics are shortsighted and are hindering their own progress as well as that of the second generation. It is time that we all got together and pushed our common aims with cooperative enthusiasm.

It is not likely the editorial did much to close the rift. In fact, intergenerational relations remained so tense that Issei sensitivity about the Manchurian issue created a major problem in selecting a keynote speaker for the 1934 convention. Almost every public figure who came to mind had spoken out against Japanese aggression and was therefore unacceptable to Issei leaders. The convention committee had no wish to offend them. The eventual choice was Chester Rowell, an editor of the *San Francisco Chronicle,* who had been critical of Japan but was widely respected for his fairness toward Japanese Americans.

The convention budget was set at $2,000, compared with $1,400 in Seattle and $1,500 in Los Angeles. San Francisco undertook to raise $1,500, with the balance to come from the other chapters in the district. The American Loyalty League in Fresno sponsored a dance to raise funds for its contribution. The San Francisco chapter put on a benefit performance of *Charlie's Aunt,* a favorite of amateur theater groups of the day, but there is no record of its financial success. San Jose and Alameda came up with $70 apiece, and so it went.

Dr. Terry Hayashi, as president of the San Francisco chapter, was also national JACL president under the then rules. Hayashi's committees arranged for the opening session to be held in spacious Polk Hall in Civic Center. They persuaded school authorities to dismiss all Japanese American students from high school classes so they could attend the opening as part of their "Americanization" education. About one thousand persons came and heard Rowell make what, in effect, were two speeches. The first fifteen minutes, broadcast by one of San Francisco's leading radio stations, was largely a tribute to the loyalty and industry of Japanese Americans, aimed at the general public. When the radio microphones had been switched off, Rowell addressed the Nisei audience with an earnest plea that, while honoring their Japanese heritage, they throw themselves into civic life by taking an interest in current issues and voting in elections, and make every effort to overcome discrimination by proving their worth as Americans.

While business sessions were conducted with the usual intensity, an odd sequence of events helped to confirm Issei charges that JACL was indeed overly concerned with the social side of life. What happened was this: almost as soon as the convention committee was organized, it booked the plush Fairmont Hotel atop Nob Hill for its closing banquet and Sayonara Ball (the first time that now common term was used). Some time later, Prince and Princess Kaya of Japan scheduled a visit to San Francisco and their reservations were also made at the Fairmont. By coincidence they were to be in the city at the same time as the JACL convention—almost certainly they knew nothing about JACL.

The Issei community, of course, wished to fete the royal couple. The Japanese consul general, who was charged with the details of the visit, insisted the event be held at the Fairmont to avoid security problems. And the only date the royal party had available was the night of the Sayonara Ball. What to do? In a later era JACL and the Issei community would have felt comfortable enough with each other to hold a joint banquet, with the Nisei as delighted as their elders over an opportunity to dine with royalty. At the time, however, such cooperation was virtually out of the question. The local reception committee swallowed its collective pride and asked JACL to please give up its hotel date. Some JACLers, Murayama chief among them, remembering that a few of the Issei had made derogatory remarks about them, refused to budge.

Eventually, cooler heads prevailed. JACL agreed to shift its Sayonara Ball to the Palace Hotel. In appreciation, S. Nakase, manager of the Nippon Yusen Kaisha office, invited delegates to a preconvention party aboard one of his crack transpacific liners, the *Chichibu Maru.* But a few days before the convention, it became apparent the *Chichibu* wouldn't reach San Francisco in time. The agile Nakase then used his contacts to schedule the party aboard the S.S. *California,* a Panama-Pacific liner that shuttled between Atlantic and Pacific coast ports through the Panama Canal. Next afternoon, when the *Chichibu* finally made port, the convention was recessed and delegates trooped aboard for a late-afternoon tea party. What had started as one major convention social event suddenly had become three and ironically the Issei critics of Nisei frivolity were partly responsible.

By this time, however, some of the rough edges had been removed when JACL made Pioneer Night an important part of the convention. A pioneer was an Issei sixty years old or more, who had come to America in 1900 or earlier. The San Francisco chapter, which had been made aware that the elderly Issei felt neglected, honored ninety-nine of them at a program at which their accomplishments and contributions were recognized. The main speaker was Jimmie Sakamoto, as forceful an orator in Japanese as he was in English. The experience of being lauded by the dynamic, blind, Nisei leader in a language they understood moved many of the Issei to tears. In response, community elders like Takanoshin Domoto, Kikumatsu Togasaki and Matsunosuke Tsukamoto spoke of their early experiences and of their hopes for the Nisei. The oldest Issei attending was Mrs. Sada Hirai, eighty-five. Photographs of all the guests were taken and presented to them as souvenirs.

A few days before this event, Sakamoto's *Courier* had published a prophetic editorial pegged on the Pioneer Night observance. Said the *Courier:*

> It is not too great a strain on the imagination to dream of a Pioneer Night on the opening night of the twenty-fifth biennial convention of the League, honoring not the first generation pioneers, but the second generation pioneers. The first generation won a place on the land of the American continent, but the pioneering second generation is winning a place in the life of the American nation.
>
> Sometimes it is to be feared that many members of the second generation do not realize that the integration of future generations depends much on how successfully the second generation can fulfill its position in American life. It is one of the prime objects of the League to hammer home the importance of the worth of the second generation. All the work of the League is consciously or unconsciously directed toward that aim.
>
> For many individuals the problem of the second generation has not been pressing, for their talents, which are universally recognized and which transcend all barriers of race, nationality or creed, have won them the admiration and esteem of their fellow Americans. It is extremely gratifying to note that these individuals are becoming slowly but surely more numerous.
>
> It is certain that these individuals will carry the second generation as a whole along with them by their very momentum—just as a few hardy pioneers in the early days of this nation made life easier for many of their less able followers.
>
> The work of today's pioneers is probably not as spectacular as that of the earlier ones, but the importance surely is not the less. The work of the second generation will in future years form at least a minor theme in the symphony of the history of Western America.

Sakamoto was being too sanguine about the achievements of the older Nisei. Few, indeed, had been "universally recognized" at this stage of their development and not many had the talent to "transcend all barriers of race, nationality or creed" in the discrimination they routinely faced. The desirable state Sakamoto envisioned had to await the test and heartache of war and all its injustices, though no one could foresee that at the time.

But the editorial looked accurately into the future in that the twenty-fifth biennial convention, held in Salt Lake City in 1978, honored not only distinguished Nisei but paused to commemorate the memories of many who had passed on.

In San Francisco, the number of registered delegates was somewhat less than the total attending the various functions. As in previous conventions jobs kept many Nisei away from the daytime events. Even so, a total of 418 delegates—nearly double the number registered at the Los Angeles convention—represented twenty-four chapters. One third of the delegates were from San Francisco itself, with another 135 from nearby Northern California areas. Los Angeles, however, sent 51 delegates and Seattle 15. The Northwest delegation had its own railroad car for the trip south, picking up the Portland group on the way.

But there was one notable delegate missing. Clarence Arai, who had helped shape the JACL movement at the organizational meeting in San Francisco five years earlier, was busy back home in Seattle taking his own advice to participate in politics. He was campaigning for a seat in the Washington state legislature. Arai had thrown himself into politics with enormous vigor if not notable success. He had been elected Republican precinct committeeman, vice-president of the Thirty-seventh Legislative District Republican Club, and delegate to the state GOP convention, but had been defeated in 1933 in a bid for election to a state convention to consider repeal of the Prohibition amendment. Arai, with 1,559 votes, finished sixth in a field of seven. The winner with 2,887 votes was a promising young Democrat named Warren G. Magnuson. (Magnuson went on to the U.S. House of Representatives in 1936 and served eight years. In 1944 Magnuson was elected to the Senate for the first of seven consecutive terms.) Undaunted, Arai, a Republican, set his sights on the state legislature in 1934. With no money of his own to spend, and very little public support, his campaign consisted mostly of handing out cards saying, "A vote for Clarence Arai is a vote for tolerance." Although he had been promised the support of many Caucasians, Arai received only 320 votes in the primary out of 3,827 cast and finished fifth in a field of five. He found what little consolation he could in the fact that he received votes in each of the district's fifty-four precincts. Sakamoto's *Japanese-American Courier* editorialized: "Arai's was a pioneering venture in politics on the American mainland. He was the first American citizen of Japanese ancestry to run for such a high elective office. . . . One of the most important features of Arai's candidacy is the fact that it brought home forcibly to every American citizen in the district and many over the entire city that the American citizens of Japanese ancestry are eager and willing to show that they are truly citizens and an integral part of the communities in which they live. . . ."

The editorial had exaggerated just a little. While Arai was the first Nisei on the mainland to run for an important public office, Nisei in the Territory of Hawaii had sought election a dozen years earlier. The first Nisei candidate to seek territorial office in Hawaii was James T. Hamada, a Republican who ran unsuccessfully for the House of Representatives in 1922. Nisei Hawaiians continued to run regularly and were defeated just as regularly until 1930 when Andy Yamashiro, a Democrat, and Takasu Oka, a Republican, were elected to the House. By 1936 nine Nisei were among Hawaii's ninety-three elected officials.

Despite Arai's defeat, his wife, Yone, gave meaning to an oddly stark message sent to the convention by Mrs. Eleanor Roosevelt. Apparently the aides to the President's wife had not been properly briefed on the nature of JACL. Her telegram in its entirety read: I HOPE EVERY WOMAN WILL INTEREST HERSELF IN ALL CIVIC AFFAIRS AND HELP HER COMMUNITY IN EVERY WAY POSSIBLE. (SIGNED) MRS. FRANKLIN D. ROOSEVELT.

Mrs. Arai was elected precinct committeewoman. She joined three Nisei women in California that year in political activity. Mrs. Flora Chiyo Suzuki of Stockton was appointed clerk on her precinct election board. (Her husband George was a member of the executive committee of the Central San Joaquin County Democratic Club.) Fumiko Kawai of Fresno was named a member of the precinct election board in Fresno, and Toyo Domoto became registrar of voters in Oakland. All, of course, were minor posts but the election of Nisei was a heartening indication of growing acceptance.

As a new convention feature, the host chapter had included an oratorical contest for Nisei high school students. Each district had been invited to hold preliminary contests to pick two entries for the San Francisco finals, but not all got around to them. There were only four contestants, three from Northern California and one from the Pacific Northwest. The contestants and the titles of their orations were: Masato Inouye, Santa Maria Valley, "Our

Failing Democracy"; Taneko Irino, Salinas, "Social Progress of the Japanese"; James Kinoshita, Puyallup Valley, Washington, "Japanese Americans"; Goro Suzuki, Oakland, "The Role of Citizenship in the Crisis of Democracy."

Suzuki, a sixteen-year-old high school student, was the winner. He wound up his oration in this manner:

> I wonder, if in the minds of this confused, materialistic world of ours, there is not room for more idealism, a higher level of thinking which can transcend human selfishness and greed, and willingness to sacrifice a little for the good of all.
>
> I wonder if this is not the place where we, as American citizens of Japanese parentage, are peculiarly fitted by reason of that idealism of the East and the spirit of sacrifice which are ours to claim and utilize. Ours is the heritage of Bushido, that noble tradition of knighthood whose code is to serve gallantly and unswervingly for our country. Like the beautiful cherry blossom symbolizing the spirit of the Samurai, let our lives be beautiful, an inspiration for the welfare and the happiness of our fellow men.
>
> We have, as Chester Rowell said, a double loyalty culturally. We have a direct and definite contribution to make to America. Imbued with a loyal interest and enthusiasm, armed with a critical attitude, equipped with adequate knowledge, let us give ourselves in altruistic activity and service for our country, the United States, and for humanity elsewhere.
>
> The world is at the crossroads. Democracy stands on trial. If there ever was a need for earnest citizenship on the part of every good American it is in this crisis today. That is the challenge before the citizenry.
>
> When our generation has done its work and gone on, let it be said that we served ardently, generously, and nobly.

Suzuki went on to become a singer and nightclub comic but his career was disrupted by the Evacuation. He was sent to the Topaz WRA camp, relocated to Cleveland, adopted the stage name of Jack Soo to avoid anti-Japanese bias and became an entertainer in a Chinese nightclub. He achieved star status in the role of Sammy Fong in the Rodgers and Hammerstein Broadway hit *Flower Drum Song,* played in numerous movie and television features and for five years prior to his death from cancer in 1979 starred as Nick Yemane, the wry-humored Japanese American police station clerk in the American Broadcasting Corporation's popular *Barney Miller* TV series. Some of Suzuki's memorabilia were shown in the Smithsonian Institution "Nation of Nations" exhibit.

The usual earnest convention round-table discussions—on legal-political issues, economics (including vocational guidance and farm operation) and social problems (marriage, education, juvenile delinquency)—attracted substantial attention but yielded few answers. Oddly enough, the education and marriage panels drew the most interest. Some Nisei questioned the value of a college education when job opportunities were lacking, and others encouraged their peers to seek practical training that would prepare them for careers as tradesmen, mechanics, plumbers and carpenters rather than white-collar workers.

There was widespread support for Japanese-language studies, to help Nisei communicate with their parents. But Tamotsu Murayama stirred up some excitement when he introduced a resolution requiring all teachers in such schools to attend Americanization classes for a year. His argument was based on fears that the teachers, if they knew nothing about United States history and traditions, might harm the aspirations of young Nisei to become 100-percent Americans. While Murayama's resolution got nowhere, it was widely agreed that Japanese textbooks used in the classes ought to be replaced by books more suitable to the American environment.

The Japanese custom of arranged marriages also came in for lively discussion. Increasing numbers of Nisei were approaching marriageable age and were under parental pressure to follow tradition by having family friends arrange a suitable match. Most Nisei preferred the American custom of finding and courting their own partners. The panelists found merit to both systems. Ultimately, when it was time for marriage, many reached a typical Nisei solution: they picked their own mates and let their parents select go-betweens of their choice to sit at the head table at the postwedding banquet to satisfy the demands of propriety.

In the business sessions the delegates reached two significant internal-housekeeping decisions. They adopted a constitutional provision for election of a national president, and they affirmed the principle of equality among chapters regardless of the size of their membership. It seemed only fitting that the first president should be Doc Yatabe, the Fresno dentist who had labored for so long to shape a Nisei organization, and no one challenged the idea. Saburo Kido, who had served as national executive secretary since 1932, was formally elected to the position. Sim Togasaki was elected national treasurer and John Ando of Los Angeles, his assistant. Chairmen of the district councils were named vice-presidents. These officers composed the National Board of JACL.

The matter of proportional representation on JACL's National Council, which comprised delegates from all the chapters, was raised by the Los Angeles chapter. Because of the large Nisei population in Los Angeles, it could foresee a time when its membership might reach a thousand or more, whereas some rural chapters would have no more than a few dozen members even if every Nisei in the area joined. The question was whether larger chapters, since they would presumably contribute more in dues to the national body, shouldn't have a proportionately larger voice in organizational affairs. But the issue was defused when the smaller chapters pledged to assume the same burden as the others, and the one-vote-per-chapter rule was retained.

If the accomplishments of a convention are to be judged by the resolutions it passes, the San Francisco gathering must be given mixed grades. The resolutions committee was chaired by Dr. Terry Hayashi and included Dr. Yatabe, Kay Sugahara of Los Angeles, Dr. Earl Yusa of Santa Maria, Walter Tsukamoto of Sacramento, Tokie Slocum of San Francisco, Minoru Terada of Auburn, Washington, and Jimmie Sakamoto. The committee drafted nine resolutions, some of which covered routine housekeeping matters as letting national headquarters remain in San Francisco (meaning Kido's office) for the next four years, and continuing designation of *Pacific Citizen* as the official publication. It approved ethnically significant resolutions, such as the one to help the Placer County chapter in its efforts to preserve and beautify the gravesite of Okei, a member of the Wakamatsu Colony from Japan who died in 1871 at age nineteen and was buried atop Gold Hill in the Sierra foothills. It ordered an investigation of reports that a federal appropriations bill would discriminate against employment of persons of "Mongolian extraction," and recommended that chapters carry on a public-relations campaign. And it urged chapters to take part in community Arbor Day observances by planting Japanese cherry trees.

But of much greater significance was a resolution supporting "any organization or governmental agency to expell and deport from the United States such undesirable alien communists who are found guilty of subversive acts toward our nation, regardless of race, creed or nationality." The "whereases" in the resolution are interesting enough to quote in full:

> Whereas: We, the American citizens of Japanese ancestry, are informed from various delegates to the National Convention of the Japanese-American Citizens' League, now convened for its third biennial convention in the City of San Francisco, Calif., that there are alarming acts of destructive measures, subversive methods of propaganda and undermining tactics to implant within the minds of plastic youths in the public and high schools of the United States of America to displace the principles of lofty Americanism, and attempts appear to be made to revolutionize and undermine the fundamental principle of American institutions which are sacred and dear to us American citizens, and
>
> Whereas: We, the citizens of the United States, fully cherish and appreciate the sanctity of our Constitution which the forefathers of this Democracy willed to us to honor and defend at great sacrifice and deprivation to themselves that we might "not perish on this earth," and
>
> Whereas: We, the American citizens of Japanese ancestry, do hereby and hereon pledge our unflinching loyalty, devotion and sacrifice to this, our United States, and swear undivided allegiance only to the United States of America.
>
> Therefore be it resolved that the Japanese-American Citizens League cooperate with and support any organization or governmental agency to expell and deport from the United States such undesirable alien communists who are found guilty of subversive acts toward our nation regardless of race, creed or nationality.

It is impossible at this date to ask members of the committee what was in their minds when they drafted this resolution, but several points should be made. On November 16, 1933, some ten months before the JACL convention, President Franklin D. Roosevelt had made the controversial decision to extend diplomatic recognition to the Soviet Union. This move was followed by a popular Red-hunting campaign in which the sinister shadow of communism was seen almost everywhere, particularly by members of superpatriotic veterans' groups. And Slocum, a member of the resolutions committee, was seeking veterans' support in his effort to win United States citizenship for Japanese aliens who had fought in the American armed forces in World War I. Also at this time, in Japan and in the Japanese American communities on the West Coast, liberals and left-wingers opposed to the Japanese military invasion of the Chinese mainland were being condemned indiscriminately as Reds and Communists. Perhaps this accounts for the pledge to support deportation of convicted alien Communists "regardless of race, creed or nationality."

As we know, fascism rather than communism turned out to be America's most immediate danger. However, in 1934, Adolf Hitler was still the funny little man with the Charlie Chaplin mustache, Benito Mussolini was the posturing, strutting dictator who finally got Italian railroads to run on time and of course the Issei were contending that Japan's military invasion of China was justified. So, for whatever reasons, JACL condemned Communist subversion and said nothing about Fascist dangers to democracy, like many other American organizations which failed to perceive fascism's threat.

Finally, there is an unfortunate hint of vigilantism in the JACL resolution to "cooperate with and support any organization or governmental agency to expell and deport . . . undesirable alien communists." Legally, expulsion is strictly a government responsibility and not that of any private group or organization. In view of JACL's deep concern for human rights, although it was some time before the term came into vogue, the charitable view is that inexperience was responsible for the gaffe. In any event, no one made a point of the embarrassing wording, and JACLers left San Francisco promising to meet again in 1936 in Seattle.

T. M. Okagaki (the initials stood for Tsuguyo Marion and she was soon to become Mrs. Larry Tajiri), a young reporter for the *New World Daily News,* recounted the mood of the Sayonara Ball in these flowery terms:

> The spacious ballroom, bathed in soft lights, backgrounded the dancing of some 500 delegates, moving to the syncopating music of Art Weidner's orchestra.
>
> Not a hundred balloons suspended from the ceiling nor Japanese lanterns could hide the spacious dignity of the Palace Hotel ballroom. But neither could wearying complexities of convention duties kill the final outburst of the Roman Holiday spirit which imbued the hearts and minds of delegates during the lighter hours of the convention.
>
> The crowd cheered the dedications the orchestra made to sectional chapters and applauded with joyous appreciation as Mr.

Nakase, beaming NYK manager, sang from the orchestra stand. But everyone burst into applause as "Texas Sally" Yabumoto stepped before the mike and sang a song, the words of which had been composed a few hours earlier by Larry Tajiri, Los Angeles press delegate.

It was a well-dressed crowd that attended. Dresses tended toward sophistication. . . .

VII

Seattle, 1936

The decision in San Francisco to elect national officers gave JACL accountability and firm direction for the first time. Until Dr. Yatabe became the first elected national president in 1934, the presidency was largely a figurehead post with ill-defined duties and not even a clear-cut term of office. Starting with Clarence Arai at the founding convention in Seattle in 1930, the national presidency went to the person chosen to chair the next convention. No one could be sure when that chairman would be named, so the president in office had no idea how long his term would last. Obviously, creative leadership was impossible.

But all that changed with the election of Yatabe to a two-year term and the confirmation of Saburo Kido as executive secretary. Responsibility was pinned down none too soon. A new rash of bills directed against Japanese farmers and fishermen popped up in the state legislature in Sacramento. The hostility without doubt was inspired in part by Tokyo's military aggression in China. As Nisei were to learn in the years to come, it was virtually impossible to separate Japanese Americans from the Japanese themselves in the minds of most of their fellow Americans. In Arizona, nightriders touched off dynamite blasts near the homes of Japanese farmers in an attempt to drive them out of the Salt River valley. Representatives of the JACL and the Japanese Association in Los Angeles were sent to investigate and express concern. Such incidents and the determined Nisei response to them, no matter how ineffective, gradually began to overcome Issei coolness toward JACL. Many of them could begin to see JACL's potential as spokesman for the Japanese American community, which had been largely mute because so few Issei spoke English adequately. Men like Yatabe, Kido and the three early presidents (Arai, Dr. Takeyama and Dr. Hayashi) were bilingual; when the Issei took the time to listen, these men could explain the goals of JACL.

It was in this upbeat atmosphere that JACL returned to Seattle in 1936 for its fourth convention. One may wonder why so much importance was placed on these biennial conventions. They were, of course, gala social events that enabled JACLers to meet Nisei from other parts of the country. But more important, the conventions gave Nisei leaders opportunities—usually lacking on the local level—to engage in serious discussion about issues important to Japanese Americans and to cooperate in search of solutions. Professor Miyamoto describes with devastating accuracy the Seattle JACL chapter meetings he attended in the early thirties:

> The high points of the organization's activities were the national and sectional conferences, the annual New Year's dance under their sponsorship, and the "Japan Day" at a local recreation park. Among other activities of prominence were the outings during the summers, their annual dinners, and the occasional gatherings to hear some speakers. Their monthly meetings were drab affairs at which a monotonous round of old and new business would be gone over, the major portion of which seemed concerned with the various conferences, or the preparation for some social event. For the majority of Nisei who participated in the functions of the group, it fulfilled a social purpose and meant little else. To be sure, the JACL constantly tried to stimulate political interest among the Nisei, and they often invited prominent candidates for elections to speak at their meetings. . . . The significant fact is that despite the dissatisfaction among the membership, there was little understanding of how to change the organization for the better.

The minutes of Fresno's American Loyalty League, going back to the organizational meeting on May 5, 1923, and carefully preserved by Fred Hirasuna, confirm Professor Miyamoto's evaluation. Following, verbatim, are the minutes of the meeting held February 20, 1931:

The regular meeting of the month was called to order by President Fred Hirasuna. The minutes of the previous meeting were read and approved. The treasurer reported a balance on hand of $24.29.

Correspondence from Mr. K. Togasaki and Mr. George Togasaki and a telegram from Brawley Citizens' League were read.

Discussion on the Cable Act was held. It was moved, seconded and carried to send one or two delegates to the San Francisco conference which is to be held on February 28th. The following were chosen: Fred Hirasuna, Robert Itanaga; alternate, Mr. Kelley Matsumura.

Discussion was held on the Mutual Benefit Fund. The body was in favor of the plan but no action was taken.

Organization of new local chapters was discussed. Dr. Tom Yatabe was chosen to meet with Mr. Iwata regarding the organization of a tentative one in Dinuba.

A Committee was appointed to investigate about placing traffic signals at the intersections of Kern and E streets and possibly one at Kern and G streets. The committee consisted of the following: Dr. Yatabe, chairman; Mr. Fred Yoshikawa.

It was decided that a list of eligible voters be made. Those appointed to take charge of the matter were: Mr. Robert Itanaga, Fresno and Bakersfield; Mr. Kelley Matsumura, Fowler; Mr. Tom Kanase, Strawberry district.

Mr. Hiroshi Yamamisaka was appointed Literary chairman.

As there being no further business the meeting was adjourned.

Respectfully submitted,
Sadie Hori, sec.

Fred Hirasuna stepped down from the presidency the following year and was promptly named secretary. His minutes for the meeting of January 29, 1932, indicate some improvement over the previous year both financially and in the quality of the meetings:

The regular meeting of the A.L.L. was called to order by President Robert Itanaga. The minutes of the previous meeting were read and approved. The Treasurer reported a balance on hand of $45.69.

Dr. Yatabe gave a report from the West Fresno Central Committee on the Highway Issue.

Miss Setsuko Saiki and Miss Ena Okonogi were introduced as new members.

The Los Angeles chapter's invitation to the National Convention of July 27, 28, 29 was read. Two official delegates are to be chosen from each chapter. Unofficial delegates are welcomed and requested to hand in their names to the secretary.

It was moved, seconded and carried that two official delegates be sent to Los Angeles.

Letters from Los Angeles and San Francisco concerning the new bills introduced in Congress to allow further liberalization of the Immigration Law of 1924 were read.

It was moved, seconded and carried that telegrams be sent to Representative Barbour and to the sponsors of the bills endorsing them. Dr. Yatabe was delegated to send the wires.

The corresponding secretary was instructed to send Mr. Hisashi Arie, the newly-elected president of the Monterey Citizens' League and a former member of the local chapter, a letter of congratulation for the success of the Monterey chapter.

New members were discussed and it was decided that a prospects list be compiled and each member assigned a prospect or prospects to interview before the following meeting. President Itanaga assigned members to compile such a list in their respective districts.

Programs and dinner meetings were discussed. It was moved, seconded and carried that the group partake of light refreshments after the next meeting, the expense to be borne individually.

Means of raising money were discussed. Box lunch sales, dances and benefit programs were suggested.

Vice-president Robert Maekawa asked for suggestions as to the nature of programs desired by the members. Various suggestions were received.

As there was no further business, the meeting was adjourned.

Fred Y. Hirasuna, Sec'y, pro tem

Only a nucleus of dedicated individuals kept local chapters together. The leadership was apt to be more dogged than inspired and it was a constant battle to retain membership let alone expand it. But somehow, when the most able Nisei met at the national conventions a certain chemistry set in to raise the level of performance. At the 1936 convention a maturing JACL—with thirty-eight chapters—buckled down to address some urgent issues. Chief among them were a greater appreciation of the opportunities and responsibilities of American citizenship, social justice, economic problems, relations with the Japan-educated Nisei group called Kibei and financing JACL's activities.

National President Yatabe in his keynote address—it was the

first time a Nisei had been called on to sound the convention keynote—spoke of the need for undivided loyalty to the United States and of better days ahead for Japanese Americans. "A radiant beam of enlightenment and hope permeates this land of ours," he asserted. "A new faith that life, liberty and the pursuit of happiness will be attained henceforth through the medium of fraternal cooperation between fellow men. Barriers of ignorance and prejudice are slowly crumbling before the assaults of social justice and fair play. And equal opportunity for all in the various fields of endeavor irrespective of race, color and creed, is an assurance of the immediate future."

Much the same theme was presented by George Kyotow, who won the national oratorical contest. Kyotow, a San Francisco teen-ager, expressed the yearnings of the younger Nisei:

> We who are culturally bred as any white American thrill to the thoughts penned by Francis Scott Key; we are just as human and democratic in ideal and crave the sterling standards set forth in the Constitution. But the pity of it all! Slight differences in physical markings throw young second generation Japanese into a different caste. As a result we begin to ponder apprehensively. Are we to resign all efforts in acquiring recognition because of such opposition? . . . An American would undoubtedly remark now and then, "You fellows are pretty lucky. Look at the great advantage you American educated fellows have over the rest of your people when you go back to the old country." This attitude perhaps reflects that of most white Americans. But we were born here and our allegiance is to America. This is our "old country" right here.
>
> We have or are now attending American schools, we speak the English language the major part of our daily lives, we know perhaps a little more than what an average American knows about Japan. Our ideas, customs, mode of thinking, our whole psychology is simply American. Physically we may be Japanese, but culturally we are Americans. We simply are not capable of fitting into a Japanese society, so we are destined to remain here. . . .

Three convention resolutions also addressed the general theme of Americanism and loyalty to the United States. One, recognizing JACL's interest "in national peace and goodwill with other nations, particularly with the Empire of Japan," called for a public-relations committee "for the purpose of maintaining and encouraging the best of Japanese American relations."

Another resolution, affirming "our faith in the founders of the

Republic" and upholding "the just principles of true Americanism," voiced opposition to "all those alien agitators which seek the overthrow of our government" and demanded "the passage of stringent laws for the deportation of such persons." In recognizing the legal aspects of deportation proceedings, this was a significant improvement over the similar resolution passed two years earlier. The resolution went on to instruct each JACL chapter "to cooperate with the American Legion and the Veterans of Foreign Wars in their splendid fight to maintain our American institutions against such alien propagandists," the reference being to "the sinister forces of communism and fascism."

In the third resolution, dual Japanese and American citizenship among Nisei was condemned as "a status of disloyalty to both Japan and the United States."

Dual citizenship was largely an inadvertence brought about by laws with which few Nisei concerned themselves, and the resolution was an effort to bring the situation to their attention. Until 1924, Japan like many European nations observed the rule of *jus sanguinis*—"law of blood." It held that a child was automatically a Japanese citizen regardless of where he was born if the father was a Japanese citizen. The United States observed *jus soli*—"law of the soil"—which made any child born in America a citizen. Largely at the request of Japanese in the United States, Japan changed its laws in 1924 to make it necessary to register a birth at one of its consulates—to take a positive action—if an Issei father wanted to claim citizenship for his child. That law also made it possible for a Nisei to renounce Japanese citizenship acquired merely by having been born before 1924. Many Nisei went through the renunciation process. The JACL resolution was directed at those who hadn't done so because they didn't know about the process or didn't think it was worth the bother.

JACL's persistent emphasis on citizenship may raise the suspicion that perhaps it was protesting a bit too much. If Nisei were so unquestionably dedicated to Americanism, why should it be necessary to make such a point of professing it again and again and again?

For Nisei who lived through the period the answer is obvious. For others it is necessary to understand the milieu. The Nisei legally were Americans but in real life were something less. Their parents were denied the privilege of naturalization and in some cases the protection of the laws. In fact, as we have seen, certain laws had been passed to legalize discrimination. The Issei, who still possessed a great deal of influence in their communities, faced an ambiguous future; while they had no immediate plans to return to Japan, many were sure that someday they and their families would go back. As aliens the Issei were denied any political role in the United States and it was likely they were more aware of what was going on in Tokyo than in Washington.

The Nisei were educated in the American school system, but when the last bell rang most of them returned to an environment quite different from that of their classmates. Socially they were inclined to be clannish, in large part because of outside pressures that forced them to stay together. Economic opportunity was severely limited, partly by the Great Depression that all but paralyzed the land, but more by racial discrimination. It was understandable that some Nisei should look to Japan for a more promising future. But JACL leaders were intensely aware of the American side of their heritage and convinced that their future lay in integration into the American scene. They carried their message to fellow Nisei with missionary zeal. There was no sham or deceit in their dedication to Americanism despite the rebuffs that had been their lot. Those who doubted the sincerity of these Nisei leaders underestimated the appeal of America and the profound influence of the American educational system which, in those times, taught an uncomplicated, unquestioning patriotism.

The point JACL wished to make was that while the Nisei must recognize their Japanese heritage, concern themselves with the problems their parents faced because of their Japanese citizenship and seek better understanding between the United States and Japan, they were in truth Americans and should not be considered in any sense as advocates, fronts or apologists for the objectives of the Japanese Empire. The posture was simple enough, but also liable to be misunderstood.

Economic issues were simpler and somewhat closer to the minds and pocketbooks of the delegates, and they quickly got down to basics. The consensus was that there were jobs to be had if the Nisei only knew where to look. The delegates agreed to survey the occupations of Nisei in their respective areas and distribute the information. They also criticized the false pride of parents who pressured the Nisei to strive only for white-collar jobs. Delegates from California's fertile Central Valley told of Nisei who were neglecting farming opportunities for jobs in the cities—a movement not peculiar to the Japanese Americans—and urged a back-to-the-soil movement.

A major occupational problem was the traditional refusal of trade unions to accept nonwhites. Thus few Nisei could find employment, or training for that matter, in the building trades, as printers, as engravers and in other skilled crafts. While it was obvious that union hostility was denying Nisei job opportunities, JACL was not ready to tackle the issue. The convention resolved only "to gather and keep any and all information on the questions of labor unions and labor."

To JACL's credit it never accepted the Issei tradition of relegating women to second-class status. From the very beginning Nisei girls were encouraged to join the movement, were accepted as equals and were given an equal voice and responsibility in organizational affairs although an inordinate number were elected as secretaries. At the Seattle convention Mrs. Yone Sugahara, wife of Los Angeles customs broker Kay Sugahara, played a major role as chairman of the social issues committee that forthrightly took on questions of cultural heritage and public relations, and the prickly Kibei problem.

The Kibei were Nisei who had acquired a large part of their education in Japan. Most of them had been sent to Japan at an early age to live with grandparents or other relatives. They returned to the United States more fluent in Japanese than English. Their outlook, if not totally Japanese, was substantially different from that of their Nisei peers (and, in many cases, siblings) who had never been to Japan. Unable to communicate with other Nisei, more interested in things Japanese, they turned inevitably to their own Kibei organizations for companionship. Despite the age difference they were more inclined to associate with the Issei than the Nisei. On the other hand, many Nisei had no interest in the Kibei. In some communities intense and sometimes hostile rivalry developed between Kibei and Nisei organizations. Yet the more farsighted members of both groups realized the need for cooperation in view of their small numbers and their mutual American citizenship.

The Seattle convention recommended that Kibei join JACL chapters in their respective communities, that distinctions between groups and "Kibei divisions of JACL chapters" be discouraged and that the use of the Japanese language at JACL meetings be considered acceptable. Today, time has taken care of Nisei-Kibei differences. In 1936, however, the decision to try to bridge the gap went a long way toward strengthening JACL and overcoming discordant rivalry within the communities.

Finances continued to trouble JACL. Minor sums assumed mountainous proportions. Delegates debated the charge to be made for membership cards, finally settling on ten cents rather than a quarter. Heated discussion preceded a decision on payment of travel expenses to national officers. Finally it was agreed to pay expenses to the national convention for the president, executive secretary, assistant secretary, treasurer, and the three vice-presidents, one from each district council. They were to be reimbursed for rail fare, not to exceed two cents per mile, and not including meals or Pullman berth. In addition, the president and executive secretary were voted $150 each for travel expenses during their two-year terms, and $120 annually for stenographic help. (The round-trip air fare between Seattle and San Francisco in 1936 was $79.16, between Seattle and Los Angeles $113.29.)

Such parsimony troubled Kido, who proposed a $100,000 endowment fund, income from which would be used to pay national headquarters expenses. Dr. Yatabe was named chairman of the endowment fund committee and he came up with the idea of collecting pledges for contributions of $100, payable at the rate of $10 per year. A $50 contribution for convention expenses from Dr. Russell Hisao WeHara was used to launch the fund.

WeHara was an Oakland optometrist who had been born in Japan and brought to the United States as an infant. Although an alien and ineligible for JACL membership, he was an enthusiastic supporter. He owned a chain of outlets which at the time of the Evacuation in 1942 was believed to be dispensing more glasses than any other organization west of Chicago. His wife, Dorothy, a Nisei who had lost her citizenship by her marriage, regained it after the Cable Act was amended.

When Dr. WeHara was notified about how his contribution would be used, he responded with the following telegram:

> HAPPY TO LEARN THAT MY DONATION HAS SERVED AS A MOVEMENT TO RAISE ENDOWMENT FUND. HOUSE IS NO STRONGER THAN ITS FOUNDATION. ECONOMIC STABILITY IS OUR GIBRALTAR. I GLADLY PLEDGE ONE THOUSAND DOL-

LARS TO THE JAPANESE AMERICAN CITIZENS LEAGUE. MEMBERS PLEASE VISUALIZE THE IMPORTANCE OF OUR UNDERTAKING AND BEND EVERY EFFORT TO COOPERATE WITH OUR OFFICERS AND PLEDGE WITH ME TO YOUR ABILITY. MAY THIS MESSAGE SERVE AS FURTHER IMPETUS FOR THE REALIZATION OF OUR ENDOWMENT FUND.

There were 583 delegates registered at the convention and 52 of them, plus Dr. WeHara, pledged $6,250. It was to be some time before the fund reached its goal, but it was just as well. No guidelines for investing the fund, or using the proceeds, had been drawn up. It had only pledges and a committee to organize matters—Dr. Yatabe, Kido as secretary and Dr. Terry Hayashi as treasurer.

The final order of business was selection of national officers, and for the first time the election was contested. The first three presidents, as we have seen, were simply the chairmen of the upcoming conventions. Dr. Yatabe, the first elected president, had such stature that he had no competition. In later years intense backroom politicking was to mark JACL national elections and this tradition got its start in Seattle, although the maneuvering there was relatively mild.

The California choice for president was Lyle Kurisaki of Brawley, national vice-president by virtue of his position as Southern California District Council chairman, who had been a Nisei leader since Loyalty League days. Because Kurisaki was respected in Northern California, Kido and others who supported him believed he could bring the two districts closer together. But Kurisaki adamantly refused to run.

Southern California then shifted to John Ando, a Los Angeles–area rancher and assistant national executive secretary, while Northern California swung its support to Jimmie Sakamoto. Kido argued eloquently that no man had contributed more to JACL than Sakamoto and that the honor of leading it should go to him. There is no doubt that Sakamoto had been one of JACL's most influential leaders. He had been the driving force in bringing the founding convention to Seattle in 1930. His newspaper had been JACL's most outspoken advocate and he was a charismatic individual. But as a national leader he faced some obvious problems. For one thing, he was blind. He had overcome much of that handicap by demonstrating a remarkable independence. He trained his memory so that he could remember what others would have to take down in notes. Perhaps a larger problem was Sakamoto's precarious financial position. His weekly newspaper was perennially on the verge of bankruptcy. If he devoted much of his time to JACL's national presidency, as he certainly would, it could throw a severe burden on his staff and particularly on his patient, hardworking wife, Misao, who, in addition to running the Sakamoto household, which included his elderly parents, was the *Courier*'s business and production manager.

Misao Nishitani Sakamoto deserves to be numbered among remarkable Japanese Americans. She was born in Japan in 1904, the fourth child of Denjiro and Jin Nishitani. Denjiro left for the United States when she was only a little more than a month old. Three years later her mother joined her husband, leaving Misao in the care of her grandparents. Misao was thirteen years old when the family was reunited in Seattle. She met Jimmie Sakamoto in the summer of 1928, six months after he started his newspaper. By this time his sight had deteriorated to the point where he could barely make out a person's outline in strong sunlight.

In New York, Jimmie had been married to Frances Imai, a Eurasian. They had a child, Blossom. After Frances' untimely death, Blossom's grandparents reared her and Jimmie returned to Seattle. Misao knew life with Jimmie Sakamoto would not be easy. He was in difficult financial straits. His elderly parents lived with him and needed care. Despite her mother's mild objections, Misao married Sakamoto on December 1, 1928, willing to share his dreams of the Nisei future as well as his problems. They moved into a rickety old house on an unstable hillside overlooking Seattle's Japanese community and lived there until it was condemned as unsafe.

There are two versions of Sakamoto's election as JACL president. As the author remembers it, when the nominating committee asked Sakamoto to run, he demurred until he could confer with his wife and staff. The staff encouraged Sakamoto to accept, and Misao agreed reluctantly. Misao remembers it another way. Kido, quite casually, told her Jimmie had been elected when they returned to his home to dress for a banquet. She was stunned and angry, feeling JACL was imposing on the Sakamotos, and there were to be other wives who felt the same way about JACL's demands on their own families.

Sakamoto won the election easily over Ando when the Northwest and Northern California chapters joined forces. Walter Tsukamoto of Sacramento and Sim Togasaki of San Francisco were unopposed for executive secretary and treasurer, respectively. Masao Satow of Los Angeles was elected assistant executive secretary over Saburo Nishimura of Seattle. Vice-presidents, representing their districts, were Mamaro Wakasugi of Portland, Dr. Harry Kita of Salinas and Henry Tsurutani of Los Angeles.

Misao Sakamoto must be considered among the first of a long line of "JACL widows," the wives of men who became so wrapped up in the organization that they often neglected families and businesses. With a few exceptions these women accepted their lot philosophically and regarded their personal inconvenience as their contribution to the movement.

Sakamoto tackled his new responsibilities with characteristic vigor. At considerable sacrifice in time and money, he visited each of the district councils, carrying word of JACL to areas where the national president had never appeared. He launched the ambitiously conceived Second-Generation Development Program. He set the Japanese Foreign Minister straight on the position of the Nisei, and indirectly was responsible for bringing a remarkable youth named Mike M. Masaoka into JACL. Before long, Masaoka was to have a profound influence on JACL—in fact, on the history of Japanese Americans.

The Second-Generation Development Program was a necessary but unfortunately vague idea for helping the Nisei become more closely integrated into the nation's economic, political and social life. It had been talked about at the Los Angeles convention in 1932, but nothing was done until Sakamoto's term. He appointed Masao Satow its chairman. Realizing that facts were needed to plan a campaign, Satow organized information-gathering task forces in the various districts. The program, as reported in the book *Nisei,* was aimed at helping Nisei to become productive American citizens by:

—Contributing to the social life of the nation, living with other citizens in a common community of interests and activities to promote the national welfare.

—Contributing to the economic welfare of the nation by taking key roles in agriculture, industry and commerce.

—Contributing to the civic welfare as intelligent voters and public-spirited citizens.

Nisei observes: "The goals, like motherhood, were beyond challenge and controversy but no one quite knew how to achieve them, particularly when the economic and social hostility against the Nisei was intensified by the pressures of the Depression. How could one contribute to the social life of the nation when one was not accepted into that life? How could one contribute to the economic welfare when one couldn't get a job?"

This somber appraisal is justified by a report to the program by the Reverend Kojiro Unoura of Los Angeles. He found that of the 161 Nisei graduates of the University of California between 1925 and 1935, 25 percent found jobs commensurate with their training, another 25 percent were working for relatives and 40 percent were in blind-alley jobs. The rest had gone to Japan in a largely futile search for work. "Race prejudice," he wrote, "hampers the American-born Japanese most of all in securing a living. Regardless of qualifications, American-born Japanese college graduates find it virtually impossible to secure positions in American business concerns on the Pacific Coast, except as janitors. As a result, highly trained engineers, chemists, teachers and other professional men, simply because of Japanese blood, are often forced to eke out a living doing the work of immigrant farm laborers."

Many years later Kido wrote of the JACL program: "The time was too early for the Nisei to do any effective work based on such a study. Nevertheless, it was something which the Nisei themselves were trying to develop for their own future. Consequently, there was no question that it did a lot of good by arousing interest."

Sakamoto's exchange with Japanese Foreign Minister Koki Hirota opened eyes on both sides of the Pacific. In March of 1938 the Associated Press, reporting an interpellation in the Diet, quoted Hirota as follows: "A majority of Japanese born in the United States in recent years cancelled Japanese citizenship. They must receive an American education. But they remain Japanese and they should be educated as Japanese in order to retain Japanese virtues. For this purpose the semi-official Migration Association keeps close connection with them."

This, of course, contradicted Nisei assertions that they were Americans free of Japanese influence. Sakamoto quickly issued a statement, declaring in part: "This [Hirota's] statement, if translated correctly, has not only been misleading but has caused a misunderstanding of the true position taken by American-born Japanese regarding their citizenship. The second generation in this country acknowledge only American citizenship, and an increasing number of the young, as stated by Foreign Minister Hirota himself, are taking advantage of the expatriation law instituted by Japan some years ago to cancel their Japanese citizenship."

Hirota backpedaled with a clarification: "My statement the other day seems to have aroused some misunderstanding. However, what I desired to express is that the second generation Japanese are American citizens, and ought to be educated in the American way. The Japanese government has no intention of educating them in the Japanese way. However, it is our desire that the second generation, as descendants of the Japanese race, retain the high virtues and culture of their race. Possessing these virtues should assist them toward becoming better and more valuable American citizens."

It was also explained that "the semi-official Migration Association" existed to help Japanese immigrants in Brazil and had no connection with the United States. JACL had indeed made a point in Tokyo.

Mike Masaoka's entry into the JACL picture was the result of a missionary visit into the Intermountain area by Walter Tsukamoto. Some years earlier the restless Tamotsu Murayama on a trip to Salt Lake City had met with a group of local Nisei and urged them to join the infant JACL. Murayama had presented JACL in terms of an ethnic organization. Masaoka, then a high school student who had known little racial discrimination, was in the audience. He saw no need for such a movement and said so in his outspoken way. Somewhat later Tom Yego, another early JACL leader, came to Utah as president of the California Federation of Nisei Farmers and presented JACL as an organization for protecting Nisei rights. This made more sense to Masaoka. As a result, JACL was asked to send a representative to Utah and Jimmie Sakamoto instructed Tsukamoto, as executive secretary, to take the assignment.

What Tsukamoto had to say intrigued Masaoka. Tsukamoto urged Masaoka to attend the upcoming JACL convention scheduled in Los Angeles early in September of 1938 to learn more about the organization. Masaoka did, with results that no one had anticipated.

VIII

In the Shadow of War

When Eijiro and Haruye Masaoka moved their family from Fresno, California, to Salt Lake City in 1918, it was a pleasant little town with unusually wide main streets and plentiful irrigation water, which rushed down the gutters. Eijiro, who had migrated to the United States from Hiroshima in 1903, saw no future farming in California where laws prohibited Asians from owning land. So he packed up his children, including a three-year-old boy named Masaru, and headed inland hoping to buy a farm in Utah. But his plans went awry and he settled for a mom-and-pop grocery store and fish market in Salt Lake City's modest Japantown.

The Mormons, who knew a thing or two about discrimination, dominated the politics and economy of Utah and provided the Japanese residents with a somewhat less onerous environment than that on the Pacific Coast. Still, prejudice was not unknown among the Japanese who farmed on the outskirts of Salt Lake City, Ogden and Brigham City, or mined copper at Bingham Canyon or coal at Price and Helper.

Eventually the Masaokas were to have eight children—Joe Grant, Ben Frank, Shinko, Masaru, Ike Akira, Kyoko, Henry Iwao and Tad Tadashi.

Masaru, soon to be known as Mike, was but nine years old when Eijiro was killed by a hit-and-run driver. Support of the family fell to Haruye, a tiny but remarkably determined woman, and her firstborn, Joe Grant. It was not an easy life, but the Masaokas were a close-knit family and no one felt deprived. From early childhood Mike proved to be an unusual youngster—witty, gregarious, voluble, inquisitive, articulate, sometimes contentious and rarely without an opinion. At the University of Utah, Mike caught the attention of Elbert D. Thomas, a sometime political science professor who had spent his Mormon missionary years in Japan and who had gone on to become an eminent United States senator. Masaoka distinguished himself as a debater at the university, and later was hired as a part-time debate coach.

On the strength of Walter Tsukamoto's invitation, Masaoka showed up at JACL's 1938 convention in Los Angeles. He sat with ill-concealed restlessness as the proceedings dragged on and interminable discussions were held as to whether outside speakers and refreshments would attract more members to chapter meetings. When he could stand it no more, Masaoka jumped up and asked for the floor. Masaoka then proceeded to tell JACLers what was wrong with their organization. It lacked a viable program, he said. Too much time was being wasted on inconsequential matters. JACL should expand into the Intermountain area if it wanted to become a national organization—and incidentally, it could pick up some fresh blood there. Finally, he charged JACL was guilty of the discrimination it professed to combat since its membership was restricted to one ethnic group.

The old guard of the JACL was startled. No one had criticized the organization in this manner before and those who had struggled through its earliest years were miffed that a kid attending his first convention should be so outspokenly critical. Sim Togasaki rose, cleared his gravelly voice and demanded to know by what right Masaoka, who was not even a member, was taking up the Council's time. Masaoka explained correctly that Walter Tsukamoto had invited him to attend. Jimmie Sakamoto was in the chair and ruled that despite the invitation Masaoka was a nonmember and therefore not entitled to the floor. Masaoka sat down in good humor but the challenge stimulated him. Vowing he would be back with the proper credentials, he returned to Utah. A little research showed him that three chapters could set up a district council and its chairman automatically became a member of the National Board. There already was a Nisei organization of sorts in Salt Lake City, founded in 1935 with Joe Grant Masaoka as first president. Mike cranked up the chapter, stirred up interest in neighboring Ogden and southeastern Idaho, applied to JACL for recognition as the Intermountain District Council, got himself elected chairman and was all set for the next national convention, in Portland.

The Los Angeles convention wasn't entirely a waste of time. In fact, it broke some fresh ground. Recognizing the importance of international problems to the Nisei, JACL instructed its National Council to "maintain close touch with the trend of international affairs, and thus be prepared to correctly inform the public through the proper mediums of news dissemination, and thus protect the status of the American citizens of Japanese ancestry." The intent was clear enough but, like many another JACL goal, the procedure was fuzzy. When JACL had no source of information other than the media, it could hardly be prepared "to correctly inform the public" about international affairs which, presumably, meant Japanese-American relations.

Of greater substance were three resolutions having to do with inequities in citizenship and naturalization laws. One urged Congress to permit Japanese aliens who had been in the United States prior to the 1924 Oriental Exclusion Act to apply for citizenship. A second sought to unite Nisei with alien parents who had overstayed their allotted time on visits to Japan and had been denied re-entry into the United States. The resolution sought entry for the parents "provided they not come to earn a living or become a public charge after admission." The third resolution pointed out that the laws permitted entry of the alien wife of a foreigner engaged in international trade, but not the alien Japanese wife of an American citizen making his livelihood in international trade. Calling this discriminatory and unfair, the resolution called on Congress to allow Nisei merchants to bring Japanese wives into the United States.

The experience of the two Togasaki brothers, both international traders, illustrates the way this discriminatory law affected the Nisei. Both George and Sim married Japanese women. George's wife, Misu, racially ineligible to enter the United States as an immigrant, could join her husband in San Francisco only six months at a stretch on a visitor's visa. When the visa expired, she sailed back to Japan and applied at an American consulate for another six-month visit. Eventually George moved to Japan to preserve his family and the Nisei community lost his not inconsiderable talents.

Sim devised a ploy to get around the law. He persuaded his

bride to learn to operate a Japanese typewriter, a complicated and cumbersome device requiring a great deal of training. Sim then contended this skill qualified her as an international trader entitled to live in the United States and help her husband.

Consular officials in Tokyo were inclined to dispute Sim's argument but, figuring he had the blessing of San Francisco immigration officials, honored the application. When Sim and his bride reached San Francisco, immigration officials contended she didn't really qualify as a trader, but allowed her to enter inasmuch as the United States consulate in Tokyo had granted the visa.

Convention delegates also sketched some ground rules for the endowment fund, which hadn't grown appreciably since it was founded in Seattle two years earlier. At least 25 percent of the money received into the fund was to be placed in bank savings accounts, not more than 25 percent could be invested in stocks and the balance could be used to purchase "national, state, county or municipal bonds." After the fund reached $25,000 (no provision was made for a drop in stock values), the income could be used to pay headquarters office rent, wages and expenses of the staff when someone was hired, and if there was anything left, the money could be applied to other JACL activities.

Lack of membership continued to be a problem. February was designated a "membership week" and chapters were urged to put up posters, sponsor vocational classes and athletic leagues, schedule more social affairs, offer reduced fees for dental and medical care and special insurance rates, line up outside speakers and hold debates on current issues, take a census of Nisei and hold voter registration drives. None of these ideas seemed to have any great salutary effect. It would take a catastrophic event beyond the control of any of the members to awaken Nisei to the importance of JACL.

Sakamoto was succeeded as president by Walter Tsukamoto, then thirty-four years old, a Sacramento attorney and a captain in the Judge Advocate General's department in the U.S. Army Reserve. Unlike Sakamoto and Kido, who operated out of shabby little offices, Tsukamoto could afford impressive air-conditioned quarters, a rarity in those times. His performance as unpaid executive secretary made his election a popular choice. Other officers under the new list of positions adopted at the convention were Ken Matsumoto of Los Angeles, vice-president; Ken Utsunomiya of Santa Maria Valley, secretary; Hito Okada of Portland, treasurer. The officers were joined on the new National Board by the chairmen of the three district councils: Henry Tsurutani of Los Angeles, Southern California district; Dr. Harry Kita of Salinas, Northern California district; Mamaro Wakasugi of Portland, Northwest district.

Four months after his installation, Tsukamoto was deeply involved in fighting a bill in the California legislature aimed at kicking San Pedro and San Diego Issei out of the tuna-fishing industry that they had pioneered. The ostensible reason was, that in case of war, Issei-owned tuna clippers might be utilized by the Japanese Navy as torpedo boats and mine-layers, but the real reason was economic competition. Tsukamoto fought the discriminatory legislation both as JACL president and as attorney for Tokunosuke Abe, a leader in the fishing industry, who was getting help from George Obayashi and George Ohashi of the San Diego JACL chapter. After a six-month battle, the bill was defeated. Historian Donald H. Estes of San Diego City College suggests it may have been one of JACL's first big legislative successes.

Tsukamoto's term was a time of growing tensions between the United States and Japan. Since 1937 Japanese armies had advanced from triumph to triumph on the Asian mainland, forcing the Chinese government to move its capital from Nanking to Hankow to, finally, Chungking far up the Yangtze River. By early 1939 most of China's ports were in Japanese hands, cutting off effective contact with the West. In September of 1939 German tank columns thrust into Poland, and Great Britain and France declared war on the Reich. World War II was under way. The United States moved closer and closer to the war without actually committing combat troops. Meanwhile, Japan took advantage of American preoccupation with the European conflict to move toward the rich resources of Southeast Asia. The only nation capable of foiling Japanese seizure of what was referred to as the "Southern Resources Area" was the United States. War between the United States and Japan, which jingoists on both sides of the Pacific had been predicting for decades, now appeared inevitable. This was as apparent to Nisei as to other Americans, but such a war was unthinkable to them and most kept trying to wish it away.

Tsukamoto put the situation into perspective in his keynote

address at the 1940 convention in Portland where registration for the first time topped five hundred. "It is the duty of every American," Tsukamoto asserted, "and that means all of us who cherish the ideals of our democratic institutions, to be prepared to protect, defend and perpetuate our form of government and our way of life. . . . This love of country and duty is not, and must not be, colored by any thought of foreign ties." Tsukamoto's address also contained these words:

> The world is again at war, and our country is faced with problems of national preparedness and defense—a crisis arising so swiftly that every American citizen must come to this realization at once and be prepared more than ever before to assume and discharge fully his obligations and duties as a citizen of this glorious country.
>
> As part of this tremendous task of preparing ourselves for any emergency, either from without or from within, Congress has already passed and the President has given executive approval to many new laws.
>
> One of these is a requirement that every alien residing in this country voluntarily register himself with designated agencies throughout the nation. We can be of practical assistance in this tremendous task by cooperating with the government agencies in this regard, and we intend to offer this cooperation in every community wherein a chapter is located.
>
> Another piece of legislation currently considered by Congress is that of compulsory military training for every able-bodied American citizen. We have heretofore, and we do now reaffirm our endorsement of this program and call upon every American of Japanese ancestry to offer his life if necessary in defense of his country.
>
> The JACL—skeptics, ill-wishers and minority opposition groups to the contrary notwithstanding—makes no compromise on the one and only reason for the existence of this organization; the maintenance and direction of every effort, program and activity as a patriotic body of American citizens to perpetuate forever our American ideals and institutions.

The convention responded by passing a resolution reaffirming "without any reservation our allegiance to the Constitution of the United States and to our American ideals and institutions."

That done, the delegates proceeded forthrightly to demand equal treatment from their government. One resolution, noting that Japanese Americans were accepted only by the Army, urged

Congress and the President "to allow American citizens of Japanese ancestry to prove their loyalty to the United States and participate in the defense of their country by being able to enter any branch of the armed forces necessary for national defense." Another resolution noted that the Alien Registration Act posed a great inconvenience, but if such a step were necessary, JACL favored "universal registration of all residents of the United States." Finally, the League charged that labor union discrimination on the basis of race damaged national unity and proposed a fair-employment-practices law.

Community economic problems continued to weigh heavily on the delegates. Even at this early stage of their development —long before the concept of the welfare state had become acceptable—JACL was concerning itself with the problems of the elderly. "Although young today," Tsukamoto said in his opening address, "the years roll by quickly and we must encourage systematic savings and frugal living on the part of our members and the Nisei in general. We must make provision now for the unfortunate and the less hardy lest we make them dependents of the government."

Economic advancement was a goal blocked by the twin burdens of the Depression and discrimination. In 1940 the Nisei were still struggling for an opportunity to exercise their skills and talents. Kido advanced once more his pet idea of fraternal insurance as a JACL program and again it got nowhere, mainly because no one had a practical proposal. However, the delegates approved a resolution to study the possibility of setting up an organization to help members launch new business ventures.

There were also many in-house matters requiring attention. Induction of the three Intermountain District Council chapters, plus Long Beach, Gardena and Arizona in the Southern district and Kings County and Lodi in Northern California, raised the number of chapters to fifty. Tsukamoto observed that the national organization had grown too large for any volunteer to administer its program while earning a livelihood elsewhere and that it was unfair to continue to demand the time and services of men and women in key positions without adequate compensation. He urged JACL to build up its finances so that it could employ a full-time executive secretary. The question of proportional representation in JACL councils, a matter that had been discussed at earlier gatherings, surfaced again. The complaint of some of the larger chapters, notably the Los Angeles group, was that they had no greater voice than tiny rural chapters which contributed far less to the national organization. Several proposals were advanced to remedy the situation. The upshot was a compromise plan giving one vote to chapters with fewer than 50 members; two votes to chapters with memberships between 51 and 100; three votes to chapters with memberships between 101 and 300; four votes to chapters with memberships between 301 and 500; five votes to chapters with memberships between 501 and 750; six votes to chapters with more than 751 members. As it turned out, this effort to achieve a more representational system never had a chance to be tested before World War II all but destroyed the organization.

Mike Masaoka, who had come close to disrupting the Los Angeles convention two years earlier, kept a lower profile this time but his counsel was listened to attentively in after-hours discussion groups. One of those listening carefully was Saburo Kido, who was impressed by Masaoka's ideas and his ability to express them.

Because of the growing tension between the United States and Japan, the delegates realized their next president had to be a man of stature, judgment, patience and vision. They turned to Kido. Years later, Kido wrote of his election:

> I had been dodging the national presidency for some time, but it happened that my immunity had expired. Before the Portland convention I could find no way out so I told Northern California leaders I would run if they wanted me. Once I was elected, I welcomed the responsibility of guiding the destiny of the organization which I had helped to found. I would not be able to blame anyone else for whatever might happen to JACL during the next two years. But I was hoping against hope that there would be no war between the United States and Japan, and I could turn over JACL to my successor in a time of peace.

Kido's cabinet included Ken Matsumoto, re-elected vice-president; James Sugioka of Hollister, California, secretary; Hito Okada, re-elected treasurer.

Despite Kido's realistic outlook, he had no inkling of the problems he would face. As for JACL, it could not have picked a better man for its most trying years.

In the spring of 1929 the New American Citizens League, founded by Saburo Kido in San Francisco, sponsored a meeting to organize a federation of Nisei groups. This photo of those attending shows Clarence Arai of Seattle third from the left in the front row with Kido next to him.

The Japanese American Citizens League was formally organized in Seattle in September, 1930, when this convention photograph was taken outside the building where the Japanese Chamber of Commerce had its offices. Clarence Arai, appointed first national JACL president, is in the front row, wearing white trousers. On his left are Saburo Kido

In 1936 the fourth JACL convention returned to Seattle. This photo was taken outside city hall. From left to right in the front row, starting from the flag bearer, are Walter Tsukamoto, Sim Togasaki, a convention speaker, Dr. Thomas T. Yatabe who presided over the convention as the first elected JACL president, Mayor John Dore, Japanese Consul Issaku Okamoto, another unidentified speaker, Clarence Arai and Tom Iseri. *(Photo: Ralph Ochi Studio)*

The first four elected JACL presidents

Dr. Thomas T. Yatabe
1934–36

Jimmie Sakamoto
1936–38

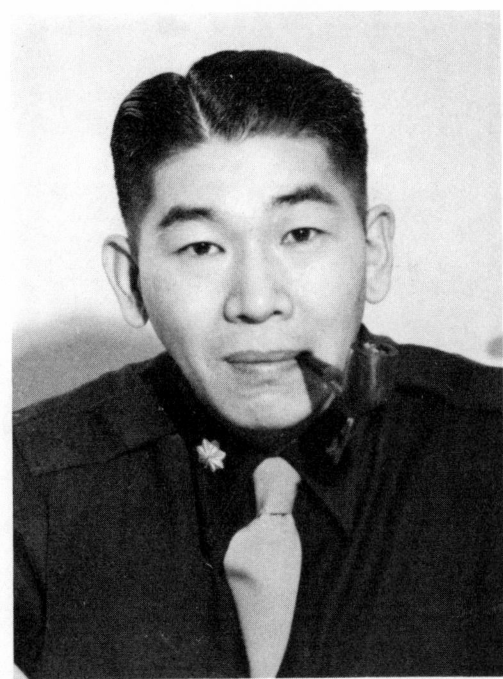

Walter Tsukamoto
1938–40

Saburo Kido
1940–46

From 1933 to 1939 JACL's monthly newspaper, *Pacific Citizen,* was published out of Jimmie Sakamoto's *Courier* office in Seattle. Tony Gomes of the *Courier* staff is in the foreground; Sakamoto's wife, Misao, is in the background.

Festivities at the corner of East First Street and San Pedro in Los Angeles, the heart of Li'l Tokyo in the 1930's. Masao Satow, whose YMCA office was in the building shown, met his future wife at the drugstore lunch counter.

JACL's top leadership just prior to the outbreak of war. In the center row, from left to right, are Teiko Ishida Kuroiwa, Dr. Thomas T. Yatabe, Saburo Kido, Jimmie Sakamoto and Walter Tsukamoto. In the front row, the first two are Yasuo Abiko and Mike Masaoka.

The FBI rounded up Issei community leaders immediately after the attack on Pearl Harbor, creating a leadership vacuum that JACL tried to fill.

Troops moved into Japanese American communities to enforce the Evacuation order. Federal officials warned against disorder and JACL counseled cooperation.

Military police preparing for patrol duty at the Santa Anita, California, assembly center. Most Japanese Americans did not anticipate armed guards when they agreed to comply with the federal order to leave their homes. *(Photo: National Archives)*

Tokie Nishimura Slocum, a World War I hero who had waged a one-man battle to get citizenship for American veterans born in Japan, pitched in to help JACL after Pearl Harbor. *(Photo: National Archives)*

A confused Issei is pushed and pulled on all sides as he seeks to comply with the Evacuation order.

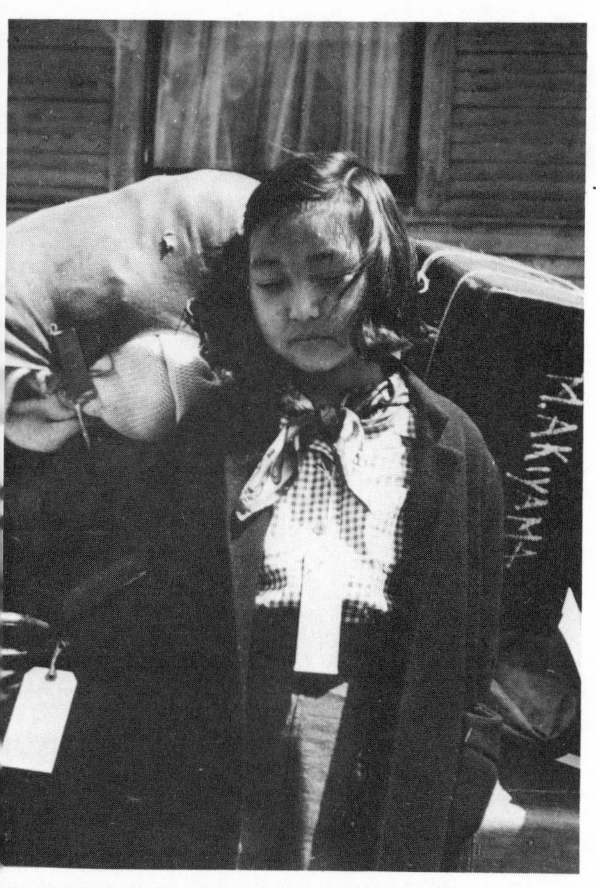

A victim of the Evacuation, called America's worst wartime mistake, on her way behind barbed wire *(Photo: Bancroft Library, University of California)*

An American concentration camp for United States citizens—Heart Mountain, Wyoming, winter 1942–43

JACL came under severe criticism in some WRA camps, but loyalists managed to keep the faith.

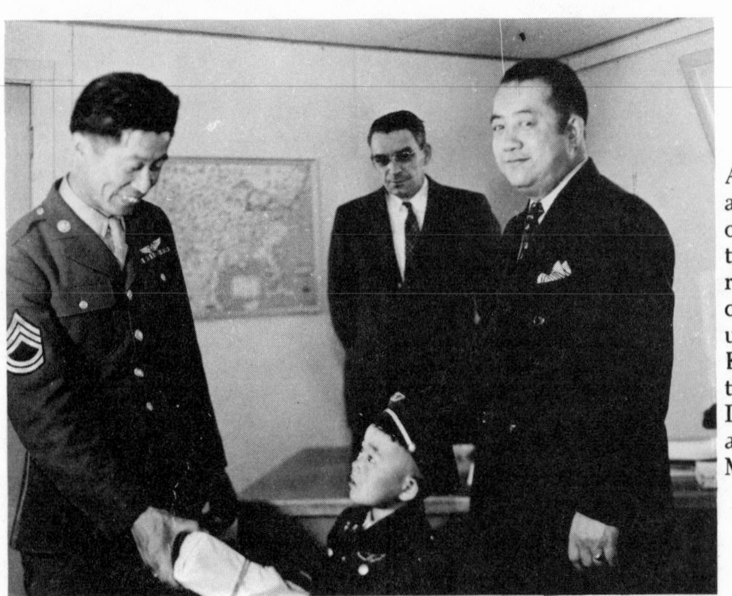

After President Roosevelt approved the enlistment of Japanese Americans in the Army in 1943, Nisei already in uniform visited camps to encourage volunteers. War hero Ben Kuroki meets an unidentified youngster, Project Director Harry Stafford and Clarence Arai at the Minidoka, Idaho, camp.

Their military record in Europe and the Pacific reinforced the Nisei's demand for acceptance. Sergeant Mike Masaoka, first to volunteer for the all-Nisei 442nd Regimental Combat Team, receives the Legion of Merit from General Wood somewhere in Italy.

Joe Grant Masaoka, left, and Ben Kuroki at the JACL office in Denver *(Photo: National Archives)*

The first postwar JACL convention was held in Denver in 1946. This was the convention committee. Front row, from left to right: Mrs. Haruko Kobayashi, Dr. Takashi Mayeda, Yoshiko Ariki, Minoru Yasui. Second row: Charles Kamayatsu, Mrs. Amy Miura, Mrs. Michi Ando, Mrs. Merijane Yokoe, George Mits Kaneko. Third row: Jack Noda, Ping Oda.

Dr. Thomas T. Yatabe installs the first postwar cabinet in 1946. From left to right: Hito Okada, president; George Inagaki, vice-president; Mas Satow, vice-president; Bill Yamauchi, vice-president; Dr. Takashi Mayeda, secretary to the Board; Kay Terashima, treasurer.

The national staff at a 1947 conference in Chicago. From left to right: Sam Nishikawa, New York; Tats Kushida, Chicago; Mas Horiuchi, Salt Lake City; Mike Masaoka, Washington, D.C.; Mas Satow, Salt Lake City; with Dr. Yatabe and Dr. Randolph Sakada, then a national vice-president. *(Photo: Vincent Tajiri)*

Hito Okada, left, and *Pacific Citizen* Editor Larry Tajiri, next to him, accept community service awards.

The Washington JACL chapter sponsored a series of memorial services for Nisei servicemen at Arlington National Cemetery. Mike Masaoka eulogizes comrades who gave their lives for their country.

The highlight of the 1952 convention in San Francisco was the passage by Congress of the Walter-McCarran Act, revising American immigration and naturalization laws, over President Truman's veto. An enthusiastic crowd met Masaoka (in dark glasses, center) when he arrived in San Francisco with his wife, Etsu, after the legislative victory. *(Photo: Kido Studio)*

IX

The Year War Came

Saburo Kido was a slight, dapper individual who never quite lost the accents of Hawaii, where he was born in 1902. His long-time friend and associate Sim Togasaki uses a Japanese word, *majime,* to describe Kido. It means "earnest" or "no-nonsense," which Kido was. But he also laughed easily and enjoyed good jokes as much as any of his contemporaries. And for all his problems, Kido was remarkably patient and even tempered.

Sannosuke and Haru Kido, like many other Japanese, had named their third son Saburo. Sannosuke made his living as a *sake* brewer in Hawaii until Prohibition wiped out his business. He returned to Japan with his wife and four younger children, two sons and two daughters, about the time Saburo left for the American mainland to study law. Although not many knew it, after he became established, Saburo sent for a brother and sister who had been stricken with tuberculosis and supported them while they underwent treatment.

Kido assumed the presidency of JACL at an extremely difficult time and he soon was called on to make three decisions which were to prove critical.

In 1940 Japan scheduled a major propaganda show pegged to the twenty-six thousandth anniversary of its founding; it was gospel under the militarists that the Japanese empire had come into being in 660 B.C. Overseas Japanese from all over the world were invited to attend the festivities. Kido as president of JACL was offered an expense-paid trip. The temptation to accept was great.

He had never been to Japan. The trip would give him an opportunity to visit his mother and other members of his family he hadn't seen since leaving Hawaii, and he couldn't afford to go on his own. In the end, he declined. Kido decided it wasn't proper to accept official Japanese hospitality when that government was at loggerheads with his own country.

The second decision was somewhat related. The Japanese Association of North America, an Issei organization, fully aware of JACL's financial problems, suggested a joint fund-raising campaign. Kido understood that the Japanese Association simply wanted to be helpful. He also knew that the Issei were well organized and could help bring a goodly sum into JACL's treasury. But again he decided it was wiser to keep a distance between JACL and any Japanese organization.

Before long, all Japanese American groups were being scrutinized with near paranoid intensity for any indications of possible disloyalty or even split loyalty. It is likely that Kido's two decisions to steer JACL clear of any Japanese taint played a substantial part in assuring the Federal Bureau of Investigation and other intelligence agencies of the League's credibility.

But the third decision was without doubt the most important in shaping the history of JACL. That came in the summer of 1941 when months of steadily deteriorating Japanese-American relations were climaxed by Japan's invasion of French Indochina. President Roosevelt retaliated on July 26 by abrogating the treaty of friendship and commerce, freezing Japanese credits and effectively halting shipping between the two countries. With virtually all normal relations suspended, war seemed inevitable unless one or the other backed down. It was under this ominous cloud that Northern California chapters met in Monterey for their biennial district convention. But war was far from the thoughts of most conventioneers. The social events were only a little less festive than usual. One of those enjoying himself was Mike Masaoka, who was combining a California vacation with a visit to the convention. Masaoka and Dr. George Hiura from Sebastopol were on a double blind date. Hiura's date was a slender girl from San Jose named Etsu Mineta, but before long she and Masaoka found themselves gravitating toward each other.

Kido, however, had more serious matters on his mind. Because a quorum of the National Council was at the convention, he called a special meeting to discuss something he had been thinking about for months—hiring a full-time JACL staff employee, a move which Walter Tsukamoto had proposed at the previous national convention. At Kido's suggestion each Council member jotted down the qualifications he thought would be desirable in an executive secretary. They were in basic agreement—he must be fluent in both English and Japanese, be able to speak in public and have the poise to meet with government officials on their terms, have an understanding of Issei and Nisei psychology and know something of the history of Japanese Americans.

Kido had his own candidate well in mind even though he did not fit the profile. That was Masaoka; he would make an articulate spokesman for the Nisei and Kido felt that was more important than being able to speak Japanese or being familiar with the Japanese American experience. Kido also had been impressed by Masaoka's intelligence; he seemed to be able to think a couple of moves ahead of anyone else. The only other candidate seriously considered by the Council was Togo Tanaka, a brilliant young Phi Beta Kappa from the University of California at Los Angeles who was working as an English-section editor at the *Rafu Shimpo.* After brief discussion, Kido was authorized to approach Masaoka.

Masaoka wasn't particularly taken by the idea of working for JACL. He enjoyed his part-time job at the University of Utah and had been mulling over the idea of getting into politics. But Kido was persuasive in explaining JACL's need for someone to run the organization and Masaoka agreed to go home and give the offer serious consideration. His friend, Senator Thomas, helped Masaoka make up his mind. The senator, who commanded respect as member of the Military Affairs, Foreign Relations and Labor committees, foresaw difficult times ahead for Japanese Americans. He suggested to Masaoka that a person of his talents could do a great deal to help them. Convinced he had an opportunity to do something useful, Mike resigned from the university and left for San Francisco in August. He and Kido hadn't discussed salary. Only after he reported to JACL headquarters in Kido's cluttered office did he learn he would be paid $135 per month, less than he had been making. He was only twenty-five years old, but remarkably mature, thoughtful, determined.

Masaoka soon realized how little he knew about the Nisei community on the Coast. The book *Nisei* reports:

> In San Francisco he found the *Nisei* being held together by ethnic ties rather than by intellectual interests or socioeconomic status, which was the case among his [Caucasian] friends back home. Their common racial heritage made them a close-knit group regardless of their other interests. He found many *Nisei* were uncomfortable with non-Japanese. They couldn't or wouldn't articulate their thoughts in a mixed group and preferred to be among their own kind. He also discovered most Nisei were polite, conservative, reliable but quite unaggressive. They seemed to lack spontaneity. They . . . were careful not to . . . cause anyone to lose face.

One of his first accomplishments was to persuade JACL that the federal government was the servant of the people, that its services existed to be utilized. From experience, many Japanese Americans knew government only as an oppressive regulator, harassing citizens at its worst and unresponsive and insensitive to their needs at best. Notified by Senator Thomas that a presidential commission on equal employment opportunities was holding hearings, Masaoka went to Los Angeles to testify that qualified Nisei were being refused work in defense industries. Before long jobs began to open up.

But there were unmistakable warnings that the international situation was growing even more ominous. One day Curtis B. Munson, a State Department official, came to JACL headquarters. He reminded Kido and Masaoka about the hostility German Americans had experienced in World War I, declared that everything should be done to avoid similar problems for Japanese Americans and asked for JACL's suggestions for protecting lives and property. The three talked for the better part of three days with Munson warning that nothing must be said about their meetings so as not to alarm the public. Kido expressed fear that violence, if it should come, was more likely in farm areas and suggested that sheriffs and other rural peace officers be alerted. Masaoka stressed the need for President Roosevelt or some other top federal official to urge the American people to distinguish between Japanese Americans and the Japanese in Japan. Several months after the war's outbreak, Masaoka chanced to meet Munson in Washington. By then he was in Navy uniform. He told

Masaoka that what he had heard in San Francisco had proved to be reliable and it was likely federal authorities would continue to depend on JACL for assistance.

Other security officers, particularly FBI agents, questioned Kido about the loyalty of individual Issei. Kido asserted that most Issei remained aliens because United States laws barred them from citizenship, that while they continued to hold a sentimental attachment for Japan they also respected the United States and would do nothing to harm the country in which they had lived for so long. There were harder questions: "If a Japanese landing party should come to the shores of California under cover of darkness, would this Issei report their presence immediately to the nearest sheriff's office or would he harbor them overnight?" No one could provide a categorical answer to such a hypothetical situation, and Kido said so.

Vice-President Ken Matsumoto in Los Angeles had established friendly relations with Naval Intelligence officers some months earlier, particularly with Lieutenant Commander Kenneth D. Ringle of the 11th Naval District. As early as March, 1941, Ringle had hosted a get-acquainted dinner with representatives of Southern district JACL chapters, with an Army Intelligence officer and Los Angeles County Sheriff Eugene Biscailuz also attending. It was an opportunity for the officers to size up the Nisei, and the Nisei to show they were hardly the type to serve as fifth columnists. Matsumoto suggested similar meetings in San Francisco and Seattle where other naval commands were located, but they never materialized.

Masaoka, in his conversations after the day's work, convinced Kido of the need to make more contacts in official circles so Nisei would have friends in government if war should come. In Utah, Masaoka pointed out, he knew Senators Thomas and William H. King well enough that he had no problem reaching them for consultations. It would take time to establish such relationships on the West Coast. But in inland areas Nisei were better integrated into their communities. It was essential, Masaoka argued, that as many inland Nisei as possible be brought into JACL so their contacts could be utilized in an emergency. After Thanksgiving, 1941, Masaoka set out on a trip to meet with Nisei in Wyoming, Colorado and Nebraska.

By then war was only a few days away, but only the Japanese high command was aware of its imminence. The attack on Pearl

Harbor was as great a shock to Nisei all over the mainland as it was to the men and women in Hawaii. The book *Nisei* tells in considerable detail the experiences of various JACL leaders on December 7, 1941. What follows is adapted from *Nisei.*

Kido was attending a meeting in San Francisco that morning. The possibility of war bore heavily on his mind. He knew the San Francisco Japanese community was divided, nervous under international tensions, unwilling to pull together. So an Issei, Kuniji Takahashi, had taken the initiative of calling various Nisei and Kibei leaders to a unity meeting, and Kido was there as national JACL president. The meeting had hardly started when Dr. George Baba entered the room, excitement written on his face. As he was driving to the meeting he had heard that Hawaii was under attack by Japanese planes. Kido recalled saying: "That's too fantastic to believe. The report must be wrong, probably just another rumor. Let's hear what H. V. Kaltenborn has to say when he comes on at 12:15."

Kaltenborn at that time was among the nation's top newscasters. He had a fast, staccato delivery that lent an air of excitement to even the most prosaic news. The meeting was recessed while everyone moved to another room to hear what he had to say. In stunned silence they heard Kaltenborn's tense, high-pitched voice confirm that Pearl Harbor in Hawaii and Clark Field in the Philippines had been attacked and even at that moment American ships were burning and American men were dying.

Ashen-faced, Kido hurried to the office of the *New World Sun,* a Japanese-language newspaper. Kido was its legal counsel and in its English section he wrote a daily column called "Timely Topics." The telephone was ringing. Reporters for the San Francisco newspapers and the local correspondent of the *New York Times* were asking for comment. Kido still could not believe war had come, but he composed himself quickly and issued a statement condemning the attack, pledging the loyalty of the Nisei and offering full support of the war effort. Then on behalf of JACL he sent a telegram to President Roosevelt that was a model of sincerity and quiet eloquence:

. . . IN THIS SOLEMN HOUR WE PLEDGE OUR FULLEST COOPERATION TO YOU, MR. PRESIDENT, AND TO OUR COUNTRY

. . . NOW THAT JAPAN HAS INSTITUTED THIS ATTACK UPON OUR LAND, WE ARE READY AND PREPARED TO EXPEND EVERY EFFORT TO REPEL THIS INVASION TOGETHER WITH OUR FELLOW AMERICANS.

As the afternoon and night wore on, Kido was gratified to hear both his statement and the message to the President mentioned on newscasts along with the latest war bulletins.

By December 7, Masaoka had progressed as far as North Platte, Nebraska. On that Sunday morning he met with some fifty Nisei in the basement of the North Platte Episcopal Church. They had converged on North Platte from farms in southeastern Wyoming and northeastern Colorado and far western Nebraska, seeking assurance that war would not come.

Masaoka had prepared well for the meeting. On the wall he had tacked a map of the Rocky Mountain area, and as he spoke he drew rings around places like Cheyenne, Denver, Pueblo and other communities where Japanese had settled. It didn't occur to him that Cheynne was the site of Fort Francis E. Warren; Denver had Lowry Army Air Base and Rocky Mountain Arsenal; Pueblo had an ordnance depot and a major steel mill. Masaoka was making an eloquent case for supporting JACL when the door was thrust open and several bulky men—Caucasians—entered.

"Are you Mike Masaoka?" one of them asked, glancing at the map.

Mike said he was. He thought the strangers were newspapermen.

"Could we see you outside a minute?"

"I'm right in the middle of some important business here," Masaoka explained, impatience rising in his voice. "Would you mind waiting outside for a little while?"

"This is quite urgent."

Masaoka left the room with the men. Once outside the door they pinned his arms to his sides and in silence escorted him directly to the city jail. His questions unanswered, Masaoka wondered if he had been picked up for failing to get a license for a public meeting. At the jail he heard for the first time of the attack on Pearl Harbor. The Nisei in the church, who still hadn't heard of the outbreak of fighting, were mystified when Masaoka failed to come back. After a while someone thought to tell them of the war, and that Masaoka was in jail. No one said anything for what seemed a long time. Then somebody said: "I guess we'd better get home to our families."

Masaoka was held incommunicado long enough to figure out how local police had known his name and whereabouts. He came to the conclusion that FBI agents had been following his progress across the country and knew where to find him at any time. Two days later he was permitted to telephone Kido, in San Francisco, but was warned not to reveal he was in jail.

"Sab," Masaoka said when the connection was made, "I was afraid you were worrying about me. I'm stuck here in North Platte, Nebraska. I'm at the, ah, the Palace Hotel."

Kido commiserated with him, figuring Masaoka had been delayed by disrupted rail schedules, and urged him to get back to San Francisco as soon as he could because there was a load of work piling up.

Later that day Kido attended a board meeting of the International Institute which had been called to discuss problems facing Japanese Americans. When he told the members of Masaoka's misfortune, someone suggested a telephone call be placed to him in North Platte to console him. Annie Clo Watson, a YWCA executive and long a friend of the Nisei, was delegated to place the call. Presently she returned with a bewildered expression. "Mike's not at the Palace Hotel," she said. "He's in jail!"

Kido got on the phone to seek Masaoka's release. The two men he tried to reach for assistance were Senators Thomas and King. Senator Thomas quickly arranged for Masaoka's freedom, and he was placed on a train for San Francisco.

At the next stop, Cheyenne, local police walking through the train saw Masaoka. They decided that since he was an Oriental he needed further looking into, and over Masaoka's strenuous protests took him once more to jail. It took another call to Senator Thomas to win his release. The senator, who had other things to do, arranged an FBI escort for Masaoka all the way back to San Francisco.

About the time Masaoka was being picked up in North Platte, Private Harry Honda, who went on to become editor of *Pacific Citizen,* was hunched over a portable radio in a barracks at Fort Warren, just outside Cheyenne. He had been stretched out on his bunk reading a newspaper when someone shouted that the war had started. The first thought that came to Honda's mind was that he wasn't going to get the furlough due on completion of sixteen weeks of basic training.

Hito Okada, then national treasurer of JACL and later its president, had chosen December 7 to take his family from their home in Portland to see friends in Seattle. While his wife and daughter visited, Okada rented a rowboat on the Seattle waterfront and went trolling for blackmouth salmon. Even as the first American battle of World War II raged in Hawaii, Okada innocently rowed back and forth off the Todd Shipyards where ocean-going vessels were being refitted. It would have been an embarrassing position in which to be caught, but no one noticed him. Late Sunday afternoon Okada returned the boat and drove to Tacoma to visit his mother. He had parked his car and was walking to her door when a total stranger stopped him and snarled: "I'll be back to get you with my gun!" Okada wondered what the man was talking about. Then his mother told him what had been coming all day over the radio.

In Tacoma itself, Shigeo Wakamatsu, later another national JACL president, was sleeping late that Sunday in the cubbyhole he used as a bedroom at the Farmers Market. He was a student at the College of Puget Sound and he worked as a combination watchman and night receiving clerk at the market where farmers brought their produce. The first words he heard that morning were those of someone shouting: "Hey, Shig, the Japs are bombing Pearl Harbor." He came awake in a hurry. The next day he asked permission to address a special assembly on the college campus. Wakamatsu poured out his anger and shame. He pledged his personal loyalty to the United States and that of other Nisei. He concluded his speech with the Japanese American Creed, written only a few months earlier by Mike Masaoka and entered in the *Congressional Record* on May 9 by Senator Thomas. The last paragraph of the creed reads: "Because I believe in America, and I trust she believes in me, and because I have received innumerable benefits from her, I pledge myself to do honor to her at all times and in all places; to defend her against all enemies, foreign and domestic; to actively assume my duties and obligations cheerfully and without any reservations whatsoever, in the hope that I may become a better American in a greater America."

As he returned to his chair, drained of emotion, his fellow students gave him a standing ovation.

Another future JACL president, Kumeo Yoshinari, was in similarly humble circumstances on Pearl Harbor Day. He was pruning trees in a pear orchard near Hood River, Oregon, trying to make a few dollars. When he returned home for lunch, his wife, Mary, told him the news. The first thing that came to mind was the admonition of his Issei friend, Masuo Yasui, to treasure his citizenship and become a 100-percent American. He also remembered the cynicism of other Issei who predicted the Nisei never would be accepted as Americans, that they would live forever under the cloud of racial discrimination. Fleetingly, he wondered who would be proved right.

But in Fresno, Tom Yatabe's long record of civic activity paid off. He got the news when he arrived home after a morning of golf. Shortly afterward there was a telephone call from Long Beach. It was the mayor of Fresno, anxious about his friend. "Doc," he urged, "tell your people to stay home. Keep them off the streets. We don't know what the hoodlum element might do, and we don't want any trouble. I've already ordered patrol cars into the Japanese areas."

Later, when sheriff's deputies began a roundup of Issei, Yatabe pleaded: "Go easy on them. They're old folks."

"I know, Doc," an officer replied. "I know most of these people and they're all right. We're working under FBI orders."

That night, various Nisei gathered at Yatabe's home to talk and seek reassurance. "What are we going to do?" the younger Nisei asked Yatabe. He had no answer for them.

In Los Angeles, the reactions of Nisei were as varied as their number and backgrounds. Masao Satow, who had been making speeches pleading for understanding of the Nisei under a program organized by JACL, heard the radio broadcasts with shock and disbelief. It did not occur to him at the time that there might be dire consequences for those of Japanese ancestry in the United States. He recalled carrying the news to his mother, and her first words were *"Nihon baka da ne!"* (How foolish Japan is!). He took his mother to church to attend somber Issei services and there gained the impression most Issei felt the same way she did. That afternoon Satow met some Nisei friends and they could talk of nothing but the war. Yet, its possible effect on their lives in the days to come did not enter their conversation.

In another part of Los Angeles the war news struck Frank Chuman with far greater impact than it had hit Satow. Chuman, also later to become JACL president, was a second-year student at the University of Southern California law school. He and his sister, Yemi, had attended morning services at St. Mary's Episcopal Church. On their return home just before noon he switched on the radio and the news was like a slap in the face. The Chumans had their customary Sunday lunch together, picking at their food in fearful silence, subdued and shocked. After lunch, Chuman's parents agreed it would be prudent to destroy as much evidence as possible of family or sentimental ties with Japan. They burned letters, photographs and magazines, and buried two magnificent samurai swords which were family heirlooms. "Disposal of these beautiful pieces of Japanese workmanship seemed to be a symbolic rite," Chuman said later. "It was as though a tangible cultural tie with Japan were being severed."

Kiyoshi Patrick Okura, who succeeded Chuman as JACL president in 1962, was a personnel technician with the Los Angeles City Civil Service Commission in 1941. On Pearl Harbor Day he had played eighteen holes of golf with a group of Nisei friends and they heard the news as they came off the course. Everyone rushed home without having their usual lunch together. Okura lived in the Wilmington harbor area. His car radio told him that troops already were patrolling key harbor spots and that the drawbridge between Terminal Island, site of a colony of Issei-Nisei fishermen, and Wilmington was under surveillance. At home Okura learned his bride of less than three months, Lily, and her sister Tomiko had gone to Terminal Island that morning to have their hair dressed. Okura telephoned the beauty parlor and instructed his wife to come home immediately. But when the women reached the drawbridge, Army sentries refused to let them leave the island without some sort of clearance. Lily called her husband to report her predicament. Okura by now was almost frantic. He telephoned almost every Los Angeles official he knew, and then it occurred to him that there was a federal prison and immigration office on Terminal Island. He reached his wife again and told her to seek help from the federal officials.

It was evening when the women were permitted to go home after they had been interrogated, photographed and fingerprinted. While at the federal facilities they had seen a number of fishermen and Japanese community leaders being brought in for detention.

Okura had fallen into a troubled sleep sometime after midnight when he was awakened by heavy knocks on both the front and back doors. "We are special agents of the FBI," a voice shouted. "Open your doors." Okura also heard his father's voice asking that they be allowed to come in.

FBI agents had already visited the elder Okura's home. They had kept Pat's two younger brothers, two younger sisters and parents in one room while they searched the house. They picked up letters from Japan and papers having to do with the activities of the Los Angeles Japanese Chamber of Commerce and the San Pedro Japanese Association. Then, because the elder Okura had been known to visit Pat frequently, the agents forced him to accompany them to the son's home. Pat Okura described what happened after a group of FBI men burst into the house:

> Just as I was trying to get out of bed, a Los Angeles city policeman in uniform stuck a flashlight in my face and told me to stay put. I questioned his authority in Wilmington. He said he had been deputized as an FBI agent. While I remained in bed, shaken and angry, they went through all our closets, opening boxes of wedding gifts that were still packed away, going through all the bookcases. Finally, when they could find nothing important, they allowed me to get out of bed and told me to instruct my father to pack a few clothes as he was to be held in detention.

Even more harrowing was the experience of Togo Tanaka, the editor. Several weeks earlier he had gone to Washington to see what could be done to keep the *Rafu Shimpo* publishing in case of war.

He was at the office on Monday when he was arrested by an FBI agent armed with something called a presidential warrant. He was never charged with violation of any law and the reason for his arrest was never spelled out in his eleven days behind bars. During this period he was mugged, fingerprinted and questioned frequently by FBI agents but was not permitted to contact an attorney or get in touch with anyone, not even his wife, Jean, who was nine months pregnant with their first child. Tanaka later recalled:

> I was worried about my wife and sore as hell about what I considered an infringement of my constitutional rights as an American citizen. I kept wondering why I was being held, and nobody would tell me. I had written and signed many flag-waving patriotic editorials on behalf of the Stars and Stripes in the *Rafu Shimpo*

> English section. For years afterward I figured that a couple of my fellow Nisei, prominent in the national JACL and overzealous in their American patriotism, who took great pride in their close association with Navy Intelligence officers, had bird-dogged a number of us whose pre–Pearl Harbor itinerary looked suspicious or confusing. I remembered, too, that I gave a talk to an Orange County service club just a couple of days before Pearl Harbor, and one of the daily papers ran a story about it saying that "a Japanese editor" had predicted the outbreak of war. Hell, that was nothing new. Among the eighty-one people I met in Washington, I found seventy-nine who definitely said that war was inevitable. You didn't have to be part of some insidious plot to know war was coming.

Tanaka's release was as sudden and unexplained as his arrest. On thirty minutes' notice on the eleventh day he was told to pick up his belongings and go home. The Los Angeles Japanese community to which Tanaka returned was in confusion. Its solidarity had been its source of strength, but now the Issei leadership was gone, picked up in a series of swift roundups by FBI agents. The same was true in San Francisco, Portland, Seattle and other communities. Government records show that by 6 A.M. on December 8, the FBI had seized 733 Japanese nationals on the mainland and in Hawaii. Within four days the number had climbed to 1,370, and by the time the program was completed, 2,192 Japanese "enemy aliens" had been apprehended.

Attorney General Francis Biddle sought to reassure both Japanese Americans and the general public with a statement that the federal agencies had the situation under control and urged understanding for loyal Issei and Nisei. "So long as the aliens in this country conduct themselves in accordance with law, they need fear no interference by the Department of Justice or by any other agency of the Federal Government," he said. "They may be assured, indeed, that every effort will be made to protect them from any discrimination or abuse. . . . Inevitably, there are some among our alien population who are disloyal. . . ."

In the Japanese communities, Biddle's words had a hollow ring, for both Issei and Nisei knew that many of the men who had been arrested had never harmed anyone, and never would. Some had been sympathetic toward Japan in a sentimental way, or had sympathized with Japan in the war against China, but most of them would never lift a finger against the United States, which would have been their country if only it had seen fit to grant them citizenship.

Those plucked out of the communities represented the first and second echelons of community leadership. Most of those who had been spared had never been in a position to lead; if they had, they hardly dared raise their heads now for fear of being noticed by the FBI. In these circumstances the mantle of community leadership fell by default on the Nisei who, as a group, averaged barely eighteen years of age. Issei in their fifties and sixties suddenly found themselves removed from authority, and their places taken by their teen-age children. JACL was their only national spokesman. Inexperienced and naïve as its leaders were, JACL was the only organization the Nisei could look to.

X

Executive Order 9066

Mike Masaoka returned on Thursday, December 11, to a confused and frightened Bay-area Japanese American community in a state of near paralysis. The Federal Reserve Bank had frozen accounts of citizens and aliens alike. Money could not be withdrawn and bills couldn't be paid. Credit vanished. With their Issei breadwinners in custody, some families were unable to buy food. Automobile and residential insurance policies were being canceled. Issei chefs and janitors and Nisei stockroom clerks were being fired simply because they were ethnic Japanese. Mom-and-pop grocery stores and dry cleaning shops run by Japanese Americans were being boycotted by longtime Caucasian customers. Suppliers refused to deliver merchandise. In Japanese American communities up and down the coast the story was the same; in some towns beer and other business licenses were suspended.

To cope with local problems the San Francisco chapter of JACL hired Henry Tani as executive secretary and opened an office at 2031 Bush Street. Sab Kido's law office was too crowded to accommodate both his suddenly increased business and JACL, so Masaoka moved in with the San Francisco chapter. After Kido briefed him, Masaoka got on the telephone to Senator Thomas once more to explain the hardships being experienced by Japanese Americans and to ask for help. Not long afterward the Treasury Department issued orders enabling both Issei and Nisei to withdraw up to one hundred dollars from bank accounts for living expenses. But life in the communities was far from normal. In Seattle Jimmie Sakamoto was made acutely aware of the need for emergency services when Issei being held at the United States Immigration station asked to see him, pressed money into his hands and pleaded that he look after their families. He responded by calling a JACL meeting to set up an Emergency Defense Committee. Other JACL chapters up and down the Coast responded similarly, moving into the community leadership vacuum, seeking to reassure distraught Issei, translating and explaining government regulations, gathering food and distributing it to those in need, sponsoring war-bond sales and Red Cross first-aid classes. In the San Joaquin Valley, where the Nisei were well accepted, JACL members enlisted as air raid wardens and helped guard the water supply at Parlier against possible sabotage. Ironically, within weeks a clamor would arise to get the Nisei off the West Coast because they might endanger water supplies.

In many communities defense committees launched belated public-relations campaigns to demonstrate the loyalty of Japanese Americans. The one in Los Angeles was called the Anti-Axis Committee. Although it was not a JACL organization, many JACL supporters were members, among them Tokie Slocum, Joe Shinoda, Togo Tanaka, Kay Sugahara and Sam Minami. They rented a small office in Li'l Tokyo and put Slocum in charge. When Mayor Fletcher Bowron, who had been elected on a reform ticket, began to use his city-financed radio program to advocate a crackdown on Japanese Americans, the Anti-Axis Committee quickly responded. The committee tapped some of its members for enough money to buy radio time and got George Knox Roth, a Quaker and early civil rights advocate, to tell the story of Japanese Americans and urge that they be treated fairly. Roth recently recalled that he and his Anti-Axis Committee friends were astonished to find the Anti-Defamation League among those hostile to Japanese Americans. When Roth investigated he found the ADL, heavily financed by Jews in the movie industry, had made extensive records of anti-Semitic and pro-Nazi activity in California. As part of this project ADL had employed translators to study the Japanese press in Los Angeles and San Francisco over a period of several years. They discovered the Japanese sections supported Japan's aggression in Asia whereas the English sections took a strong pro-American stand. This apparent schizophrenia was interpreted by ADL as evidence of the unreliability of the entire Japanese American population, and this judgment led to the decision to support their removal from the West Coast.

One day Masao Satow led a three-man delegation to invite John Anson Ford, chairman of the Los Angeles County Board of Supervisors, to join them in signing a loyalty pledge. Ford was cautious. He said he knew Satow was loyal, but he was unacquainted with the others and, since he couldn't vouch for them, declined to be photographed.

In Seattle, the JACL Emergency Defense Committee soon after its organization sponsored a mass meeting at the new Buddhist church. The crowd of some fifteen hundred overflowed into the gymnasium to hear Mayor Earl Millikin praise the loyalty of Japanese Americans, but like many another politician he was soon to change his mind about the people he had addressed as "my fellow Americans."

Efforts to convince the public of the loyalty of Japanese Americans took many shapes. The Seattle JACL's executive secretary asked Ham Fisher, creator of the popular Joe Palooka comic strip, to introduce a couple of Nisei GIs into the cartoon story "so that the general public will realize that we of this group are doing our part in national defense." Fisher did indeed draw a cartoon panel showing Palooka, who had abandoned his heavyweight boxing title to join the Army as a buck private, saluting a Nisei soldier. The *Seattle Times* ran it under a headline reading: NISEI LOYAL, JOE PALOOKA SALUTES MEMBERS IN ARMY. The cutline said: "A salute from Pvt. Joe Palooka to the soldiers of Japanese descent in the United States Army, loyal and faithful Americans, and another salute to the vast number of other loyal Americans, the Nisei, who are as bitterly angry at the brutal, Nazified Japan as their fellow Americans are, and whose one wish is victory for America and her allies." In Stockton, Sacramento, Salinas, Alameda, Tacoma and a dozen other communities, JACL chapters sought to cushion the war's impact on all Japanese Americans.

For a brief time it began to look as though such efforts had been successful in quieting hysteria about the possible danger to the national security posed by Japanese Americans, and that drastic action against them by either the federal government or the public at large had been averted. A dreary Christmas came and went, followed by an equally gloomy New Year's, which traditionally is the most festive of Japanese holidays. Then, suddenly, what had been feared by many took ominous shape. Until then the media largely had been friendly or, at the worst, not particularly hostile toward the Japanese Americans. But on January 4, Damon Runyon, the widely read Hearst columnist, charged falsely that a radio transmitter had been found in a Japanese rooming house and declared: "It would be extremely foolish to doubt the continued existence of enemy agents among the large alien Japanese population." Where he got this misinformation was never revealed. The next day John B. Hughes, a Mutual Broadcasting Company commentator in Los Angeles, began a series attacking the federal government for failing to act on what he perceived as a terrible danger. On his program, *News and Views by John B. Hughes,* the commentator hammered day after day on the theme that 90 percent of the Nisei were loyal to Japan. Other writers and broadcasters soon took up the cry, some focusing their attacks on the alleged disloyalty of Japanese Americans and others bitterly assailing federal failure to put them away where they couldn't damage the war effort. Chester Rowell of the *San Francisco Chronicle,* who had addressed the 1934 JACL convention, was one of the few to express faith in the Japanese Americans. Others, apparently overcome by patriotic fervor, lost all sense of fair play and seemed to be trying to outdo each other in expressing hatred for what they saw as the local surrogates of the Asian enemy.

Under such hammering it did not take long for the West Coast's anti-Orientalism, which had remained largely latent since the end of immigration in 1924, to surface. Predictably, politicians joined in the attacks. By mid-January Congressman Leland Ford of Santa Monica was demanding that "all Japanese, whether citizens or not, be placed in inland concentration camps." Congressman Clarence Lea, unofficial chairman of the California congressional delegation, mustered his forces in support of Ford. Senator Hiram Johnson, who as governor had helped pass California's anti-alien land law, stirred things up in the Senate in the name of national security.

JACL viewed this swiftly rising tide of hate with alarm and consternation, not knowing how to combat it other than by doing what it had been doing. Banishment of Issei to concentration camps began to look like a definite possibility although few thought the Nisei would be affected; after all the Issei were enemy aliens but the Nisei were American citizens. One day Kido received a telephone call from Joseph Shinoda, a prominent Southern California floral nursery operator. Shinoda said he was convinced officials in Washington didn't have the faintest idea of the truth about Japanese Americans and didn't understand the reasons for the pressures building up against them. He urged Kido to send Masaoka to Washington to present the Nisei case and offered to pay his expenses. Kido tried the idea on some of his Caucasian friends and advisers but they didn't show a great deal of enthusiasm for it. Kido himself couldn't see much value in sending Masaoka on such a long, time-consuming trip. He felt Masaoka's time and energy could be better spent coping with the endless problems being dropped on national headquarters. In retrospect, one must ask what might have happened if JACL had sent the young and inexperienced but extremely aggressive and persuasive Mike Masaoka to prod the consciences of government leaders about the constitutional guarantees that were in danger of being violated. Could such a one-man mission have blocked the government's misguided decision to safeguard the West Coast's security by a blatantly racist move and saved it from the ghastly error of the Evacuation? There is no way to tell.

Meanwhile, unknown except to those directly involved, a harsh federal policy toward Japanese Americans was taking form. Since mid-December two arms of the government had been vying for responsibility for the Japanese American problem. On the one hand was the Justice Department, which had a legitimate concern that the civil rights of citizens be protected, and which felt the FBI had under control any danger of sabotage and subversion. On the other, the Army, largely in the person of Provost Marshal General Allen W. Gullion, felt Justice was being too soft on a dangerous segment of the population. By January, Attorney General Biddle waffled and the Army was clearly in command. Gullion detailed an ambitious young civilian in uniform, Major Karl R. Bendetsen, to General John L. DeWitt's Western Defense Command headquarters in San Francisco and arranged to have all matters concerning aliens bypass normal channels and come directly to the provost marshal. The possibility of interning all Japanese aliens came under lively discussion between Army and Justice Department officials at a meeting in San Francisco on January 4, and DeWitt made known his feelings toward Nisei citizens with these words: "I have no confidence in their loyalty whatsoever. I am speaking now of the native born Japanese—117,000—and 42,000 in California alone." He was as wrong on his numbers as he was on his evaluation of Nisei loyalty. However, as a result of the conference, the Justice Department agreed to stage a series of well-publicized FBI raids on Issei homes, and "Category A" zones were set up around defense installations from which all civilians could be excluded. The strategy was to issue special licenses to non-Japanese so they could remain in those areas. By mid-January Congressman Ford was arguing that the Nisei could prove their loyalty by willingly agreeing to their own incarceration. Ford was probably the first responsible official to suggest that Nisei citizens as well as the alien Issei be locked up. JACL in the person of Jimmie Sakamoto responded quickly. Assailing the idea of imprisoning citizens, Sakamoto declared in a widely publicized statement: "This is our country. We were born and raised here . . . have made our homes here . . . and we are ready to give our lives, if necessary, to defend the United States."

Although the Nisei were unable to admit it, the die had been cast. From this point on, realistically the question was not whether Japanese Americans would be evacuated, but how and when. DeWitt and Bendetsen continued to meet almost daily with both civilian and military officials to discuss details.

About this time Kido and Masaoka were invited by telegram to meet in Sacramento with Governor Culbert Olson. They had no idea what the governor wanted. There were some two dozen Japanese Americans at the meeting but Kido recognized only a few of them. Olson suggested all Japanese males voluntarily leave their families and move into inland camps from which they would go out by day to work on farms to continue California's food production. In other words, they would be treated as virtual prisoners of war working for the state, in return for which their families would be permitted to remain in their homes.

Some of those in the meeting said they thought the idea was worth considering, but Kido was outraged. He reminded the governor the Nisei were entitled to equal protection under the law and demanded to know why the state could not safeguard the lives and rights of law-abiding Japanese Americans. News accounts of the meeting, which broke up inconclusively, described the usually mild-mannered Kido as "truculent."

Kido and Masaoka met almost daily with government officials as well as their friends in the liberal Caucasian community in a desperate effort to devise a strategy enabling Japanese Americans to remain in their homes. When it seemed the Issei would be incarcerated en masse, they proposed that hearing boards be set up immediately to quickly separate the obviously harmless from the possibly dangerous. At one point Masaoka suggested to military authorities that, if it would convince everyone of their loyalty, Nisei men be inducted into a special combat unit, leaving their parents as hostages, as it were. But it was a losing struggle.

In Washington, meanwhile, members of Congress from the West Coast met regularly to discuss removal of the Japanese. On January 30, Bendetsen attended one of their meetings and the next day he sent telegrams to various Army commands asking them to locate places where large numbers of evacuees might be housed.

Now the decision-making process moved more swiftly, still without the knowledge of Japanese American leaders. By February 11 the policy was firm enough for Secretary of War Henry L. Stimson to telephone President Roosevelt to tell him the Army wanted to evacuate alien and "nonalien" Japanese Americans from the coastal states because of military necessity. Whether or not Roosevelt was aware that the FBI and Naval Intelligence saw no need for such drastic measures, the great champion of human rights granted Stimson's request, only urging him to "be as reasonable as you can." The next day, February 12, the widely respected liberal commentator Walter Lippmann wrote the first of two newspaper columns advocating mass evacuation. He had come west in search of information, talked to military and civilian leaders and accepted their arguments totally. If he had thought to talk to Nisei, he didn't bother. He warned that the Pacific Coast "is in imminent danger of a combined attack from within and without." Lippmann had such a reputation for omniscience that millions of Americans believed his alarums of impending fifth-column activity.

But the first public inkling that a mass evacuation was impending came only after President Roosevelt signed Executive Order 9066 on February 19. It authorized military commanders to designate areas from which "any or all persons may be excluded." On the surface it did not seem to be a document capable of wreaking havoc on human rights. Its significance all but escaped the notice of JACL leaders. Only when it began to be implemented did the full horror of E.O. 9066 become apparent.

On February 14, five days before the signing of E.O. 9066, the Navy had posted notices on Terminal Island in Los Angeles harbor ordering all residents to leave by March 14. That deadline was a month in the future, hardly reflecting wartime urgency. Even among the residents it had been widely assumed that Terminal Island would have to be evacuated since it was virtually surrounded by naval installations. Many of the men in the community had been picked up immediately after war's outbreak and a number of families had moved into Los Angeles to be with friends. So the Navy's removal order did not stir a great deal of concern other than among the families directly affected. But soon it became evident E.O. 9066 was a different matter. Years later Kido was to write of the changing mood:

> Because of the favorable public response to the appeals for fair play, we were becoming confident that the situation was not going to be as bad as we had feared. Then, all of a sudden, the barrage began for mass evacuation of all Japanese from the West Coast. We were not prepared for this hysteria. We had been lulled by the thought that the public relations work of the chapters and national headquarters was succeeding in stemming the tide of hatred which might be directed towards us because of our ethnic affiliation. Once this tide started to roll, there was no stopping it. Fred Nomura had heard from the Oakland chief of police that evacuation was being considered. And he came to tell us that citizens and aliens alike might be evacuated. But I scoffed at him, pointing out that Nisei had Constitutional rights.

The book *Nisei* makes this observation:

> Even though their future was clearly charted by the act of signing Executive Order 9066, to the *Issei* and particularly *Nisei* evacuation still seemed to be an impossibility. Such a thing could not happen in America; it was a hideous nightmare that would vanish with the dawn.
>
> Their hopes were buoyed when it was announced that a Congressional committee, headed by Representative John H. Tolan of California, would hold a series of hearings "to inquire further into the interstate migration of citizens," and to look into the "problems of evacuation of enemy aliens and others from prohibited military zones."
>
> Thoughtful *Nisei* knew that the power to evacuate "any or all"

in the interests of military security had been provided by Executive Order 9066. But no action had been announced. And so, their vision clouded by a large measure of wishful thinking, they believed that the findings of the Tolan Committee would have a large part in determining the government's policy. Up to this point hardly anyone in authority had listened to *Nisei* protestations of loyalty and innocence. Now the Tolan Committee was inviting them to speak. At last here was someone who would listen and a forum in which to be heard. . . . But Secretary Stimson already had declared evacuation was necessary to the national defense. The Tolan Committee hearings could not affect the decision in any way. In this sense the hearings were a sham, a forum for expressions of opinions and prejudices, for the voicing of pleas for justice as well as the cries of bigotry, none of which could have any effect on the issue.

Anxious to get into the act, Congressman Tolan opened his hearings in San Francisco on February 21, just two days after E.O. 9066 had been signed. California Attorney General Earl Warren, San Francisco Mayor Angelo Rossi and a host of others who had been described by General DeWitt as "the best people of California" urged that Japanese Americans be locked up without delay because they posed a fearful security risk. The burden of the "defense" was carried by JACL although a number of Nisei representing themselves or other organizations also testified.

Laboring under the illusion that the hearings were crucial, Kido yielded to the more eloquent Masaoka and asked him to speak for the organization. Masaoka was the first Nisei to appear before the committee, followed by Tani, the executive secretary of the San Francisco chapter, and Dave Tatsuno, chapter president. From the beginning it was evident the congressmen had their minds closed to anything they might hear from the Nisei. It was equally apparent they were totally ignorant about Japanese Americans, surprised that they could speak English so well, astonished that they were totally "American" except in appearance. Under questioning Masaoka said he was a native-born American, that he could not speak, read or write Japanese, that he had never attended a Japanese-language school, had never been to Japan. They asked about Masaoka's faith, expecting to hear that he embraced some alien religion like Shinto, and Masaoka replied that he was a member of the Mormon Church but some of his family were Methodists. Tani and Tatsuno were subjected to similar questions: both testified they were graduates of American universities. Tani said he was a member of the Evangelical and Reformed Church. Tatsuno said he was an elder in the Presbyterian Church and both denied any loyalty to the government of Japan.

Masaoka's formal statement had been reviewed by Kido, Annie Clo Watson, Dr. Galen Fisher and others. Its gist was that E.O. 9066 appeared to be directed unfairly at Japanese Americans and they should not be treated in a discriminatory manner. He declared:

> . . . With any policy of evacuation definitely arising from reasons of military necessity and national safety, we are in complete agreement. As American citizens we cannot and should not take any other stand. But, also, as American citizens believing in the integrity of our citizenship, we feel that any evacuation enforced on grounds violating that integrity should be opposed.
>
> If, in the judgment of military and federal authorities, evacuation of Japanese residents from the West Coast is a primary step toward assuring the safety of this nation, we will have no hesitation in complying with the necessities implicit in that judgment. But if, on the other hand, such evacuation is primarily a measure whose surface urgency cloaks the desires of political or other pressure groups who want us to leave merely from motives of self-interest, we feel that we have every right to protest and to demand equitable judgment on our merits as American citizens. . . .
>
> In this emergency, as in the past, we are not asking for special privileges or concessions. We ask only for the opportunity and the right of sharing the common lot of all Americans, whether it be in peace or in war.
>
> This is the American way for which our boys are fighting.

Because controversy arose over JACL's position before the Tolan Committee, the full text of Masaoka's statement is reprinted in Appendix A. JACL has been accused of selling Japanese Americans "down the river," but Masaoka's statement made it clear the organization would bow only to military necessity. JACL's stance will be discussed in greater detail in the next chapter. At this point it is sufficient to say that such was the temper of the times that even the national American Civil Liberties Union did not object to suspension of civil rights in the face of military necessity. The Committee on National Security and Fair Play, an organization of prominent West Coast civic, religious and educational leaders, told the Tolan Committee: "We believe that the extreme gravity of the situation justifies this drastic step [evacuation]. And as Californians, no less than as American citizens, we accept it as a wise solution of the vexing problem of handling enemy aliens and dangerous citizens."

Years later they would look back on such an uncharacteristic statement with embarrassment and remorse. Obviously their regard for constitutional rights had been overwhelmed by the fear that maybe, just maybe, the Japanese Americans posed a real danger. In the back of their minds was a worrisome question that fed on the hysteria of the times: "We know we can depend on the loyalty of the Japanese Americans, but what if we are wrong? What if we are wrong?" So they, too, took what they considered to be the safe way.

The Tolan Committee moved on to Portland, where Hito Okada was one of those testifying, and then to Seattle where JACL had prepared an elaborate report on the economic contributions of the Japanese Americans to the local community. It was an impressive compilation of data showing how thoroughly the Japanese Americans had become integrated into the local economy—as farmers, hotel operators, grocery store proprietors and the like—but under the circumstances these were hardly arguments likely to sway congressmen who were convinced Nisei in Hawaii had impeded the United States response to the attack on Pearl Harbor, and were totally convinced of the validity of what Earl Warren had testified about California:

> I am afraid many of our people in other parts of the country are of the opinion that because we have had no sabotage and no fifth column activities in this state since the beginning of the war, that means that none have been planned for us. But I take the view that this is the most ominous sign in our whole situation. It convinces me more than perhaps any other factor that the sabotage that we are to get, the fifth column activities that we are to get, are timed just like Pearl Harbor was timed and just like the invasion of France, and of Denmark, and of Norway, and all those other countries. I believe that we are just being lulled into a false sense of security and that the only reason we haven't had disaster in California is because it has been timed for a different date, and

that when that time comes if we don't do something about it, it is going to mean disaster both to California and to our nation. Our day of reckoning is bound to come. . . .

Even while the Seattle hearings were under way, another minor drama typifying the hysteria of the times was unfolding. A group of Parent-Teacher Association mothers began pressuring the Seattle school board to discharge twenty-seven Nisei girls working as forty-cent-an-hour clerks in school offices on grounds of potential disloyalty. One mother said she felt the Nisei girls should not be answering the telephone in principals' offices. "After all," she said, "in the event of a raid on the city, they would be the ones to take any calls intended to put schools on the alert." School administration support for the girls was lukewarm and eventually they resigned as a body, issuing a statement which said in part:

> We, the undersigned American citizens of Japanese ancestry have learned that our presence as employees in the Seattle school system has been protested by certain persons and organizations. Therefore, we respectfully request the Seattle school board to accept our resignations immediately. . . .
>
> We take this step to prove our loyalty to the schools and to the United States by not becoming a contributing factor to dissension and disunity when national unity in spirit and deed is vitally necessary to the defense of and complete victory for America. We bear no ill will toward those who have protested our employment in the school system. . . .

Despite considerable public support for the girls, the school board in a closed meeting accepted the resignations. One of the mothers leading the ouster campaign responded: "I think that's very white of those girls."

In an editorial the *Seattle Star* called the resignations "a graceful act" which spared the school board and the community "a great deal of acrimony at a trying time."

The Tolan Committee moved from Seattle to Los Angeles and back to San Francisco, concluding its hearings on March 12. But on March 2, ten days before Tolan's self-imposed fact-finding mission was completed—eleven days after the signing of E.O. 9066—General DeWitt in what was called Public Proclamation No. 1 announced that "all persons of Japanese ancestry" would be removed from the western half of California, Oregon and

Washington and the southern third of Arizona.

Masaoka and Kido received the word before the public announcement in a special meeting with civilian emissaries from Washington. They were told bluntly that the Evacuation decision had been made—both citizens and aliens of Japanese descent would be hustled off to temporary assembly centers to be set up in fairgrounds and racetracks. Meanwhile, semipermanent camps would be built in inland areas and the evacuees would be moved into them as quickly as possible. Then came the hook: would JACL cooperate with the Army to make the Evacuation as uneventful as possible?

Masaoka and Kido knew what the answer had to be. Behind the Army's softly worded request was the threat of force. They had fought the Evacuation as best they could; further resistance would be suicidal and there was no alternative but to cooperate. But they refused to commit themselves at that meeting, requesting time to confer with JACL leaders. Masaoka explains:

> We were led to believe that if we cooperated with the Army in this mass movement, the government would try to be as helpful and as humane as possible to the evacuees. Moreover, we feared the consequences if Japanese Americans refused to cooperate, and the Army moved in with armed troops and even tanks to eject the people forcibly from their homes. At a time when Japan was still on the offensive and apparently winning the war, we were afraid that the American people would consider us traitors and enemies of the war effort if we forced the Army to take drastic action against us. This might forever place in jeopardy our future as United States citizens. As the involuntary trustees of the destiny of Japanese Americans in this country, we felt that we could do no less than whatever was necessary to protect and preserve that future. The JACL could not give a doubting nation further excuse to confuse the identity of the Japanese enemy with Americans of Japanese origin.

Masaoka's fear of the consequences of resistance were confirmed some time later by Bendetsen himself. In a speech to the prestigious Commonwealth Club of San Francisco on May 20, 1942, when the Evacuation was well under way, Bendetsen told about the Army's preparations for moving Japanese Americans into temporary locations and then said:

> "The Army needed time to prepare a permanent program and the situation called for an emergency plan. It was impossible, of

> course, at this time for the Army to reveal the fact that it was prepared to effect a complete evacuation, practically overnight, in the event of an emergency. Plans were made to move the 113,000 Japanese into already established Army cantonments in a mass movement which would have been undertaken immediately. Prepared in this way against the possibility of fifth-column activity, or for any outbreak of anti-Japanese feeling, the Army continued its plans for a permanent program."

With heavy heart, Kido sent telegrams to each JACL chapter asking them to send representatives to an emergency National Council meeting to be held in San Francisco on Sunday, Monday and Tuesday, March 8, 9 and 10.

Meanwhile, in long talks at night, Kido and Masaoka asked each other why there was no greater public outcry against the unconstitutionality of General DeWitt's Evacuation order directed at a racial minority. What they had in mind were the Fifth and Fourteenth amendments, the so-called due process and equal protection provisions.

The Fifth Amendment says in part: "No person shall be . . . deprived of life, liberty, or property without due process of law. . . ."

The Fourteenth Amendment contains these words: "No state shall make or enforce any law which shall abridge the privileges or immunities of citizens of the United States; nor shall any state deprive any person of life, liberty, or property, without due process of law; nor deny to any person within its jurisdiction the equal protection of the laws."

Certainly the Japanese Americans were being singled out for special treatment on a racially discriminatory basis—without due process, they were being denied the equal protection of the laws, they were being deprived of their liberty. Did constitutional safeguards of an American citizen's rights mean nothing in a war emergency? The question demanded an answer.

XI

The Decision to Cooperate

By Sunday, December 7, 1941, the potatoes were in the cellars, the chores that had piled up during the busy summer and fall had been taken care of and there was time for a bit of socializing before the holiday season. Members of the Idaho Falls JACL chapter at the eastern edge of the state met at noon that day at the Gakugeikai, the tiny building where children of the community gathered on Saturdays for Japanese-language lessons. The chapter was one of the youngest in JACL's family, and like many of them it had started out as something else; it was originally a Nisei club known as Kyowa (meaning "harmony," or "togetherness"). Without really being sure that their decision was wise, the members had agreed to take their club into JACL in 1940 after Mike Masaoka had organized the Intermountain District Council. No one remembers just how news of the attack on Pearl Harbor reached the meeting that Sunday, but Yukio (Eke) Inouye recalled some decades later that everyone, quite unbelieving, went home quietly.

The Nisei in the Idaho Falls community did not feel the impact of Pearl Harbor's aftermath in anywhere near the intensity experienced in coastal areas. "We'd been here for years and had gone to school with the people in the area. They were friends and our relations with them were good. That was one reason we weren't sure we needed JACL," Inouye explained. Aside from some minor harassment, the war seemed far away. When Inouye under federal orders surrendered his shotgun to Sheriff Harry

Mackin, the officer took it reluctantly and invited him to pick it up whenever he wanted to go hunting. Inouye happened to be killing time in Mackin's office the evening the sheriff received a call that "some Japs are signaling enemy planes." It turned out to be a blinking red bulb that was used to mark an electrified fence around a pasture. "That fence has been blinking for years," the sheriff complained, "but now some people are seeing all kinds of things and I'm getting tired of it."

All in all, however, the war and the threat of evacuation were distant problems until a few Issei and Nisei from the Coast, in anticipation of being driven from their homes, began to move into the district in search of farmland they could buy or lease. Then came Kido's summons to the emergency meeting in San Francisco.

Inouye didn't think it was worth attending. San Francisco was farther from home than he wanted to travel and besides he wasn't altogether sure how important the meeting was to Idahoans. But an Issei leader, K. K. Nukaya, quickly made up his mind for him. "Yukio, you go," Nukaya ordered. "You take some of the older Nisei and go to the meeting. Important. If you need money and gas, we get for you." Inouye collected gasoline ration stamps from farmers who had more than they needed and set out for California with Sadao (Sud) Morishita, Mitsugi Kasai and Pat Watanuki. They were looking for a restaurant in Twin Falls in south-central Idaho when the local police chief stopped them, demanded to know where they were from and where they were going and ordered them to produce birth certificates to prove they were citizens. Shaken by the experience, the Nisei hurriedly gassed up and drove the rest of the way to San Francisco nonstop except to pick up fuel. The return trip proved even more frightening, but that is getting ahead of the story.

In San Francisco the Idaho Falls delegation found a grim, deeply troubled group of delegates assembled at JACL headquarters. There were some two hundred men and women representing sixty-six chapters—seventeen of them were new groups that suddenly saw wisdom in joining the national organization and had come to the meeting requesting membership. They were from ten states, stretching from the North Platte Valley of Nebraska (the chapter had been unable to send a delegate and asked Masaoka to represent them) to the shores of the Pacific on the west; from the Big Horn Mountain chapter of Montana (also represented by Masaoka) on the north to Brawley, El Centro and San Diego adjoining the California-Mexico border; from Seattle in the northwest to Arizona's Phoenix area in the southeast. Many were strangers, but common concerns united them. What did the Army's Evacuation order mean to them and their people? How should they respond to the order? What could JACLers do to carry out the community responsibilities unexpectedly thrust upon them?

Contrary to later charges that power-hungry JACLers had seized community leadership for their own purposes, the mantle rested uneasily on reluctant shoulders. Most of those at the conference would have preferred to be at home with their families taking care of their own business instead of wrestling with difficult problems affecting an entire people. But the federal government had chosen to consider Japanese Americans as a group rather than as individuals, and in the absence of other leadership JACL was forced, or perhaps more accurately had to accept by default, accountability for the ethnic group. They had no choice but to step forward if there was to be any kind of leadership at that critical time.

Kido established the keynote for the meeting with a sober summary of the problems facing JACL and the decision that needed to be made. (The full text is provided in Appendix B.)

"Never in the thousands of years of human history has a group of citizens been branded on so wholesale a scale as being treacherous to their own native land," Kido asserted with no sense of hyperbole. "We question the motives and patriotism of such men and leaders who intentionally fan racial animosity and hatred."

He recommended that JACL continue to function "because there are important missions to be carried out." Then he wound up on a stirring upbeat note:

> Fellow members, no matter whatever we may do, wherever we may go, always retain your faith in our government and maintain your self-respect. Let us keep our chins up despite all the travesty being committed upon our good name and rights. We are going into exile as our duty to our country because the President and the military commander of this area have deemed it a necessity. We are gladly cooperating because this is one way of showing that our protestations of loyalty are sincere. We have pledged our full support to President Roosevelt and to the Nation. This is a sacred promise which we shall keep as good patriotic citizens.

> The sacrifice which we have been called to make is just as great as that which our selectees have been called to make, for ours is the call to quietly uproot ourselves from all that we know and hold dear and to make our way into a wilderness of which we know not. . . . Let us look upon ourselves as the pioneers of a new era looking forward to the greatest adventure of our times. Let us conquer whatever frontier may await us with the same fortitude and patience as did our fathers and mothers who contributed more to the development of the west than most of us realize. Let us serve our country in the hardest way possible for us to serve. . . .

The delegates quickly voted to maintain JACL as an organization. They authorized moving headquarters to Salt Lake City, where Masaoka had friends. Utah was at the eastern edge of the Western Defense Command and Salt Lake City presumably would not be subject to further Evacuation orders. The then officers and board were continued in office for the duration of the war with extraordinary powers to carry out a three-pronged program:

1—To assist Japanese Americans in every way possible, help maintain morale and ease the impact of the Evacuation.

2—To cooperate and keep in touch with the federal government to ensure just and humane treatment.

3—To carry on a public relations program to demonstrate that Japanese Americans were good citizens.

Masaoka was authorized to go to Washington where he would have access to federal decision makers. And as a key part of the public-relations efforts, it was decided to publish *Pacific Citizen* in Salt Lake City as a weekly carrying news of interest to Japanese Americans and serving as an advocate of their cause. Larry Tajiri, undoubtedly the most professional of Nisei journalists at the time, was hired to edit *Pacific Citizen,* with his wife Guyo as his assistant. Tajiri was a veteran of English-section journalism on Japanese newspapers in Los Angeles and San Francisco. Several years before war's outbreak he went to work in the New York bureau of the giant Asahi newspapers of Japan. The bureau was closed when war broke out and Tajiri and his wife returned to the Pacific Coast. Appalled at JACL's lack of a public-relations program, Tajiri volunteered his services to handle press relations and keep the Nisei public informed. Tajiri was given virtual *carte blanche* in editing and publishing *Pacific Citizen.* His only instruction from Kido, he once recalled, was a six-word sentence:

"Just don't get me in trouble." Tajiri had to convert JACL's sporadically published monthly house organ into a vigorous professional newspaper on an extremely limited budget. He had to find a printer in Salt Lake City, redesign the paper and establish news sources. The first issue of the new *PC* under Tajiri's editorship appeared on June 4, 1942.

Having charted their course, the delegates in San Francisco had to tackle the knotty problems involved in carrying out the program, learn details of the federal government's intentions and devise means of coping with them. The first issue was money. The national treasury, as usual, was virtually flat. A budget committee and a ways and means committee were appointed to come up with some proposals for raising and allocating funds. The members were Kay Hirao, Ken Matsumoto, Tom Shimasaki, Masaoka, Hito Okada, James Sugioka, Dr. Yoshio Nakaji, Dr. Harry Kita, Dr. Newton Wesley, Eke Inouye, Shigeki (Shake) Ushio and Sim Togasaki, with George Inagaki as chairman. After hours of discussion they agreed on a budget of $26,000 with expected income of $25,950, but in the cold light of reality it was found to be quite unrealistic. Maintaining a program would cost substantially more than $26,000 while income was likely to be far less. The budget provided for assessing each JACL chapter $300 for a total income of $18,000 but it was apparent that most chapters would be disbanding and would hardly be in a position to put together that kind of money. Ultimately, the various chapters as well as other Issei and Nisei groups with funds left in their treasuries were asked to contribute them to national JACL.

The thrust of Kido's speech opening the conference had been an admonition to cooperate in the Evacuation, to go willingly into exile as a patriotic gesture and wartime sacrifice. But among the delegates there was no consensus in support of this position. That was developed later. The conference minutes do not reflect great differences of opinion on this subject; in reality JACL policy was hammered out in intense informal discussions that raged late into the night.

There were some who argued that JACL as a civil rights organization had an obligation to challenge the Evacuation order as unnecessary, unconstitutional and racially discriminatory. Others urged JACL to take the issue before the federal judiciary. Many others could see no logic or justice in evacuating American citizens of Japanese descent en masse as a "military necessity" while exempting German and Italian aliens.

These were all good arguments and might have been effective under other circumstances. But Kido and Masaoka knew that the Evacuation decision was a *fait accompli,* that right or wrong the Army was poised to carry out its orders. They had been told bluntly the Army was prepared to use whatever means necessary to force Japanese Americans out of the prohibited zones, and it had a presidential order authorizing it to do so. There was no room for compromise or bargaining. Under the circumstances it was obvious that if the Japanese Americans resisted, as some of them wanted to do, and if any substantial number of troops had to be detached to carry out the Evacuation forcibly, the Nisei would in fact be guilty of sabotaging the war effort. Furthermore, JACL could have nothing to do with a policy that might lead to bloodshed. There would be a time later on when the Evacuation order's constitutionality could be tested in court, but such a test well might drag on for years and hardly would be effective in blocking the military. Though painful, the wisest course, Kido and Masaoka argued, was to cooperate with the government in the hope of a better deal when war's hysteria had cooled.

Their position was endorsed by two eloquent firebrands who were unlikely advocates of submission to an injustice. Tokie Slocum, the World War I hero who was representing the San Fernando Valley chapter and whose love of justice was beyond question, saw cooperation as an opportunity for the Nisei to make a new start in America.

"We are facing this problem today because of the short-sightedness of the Japanese leaders in America up to this time," he thundered. "They thought only in terms of being Japanese. In order that we do not repeat the mistake that our fathers made, we must break our ties with Japan. It is in this time of crisis that we must take advantage of the opportunity to test our mettle. How we meet this problem will determine the destiny of Japanese Americans as Americans. We must not expect comfort or luxury in time of war. Cooperation with the federal government is essential."

Jimmie Sakamoto, the blind ex-prizefighter, had a similar message: "The government is going to cooperate with us to the fullest extent possible, so now it is up to us to cooperate with the government loyally and cheerfully. You people gathered here have a job to do; go back to your communities and get people working with the government on the evacuation order."

Word of these discussions got out and the press published reports of "disunity" and hinted at possible disloyalty within JACL. Tajiri quickly issued a press release quoting Masaoka:

> We believe in free discussion because we are a group of Americans meeting together as Americans. Our organizational policies are not dictated from the top but are formulated by the membership.
>
> Within a short time we Americans, together with our alien Japanese parents, must leave our homes on the West Coast to make new homes for the duration in inland areas. We are meeting because we are anxious to do our share as Americans in facilitating the evacuation process. There may be differences of opinion among us on how we can accomplish this but we believe in differences of opinion as we believe in democracy. Under fascism there are no differences of opinion.
>
> We Americans of Japanese parentage are unified in our desire to aid national defense in any way possible. We are unified in our belief in the inevitable victory of the forces of democracy. Now that the Army has ordered our evacuation from coastal zones, we ask only for humane treatment consistent with America's belief in tolerance and fair play.

Masaoka also responded to charges that the Buddhists were quarreling with Christians, and aliens with citizens within JACL. He released the text of two telegrams. One, from the Reverend Masaru (Mac) Kumata, field executive of the Buddhist Church of America, read: FORTY THOUSAND CITIZEN BUDDHISTS PLEDGE THEIR SUPPORT TO JACL. The other, from the General Council of the Japanese Christian Church Federation of North America and from the Northwest, Northern California and Southern California Young Peoples Christian Conferences, read in part:

> WE WISH TO REITERATE OUR APPRECIATION OF YOUR SPLENDID LEADERSHIP AND EXPRESS OUR WILLINGNESS TO COOPERATE WITH YOU IN ANY WAY POSSIBLE TO SOLVE THE DIFFICULT PROBLEMS WE NOW FACE AND TO DO OUR PART IN UPHOLDING THE GREAT AMERICAN IDEALS.

Masaoka also pointed out that there was no quarrel between "aliens and citizens" since JACL membership was restricted to citizens.

At this point it is pertinent to ask just who JACL represented. Issei leadership, it will be recalled, was virtually demolished by FBI raids, in addition to which, as enemy aliens, Issei were in effect nonpersons. JACL was the only coastwide Nisei organization that crossed church lines. In the weeks after war's outbreak, JACL's membership nearly tripled to some twenty thousand as Nisei rushed to join. They joined in part to support the only major organization that was looking out for their interests in a time of peril, in part because they believed that JACL membership was proof of loyalty to the United States, which they wished to demonstrate. JACL never claimed to represent all or even most Japanese Americans, but federal officials, looking for all the help they could get, found no viable community leadership other than JACL and depended heavily on it to reach the people. If there were Nisei who disagreed violently with JACL's policy of cooperation, they failed to speak up in any effective way. No one resisted the Evacuation physically, and only two young men were outraged sufficiently by the order's injustice to go to prison and demand judicial review. Revisionists would have us believe, however, that JACL forced its views on a reluctant community. The opposite is true. The community sought leadership and guidance and JACL chose the only possible course of action.

In the end, Masaoka wrote years later, the conference delegates were virtually unanimous in agreeing that cooperation was necessary and the public supported their decision:

> Both Kido and I were quite surprised and pleased that there was practically no public outcry or challenge against the decision to cooperate with the Army. We believed that such total compliance indicated the general agreement of the evacuees that cooperation was indeed proper under those tumultuous and threatening conditions. Despite all we had to suffer as suspect citizens, many besides myself must have hoped that if we demonstrated our belief in American ideals and objectives, the people of the United States would somehow more than make up for what we had sacrificed after the heat and hysteria of the war was over. As for a court suit, we were confident the opportunity would come for seeking a judicial verdict. For the time being, we felt it was more important for JACL leaders to devote their time and energies to helping the people of their communities to face the immediate problems of the evacuation rather than going to jail as a matter of principle.

Nor did Kido ever doubt the wisdom of the decision although there was a time when he thought seriously of violating the Evacuation order as an individual to symbolize Nisei outrage. "I am sure that if we (as a group) had uttered defiance to the evacuation orders we might have been popular with some, but most foolish under the circumstances," he wrote in his memoirs published some twenty years later in *Pacific Citizen.* "We may not have had the orderly evacuation. Any interference with the military when it was decided to be a military necessity may have been construed as sabotage and a treasonable act on our part."

But in time, and before too long, there would be some who retroactively disagreed strongly with the JACL decision. How that came about, and what resulted from the disagreement, will be the subject of subsequent chapters.

Even before the decision was finalized there was a great deal of discussion among the delegates about voluntary evacuation, which was being encouraged by the Army. No one had any idea what the Evacuation camps would be like, but the prospect of being moved into confinement somewhere in the interior was, to put it mildly, not inviting. Press reports had indicated Evacuation centers were being planned for the Owens Valley, east of the Sierras and close to the Nevada border, and the Parker Dam area of southern Arizona. If the Owens Valley area was fully developed, one report said, fifty thousand evacuees could be accommodated. The soil was productive, but the valley was a virtual desert since its water had been diverted into the Los Angeles system.

Delegates from inland areas were not optimistic about opportunities for voluntary evacuees to find homes, jobs and make new lives. Dr. Jun Kurumada from Salt Lake City said land in Utah was cheap but unproductive. He said a number of evacuees had moved into Salt Lake City and been unable to find housing; some were reported sleeping in cars. Shake Ushio, chairman of the Intermountain District Council, said the Japanese population of Utah had increased by a third with voluntary evacuees moving in with friends or relatives and there was no way of accommodating many more. Jimmie Sakamoto said many Seattleites were thinking of moving to the Yakima Valley of eastern Washington, but felt any large influx would be unfair to the people already there. Sakamoto also reported that a group of Seattle and Los Angeles Catholics had studied the possibility of moving in a body to the St. Louis, Missouri, area under Maryknoll auspices, but negotiations had collapsed.

The opposition to voluntary evacuation was not confined to whites. Utah historian Leonard J. Arrington, as editor of the *Western Historical Quarterly,* found a letter in the state archives dated March 23, 1942, and addressed to Governor Herbert B. Maw, a portion of which is reproduced here:

> *My dear Governor:*
>
> The Japanese residents of Ogden City and Weber County find it imperative to submit the following objections to the influx of Japanese evacuees from the restricted coastal areas:
>
> 1—This is the Central Defense Area.
>
> 2—Problems of housing, lack of available farming areas, and all other means of livelihood are acute.
>
> 3—The influx of new Japanese inhabitants would be a hazard to those already established here.
>
> The Weber County and Ogden Japanese of First and Second generation have established a reputation through industry and good behavior in appreciation of the privileges given them to contribute to the general welfare of the community. It appears exceedingly unwise to disturb and disrupt this status, for this most important reason the strangers from other localities might be undesirable in adjustment to these settled conditions.
>
> We, therefore, emphatically and sincerely oppose the entrance and settlement of these people, at the same time express our regrets that the war situation compels our position in this emergency.

On the whole, however, Japanese Americans in inland areas were remarkably understanding, compassionate, hospitable and supportive of JACL, as will be chronicled in later chapters.

Another question widely discussed by the delegates was whether evacuation from the Coast should be considered temporary or permanent. Kido explained the federal government expected evacuation to be strictly temporary. The Fresno delegation reported 99 percent of their people planned to return. On the other hand, the Guadalupe group said only 5 percent of the Japanese farmers owned their land and the others, having nothing to return to, were not inclined to come back. Kido advised that the prospect of returning to familiar areas would enable the Issei to face the uncertainties of evacuation and resettlement with greater hope.

But a long afternoon session with a panel of federal officials did little to assure the JACLers that the government understood or was ready to cope with the enormous problems involved in uprooting more than one hundred thousand men, women and children in a humane manner. Here are some excerpts from the transcript of the meeting:

> Q—After the evacuees are investigated, will they be allowed to come back and engage in or be employed in any business enterprise?
> A—That matter has to be worked out by the Federal Reserve Bank. . . .
> Q—What will be the maximum amount of personal and business equipment which the federal government will transport for us?
> A—I do not think I am in a position to answer that. It has not been worked out.
> Q—Will farmers be reimbursed for their crops?
> A—I do not know what will be done, but certainly some steps will be taken to protect the crops. . . .
> Q—It has been said that many of these people will be transferred to agricultural lands and put to work on farms. Will the government make some provision?
> A—We haven't decided on that yet.
> Q—Will some form of legal guardianship be provided for minor orphans?
> A—I haven't attended any meeting where that has been discussed —we haven't thought about it as being necessary.
> Q—If the people use their present assets for [voluntary] evacuation purposes they will have no funds with which to reestablish themselves. Will the government foot the expenses of evacuation?
> A—I think you are asking for too much, and that is not good for you.

Understandably dissatisfied with such answers, JACL asked for another meeting where more specific information could be provided. Colonel W. F. McGill, representing the Army, Richard M. Neustadt, regional director of the Federal Security Agency, and Thomas C. Clark, later a Supreme Court justice, who was serving as alien coordinator for the Justice Department, agreed to meet with a small JACL committee. The committee was made up of Dr. Yatabe, Fred Tayama of Los Angeles, Mamaro Wakasugi of Portland, Tom Yego of Placer County, Masao Satow of Los Angeles, Jimmie Sakamoto and Mike Masaoka. The upshot of this meeting was that the federal officials asked for details of specific problems perceived by JACL and specific proposals for meeting them. "We want you to lay all your cards on the table so that we can both understand each other fully," Clark asserted. This time it was the officials asking the questions and JACL providing the answers. *How many people in Los Angeles are lacking housing as a result of the impending Evacuation?* About two thousand.

About how many people would be involved in the Evacuation and what percentage would be able to do manual labor? About one hundred thousand ethnic Japanese were believed to be living in the evacuation zones. About one third of this number are of the first generation, and one third of them are farmers. Of this 30 percent who are farmers, about 15 percent would not be able to do manual labor.

Do you have a breakdown of the various professions and businesses in which your people are now engaged? We don't have such a breakdown on a national scale but local chapters have conducted surveys which can be assembled quickly.

Do you have any areas under consideration as suitable for moving into? From time to time promoters have come to JACL with various ideas but we have not been able to investigate them.

Are there many Japanese in the Mississippi Valley? No, there are only about 250 Japanese families in the entire Mississippi Valley.

(Just how little the authorities knew about the problem was illustrated some weeks later when the Army, top-ranking Seattle police officials and JACL representatives met to discuss plans for evacuating the city. A police officer pinned up a map of Seattle showing concentrations of Japanese. One of the Nisei noticed a very heavy concentration indicated on Western Avenue near the waterfront where there were no hotels, apartments or other residences. It turned out that this was the wholesale fresh-produce area where several hundred Issei and Nisei worked during the day, when the survey was made, but which was abandoned after business hours.)

The delegates got their first clear idea of what the government had in mind for resettlement projects when Neustadt answered in response to a direct question:

> You must realize that this is something new to us, just as it is something new for you, and everything has not been worked out

> as yet. All I know is that we are all doing the best we can and that we are trying to be as liberal and humane as possible. . . . We hope that we will be able to keep the families in their own units and that each one of them will be able to bring as much of their own personal belongings as can be reasonably expected. Adequate houses will be set up before you arrive, and while they are certainly not luxurious, *they are much better than what many Japanese are accustomed to at the present time* [italics added]. We hope that families can be kept together instead of having separate barracks for the men and the women. There will be Japanese cooks and Japanese waiters because you must have community feeding, at least in the beginning. While you are there, you will be put to some constructive work, or in some other field if you are not a farmer. Briefly, it will be very much like a normal community with its schools, churches, and homes, and everything else within the physical limits of such a project. Everything is being done on a temporary basis so that you will be able to return when all of this is over.

Neustadt undoubtedly was sincere when he painted such a rosy picture of what the camps would be like. They turned out in reality to be drab, dreary, dusty camps of flimsy tarpaper-covered wooden barracks surrounded by barbed wire and guarded by armed troops in watchtowers with floodlights.

Years later Kido, recalling this statement and later conversations with Milton Eisenhower, wrote:

> The restrictions we had imposed on us at the assembly or relocation centers were unexpected. In fact, when discussions were held . . . the relocation centers were supposed to be a "haven of refuge" during the war years. We were supposed to be protected from the outside, but with free going in and out of the centers. Industry and farming were to be developed so that the residents of the relocation centers would have a trust fund which would help them to relocate after the war. . . . The public hysteria created an atmosphere which made such a friendly haven impossible. We became virtual prisoners contrary to the original understanding and promises.

Would the JACLers have agreed so readily to cooperate in their own incarceration if they had had a clearer idea of what the camps would be like? The answer must be yes, for it was plain the Army was prepared to drive the Japanese Americans out of their homes and behind barbed wire enclosures at bayonet point and to counsel resistance would have been to invite unthinkable consequences. But certainly JACLers would have underscored the need for more humane treatment and demanded assurances that it would be forthcoming. At the time, however, there was no reason to doubt the sincerity and good intentions of men like Neustadt and Milton S. Eisenhower, first director of the War Relocation Authority, a civilian agency established to operate the semipermanent relocation camps and then to resettle the evacuees on farms and in the cities of the American interior far from West Coast hostility. And there was no way to anticipate the savage hate attacks loosed on the Japanese Americans by the lunatic fringe once the Evacuation had been completed.

On the meeting's final day the delegates received word that Assistant Secretary of War John J. McCloy would speak. McCloy was the highest-ranking government official to appear and his arrival was awaited with great anticipation. But he was unable to add much to what had been reported by earlier speakers other than to say that while the Army was moving with all reasonable speed, it might be a month or more before the first Evacuation movement got under way.

"We know that the great majority of citizens and aliens are loyal," he said, "and being appreciative of that, we are most anxious to see that you don't suffer any more than necessary the loss of property values. . . . We want to have conditions [in the Evacuation camps] just as humane and comfortable as is possible to have them. Above all, we want to give you protection. One of the best things you can do is to advise those you represent of the intent and spirit in which the government is going about this. So far as you can, urge them to take this, as I know they are, in good spirit as one of the ravages and misfortunes of war."

McCloy's appearance did little to cheer the delegates, but Masao Satow was not one to brood about misfortune. "Hey," he told a group of friends, "this may be the last time we'll be in San Francisco. Let's go out and get a big dinner, maybe at a Chinese nightclub." Then on an impulse he invited McCloy to join them.

McCloy was startled. "Did you say Chinatown?" he asked. "Aren't the Chinese hostile toward you fellows? Aren't you afraid to go down there?"

"No, sir," Satow assured him. "They're Chinese and we're Japanese, but we're all Americans. Come on, join us."

McCloy did. His experience of eating at a San Francisco Chinese restaurant with a group of Japanese Americans may have given him new insights into the meaning of Americanism, particularly as it applied to the sons and daughters of Asian immigrants. McCloy was to become a staunch friend of the Nisei.

One of the final items of conference business was rejection of a proposal to rename the Japanese American Citizens League. A friendly federal official had made the suggestion, warning that an intensive "hate Japan" campaign was developing to whip up the American fighting spirit and it might be to the advantage of the Nisei to reject anything to do with Japan.

Masaoka argued against the idea. "Through the years of patient and sincere work," he said, "persevering members have built the prestige of the JACL movement under its present name. A change now would not only incur confusion requiring constant explanation, but would suggest an endeavor to hide our identity and possibly bring about allegations of evasion. JACL's name does not connote hyphenated Americanism; the word Japanese is an adjective modifying the noun American to distinguish the group from others."

The three days of the conference had been intensely trying. Not only were the hours long but the delegates were burdened with the knowledge that their decisions might well have a profound influence on the futures of themselves, their families and their friends, as Americans. They sensed that some of their decisions would not prove popular. They knew only vaguely the shape of the future; they could be sure only of uncertainty. At the closing session the delegates gave Kido a Lord Elgin watch as a farewell gift and token of their respect and affection. Kido began to speak, thanking his friends for their loyal support, wishing them good luck, admonishing them to keep the faith until they could meet again, but he was unable to finish. The tears flowed down his cheeks and many of the delegates wept with him. Then they scattered for home, knowing difficult tasks lay ahead.

Eke Inouye and his friends began the long drive back to eastern Idaho, the knowledge that they would not be evacuated scant consolation. They had gone to the meeting unconvinced it had much to do with them. They left with the knowledge that the travail of the Japanese Americans in the coastal areas was also their burden and it pained them that they couldn't invite everyone to resettle in Idaho. The homeward trip was uneventful until they approached Mountain Home, a town about midway between Boise and Twin Falls, at 3 A.M. That's when their universal joint went out. Inouye pushed the car off the highway and he and Mitsugi Kasai started for town on foot to buy the necessary parts, leaving Sud Morishita and Watanuki to watch the car so it wouldn't be stripped. Sud remembers:

> After they left, cars would slow down to see what was wrong, but as soon as they saw we were Japanese, they would speed away. Then one car did stop and the red lights went on. It was either a state patrolman or a sheriff's deputy, I don't remember which. He wanted to know what we were doing and I told him. He offered to drive me into Mountain Home so I told Pat, "You stay here so nobody will try to steal the tires," and the poor guy had to sit there alone. We looked all over Mountain Home and couldn't find Eke and Mits. We checked with the telephone operator to see if they had called any place in Idaho Falls. We finally located them in a service station about the time I began to worry whether the deputy believed me.
>
> We couldn't find any parts in Mountain Home so we called Tom Mori in Shoshone, fifty, sixty miles down the road, to come and get us. He pulled us into Shoshone and ordered the parts from Twin Falls. The guy at the hotel in Shoshone wasn't going to let us stay, but finally he said, "To hell with the boss; come on in, boys," and at least we had a place to sleep.

In JACL's darkest days that lay ahead, it was Nisei—and Issei, too—from places like Idaho Falls and Pocatello, Ogden and Provo, Denver and North Platte and other inland areas who kept the organization afloat.

XII

Forced Migration

March, 1942, was a month of anxiety, fear and foreboding for Japanese Americans. On the second, just five days short of three months after the outbreak of war, General DeWitt's Public Proclamation No. 1 established Military Area No. 1. Shorn of its bureaucratese, this meant he had given himself authority to kick everyone of Japanese blood out of the western portions of Washington, Oregon and California and the southern third of Arizona. The proclamation also established Military Area No. 2, encompassing the remainder of these states. This was the action that led to JACL's emergency meeting in San Francisco on March 8, 9, and 10.

The Army urged the Japanese Americans to move out voluntarily, in effect suggesting that they abandon property and exchange the security of homes, jobs, friends and community for the great hostile unknown to the east. As an incentive, DeWitt promised only that "in all probability" those who left Military Area No. 1 would "not again be disturbed."

It is obvious that one reason the Army urged voluntary evacuation was that it didn't know what to do with the people it now had the power to dispossess. DeWitt's official report admits that "between March 2 and March 10, 1942, the discussions as to evacuation procedures were general in nature and specific planning had not emerged." This lack of preparation had been only too apparent to JACL leaders who had questioned government officials during their conference.

On March 11 DeWitt established the Wartime Civil Control Administration (WCCA), a civilian agency directly under the Army, "to provide for the evacuation of all persons of Japanese ancestry from Military Area No. 1 and the California portion of Military Area No. 2 . . . and initially to employ all appropriate means to encourage voluntary migration."

The Army had abruptly designated eastern California as an Evacuation area but in an unconscionable demonstration of bad faith it continued to encourage movement into that part of the state. And since much of it was familiar, a number of Japanese Americans had responded. Sim Togasaki had deposited two months' rent on property in Visalia with the intention of moving his business there. JACL wanted Kido to move to Salt Lake City with headquarters, but he insisted he should go through the Evacuation experience. He sent his wife and three young children to stay with friends, also in Visalia, while he stuck it out in San Francisco. Some families with friends in Idaho, Utah, Colorado and other inland states hurried to join them. A few students, with the help of sympathetic professors, wangled invitations to enroll in Midwestern and Eastern schools. There are many dramatic stories. Kimi Hara, recently capped as a registered nurse in Seattle, faced an agonizing decision. A friendly doctor helped her get a job offer from the Mayo Clinic in Rochester, Minnesota. It would be a dream assignment. But another physician urged her to stay and serve her people; her skills would be in critical demand in the camps. At the last minute she and two other nurses took a train for the East, to a part of the country they had never seen, and were able to lend a welcoming hand to many other Japanese Americans who later moved to Minnesota.

Those who headed east in their cars—reversing the pilgrimage of the Okies and Arkies a decade earlier—had a particularly difficult time. While urging the Japanese to leave the West Coast voluntarily, neither the Army nor civilian authorities had prepared inland areas to receive them. DeWitt admits in his *Final Report:* "The attitude of the interior states was hostile. This group considered too dangerous to remain on the West Coast, was similarly regarded by state and local authorities, and by the population of the interior. The evacuees were not welcome." The Army began to receive calls about "Japs escaping" from California. Some evacuees were refused gasoline and service in restaurants. Others were permitted to drive through a town only after agreeing they would not stop.

Vicky Marumoto Mikesell, who went on to become president of the JACL chapter in Dayton, Ohio, has vivid memories of this period although she was but a youngster. Her father, Masaichiro Marumoto, grew vegetables on a rented farm outside of Gardena, California. A fierce love of freedom burned in his heart. Rather than be confined in a camp, he decided to abandon his crops and join relatives at West Point between Salt Lake City and Ogden, Utah. The Marumotos sold their plow horses for ten dollars each and loaded what they could in a trailer towed behind their Chevrolet sedan. There wasn't room enough to take all their belongings. Vicky remembers her mother lighting a fire in their front yard to burn prized possessions she didn't want to fall into strangers' hands. Among the items was her silk wedding kimono. Tears coursing down her cheeks, she poked at it with a long stick to encourage the flames. Until Vicky grew old enough to understand, she thought smoke from the fire had caused those tears. When the kimono was ash Masaichiro loaded his four children into the car and headed east without looking back, defiantly singing a popular Japanese song of the time. It was titled *Tabi no Yokaze* (Journey's Night Wind) and the first lines were:

Hana mo arashi mo fumi koete
Yuku no ga otoko no ikiru michi,
Naite kurena, hori-hori doriyo

In rough translation: "Weep not for me, *hori-hori* bird. The path of a man's life leads through storms and over flowers. . . ." In other words, a man must be courageous. That first winter in Utah, home for the Marumoto family was a tent.

In all, some nine thousand Japanese Americans found the idea of confinement in a government camp reprehensible enough to leave the West Coast on their own. Others were no less liberty-loving but lacked the resources, the opportunity or the will to strike out independently. Or, bewildered by the prospect of becoming government wards and confident they would not be treated harshly, they decided to sit and let the inevitable take its course. The dilemma of whether to leave or stay was told dramatically in the Seattle JACL's statement to the Tolan Committee:

> A large number of people have remarked that they will go where the government orders them to go, willingly, if it will help the national defense effort. But the biggest problem in their minds is where to go. The first unofficial evacuation announcement pointed out that the government did not concern itself with where evacuees went, just so they left prohibited areas. Obviously, this was no solution to the question, for immediately from Yakima [in eastern Washington], Idaho, Montana, Colorado, and elsewhere, authoritative voices shouted: "No Japs wanted here!"
>
> The Japanese feared with reason that, forced to vacate their homes, unable to find a place to stay, they would be kicked from town to town in the interior like the Okies of John Steinbeck's novel. Others went further and envisioned the day when inhabitants of inland states, aroused by the steady influx of Japanese, would refuse to sell gasoline and food to them. They saw, too, the possibility of mob action against them as exhausted, impoverished and unable to travel further, they stopped in some town or village where they were not wanted.

So many incidents developed that on March 21, Bendetsen recommended to DeWitt that the voluntary evacuation program be halted. That same day, the WCCA organized what DeWitt's *Final Report* calls "a voluntary evacuation" of some twenty-one hundred Los Angeles residents to the Manzanar camp, still under construction in the Owens Valley between the Sierras and Death Valley in eastern California. Three days later, March 24, DeWitt ordered an 8 P.M. to 6 A.M. curfew for all Japanese, German and Italian aliens "and all other persons of Japanese ancestry," a cruel euphemism for citizens who were being singled out for discrimination solely because of their ethnic origins. Just why it had suddenly become necessary to impose a curfew was never explained. And three days after that, on March 27, DeWitt issued Public Proclamation No. 4, ending voluntary evacuation. As of the effective date, March 29, the order froze in place those still on the West Coast. From that date, the book *Nisei* notes, "it became illegal for Japanese to leave the area and soon it would be illegal for them to remain; they had to sit tight and wait for the Army to move them."

As resignation set in, JACL chapters set about preparing for the coming Evacuation. In many communities clinics were set up under JACL auspices and physicians volunteered their services to provide typhoid shots. The JACL Emergency Defense Committee in Seattle, with the encouragement of Army officers sent in to prepare for the Evacuation, picked individuals to supervise operations in camp—to disseminate information, run recreation and education programs, look after sanitation, assign housing, police the kitchens, maintain internal order. Jimmie Sakamoto as council chairman made the appointments from those close to JACL. It was not a democratic procedure, but the appointees were in place to ease the way through the inevitable maze of petty problems. In the advance cadre sent to Manzanar to prepare the way for the mass movements, members of JACL also were prominent.

In their inexperience the well-intentioned JACLers failed to see the pitfalls of such initiatives. They were working diligently to help their communities, but others saw their activity as a JACL elitist power-grab. Some outsiders who had declined to lift a finger now complained that JACL leaders were latching on to the most desirable jobs. This hostility was to boil over into ugly incidents after the urgency of the Evacuation gave way to boredom, discontent and anger.

On March 20 the Army Corps of Engineers received orders to build temporary confinement facilities for approximately one hundred thousand men, women and children. They picked fifteen sites ranging from the Puyallup, Washington, state fairgrounds on the north to the Pomona fairgrounds and the Santa Anita race track in the Los Angeles area on the south. The engineers were given thirty days to have the facilities ready. More permanent camps were scheduled for Manzanar and Poston near the town of Parker.

The movement into the assembly centers began even before the completion date. After weeks of dillydallying, the Army suddenly became aware of the "military necessity" of disposing of certain civilians. Fifty-four Japanese American families farming on Bainbridge Island, in Washington's Puget Sound, were rounded up on March 30 and sent off to Manzanar, the only center anywhere near ready. But it was late April before the Evacuation got under way in earnest. Soldiers swept into communities one after another and tacked up Evacuation notices. Urban centers were divided into areas containing approximately five hundred Japanese Americans who were notified to register and get details of the procedure that would change them from free men and women to prisoners of their own government. The dismal parade by train and Greyhound bus into American concentration camps had begun.

Four decades after the event, it is pertinent to ask why the American people permitted their government to take this action. "Permit" is hardly the proper word. The Evacuation program escaped the attention of vast numbers of Americans; years later many of them would say they were totally unaware of what was going on. And among those who knew, there was widespread support for the Evacuation. The United States and Japan were at war, Japan had scored a series of impressive victories and Americans generally identified Japanese Americans with the enemy. This attitude reflected the failure of the Nisei to convince enough of their countrymen that they were Americans by choice as well as accident of birth, that their immigrant parents were aliens only because the laws of the United States denied them the privilege of citizenship. In short, it was the official position that Japanese were not worthy of being accepted as immigrants as Europeans were, and not good enough to be extended citizenship no matter how long they lived in the United States.

As for the Nisei, the civil rights campaign for recognition of the equality of all Americans was years in the future. The Army could trample with impunity on the rights of Americans of Japanese ancestry by callously referring to them as "nonaliens." The enormous power of television to influence public opinion was also in the future. One must wonder what might have happened if pictures of children being herded behind barbed wire by armed troops were beamed night after night into America's living rooms.

There is reason to ask why Congress failed to question the validity if not the necessity of the Evacuation order. Mike Masaoka recalls that Admiral Arthur McCullum, a top officer in Naval Intelligence, told him he was convinced that one member asking the right questions in Congress could have blocked the Evacuation. But there were no human rights activists to prod congressional consciences, and no senator or representative to take such action on his own initiative. Indeed there was no wave of outrage when as late as February, 1945, according to Allan R. Bosworth in his book *America's Concentration Camps,* Congressman Jed Johnson of Oklahoma reportedly made an "extension of remarks" suggestion that the Japanese in the relocation camps be sterilized to prevent their numbers from increasing.

On the whole, the Evacuation proceeded without incident. JACL's decision to cooperate with government orders was a factor. But in reality, it was only obvious even to hotheads that resisting orders backed by guns and bayonets was foolhardy. This is not to say that the legality of the Evacuation order was not questioned by many of its victims. Some youths in Los Angeles considered passive resistance—they would stage a sit-down strike and dare soldiers to carry them aboard the Evacuation buses—but thought better of it at the last moment. Walt Tsukamoto in Sacramento broke the curfew one night, hoping to test its constitutionality. But he changed his mind when officials reminded him he was an Army Reserve officer and he might jeopardize his opportunity to serve his country. Kido himself violated the curfew, as often as not because he was too busy to pay much attention to the time. Police officers who patrolled Japantown refused to take his transgressions seriously, sometimes delivering him in their squad car to the Aki Hotel where he slept when he couldn't get home. Numerous others broke the curfew, more because it was an inconvenience and bothersome than for political reasons. Some were picked up, held overnight or given token jail terms. But enforcement was sporadic. With residents of Chinese, Korean and Filipino extraction under no restrictions, the police had no way of enforcing the curfew other than by stopping and questioning everyone with Oriental features. This they were disinclined to do.

But if the curfew was an irritant, evacuation was a much more serious matter. In Seattle an earnest young student named Takayoshi Okamoto was deeply troubled by what he perceived as an affront to his constitutional rights. After talking over the idea of resistance, he and two friends asked a JACL leader's advice. There was not much doubt that the Constitution was being violated, they were told, but to resist the Army at this point well might disrupt the nation's war effort, could result in personal harm to the resisters in view of the war hysteria and probably wouldn't deter the Army in any case. They decided it was wiser to cooperate.

Minoru Yasui, a young Portland attorney, decided otherwise. Yasui, who held a second lieutenant's commission in the U.S. Army Reserve, had been employed by the Japanese consulate in Chicago to handle English correspondence and other routine duties. He promptly resigned when war broke out. But the railroads refused to sell him a ticket back to Portland. Only after he received Army orders to report for active duty at Fort Vancouver, across the Columbia River from Portland, was he able to get passage. The Army put him in charge of a platoon of troops but next day, before he was formally inducted, Yasui was told he was unacceptable and ordered off the base.

Like Takayoshi Okamoto, Yasui felt DeWitt's curfew and Evacuation orders were illegal. After conferring with several attorneys, Yasui decided to violate the curfew and invite arrest as a matter of principle. On March 28, Yasui arranged to have his friend Ray Shimojima notify city and federal officials of his intentions. He walked the streets of downtown Portland until 11 P.M., finally stopped a patrolman and asked to be arrested. The officer told Yasui to go home. Yasui walked into police headquarters and demanded that he be jailed as a curfew violator. The police had no alternative but to lock him up. Next day the *Portland Oregonian* reported Yasui's arrest under a headline across the top of the front page which screamed: JAP SPY ARRESTED.

Before deciding to test the curfew Yasui had written to Mike Masaoka in San Francisco stating his intentions, and asking JACL's support. There is no record the letter was ever delivered. Yasui was in effect a Lone Ranger, without the backing of any person or organization, challenging the power and authority of the United States government. To carry his case to court, he was prepared to spend his life savings of five thousand dollars.

Yasui's name has gone down in legal history together with that of Gordon Hirabayashi, who similarly expressed his concerns about the Army orders but under somewhat different circumstances. Hirabayashi was a junior at the University of Washington, a Quaker, a conscientious objector and active in the YMCA. A native of the Seattle area, in early 1942 he was the only person of Japanese ancestry among the dozen men living at Eagleson Hall, a residence for international students. When General DeWitt imposed the curfew, Hirabayashi obediently rushed back to his room at 8 P.M. from the library or wherever he might be. After a week of this, it dawned on Hirabayashi that the only reason he of all the international students had to observe the curfew was his ancestry. That seemed unfair. After that Hirabayashi ignored the curfew and nothing came of this bit of lawbreaking.

At that juncture Hirabayashi fully expected to comply with the Evacuation order, peacefully boarding the bus for camp along with other Japanese Americans in the university district when the time came. Then it occurred to him that while he was ignoring the curfew on principle, the Evacuation order was an even greater violation of his constitutional rights. One night he wrote out a statement to clarify his thinking; his conclusion was that if he was going to uphold principles vital to the rights of Americans, he could not accept orders that discriminated against him because of his ethnic background. Another Nisei student, Bill Makino, had moved in with Hirabayashi during this period and they discussed the issues night after night. Although they had no more knowledge of the law than the average college student, they agreed they had an obligation as Americans to challenge an injustice. However, Makino's sense of responsibility to his elderly parents ultimately took precedence. As the only son he felt an obligation to look after them and accompany them into whatever it was the future held. Hirabayashi didn't have that problem. His parents were relatively young, there were four other children and he felt the family could take care of itself. One weekend he went home to tell his parents he could not accept the Evacuation. His mother was distraught; defiance of the government was unthinkable and besides, she feared that Gordon would be mistreated, perhaps even tortured. Gordon explained that he wasn't going to try to influence anyone else. In fact, he was spending much of his time helping families to pack and prepare to be evacuated. But he had no intention of complying with the order. It was strictly a matter of personal principle, he declared.

Hirabayashi found more encouragement from a group of Caucasian friends who were deeply upset by what their country was doing. With his approval they formed what came to be known as the Gordon Hirabayashi Defense Committee to provide him with moral and financial support. One of the leaders was Mary Farquharson, a liberal state senator and wife of a university professor, who asked Roger Baldwin, executive secretary of the American Civil Liberties Union in New York, to throw ACLU's not inconsiderable weight behind a court test. This was the kind of civil liberties case Baldwin relished, but he ran into a stone wall in his board, a majority of whom insisted ACLU should not become involved in any situation interfering with the war effort. Hirabayashi recalls that Baldwin then expressed his personal commitment by contributing five hundred dollars of his own money to help meet court costs.

On a Saturday about a week before the university district was scheduled to be evacuated, Hirabayashi, accompanied by the committee's attorney, Arthur Barnett, went to the Seattle FBI office to give himself up. The agent in charge didn't know quite what to do. Several agents took Hirabayashi to the Maryknoll mission school where Japanese in the area were being registered for evacuation and urged him to sign up. Hirabayashi declined politely. They took him to another registration station and again Hirabayashi declined. Eventually they booked him into the federal tank of King County jail where he remained for nine months before being brought to trial. During this period Mary Farquharson and her committee—ministers, businessmen, professors from the university—raised funds and spoke before countless groups about the injustice being dealt to an innocent group of which Hirabayashi was a symbol.

JACL meanwhile was preparing for the long haul. Teiko Ishida (later Kuroiwa) was given the responsibility of transferring JACL headquarters from San Francisco to Salt Lake City. She jammed her rust-colored Studebaker with files and records and somehow managed to fit Larry Tajiri, his wife Guyo and their possessions into the car. They left California on March 29, the final day of voluntary evacuation from the military zone, crossing into Nevada on old Highway 40 just before midnight. "There was a real sense of relief, a letting out of breath held too long," Guyo Tajiri recalls. "I think we had expected guards and checking of permits, but there was nothing—no border patrol, gates, nothing. Teiko remembers Larry saying something to the effect that 'if it weren't for the circumstances, this would all have been very romantic.' "

In Salt Lake City they headed for the JACL office being run by Jerry Katayama, who helped them get settled. Office space was scarce but they found three rooms in an ancient, high-ceilinged downtown structure called the Beason Building. The Tajiris also managed to rent a small home from an elderly German widow who sympathized with their plight. Tajiri made arrangements with Century Printing Company, a little shop somewhat less impressive than its name. In the beginning things weren't particularly well organized and the first issue of the new *Pacific Citi-*

zen, dated June 4, 1942, was less than a masterpiece. The headline across the top of page 1 read:

ARMY TO ORDER EVACUATION OF MILITARY AREA 2

The story reported that while the Army had stated previously that persons moving voluntarily into eastern California probably would not be disturbed again, the policy change came on the heels of a meeting in Sacramento between General DeWitt and agricultural pressure groups. The second most prominent story reported that the Native Sons of the Golden West, the American Legion and the Joint Immigration Committee had filed suits in federal district court seeking to deprive Nisei of the right to vote. Reviewing the progress of the Evacuation, *Pacific Citizen* said:

> The first phase of the greatest forced migration of people in America was virtually completed this week. General DeWitt's headquarters announced that all major cities on the West Coast had been evacuated by its residents of Japanese race. In California only the delta lands of Yolo county had not yet been completely evacuated. Yet a few remained behind. These were the infirm, the too ill to move. There were also the few Americans with Japanese faces who had been exempted because they were engaged in vital war work—at U.S. government listening posts, in other federal agencies. These Nisei and their families were authorized to remain at liberty, but must carry with them, at all times, special identification papers.

While the Tajiris and Teiko Ishida were getting established in Salt Lake City, Mike Masaoka wound up his affairs in San Francisco and prepared to move to Washington. He knew he would need help when he got there and without hesitation he picked a steady, hardworking, low-key Los Angeles JACL leader named George Inagaki who was general manager of a floral nursery. Inagaki knew Masaoka's oldest brother, Joe Grant, who ran a food market, better than he knew Mike. But the choice turned out to be a fortunate one. Inagaki was born in Sacramento, had been a high school football star and the first Nisei valedictorian in the area. Walter Tsukamoto had recognized Inagaki's potential as a Nisei leader and got him interested in JACL. Where Mike Masaoka was mercurial, often brash, Inagaki was steady. Unlike Masaoka, Inagaki spoke Japanese fluently. He understood Issei and Nisei psychology, which Masaoka did not. In many other ways they complemented and balanced each other's talents. As Inagaki recalled shortly before his death in 1978, he received a telephone call from Masaoka soon after JACL's San Francisco emergency meeting. Their conversation went something like this:

"Hello, George? This is Mike Masaoka. Will you go to Washington with me to represent JACL?"

"Well, I, ah . . ."

"You have a car, don't you?"

"Yeah . . ."

"You don't have any kids, do you?"

"No."

"Then you have no excuse for not helping me out. When can you leave?"

Inagaki talked things over with his wife Yuki and father Kuniji. They agreed George had an obligation to go. He helped them prepare to move into an Evacuation center. Then, with a travel permit authorizing him to leave the area, he drove to Reno, Nevada, where he met Masaoka to begin the long drive east. In Salt Lake City they touched base with Tajiri and Teiko Ishida, who in effect were the entire JACL headquarters staff, then headed east again, allowing themselves five dollars a day for living expenses, meeting with ministers, human rights leaders and anybody else who would listen. Inagaki was driver, treasurer, consultant and sounding board as Masaoka bounced idea after idea off him. Their first major appearance was in Cleveland, Ohio, at the annual conference of the American Committee for the Protection of the Foreign Born. Masaoka gave a stirring speech attesting to the fealty of Japanese Americans:

> I bring you pledge and proof of the loyalty of your fellow Americans of Japanese origin—a promise that we will continue to serve, to sacrifice, to fight in the defense of our nation; proof that our actions to date bear out the sincerity of our promise. We ask no favors, no sympathy; we call only for what all Americans have a right to demand—the privilege and the opportunity to share in the common lot and life of all Americans, regardless of what it may be.
>
> From reception and assembly centers on desert lands, and racetracks, and county fairgrounds, we Americans look forward to the victory which must come and to the realization of that greater

> democracy that is the promise of America. We are contributing our share to that glorious new day when Americans of every race, color and creed can join their strength and sinew in the creation of a better and greater America—and a great new world in which the individual man is the master of his own station, to join with us and with the millions of other Americans in serving and sacrificing that mankind may be freed forever from the bonds of slavery and fear.

But the applause he received soon turned sour. Masaoka's inexperience and his desire to tell the Nisei story to any audience that would listen nearly resulted in disaster. The American Committee for the Protection of the Foreign Born turned out to be a front organization seeking to exploit the plight of Japanese Americans to embarrass the United States. Later, Masaoka found his name was listed without his permission on the committee's letterhead as a member of the board, a fact that stirred the suspicions of government officials and untainted liberal groups whose support JACL sought.

The next stop was the National Conference of Social Work in New Orleans. Annie Clo Watson had arranged the invitation. After checking in, the two went sight-seeing in St. Bernard Parish just outside New Orleans until it was time to speak. They didn't know that the previous day a German U-boat had been reported nearby and the parish was buzzing with rumors that Axis spies had been landed. Two Orientals driving about slowly alarmed the local constabulary. Masaoka and Inagaki soon found themselves locked up in separate cells with visions of becoming guests of honor at a Southern lynching party. When Masaoka failed to appear for his speech, the social workers notified the FBI, which quickly located and rescued the suspects.

In mid-May Masaoka and Inagaki reached Washington. Masaoka had been in Washington briefly twice before. Once, as a high school student, he had been given a trip as a reward for having helped in Elbert Thomas' election campaign. He visited the capital a second time with the University of Utah debate team. But he had no more than textbook knowledge of how Washington works, or where to begin. Nor was his introduction encouraging. The two tried many inexpensive hotels before they found one that would accept them. But when FBI agents quickly showed up to question them, the clerk became alarmed and asked them to leave. In desperation, Inagaki got in touch with Jack Murata, a civil service employee, and he and his wife Betty took them in.

That problem solved for the moment, Masaoka and Inagaki drove to the Lincoln Memorial. They stood a long time before the giant, brooding statue of Abe Lincoln, absorbing strength and inspiration from the memory of the martyred President. Then they set out to find Senator Thomas.

XIII

Difficult Times

By June 7, 1942, Colonel Bendetsen could report that Military Area No. 1 had been purged of Japanese Americans. And by early August the California portion of Area No. 2 had been cleared. By order of the military, one hundred ten thousand men, women and children had been hustled into crude, hurriedly set-up assembly centers. At the Santa Anita and Tanforan racetracks the evacuees were placed in stables still redolent with the aroma of their previous tenants. At the fairgrounds in Puyallup, some evacuees were housed in dank cubicles under the concrete of the grandstand, others in long, cooplike shacks hammered together in the infield. Barbed wire surrounded the centers and armed guards were on constant duty. This wasn't quite what JACL leaders had expected.

The Army made no bones about admitting the Evacuation had been based on race. DeWitt's *Final Report* carries this passage on page 145:

> Included among the evacuees were persons who were only part Japanese, some with as little as one-sixteenth Japanese blood; others who, prior to evacuation, were unaware of their Japanese ancestry; and many who had married Caucasians, Chinese, Filipinos, Negroes, Hawaiians, or Eskimos. Most of these people were American-born, had been through American schools, had not developed Oriental thought patterns or had been subjected to so-called Japanese culture. Because of their Americanization and their awkward social position, life in the Japanese Centers proved

> a trying and often humiliating experience. . . . A policy was initiated which provided exemption from evacuation for certain mixed-marriage families and mixed-blood individuals whose background made it reasonably clear that their sympathies were and would remain American.

Since the Evacuation was based on race, racism also governed its exemptions for, in the Army's language, "mixed blood [one-half Japanese or less] individuals, citizens of the United States or of friendly nations, whose backgrounds have been Caucasian."

Having locked up the Japanese Americans, the Army was unsure about what it should do next. Its solution was to push off its charges as quickly as possible on the War Relocation Authority, a civilian agency which itself had been the product of an afterthought. Secretary of War Stimson's notes show that on February 27, eight days after the President signed Executive Order 9066, Roosevelt brought up the Evacuation in a cabinet meeting. He wanted to know what progress had been made in resettling the Japanese Americans. Stimson explained that because of the magnitude of the job, progress was slow. His notes say: "The President seized upon the idea that the work should be taken off the shoulders of the Army so far as possible after the evacuees had been selected and removed from places where they were dangerous."

Parenthetically, this would indicate that Roosevelt had not anticipated the kind of indiscriminate mass evacuation clearing entire states that DeWitt ordered, but rather, a limited and more selective removal. Stimson's notes continue: "There was general confusion around the table arising from the fact that nobody had realized how big it was, nobody wanted to take care of the evacuees, and the general weight and complication of the project. [Attorney General] Biddle suggested that a single head should be chosen to handle the resettlement instead of the pulling and hauling of all the different agencies, and the President seemed to accept this. . . ."

The upshot was that Harold D. Smith, director of the budget and key White House aide, appointed Milton S. Eisenhower, veteran of Department of Agriculture service, the "single head." On March 18 Roosevelt signed Executive Order 9102 establishing the War Relocation Authority to assist the evacuees. Just how that would be done was solely Eisenhower's problem as director of WRA. He brought little more than compassion, common sense and bureaucratic experience to the unprecedented job of looking after 110,000 Japanese Americans. He had known nothing of the building pressures on the West Coast until Executive Order 9066 had been signed and, like most Americans from the Midwest and East, knew next to nothing about Japanese Americans. He was also dismayed that the Army was anxious to dump the evacuees on WRA and close the impounding camps as quickly as possible. But first Eisenhower had to devise a plan for inland centers—his initial idea of fifty or more temporary cities scattered throughout the interior was quickly shot down by hostile governors—and work out a policy for operating them. Ultimately he settled on ten large camps, housing an average of approximately 10,000 people, to be built on federally owned land away from population centers. The Army announced a schedule of movement to the WRA centers long before they were completed. Construction crews were still hammering and laying pipe when daily train-loads of evacuees began to arrive. The movement was completed October 30 when a train carrying 415 evacuees left the Fresno assembly center for Jerome, Arkansas, finally arriving November 3. In all, 117,116 Japanese Americans were forced to leave their homes in the Evacuation areas; the 1940 census showed a total of 126,947 persons of Japanese descent in the forty-eight states.

The ouster of such numbers left a sizable vacuum. Ben Yoshioka, a Nisei employed by WCCA and permitted to remain behind temporarily in Los Angeles, had a depressing report about Li'l Tokyo, once the largest Japanese community in the United States: "It's really sad. Everything looks so deserted. Stray cats wander around aimlessly looking for masters who have gone. The Miyako Hotel [Li'l Tokyo's largest] is now the Civic Hotel. And the JACL sign, 'We Are Ready to Serve America' is still hanging on the corner of First and San Pedro." Sacramento's West Side was described as looking as though it had been blitzed. Some farms had been taken over by Chinese and Filipinos and even teen-age members of the Future Farmers of America. More than one abandoned farm was looted of its fruits and vegetables before they could be harvested. In the Florin–Elk Grove area outside Sacramento the $600,000 strawberry crop left behind by Japanese farmers was declared a total loss.

As community after community was evacuated, JACL chapters disbanded "for the duration," forwarding what remained in their treasuries to national headquarters. JACL leaders were thoroughly scattered. Kido moved from San Francisco to join his family in Visalia. When the eastern half of California was evacuated, the Kidos were sent to the camp at Poston, Arizona, as were Sim Togasaki and his family. Vice-President Ken Matsumoto had relocated to Cincinnati, Ohio. Secretary James Sugioka was in Denver. Fred Tayama, a Los Angeles stalwart, had been sent to Manzanar. Doc Yatabe had gone into the Fresno assembly center, not far from his home, before being shipped off to one of the WRA camps in Arkansas. Clarence Arai, suffering from hypertension, Tom Iseri and Jimmie Sakamoto were evacuated to the camp in the Puyallup fairgrounds before being sent on to Minidoka, Idaho. Walter Tsukamoto was at the Tule Lake WRA camp. A survey showed 90 percent of JACL chapter presidents, the faithful wheelhorses of the JACL movement, had gone into the camps with their friends and neighbors out of a sense of obligation to the people of their communities.

Hito Okada, the national treasurer from Portland, was the only elected national JACL officer to move to Salt Lake City. He was needed to supervise disbursement of JACL funds and Masaoka arranged for permission for him to leave Portland. Authorization came in the form of a telegram instructing him to proceed to Salt Lake City. It made no mention of his wife, Hana, and young daughter, Carolyn. He left them with friends, much to his wife's distress, and went to Salt Lake City where he found that the Tajiris and Teiko Ishida had the situation well in hand. But the financial problem was much more critical. JACL had managed to accumulate a treasury of roughly $23,000, which was to carry the organization for a year. It had been agreed to pay employees—Masaoka, Inagaki, the Tajiris, Teiko Ishida—$150 per month. Okada was being paid a like sum from the federal alien-property custodian for looking after the assets of the Japanese lumber-exporting company where he had been employed, so he decided to draw nothing from JACL. After office rent, travel expenses, telephone and other bills were incorporated into the budget, it was obvious the $23,000 wouldn't last beyond a year. What would happen when that money was gone? No one knew how long JACL's services would be required. But the employees came up with a proposal that saved the situation. They voluntarily agreed to cut their pay in half to $75 a month, watch their expenses and try to make the organization's nest egg last for two years. None of the employees were working for JACL for the money; they asked only enough to live on while they served their fellow Japanese Americans. But obviously the Tajiris could not make ends meet on $75 a month. Ultimately it was agreed JACL would pay the rent on their house, while Larry would draw $75 a month and Guyo $25. Tears fill Okada's eyes when he talks about this trying period.

But before the $23,000 was exhausted, help came from various quarters. The Seattle chapter turned over the $3,000 remaining in its treasury, and Oakland contributed $1,000. The biggest boost came from the nine chapters of the Intermountain District Council, youngest and smallest of the JACL family with less than five hundred prewar members. Bill Yamauchi as district chairman pledged the council would raise $10,000 a year for national headquarters. The district at the time had four Utah chapters (Salt Lake City, Ogden, Northern Utah and Davis County), four Idaho chapters (Idaho Falls, Pocatello and Yellowstone in the eastern part of the state, Boise Valley in the west), and the Big Horn Mountains chapter embracing north-central Wyoming and southern Montana). Some time later, in a district meeting at Idaho Falls, this pledge was ratified with Shake Ushio as district chairman. There was no hesitation about taking on the fund-raising project. Joe Saito from western Idaho; Sud Morishita, Joe Nishioka and Eke Inouye of Idaho Falls; George Shiozawa of Pocatello; Ken Uchida of Ogden; and Yukus Inouye and Joe Kurumada of the Salt Lake City area were among those who promised to go back home and seek contributions for JACL. Volunteers went from farm to farm in their areas asking for support—$10, $50, $100, anything the families could spare.

Inouye recalled: "Farm prices were cheap and everybody was having a hard time. It would be easier to raise $500,000 in the 1970s than to raise $10,000 back in those days. With many families it wasn't necessary to explain why we needed the money. JACL had a terrific amount of support. The people knew JACL was the only organization they could depend on, and they were scared about the future."

Until the money began to come in, each time the bank balance became dangerously low Okada would rub the ample belly of a homely figurine depicting Hotei, the Japanese god of good luck, which he kept in his office. And miraculously, a contribution would show up in a day or so. There were weeks when Okada did a lot of fervent belly-rubbing.

Back east, meanwhile, Masaoka and Inagaki were working tirelessly, traveling from Washington to Philadelphia to New York and back again for a series of conferences with WRA officials, the American Friends Service Committee, the American Civil Liberties Union, the Post-War World Council headed by Norman Thomas, Read Lewis of the Common Council for American Unity and headquarters officials of numerous church groups. In Washington they depended heavily for logistical support on Jack Murata and his wife. In New York, Mr. and Mrs. Mervyn Suzuki provided the hospitality that enabled them to keep expenses down.

Foremost among Masaoka's objectives was to get out the word that Japanese Americans had been incarcerated by their own government not because they were disloyal, but because the Army had deemed their removal a military necessity. The shadow of suspicion had to be eliminated as quickly and completely as possible. Masaoka also was seeking support for a resettlement program that would enable the evacuees to leave the camps and find decent homes and jobs in interior America. And finally, he was looking to the long future of Japanese Americans in a land without the old hatreds; JACL would need all the help it could get in its efforts to find equality, justice and an end to racial discrimination when the war ended.

Accompanied on occasion by Ken Matsumoto, Masaoka and Inagaki called on Eisenhower to exchange views. Eisenhower welcomed all the input he could get to help cope with the responsibilities that had been thrust on him. In 1978, responding to questions from Harry Takagi, he had some trenchant comments about the Evacuation and JACL's role.

About the Evacuation decision:

> It could have been avoided if from the very first the intelligence services—the Army, Navy, FBI and all the rest including top military leaders—if they had said keep calm, there is nothing to fear about this, there are probably some Kibei whose allegiance is to Japan and we know pretty much who they are, and if it becomes necessary to segregate them, we'll do so. If there is going to be an invasion, we'll know that in time. There's not going to be a second Pearl Harbor. If all these things that we now see might have been done, or had been done, then this [the Evacuation] would have never happened. But I'm convinced that the thing was so inflamed by the time the President signed the order, no matter whether it

was right or whether it was wrong, things were in a pretty hopeless situation.

On the contention that the Nisei should have resisted the Evacuation:

> My judgment is that had there been mass opposition, there would have been horrible consequences for the country. The people had been whipped into a frenzy by not very nice folks in the mass communications business and even some in the military. And in view of the hostility already existing, if there had been opposition . . .

His voice trailed off.

On JACL's activities:

> The cooperation of the Japanese American Citizens League helped make the horrible things that had to be done as humane and as acceptable as they could be under the circumstances. People such as I, who had no previous experience in such activities, didn't even know the problems. Dillon Myer when he first came over to WRA was equally uninformed. He wasn't a Westerner. He never had lived in California. I think we would have made some horrible mistakes, and I do believe to this day that considering what went on in California, on the West Coast, by newspaper people, radio people, military people—and with certain actual possibilities of danger—considering the turmoil it would have been tragic if strangers came in and made judgments without guidance of the League. I always had great admiration for Mike Masaoka and his associates who worked with him.

But Eisenhower remained on the job only three months, just long enough to gain an understanding of the magnitude and complexity of his responsibilities. One night he sat down with his friend and Department of Agriculture colleague Dillon S. Myer and said he had become so deeply involved in WRA's problems that he had trouble sleeping. Eisenhower said he had been offered a post as Elmer Davis's deputy in the Office of War Information. He said he would like to accept if he could find a good man to head WRA. Then he asked Myer if he would take over.

Myer had been in Washington long enough to understand that the WRA post was not the kind of job an ambitious civil servant could use to advance his career. "The reason it was set up as an independent agency," he once explained, "was that most of the people who had any political savvy and were interested in their own political ambitions didn't want to deal with the 'Japs.' That's kind of rough, but that was exactly their thinking, and they didn't want to be caught in this kind of an unpopular situation. So the President set it up as an independent agency. That kind of setup had drawbacks, such as having nobody above to give you support when you felt you needed it. The other side of it was that you could call your own shots, you could make your own decisions, you could put them into operation and you didn't have to go through three or four layers of authority to get it done." Myer took the challenge. He became WRA director on June 17.

Masaoka was disappointed that Eisenhower decided to move on. Eisenhower had been understanding and sensitive. Myer was an unknown quantity. He would have to be felt out, studied, evaluated. Myer, aware of his ignorance, also was wary. At first he was turned off by the feeling that Masaoka was overly impressed with his own importance since he was seeing and advising a lot of government brass. But before long they realized they were thinking along the same lines and would have no problem working together.

Masaoka had outlined four broad JACL goals in his conversations with Eisenhower. First was resettlement of all the evacuees back into normal community life and restoration of their civil rights as quickly as possible. Second was restoration of Selective Service responsibilities for all Japanese Americans. Then he wanted President Roosevelt to issue a strong statement to the effect that the loyalty of the evacuees was not being questioned and calling on all Americans to treat them fairly as patriots who had sacrificed their freedom in the interests of national unity. And finally, Masaoka asked WRA to meet periodically with representatives of all the camps to discuss problems and policies. Myer had no disagreement with any of these objectives. One of his first actions was a directive authorizing Nisei who had never lived or attended school in Japan to leave the camps provided they had a job outside the evacuated areas. The other goals were more difficult to achieve. Roosevelt never saw fit to make the forthright statement Masaoka wanted, although he did speak out for the Nisei when they were invited to volunteer for military service.

As soon as Myer could break away from his desk he visited the Poston, Manzanar and Tule Lake camps to get a firsthand feel for the problems of the evacuees. What he saw sickened him—dismal tarpapered shacks in a vast, dusty, sun-seared wilderness, barbed wire fences, guard towers, floodlights and men, women and children trying to make do. At one camp he watched a group of newly arrived evacuees getting off a bus, fear and confusion written on their faces. "I saw a poor old lady walk over to a garbage can and lose her breakfast," he once recalled. "I was terribly upset. It bothered me that people were having to go through this kind of experience for no reason other than that they were of Japanese extraction." What he witnessed strengthened his conviction that the evacuees must be returned to normal life outside the camps as quickly as possible.

Masaoka, meanwhile, viewed with alarm the growing hostility toward the evacuees in various parts of the country. The professed goal of getting Japanese Americans off the West Coast as a national security measure was rapidly being turned into a campaign to get rid of them permanently. Even before the Evacuation was completed the Native Sons of the Golden West and the American Legion, both with a history of hostility toward Japanese Americans, filed separate suits to strip Nisei of their citizenship. U. S. Webb, former attorney general of California, appeared for both the plaintiffs, arguing that since only white persons could be naturalized, it followed that children of ineligible aliens (like the Chinese and Japanese) should not be accepted as citizens simply because they happened to be born in the United States. Webb in effect was seeking to rewrite the Constitution and his suit was quickly quashed.

But that did not discourage others intent on winning World War II by attacking the Japanese Americans. Congressman Ford charged that WRA's proposal to relocate the evacuees in interior areas would "undo the very thing" the Evacuation was intended to accomplish, namely keep them locked up in concentration camps. Senator Tom Stewart, a Tennessee Democrat, with little fanfare slipped a bill in the hopper requiring the Secretary of War to take into custody "all persons of the Japanese race, regardless of the place of their birth." Stewart wanted to deny citizenship to Nisei, contending "a Jap is a Jap anywhere you find him, and his taking the oath of allegiance to this country would not help, even if he should be permitted to do so." Stewart was joined in Congress by two other Southern racists, John Rankin and Theodore Bilbo of Mississippi, who found it easy to shift their contempt for blacks to the "Japs."

There were numerous other expressions of hostility. In Los

Angeles, Assistant District Attorney Clyde Shoemaker told Kiwanians that Americans were foolish to believe American-born Japanese could be trusted. In Detroit, organized veterans and others persuaded the Safety Commission to block four young Nisei men from resettling in the community. In Marshfield, Wisconsin, a Chinese American reported he had been mistaken for a Japanese and the tires on his car slashed. When Governor Olson of California asked the Army to halt evacuation of Area No. 2 because millions of dollars in crops was likely to remain unharvested, spokesmen for his election opponent, Earl Warren, threatened to make it a campaign issue. In Arizona, the legislature passed a law making it illegal to do business with "a person under legal restraint" (meaning a Japanese American) unless notice of such a contemplated business transaction was published in a legal newspaper and formal notice filed with the secretary of state. This had the effect of preventing Japanese Americans from buying even a package of gum without going through all that red tape, a fact which the state supreme court recognized in ruling the law invalid.

The widespread state of mind of that unhappy time was explained by Richard Drinnon in the April 27, 1981, issue of *Inquiry Magazine* with this passage:

> From FDR down, through the national to the state level, officials could see Japanese immigrants [Issei] and Japanese Americans [Nisei] only as inscrutable Orientals, not persons but mysteries to be solved, perils to be guarded against, abstractions, symbols, all subsumed under the epithet "Japs." Whites could not tell them apart, in short, good from bad, because whites had been conditioned not to look at them, to *see* their individuality, but to look through them to their racial essence.

Masaoka was acutely aware of the nature of the problem even though he might not have seen it the same way that Drinnon did. Viewing the seemingly endless series of attacks—petty, spiteful or profoundly dangerous, based on blind prejudice or total ignorance—Masaoka feared for the future of Japanese Americans if the tide of hate were not stemmed. The federal government wasn't being of much help. What could be done?

The one thought that kept coming back was that despite their ordeal the Nisei must share with other Americans the burden of defending their country. Nisei had been drafted like other Americans prior to the outbreak of war. After Pearl Harbor, many Nisei in uniform were discharged "for the convenience of the government." Japanese Americans were turned away from recruiting centers and they found their 1-A classification (acceptable for military service) being changed to 4-C (alien ineligible for military service) and 4-F (unfit for military service). Masaoka articulated his thinking in these words:

> I believed that Selective Service and actual participation in the armed forces during the war would be the most telling and irrefutable answer conceivable to those who question the loyalty of Japanese Americans. West Coast professional rabble-rousers have used the technique of discounting the usual attributes of good citizenship insofar as persons of Japanese descent are concerned, alleging that these are all a part of a program to insinuate themselves into the good graces and confidence of the public at large, of explaining the complete lack of fifth column activity after Dec. 7 with the statement that the Japanese communities were only awaiting orders from Tokyo before beginning such activities. They demanded positive and actual proof of the loyalty of the group. Serving in the armed forces after all that we have been forced to go through would supply that answer, for if Japanese Americans participate and die if necessary in the defense of the country, they would have demonstrated their willingness to pay the supreme price that the United States might triumph. Even though America may have failed us temporarily and permitted our evacuation, America still represents by far the best opportunities for us after we have helped to win the war. After all, we are Americans. We may be called upon to make greater sacrifices than most, but they provide us an opportunity to ensure our future.

He found support for this point of view among friends and advisers as well as Myer. Masaoka was also aware of spreading unrest among the evacuees who felt betrayed by their government. JACL leaders and others wrote to tell Masaoka of growing bitterness. It was understandable that some evacuees would resent efforts to put them in uniform. It was understandable that they would demand restoration of their rights before they would agree to serve their country. A strong position on military service could not be taken without approval by JACL's leaders. And there were many other matters that JACL needed to talk over.

Masaoka wrote to Kido in Poston and suggested it was time to call another conference. Meanwhile, he received Myer's permission to summon JACL leaders from each of the camps to a meeting in Salt Lake City in November, and his promise to attend and answer questions.

XIV

Salt Lake City, 1942

Winter came early to Salt Lake City in 1942. By mid-November, the skies were leaden, matching the mood of JACL representatives assembling for the special emergency national conference. The meetings began the afternoon of Tuesday, November 17, at the Japanese Christian Church. The delegates met morning and afternoon—and most evenings—for the next week to ponder and arrive at positions on a vast array of knotty problems facing Japanese Americans. The convention minutes, in single-spaced elite type, cover 120 legal-size pages.

The conference opened under less than auspicious circumstances. A few days earlier the Native Sons of the Golden West, rejected in state court, had begun proceedings in federal court to revoke the citizenship of Japanese Americans. The California American Legion, ignoring the fact that nearly five thousand Nisei were serving in the U.S. Army, had urged the deportation of all persons of Japanese ancestry at war's end. In Arkansas, a Nisei GI in uniform was shot at and narrowly escaped injury when he stopped at a restaurant en route to see friends at the Jerome WRA camp. In Portland, Judge James Alger Fee had ruled in federal court that the military's curfew order restricting the movement of citizens of Japanese ancestry was illegal, but that the American-born Minoru Yasui was guilty of violating that order since he had lost his citizenship by working for the Japanese consulate in Chicago before the war. And from a public-relations viewpoint, the most damaging development was a five-day disturbance at the Poston WRA camp. Three days before the conference was to open, a gang of dissidents attacked and seriously injured Kay Nishimura, an elected councilman. When two suspects were arrested, the dissidents seized virtual control of the camp and intimidated workers into calling a general strike. Military guards were called in to restore order. Project Director W. Wade Head was quoted by the Associated Press as saying a small but well-organized pro-Axis group had "deliberately attempted the destruction of the Americanism of the American-born Japanese," but "hundreds of fine, loyal American-born Japanese cooperated and worked as a team in defeating all pro-Axis groups without bloodshed or loss of property."

The disturbance delayed Kido's departure and the conference started without him. Telegrams had gone out from Washington authorizing project directors to release two or more evacuees from each of the camps for the trip to Salt Lake City. The request had been made by JACL and the delegates were selected largely on the basis of JACL experience and dedication. The logistics of getting these individuals to their destination in a time of war were formidable. The men from the four camps within the Western Defense Command military zones—two in California and two in Arizona—had to be escorted by Caucasian guards to the state line. Kido, Sim Togasaki, Lyle Kurisaki and Dr. T. G. Ishimaru represented Poston; Nobu Tashiro and Ken Tashiro came from Gila River, Arizona. Representing Manzanar were Fred Tayama, Joe Grant Masaoka and Kiyoshi Higashi; from Tule Lake came Walter Tsukamoto, Ted Nakamura and Tom Yego, who had been working as a volunteer sugar-beet harvest hand in Idaho. (On the return trip the California contingent slept overnight in the Reno jail while waiting for their escorts to show up.)

The longest trip—more than three thousand miles total—was made by representatives of the two Arkansas camps: Dr. Yatabe and Tom Shimasaki from Denson and James Yoshinobu and Frank Ishii from Rohwer. Traveling by way of St. Louis by bus, limited to thirty-five miles per hour by wartime fuel conservation rules, these four were on the road sixty-four hours en route to Salt Lake City. The delegates from Heart Mountain, Wyoming—Henry Mitarai and Bill Hosokawa—had to take a roundabout route through that sparsely populated state. From the camp near Cody in the northwest corner of Wyoming, they rode twenty hours across the state to Cheyenne in the southeast corner to wait for a westbound bus. There, they were farther from Salt Lake City than when they started. In all, their trip took forty hours and the only unpleasantness they experienced was when Mitarai was denied a cup of coffee at a Chinese-run restaurant in Evanston. Granada, Colorado, sent Masao Satow and Henry Shimizu. Topaz, Utah, in the Sevier Desert only 160 miles from Salt Lake City, sent Dr. Carl Hirota and Vernon Ichisaka. Minidoka, 240 miles to the northwest in south-central Utah, was represented by Jimmie Sakamoto and Milton Maeda. For most of the delegates the Salt Lake City conference was their first experience of freedom since the big roundup. JACL put them up, two to a room, in a third-rate hotel.

Delegates and invited observers from the "free zone" were Mitsugi Kasai, Idaho Falls JACL; Tatsuo Koga, Michi Sato, Fumiko Takahashi, Ogden; Shig Tanita, Jack Suda, Arizona; Ichi Nosagi, T. Nakano, Davis County; Haruo Yamasaki, Kiyoshi Sakota, Yellowstone; Masao Yamashita, Boise Valley; Paul Okamura, Bill Yoden, George Shiozawa, Pocatello; Dr. Jun Kurumada, Jerry Katayama, Shake Ushio, Bill Yamauchi, Salt Lake City; Yoshiko Ariki, Kimi Mukaye, Denver; Isamu Noguchi, the sculptor, and Koji Ariyoshi, a Hawaii longshoremen's union leader who also had been in the beet fields.

Hito Okada was in charge of arrangements. Mike Masaoka had come back from Washington for the meeting. Other headquarters personnel included George Inagaki and volunteer Scotty Tsuchiya, who had just returned to Salt Lake City after an inspection trip through the sugar-beet harvest areas, the Tajiris and Teiko Ishida, who had rounded up a secretarial corps for the meetings.

The agenda covered every aspect of the WRA camps, student relocation, outside agricultural work, chapters in the free zone, finances, operation of *Pacific Citizen* and other matters that affected Japanese Americans. But there were two subjects that overshadowed all else. On the third day, Masaoka introduced the first of them almost casually. He asked: should JACL at this point in history demand the right of military service for Japanese Americans? If so, should JACL seek restoration of Selective Service responsibilities, or should JACL endorse the idea of Nisei volunteering for military service? He made his own position clear:

> The national JACL has always insisted upon our treatment as equal partners in the war effort with every other American. We believe that we are entitled to share in the good things of democracy just as much as we should share in the sacrifices and the heartaches of our country. Even before evacuation took place, when it appeared that some of the Selective Service boards were not accepting Nisei on the same basis as other Americans, we protested indignantly. Being deprived of the right to serve our country in the armed forces today, we are being deprived of our biggest chance to prove to those who are skeptical that our loyalty is as great as that of any other group. Somewhere on the field of battle, in a baptism of blood, we and our comrades must prove to all who question that we are ready and willing to die for the one country we know and pledge allegiance to.

Then Masaoka invited discussion. What followed was an intense, emotional, sometimes agonized outpouring on both sides of the issue as doubts and resentments were aired. Some of the delegates quoted Issei parents who bitterly protested that the Army had segregated their sons in uniform, disarmed them and sent them to perform menial tasks in inland camps. "Why should we part with our other sons when America doesn't believe in them?" they asked. Others reported the sentiment in the camps was to oppose military service until the civil rights of Japanese Americans were restored. Some contended that military service was not the only demonstration of loyalty; the Japanese Americans had made an enormous sacrifice in the interest of national unity by cooperating in their own imprisonment and if they were to be subject to Selective Service their civilian status should be the same as that of anyone else.

The book *Nisei* points out that the military had done little to endear itself to Japanese Americans and summarizes the discussion at the conference in this way:

> To begin with, the Navy and Marines had a policy of not accepting *Nisei* even before Pearl Harbor. And the Army had demanded evacuation and then carried it out. Shortly after Pearl Harbor the Selective Service System had changed the classification of all *Nisei* to 4C—aliens not subject to military service—thus imposing on them a blanket exemption from the draft. The *Nisei* had resented this discriminatory treatment deeply. On top of this, many Nisei already in uniform had been released from active service by transfer to the Enlisted Reserve Corps "for the convenience of the government"—a transparent euphemism for being kicked out. No

explanation was ever given; the names of *Nisei* GIs (most of them *Kibei*) had been posted without warning at Army installations along the Pacific Coast and the next day they were on their way home. Other *Nisei* who remained with their outfits found themselves on permanent K.P. or yard detail, stuck with the most menial jobs. When their buddies were shipped overseas, the *Nisei* were transferred to other units.

Now Masaoka was urging that the delegates overlook this discrimination, overlook the fact that their people had been locked up, ignore all this and petition that these same people be conscripted to go out and fight for freedom. Some of the delegates said Masaoka's proposal was ridiculous and unrealistic, that the *Nisei* had every right to enjoy exemption from the draft since the government had made it plain they were not wanted. Others could see the long-range wisdom of Masaoka's argument that the *Nisei* needed a record of having fought for their country to bulwark their postwar struggle to win full citizenship rights, but they feared hostile reaction in the camps where long-suppressed resentments were bubbling to the surface.

But after their sense of outrage had been spent by debate, the delegates agreed some grand, sincere gesture was essential to dramatize Nisei loyalty. They were now prepared to make this gesture even though they knew that, inevitably, there would be opposition by some embittered elements in the camps.

Finally, when it was apparent that all shades of opinion had been expressed, Masaoka summed up his feelings:

> I have come to the inescapable conclusion that this matter of Selective Service is the cornerstone of our future in this country. Perhaps we may be somewhat short-sighted today in view of what we have gone through, but let me ask you to think of your future —and that of your children and your children's children. When the war is won, and we attempt to find our way back into normal society, one question which we cannot avoid will be, "Say, Buddy, what did you do in the war?" If we cannot answer that we, with them, fought for the victory which is ours, our chance for success and acceptance will be small. We need Selective Service; the least we can do is to ask for it. As for the work of the Washington office, such a resolution from this body will go far in carrying on our public relations work. Gentlemen, in order to bring this discussion to a head, I call for a resolution to the President and the Army of the United States asking for a reclassification of the draft status of the American-born Japanese so that we shall be accorded the same

privilege of serving our country in the armed forces as that granted to every other American citizen.

Sim Togasaki rose to make the motion:

> I feel strongly that most of us desire to be treated in the same way as all other Americans, both as to sacrifices and benefits. This is a matter which vitally affects our very lives. Even though we have gone through so much, I am confident that most of us are willing to forget and forgive, and join the Army and fight for our country and our future. Mr. Chairman, I move that the resolutions committee be instructed to draw up a resolution embodying the wishes of this assembly.

When Togasaki sat down to applause, Henry Shimizu rose:

> I second the motion. I believe we have made a most significant decision, and one which we will be proud to recall in the years to come.

The motion was carried unanimously. There was a relieved, happy silence around the table.

Several days later Dillon Myer met with the group and one of the questions he was asked was about his feelings on Selective Service for the evacuees.

"I'm surprised the subject didn't come up a long time ago," he said. "If this program that I talked about, resettlement, is going to really be successful, there is one key thing that must happen. I consider it important that all citizens have the right to fight for this country. I have been working toward that end for a long time. I have talked to a lot of people who are in a position to influence the decision. We have a great deal of sympathy on that program. It is definitely under consideration and I am very hopeful that it will happen within a WRA month." Earlier, he had explained that the tempo of action in WRA was so rapid that one month in WRA time equaled one year in ordinary time. "I won't promise that, but I will promise that I am going to keep on battering at the door or be kicked out. I think it is that important and that essential. Now, I would like to ask the group a question. There are two possibilities, volunteering, or reinstitution of Selective Service. Which do you people think ought to be done?"

Masaoka replied: "We have an answer to that. It was unanimously agreed that as American citizens and representatives of JACL in the relocation centers we will ask the President and the military authorities for the reclassification of our Selective Service status on the same basis as all other Americans."

Before the question period Myer had spoken about WRA's plans. He reminded the delegates that it had never been WRA's intention to keep the evacuees cooped up for the duration. He said that while the camps would be made as livable as possible, WRA's primary efforts would be to relocate Japanese Americans in "hundreds of communities throughout the United States before the war ends," helping them to find jobs, homes and community acceptance. Myer said most people didn't know about the Japanese Americans, that this ignorance was the basis of fear about them, and that it was essential for the Nisei and Issei to scatter out over the country. To that end, Myer said, he would oppose making camp life so snug or profitable that the evacuees would become too comfortable to leave.

Total support of this proposal to relocate and disperse was JACL's second key decision. Such a program obviously would have problems in the short run and profound sociological implications in the long term. If the goal of Japanese Americans was assimilation and integration—the absence of which had in large part been responsible for the harshly racist Evacuation order—scattering out into literally hundreds of communities would speed up the process. It was likely that many of the Nisei so dispersed would not return to the West Coast's Oriental ghettos. This was before general awareness of the concept of cultural pluralism, and the prospect of Japanese traditions dying out among the descendants of immigrants posed no particular problem. Such dispersal of population also raised the possibility that JACL chapters as they had been known would, before long, be unnecessary, possibly undesirable and physically difficult to maintain. These prospects did not deter the delegates. They voted to support WRA's program by opening service offices in various parts of the country, and to boost the budget to fifty thousand dollars to expand facilities and increase personnel. Where that money would come from was uncertain.

JACL at the time had only five paid staff members—the two Tajiris and Teiko Ishida in Salt Lake City, Masaoka and Inagaki. Masaoka was spreading himself woefully thin. His Washington base was 1509 22nd Street N.W. In New York he got his mail at 545 West 111th Street. In Chicago he could be reached in care of the American Friends Service Committee at 189 West Madison, and in Philadelphia in care of Bob O'Brien at 1201 Chestnut Street, from which he was running a program to get Nisei students into colleges around the country. Now Masaoka proposed setting up a Resettlement Division headed by Inagaki to supervise field offices which were to be opened in key cities such as Chicago, Denver, Cincinnati and St. Paul. Inagaki's function was to cooperate with WRA and local government and private organizations to find jobs, housing and community acceptance for relocatees.

In addition, Hito Okada was given responsibility for coordinating the activities of chartered chapters. Joe Grant Masaoka was scheduled to come to Salt Lake City from Manzanar to set up an Associated Members Division to enroll individual members in areas where there were no chapters, solicit funds and take on special assignments as the need arose.

Before Myer left, he threw two challenges at JACL. He urged the organization to come up with a program so that no more relocatees moved into any community than it could absorb without problems. "If you are going to live in Chicago," he said, "scatter out. It is going to take guts to do it. It is going to take a great deal of courage for a lot of people to go out and do that sort of thing. But if this generation doesn't do those things now, your next generation is still going to suffer. If we can do it now while the war is going on, then the problems are licked. Due to the need for manpower and womanpower, we're going to get acceptance now that we never got before."

Second, Myer noted a growing generational rift within the camps. Issei resented WRA's decision to limit eligibility for elective offices in camp self-government to citizens. Myer pointed out that most Nisei were young and inexperienced and suggested that they would benefit from Issei participation. "We don't dare have a continued division between the parents and the younger generation in trying to run the government at community centers," he said. "We have to use good judgment in bringing into the community committees a reasonable number of the older group of leaders who really have something to contribute. If we don't, human nature is such that they are going to work in the opposite direction." In short, Myer was asking JACLers not to oppose Issei involvement in camp politics.

On this matter Myer had been overly apprehensive. It was true that Issei were unhappy about being denied an active role in camp government, but that was the result of WRA recognition of the prerogatives of citizenship and not JACL efforts to freeze them out. When WRA modified its rule the Issei moved without friction into camp political activity.

One long conference session was held on JACL's role in the camps. Some, like Gila River under the determined leadership of Nobu Kawai, had established a chapter. But in some other camps there was no such movement. Some former members had lost interest or had become openly hostile to JACL. In many instances JACL leaders who had stepped forward to take charge at first because no one else would, found themselves being condemned as dictators. One widespread criticism was that JACL had not opposed the Evacuation vigorously enough; in extreme cases JACL was condemned for "selling the Japanese communities down the river." Some of the delegates reported the evacuees had no idea what JACL was doing and Masaoka was being criticized for inaction. And there were others who said JACL was losing popular support because it was too "pro-American."

Masaoka responded heatedly:

> Let me say two things. First, regardless of opposition from within or outside the relocation centers, JACL will never take any course but that of pro-America. No matter what it may cost in the way of membership, JACL will never be anything but pro-American and anti-Fascist. This is the only course for us, and I will never permit any policy or program to function in any way opposed to our government as long as I am national secretary. Under no circumstance will we ever tolerate anything less than 100 percent Americanism. We will not compromise our loyalty.
>
> The other matter refers to local chapters and their leaders. In a volunteer system such as ours, these troubles are bound to occur. But, just as in religion, we must have faith in the true principles regardless of the activities of some of the leadership. I have faith that JACL is on the right path and that the path leads to the salvation of our people if they will only follow our leadership.

Oddly enough, very little of this kind of dialogue was reported in *Pacific Citizen.* There simply wasn't space enough in the eight-page tabloid newspaper. JACL's position on the loyalty issue was covered in one paragraph of a roundup story on resolutions passed at the conference: "The resolution declared that the 'Japanese American Citizens League . . . reiterates and underscores . . . its stand on the principles of duty to country and to Americanism is unwavering and holds even greater significance in these times of stress.' "

Even the decision to ask for reinstatement of Selective Service was part of a longer paragraph about various resolutions: "Other resolutions passed at the national meeting included expressions of confidence in the WRA, greetings to Nisei soldiers, commendation to the President of the United States on his selection of liberal personnel in WRA, the voicing of gratitude to religious bodies for their work on behalf of loyal Americans and residents of Japanese ancestry, a request for reclassification of American-born Japanese from their present status in the draft and an appeal for funds for recreational purposes in the centers."

Something of the color and mood of the conference was caught in the "From the Frying Pan" column, part of which is quoted here:

> This is the darndest convention I've ever seen. In fact it isn't a convention—it's an intense, serious, vital series of meetings having to do with the destinies of 110,000 human beings, being conducted on a marathon day-and-night schedule.
>
> Actually, it will be a long time before the exact relationship of this conference to the over-all picture of evacuation, relocation and resettlement can be determined, but certainly it will not be an insignificant role.
>
> Delegates to this conference are so engrossed in their problems that discussions are held all day and half the night—at the conference hall, in restaurants, in hotel rooms, and even in the men's lounge to which all the delegates drifted during a dance given in their honor by a Salt Lake City group.
>
> All this is a healthy sign. If it took December 7 to snatch the swaddling clothes off JACL as some claim, surely a new social consciousness has come over its leaders and the organization has reached adult stature during the tribulations of the past few months.
>
> Most of the leaders are looking forward to a new and perhaps the League's greatest task, from a more practical, mature and reasoned viewpoint than ever before. This was obvious to anyone who attended the conference.
>
> The task is that of individual resettlement of evacuees from the government relocation centers to normal lives in all sections of the

country, not as Japanese Americans but as Americans who will be an integral part of the amalgam in the American melting pot.

The implications of this program are almost terrifying to those who have always sought refuge in either the physical or spiritual Li'l Tokyos. For various reasons there have been little circles of interests and sympathies and social and economic relationships built up on the basis of identical backgrounds. This is to be no more. . . .

Despite the high resolve of the conference, one of the last items for discussion was eminently practical. It had to do with expenses. Hito Okada, with an eye on the anemic treasury, proposed that the delegates or their home chapters foot rail or bus fare and all other costs while traveling, with national JACL paying for room plus meals up to $1.50 per day. But in view of the fact that the evacuees were being paid $16 or $19 a month in the camp jobs, Tatsuo Koda of Ogden moved that national JACL pay all expenses, including those of the guards required for the California and Arizona delegates.

It was past midnight on the seventh day when Kido wrapped up the conference with an entreaty and a warning:

Some of us have to go back to a pretty bad situation, but it is our duty to go back and face the music. I hope it will not be bad music. But as long as we have assumed the responsibility as leaders of the JACL the fact that we may be criticized should not bother us. We have sacrificed enough, but we will be sacrificing more by returning to the centers and assuming all our responsibilities and duties. . . .

The "bad music" Kido feared came sooner than expected. On December 5, less than two weeks after adjournment of the Salt Lake City meeting, a small group of dissidents began what appeared to be a noisy pro-Axis rally at the Manzanar camp. Fred Tayama, who had attended the Salt Lake City meeting, tried to dissuade the demonstrators. That night six masked men invaded Tayama's barracks room and beat him so badly that he had to be hospitalized. Three evacuees were arrested and one of them, believed to be the ringleader, was taken out of the camp and placed in the jail at the nearby town of Independence.

Next morning, a committee called on the project director, Ralph P. Merritt, and demanded the prisoner be returned to the camp. Merritt agreed on the condition that no more demonstrations would be held, order would be maintained until proper hearings were conducted and the men who beat Tayama would surrender. The suspect was returned from Independence that afternoon. On Sunday night, December 6, a group of dissidents armed with clubs invaded the hospital in search of Tayama. Fortunately, he had been spirited into hiding. Another group surrounded the internal security office where Kiyoshi Higashi, a former president of the San Pedro JACL and also a delegate to the Salt Lake City meeting, was in charge. When violence against other JACL leaders was threatened, Merritt called in the military police. A rock-throwing melee followed. When tear gas failed to disperse the dissidents who refused to obey orders to halt, a volley of shots was fired. One youth was killed and several wounded and the demonstrators fled.

Most of the evacuees remained calm during the outbreak but WRA, fearing for the safety of some aggressively pro-American JACL leaders, hurried to move them and their families to the shelter of an abandoned Civilian Conservation Corps camp at nearby Death Valley. Among those who left were Tayama, Joe Grant Masaoka, Tokie Slocum, Togo Tanaka, Tad Uyeno, Tom Imai, Tomomasa Yamasaki and several others.

The timing of the outbreak did not escape the West Coast press. Some editorialists saw the riot as justification for the Evacuation. Others called for early segregation of the loyal from the disloyal. The *Salt Lake Tribune* said: "Ample justification for clearing out Japs from critical Pacific coast areas has been furnished by the Japs themselves." The *San Jose Mercury-Herald* wrote: "These rioters should be separated from those other Japanese who demonstrated pro-American leanings and tried to prevent the Manzanar demonstration." But a letter from Mary Farquharson, Gordon Hirabayashi's friend and adviser, published in the *Seattle Post-Intelligencer,* put the problem in focus: "Instead of justifying mass evacuation I think riots in Japanese camps show that this policy is a serious mistake. The worse you treat people the worse they act and concentration camps might be expected to make the soil fertile for propaganda of a small group of pro-Axis agitators. Of course they ought to be isolated. The exemplary conduct of a very large majority of citizens and aliens (who were never allowed to become citizens) over a period of many years should not be forgotten."

Among the evacuees themselves, WRA's decision to remove some leaders from Manzanar for their own protection stirred new doubts. Prior to the Evacuation, some government spokesmen had declared Japanese Americans were being sent to camps—held in protective custody—to protect them from hoodlums purporting to be patriots. Nisei argued this was faulty logic; the nation had an obligation to defend its law-abiding elements, but not by depriving them of their freedom. In Manzanar, WRA itself seemed to be admitting it could not guarantee the safety of its supporters and again was taking them into protective custody.

Less than two months later violence broke out again. On January 28, 1943, the War Department announced formation of a volunteer all-Nisei combat team, to be followed by restoration of Selective Service for all Nisei. A week later Saburo Kido was attacked by eight men who broke into his Poston barracks apartment. The attack was not unexpected. Guards were posted in the laundry room near Kido's barracks but the men had fallen asleep. The assailants methodically jammed the doors of nearby barracks so neighbors could not come to the rescue, and were in the process of unhinging Kido's door when he awoke. The men rushed in, clubbing him unmercifully around the head and arms as he and his wife, Mine, fought back. The scuffling aroused one of their neighbors, George Imai, who jumped out a window to come to the rescue. The noise also awakened the guards and eight men, ranging in age from eighteen to thirty-seven, were quickly apprehended. A preliminary hearing was held immediately. The men signed confessions and were taken outside the camp and charged with assault and battery with intent to commit grave bodily harm. Kido was hospitalized for three weeks and his hospital stay was extended another three weeks to avoid the possibility of further attack before the red tape was cut and he and his family could move to Salt Lake City.

The worst was not over. On the morning of March 6 at the Jerome camp near Denson, Arkansas, a small group of youths attacked the Reverend John M. Yamazaki, former pastor of the Los Angeles Japanese Episcopal Church. Several hours later they visited the camp hospital and asked to see Dr. Tom Yatabe. As he stepped to the door the gang jumped him. "My glasses flew off and the next thing I knew I was on the floor under a pile of bodies," Yatabe recalled. "A pair of shears was coming down on me and I remember gripping a wrist." That action might have saved his life. Yatabe was hospitalized for nearly a month before he and his family were allowed to leave for Chicago.

These were not the best of days for JACL leaders. Yet, along with the doubts and grief, there were encouraging signs.

XV

Back to the Real World

> January 28 marks the beginning of the end of a most tragic period in the life history of an American race group. It began with the thunder of bombs on a sunny December morning at Pearl Harbor. It will not end until the last person of Japanese ancestry loyal to the United States has been returned to his rightful place in the nation's life. This period saw the temporary forfeiture of certain basic rights of persons who were native-born citizens of this country. And one of these lost privileges was that of participating in the national defense in time of war. . . . Now the months of despair are part of the receding past and the future promises much toward the readjustment and reassimilation of the evacuee group.

The above passage appeared in an editorial Larry Tajiri published in *Pacific Citizen* on February 4, 1943. It was in reference to an Army announcement one week earlier that a special combat regiment of Japanese American volunteers would be formed.

For the Army this was another drastic reversal of the position it had taken after Pearl Harbor. In fact, its stance had been marked by a series of inconsistencies. Even as Nisei were stigmatized by Selective Service as 4-C aliens and some Kibei were being kicked out of the Army as potential security risks for no reason other than race, others were being rushed through the Military Intelligence Language School to serve as translators and interpreters in the Pacific Theater. A Nisei Hawaiian National Guard outfit which had been disarmed after Pearl Harbor was now honing its fighting skills on the mainland as the 100th Battalion, in preparation for combat duty in Europe. General DeWitt had vowed to lock up every last man, woman and child with as little as one-sixteenth Japanese blood, but now the Army was prepared to open its ranks to Nisei volunteers.

It was fitting that the chief spokesman for JACL, which had pleaded for restoration of military obligations, should get first word of the policy change. Some time in mid-January Masaoka was asked to come to the Pentagon office of Assistant Secretary of War McCloy. Inagaki accompanied Masaoka to the meeting with McCloy and his administrative assistant, Colonel William P. Scobey. McCloy explained that a great many persons had vouched for Nisei loyalty, that many Nisei had written to ask for the right to fight for their country and that, confidentially, the War Department was preparing to announce that volunteers would be invited for an all-Nisei regiment-sized combat team. Before long, McCloy went on, it was likely that all Nisei males would become subject to the draft.

Masaoka's elation was tempered by reservations about a segregated unit and the call for volunteers rather than an immediate restoration of Selective Service. Scobey convinced Masaoka and Inagaki that a few thousand Nisei scattered among millions of American servicemen would be lost from view and it was to their advantage to fight together. And volunteers were being invited initially as the fastest way of getting the unit together. In the euphoria of the moment both Nisei volunteered on the spot. Scobey, half in jest, said he supposed they wanted commissions and a soft Pentagon assignment. But Masaoka was in no mood for joking. "No, sir," he replied. "We've been pleading for an opportunity to fight and now that we have it, we don't expect any favors."

But not all government officials supported McCloy's decision. Edward J. Ennis, director of Enemy Alien Control in the Justice Department, who later was to assist JACL in winning passage of the Evacuation Claims Act and the law that enabled Issei to gain United States citizenship, was one of those opposed for reasons that had nothing to do with loyalty. In an interview in 1978 with Harry Takagi, he explained:

> If I had been interned in my country, I certainly would not volunteer for a special combat team. I'm not sure I would serve at all

> if I had to serve from a detention camp. But if I had to serve, I would want to take my chances like everybody else and not in a special combat team. I feared that if young Japanese American men went into a combat team, they would suffer the highest casualties of the war because they would be put by their white officers into especially dangerous combat missions and I thought they would be over-patriotic and suffer undue casualties. But they felt differently, and as it turned out, we were both right. I don't think any group should have to pay that special price, but I want to confess I was against that even though it may have turned out to be a good thing for them to do.

Masaoka and Inagaki were back in Salt Lake City, leaving the Washington duties to Joe Tooru Kanazawa, when Secretary of War Stimson released a statement which said in part:

> The War Department announced today that plans have been completed for admission of a substantial number of American citizens of Japanese ancestry to the Army of the United States. This action was taken following study by the War Department of many earnest requests by loyal American citizens of Japanese extraction for the organization of a special unit of the Army in which they could have their share in the fight against the nation's enemies.

The reference to "requests" for "a special unit" was not totally accurate. Almost from the moment of the announcement questions were raised about the decision to form a segregated unit, which appeared to be exactly what Nisei were trying to avoid. Before long Stimson felt the need to issue a somewhat wordy clarifying statement:

> It is only because the War Department desires to aid the loyal American-Japanese that a separate unit is being formed. Millions of people are not familiar with the American-Japanese. By forming an all American-Japanese combat team on a voluntary basis, the American people will be presented with the incontrovertible fact that there are loyal American-Japanese who are willing to fight for the United States. If the volunteers were spread throughout the Army their enlistment would attract little attention but the formation of an all American-Japanese combat team composed entirely of volunteers will help tremendously to convince those who oppose the American-Japanese. It is hoped that the American-Japanese combat team will fight with and as a part of a Caucasian force. . . .

Stimson's announcement was followed by a ringing statement of support from President Roosevelt who, less than a year earlier, had signed Executive Order 9066 authorizing the Army to lock up Japanese American citizens and aliens alike. In a letter to Stimson, Roosevelt wrote:

> The proposal of the War Department to organize a combat team consisting of loyal American citizens of Japanese descent has my full approval. The new combat team will add to the nearly 5,000 loyal Americans of Japanese ancestry who are already serving the armed forces of our country.
>
> This is a natural and logical step toward the reinstitution of the Selective Service procedures which were temporarily disrupted by the evacuation from the West Coast.
>
> No loyal citizen of the United States should be denied the democratic right to exercise the responsibilities of citizenship, regardless of ancestry. The principle on which this country was founded and by which it has always been governed is that Americanism is a matter of the mind and heart; Americanism is not, and never was, a matter of race or ancestry. A good American is one who is loyal to this country and to our creed of liberty and democracy. Every loyal American citizen should be given the opportunity to serve this country wherever his skills will make the greatest contribution—whether it be in the ranks of our armed forces, war production, agriculture, government service, or other work essential to the war effort.
>
> I am glad to observe that the War Department, the Navy Department, the War Manpower Commission, the Department of Justice, and the War Relocation Authority are collaborating in a program which will assure the opportunity for all loyal Americans, including Americans of Japanese ancestry, to serve their country at a time when the fullest and wisest use of our manpower is all-important to the war effort.

The Army revealed that approximately five thousand men would be inducted, among them fifteen hundred from Hawaii. Some three hundred Nisei already in uniform were dispatched to Camp Shelby, Mississippi, as an advanced cadre. Four-man recruiting teams in the charge of a Caucasian officer and including a Nisei noncom were sent to the camps. Masaoka confirmed his desire to be the first volunteer by sending a telegram to Stimson from Salt Lake City. Other Nisei with reserve commissions, including Captain Walter Tsukamoto, were quick to volunteer and before long they began to get their orders to report for duty.

The men anticipating military service had to make preparations in their personal lives and Mike Masaoka was no exception. He and Etsu Mineta of San Jose, whom he had met at the JACL convention in Monterey the summer of 1941, were planning to be married but hadn't set a date. Etsu had been evacuated to Heart Mountain, Wyoming, with her parents, Kunisaku and Kane Mineta, and brothers, Albert and Norman. When Masaoka had something urgent to discuss with her, like a wedding date, he would send a telegram telling her when he would telephone. Usually it was late at night. Etsu would trudge through the frigid dark to the camp administration building where the only telephones were available and await his call.

Originally they had planned to be married at Heart Mountain but reports of rising feeling against Masaoka made it prudent to shift the site to Salt Lake City. They set the date for February 14. Ten days before that date Etsu bade good-bye to her family and set out alone to begin a new life. The train took her north to Billings and then Butte, Montana, where she had an all-day wait for the connecting train to Salt Lake City. The train was ten hours late and Etsu reached her destination late at night. There was no one at the station and she had never been in Salt Lake before. In desperation she telephoned the JACL office. Larry Tajiri was still working and he picked her up.

For the ceremony Etsu wore a powder-blue suit which she had taken to camp along with rough outdoor clothing because her father had suggested she ought to have at least one presentable outfit for dress-up occasions. Mike's brother Ben, who was to die a soldier's death in France, was best man. Hito Okada's wife, Hana, who had never met Etsu before the occasion, was matron of honor. Okada sang and Tajiri gave the bride away. In deference to Issei custom, which required *baishakunin* go-betweens representing the two families, Henry Mitarai stood up for the Minetas and George Inagaki for the Masaokas. When it was time for Mike to report for military training, his bride went to Chicago to move in with her sister, Helen, who was working as a secretary. Teiko Ishida assumed Masaoka's JACL duties as acting national secretary.

Meanwhile, it was becoming apparent that miscalculation, ignorance and just plain blundering surrounding the call for volunteers was creating great confusion in the camps. Unexpected hostility quickly developed toward the complex program which the government, in all innocence, had drafted with every good intention of helping the evacuees.

The program's first step was the call for loyal volunteers for military service with the understanding that before long the Nisei would be subject to Selective Service. Loyalty was to be determined by questionnaires, in itself a dubious tactic but perhaps the best that could be devised in view of the absence of more meaningful tests. A two-page questionnaire was put together by the Army. Aside from the inherent limitations of any questionnaire, it was adequate for its purpose. But a major tactical error was made by WRA when it decided to piggyback on the Army's questionnaire to expedite the government's second step, which was to step up relocation of the evacuees. To speed screening for loyalty, which had been a bottleneck from the beginning, WRA retitled the Army's questionnaire "Application for Leave Clearance," and instructed all men and women over seventeen years of age, citizens and aliens, to complete it.

Most of the questions were innocuous and offended no one. But two proved to be booby traps when applied to Nisei other than males of military age. The problem could have been detected by any knowledgeable Nisei or, for that matter, anyone familiar with the Japanese American community. Unfortunately, neither Masaoka nor any other Nisei was consulted. Myer later called this oversight "a bad mistake."

The faulty questions were 27 and 28. Number 27 asked: "Are you willing to serve in the armed forces of the United States on combat duty, wherever ordered?" Number 28 asked: "Will you swear unqualified allegiance to the United States of America and faithfully defend the United States from any or all attack by foreign or domestic forces, and foreswear any form of allegiance or obedience to the Japanese emperor, to any other foreign government, power or organization?"

The title was the first problem. Understandably, many Issei assumed that the questionnaire was the beginning of a movement to force them out of the camps against their will. Fearful of hostility on the outside, uncertain of their ability to support themselves, they had no desire to apply for leave clearance. Question 27 posed a second problem: Issei, most of whom were in middle age, and women had no intention of agreeing to serve in the armed forces on combat duty. Some Nisei also found Question 27 troubling; they would be proud to serve, but only if their country recognized their rights as citizens.

But Question 28 concealed even more profound difficulties. Some Nisei contended that to foreswear allegiance to the emperor of Japan would be an admission that such allegiance existed where in fact none did. And Issei, who had been denied American citizenship, were being asked to renounce the only affiliation they had.

When the unfairness of Question 28 was realized, WRA rephrased it to read: "Will you swear to abide by the laws of the United States and to take no action which would in any way interfere with the war effort of the United States?" This was widely acceptable, but the damage had been done by the same incredible lack of understanding and sensitivity that had characterized so much of government policy toward the Japanese American minority.

The miscalculation referred to above had to do with the effect on morale of nearly a year of confinement—for no reason other than race—in what amounted to prison camps. In the days and weeks immediately after the outbreak of war, it could safely be said that the vast majority of Japanese Americans were solidly loyal to the United States. Noncitizens, who were stigmatized as "enemy aliens," at worst were passively sympathetic toward Japan; active disloyalty to the land in which they had lived for so long was far from their minds. But if the United States government had set out deliberately to alienate this ethnic minority, it could not have done a more effective job. Instead of recognizing and encouraging loyalty, it was government policy to hold Japanese Americans suspect. Instead of judging them as individuals, the Army with President Roosevelt's approval appeared to be condemning them as a group. The militant patriotism expressed through JACL won scant recognition and support in the white community, diminishing the organization's stature among the discouraged and disillusioned. In retrospect, the wonder is that the overwhelming majority of Japanese Americans remained steadfastly loyal.

But for some Nisei, rejection by the only country they had known was a terrible test of fealty. They had no sympathy, affection or loyalty for Japan, but they deeply resented the way their own country had treated them. The call for military volunteers under such circumstances and the bungled loyalty questionnaires set off enormous pressures in the camps. Some of the resentment exploded in violence against JACL leaders like Tayama, Kido, Yatabe and others. Some of it was manifested in gangs that tried to intimidate the aggressively loyal. Old friendships broke up. Some parents forbade sons to volunteer and others urged them to be Americans and act on the dictates of conscience. In some camps dissidents pressured parents to prevent their sons from volunteering. Many youths became confused and sought the counsel of older Nisei. Scores made their way to Clarence Arai's barracks apartment in the Minidoka camp, often quietly late at night, and most went away moved by his uncomplicated patriotism and chagrin that his hypertension would keep him out of uniform. No doubt the leadership of JACLers like Arai and Jimmie Sakamoto had much to do with more than three hundred men volunteering from Minidoka—19 percent of those eligible—the largest number in any of the camps. Among the Minidoka volunteers were the three Yanagimachi brothers, Harry, Frank and Bill; the three Onodera brothers, Ko, Kaun and Satoru; and the four Sakura brothers, Chet, Howard, Kenny and Ted. Chet, the father of three children, said he and his brothers had not lost faith in America and were ready to discharge their responsibilities "to the United States, to our children, and to all future Japanese Americans." In all, more than a thousand Nisei stepped forward from behind the barbed wire of the camps to offer themselves for military service, swearing allegiance to the government that had imprisoned them, vowing to fight for the freedom that had been denied them. Their ranks were bolstered by hundreds of volunteers from outside the camps, including five Masaoka brothers—Ben Frank, Mike, Ike, Henry and Tadashi.

Even so, the response from mainland Nisei was short of expectations and reflected as nothing else could the demoralization resulting from the Evacuation. In Hawaii, where there had been no mass incarceration, the Army had intended to accept fifteen hundred volunteers. More than ten thousand responded. To make up for the shortage from the mainland, twenty-six hundred Hawaii Nisei were enrolled for the first contingent and were given a rousing waterfront send-off as they set sail for training on the mainland.

Ironically, evacuees opposing military service found themselves in strange company. Various groups hostile to the Japanese Americans opposed opening the Army to their enlistment for the same reason that the JACL convention in Salt Lake City sought the right to serve; it would be difficult to deny full citizens' rights to people who had fought for their country. Officials of the Native Sons spoke out in opposition to giving Nisei an active part in the war. In the Idaho state legislature a joint memorial was introduced demanding immediate discharge of all Nisei in service. The Oregon state senate voted 16 to 14 in favor of barring Nisei from the armed forces and 21 to 9 to deport all Japanese Americans at war's end. General DeWitt added his voice to the hysterical opposition at a House subcommittee hearing in San Francisco. Speaking against permitting the evacuees to return to the West Coast, DeWitt declared "a Jap's a Jap" and "it makes no difference whether he is an American citizen or not." He went on to say: "I don't want any of them. We got them out. They were a dangerous element. The West Coast is too vital and too vulnerable to take chances."

But DeWitt quickly learned the War Department had changed and he was out of step. Within two weeks after his testimony DeWitt—presumably under instructions from Washington—issued an order permitting uniformed United States soldiers of Japanese ancestry on furlough to enter and travel within the evacuated zones. And a month later DeWitt was replaced as chief of the Western Defense Command by Lieutenant General Delos C. Emmons, whose tenure as commander of the Hawaiian Defense Area had been marked by a fair and evenhanded policy toward the territory's population of Japanese origin. DeWitt was transferred to a desk job in Washington.

In all the camps volunteers were feted and given going-away parties, often organized by JACL stalwarts. But despite these gestures of good faith, despite the unsavory character of those opposing military service for Nisei, some dissidents in the camps were so persistent that a few volunteers had to go to extraordinary lengths to avoid harassment. Take the experience of S. Neil Fujita, a young Hawaiian-born art student who had been among the first to volunteer at Heart Mountain. When the annoyance became more than he wanted to put up with, Fujita received permission to move out to nearby Cody and take a job as a handyman until he was called up. What he encountered there was good for both him and some of the people of Cody who hadn't exactly been friendly toward the evacuees. Fujita had reciprocated the dislike but began to wonder whether he was wrong when a barber, who had turned him down as a customer, quietly invited him to come back to the shop by the rear door after closing hours. One day Fujita felt ill and stayed in bed. His employer's mother, who hadn't paid him much attention, came to his room to see whether he needed anything. Then she noticed the volumes on a makeshift bookshelf near Fujita's bed—the works of Voltaire, Kant, William Blake, Friedrich Wilhelm Nietzsche.

"Do you really read these?" she asked in amazement.

"Yes, ma'am," Fujita replied, "whenever I can find time." Then he explained that before he left home one of the last things his mother did was urge him to read the books she had learned to love in school. Fujita told the woman he had been born on a Hawaiian sugar plantation where his father was employed. At eighteen Neil figured there was more to life than laboring in the cane fields and decided to go to the mainland. Despite her modest station, Neil's mother was an educated person. She had read the European classics in translation in Japan, but her English was inadequate to communicate on an intellectual level with her son. She hoped to bridge the gap by sharing with Neil the books that had been so much a part of her youth.

That was a somewhat different picture of the evacuees than the Cody woman had held. By the time Fujita returned to the camp to prepare for induction, he and the elderly woman were friends, each with a greater respect for and understanding of the other. Fujita went on to become an outstanding graphic designer with some of the nation's top corporations as his clients.

Largely because of the snafued loyalty questionnaire, about seventy-six hundred evacuees—11 percent of those required to register—either refused to turn in their questionnaires or gave negative or qualified answers to the loyalty questions. Some three thousand of them, about 38 percent, were in the Tule Lake camp where the agitation was fueled by well-organized dissidents. WRA interpreted this response correctly as representing individuals who were weary of the battle against discrimination, unhappy with the way they had been treated in the Evacuation, angry with the government and discouraged about their future in the United States, or who felt sincerely that life in Japan held greater promise. In other words, they were fed up with America; the times were such that the loyalty which should have come naturally took determination and effort to maintain.

And while it was the dissidents who attracted the attention, those who retained the faith were in the overwhelming majority. As a consequence of the registration program, WRA announced that some fifteen thousand evacuees had filed for permission to relocate in interior areas. The loyalty check, aimed at reassuring those nervous about having "Japs" enter their communities, sped the clearance process but the greater problem was locating housing and jobs. To back up WRA's efforts, JACL sent Joe Grant Masaoka to open a service office in Denver. Earl Tanbara, who with his wife Ruth had evacuated voluntarily to St. Paul, became JACL's representative in the Twin Cities. In Chicago, the office opened by George Inagaki needed a director after Inagaki enlisted. Dr. Tom Yatabe, recovering from the effects of the beating he suffered at the Jerome camp, had barely checked into the Brethren's Hostel in Chicago when he received a telegram from Kido asking him to take over the JACL office. Yatabe was forty-six years old with a family to support, and hoped to re-establish a dental practice. But he found it impossible to refuse Kido. T. Scott Miyakawa and Peter Aoki worked out of the New York office.

Those most anxious to leave the camps were the aggressive young adults with marketable skills, angered by the pointlessness of camp life and anxious to resume life as free Americans. At first, some had been torn between the need to seek freedom and a sense of obligation to remain with the group. But as the threat to the group dwindled—the Evacuation order itself was the primary threat—individual concerns became paramount.

Take the experience of Martha Kaihatsu, now a successful New York public-relations consultant, who had been an active member of the Los Angeles Li'l Tokyo community before the war. As busy as she kept herself, she resented the strictures of ghetto existence. She saw the Evacuation as an opportunity to break out of the mold, but quickly gauged camp life as an even more repressive extension of what she had known. But it could be made a stepping-stone to opportunity in the free world away from the West Coast. She was among the early applicants for leave clearance. While waiting for approval she ordered some material through a mail order service and she and a friend, Florence Uba, cut out and sewed a suit. It was the only decent outfit she had when she set out alone for Chicago. She worked for six weeks as a file clerk until the *Chicago Sun* hired her for its church-news department. Later she moved into the *Sun*'s advertising department where she developed the skills that enabled her to make good in New York. She never had any desire to return to California.

In his *Pacific Citizen* column, "Whistling in the Dark," Kenny Murase revealed his thought about relocation. When he left Poston, he wrote:

> I hadn't the least notion of what I would be running into. All I knew was that I was pretty scared to face the world outside; for even then stories were circulating about students being mobbed and beaten and chased out of certain communities. Of course I didn't want to leave. It wasn't just that I was afraid of going to a strange and distant city, but there was something soul-satisfying about camp which I had never experienced before, and this was probably true with others too—for the first time in our lives we were doing the kind of work we really wanted to do. We occupied some sort of position where we could order others around, and we got a pretty big sense of self-importance which made us feel good, and, of course, we hated to let it go.
>
> But to me it seemed that anyone with a little reasoning could see that the whole program of the relocation centers was built on a foundation that was artificial, and therefore weak and false. It was emergency and makeshift, with no long-range planning, and therefore impossible to maintain for any length of time. Then the fact that students and other individuals were being released seemed to indicate that a process was begun which was bound to be stepped up as conditions became more favorable. So if someone at that time had the choice of leaving or not leaving, the simple force of logic left no alternative but to leave.

Murase went on to deplore the sensationalized stories of Nisei being harassed and related all the good things that were happening to those who had resettled in Philadelphia. He wrote of two Nisei engineers working in a big aircraft factory, of prominent members of the community inviting relocatees to their country estates, of a Nisei and a Chinese teaming up to visit churches speaking about tolerance. The real America, he was saying, lay east of the Sierras. The Nisei were discovering America and America was discovering the Nisei.

Meanwhile, as he prepared for induction, Masaoka issued a long memo to JACL leaders outlining the organization's goals. The primary objective was "restoration of every citizenship right and privilege" to loyal Japanese Americans. These would include:

Reinstitution of Selective Service on the same basis as for other Americans; equal treatment and opportunities for advancement within the Army; opening up of the service to Nisei women.

Freedom of movement on the same basis as for other Americans, including return to the Pacific Coast, and revocation of discriminatory "contraband" regulations.

Equal opportunities for employment in defense industries and government service and for membership in trade unions.

Elimination of unwarranted government supervision of Japanese Americans as a class.

Legal vindication in the courts in the Evacuation test cases and the Native Sons' efforts to strip Nisei of their citizenship. Defeat of legislation predicated on race.

Retraction and, to whatever extent possible, elimination of lies, rumors and racially discriminatory treatment in the media.

Speeding of the federal resettlement program with decent wages and working and living conditions. Government travel subsidies for persons leaving relocation centers.

Postwar planning to avoid undue movement, sacrifice and hardship.

"Friendly alien" status for noncitizens of Japanese ancestry loyal to the United States; legislation enabling loyal aliens of Asian ancestry to enlist in the armed forces and to become naturalized citizens.

Kido's comments in "Timely Topics," his *Pacific Citizen* column, about the impact camp life had on the evacuees, were perceptive:

> One year of center life has brought about a great change in the people's minds and attitudes. Already there are a certain number who feel that they will remain in the centers for the duration regardless of what attractions are offered or exist on the outside. The fear of public reaction to unfavorable war news; the publicized high cost of living, fear of racial antagonism and other matters that must be considered when living in the free zone make

> the center more attractive. If another year passes by, there will be a larger number who will lose the initiative or the desire to relocate. . . .
>
> Once a group which had established a record of keeping off the relief rolls is taught the easy way of life by becoming wards of the government, the pride which kept them away from charity is gone. The attitude that it is the obligation of the government to feed and look after them is engendered. When 110,000 people are placed in the same class at one time, no one feels the stigma.

The truth was that the federal government had indeed forcibly made the Japanese Americans as a group its wards. No charity was involved and the objects of the government's meager largesse would have preferred not to have to accept it. But Kido was right in becoming concerned about the deteriorating independence in many members of a once proud people.

XVI

The Turning Tide

One day early in June, 1943, several men hammered at the door of apartment 5 in the run-down building at 1324 Fourteenth Street N.W. in Washington, D.C. The apartment was occupied by Emilie Aldridge Kanazawa, whose husband, Joe Tooru Kanazawa, had resigned his job with JACL a few weeks earlier and enlisted in the Army at age thirty-five. Kanazawa, who had been struggling to make a living as a free-lance writer in New York after leaving Seattle, had moved to Washington to work for JACL shortly after Mike Masaoka arrived. His pay was seventy five dollars a month. Since JACL had no office as such and Masaoka himself was entering military service, his files were stored in the Kanazawa apartment.

The strangers identified themselves as members of the staff of the House Un-American Activities Committee. It was better known as the Dies Committee for its chairman, Congressman Martin Dies, a Texas Democrat. Over Emilie Kanazawa's protests they seized the JACL files and left. Those records were never recovered.

The Dies Committee had established a reputation as an overzealous, headline-seeking, witch-hunting panel intent on finding Communists under every bed. But when the Soviet Union and the United States became allies in the war against the Axis powers, Dies had to look for other goblins. A subcommittee headed by John M. Costello, a California Democrat, located an easy and made-to-order target in the Japanese Americans and the WRA, which he saw as a bunch of fuzzy-headed liberal New Deal bureaucrats pampering disloyal "Japs."

The same week that JACL's records were seized in Washington, Costello was holding hearings in Los Angeles with handpicked witnesses testifying that the federal government was guilty of mishandling dangerous Japanese Americans who should not be permitted to return to the West Coast now or, presumably, ever. Los Angeles Mayor Fletcher Bowron was one of the witnesses. He testified that Patrick Okura, former member of the Los Angeles Civil Service Commission, had been investigated by his police department and was considered "the most dangerous Japanese American in the country." Bowron went on to say Okura was high on a Japanese government exchange list, and that the federal government had foolishly permitted him to move to the Midwest. If Bowron knew it, he did not say Okura was employed at Boys Town, Nebraska.

Bowron also fingered Miya Sannomiya Kikuchi as a dangerous person who had been released from the Manzanar camp to go on a lecture tour under auspices of the International YWCA. The Costello subcommittee's performance was so blatantly prejudiced that Chester Rowell of the *San Francisco Chronicle* was moved to write that the "investigation" had turned up testimony of which "not one word would even be admitted or heard by any judicial or quasi-judicial body in existence."

That didn't discourage sensationalized coverage of the hearings, particularly in the Hearst newspapers and the *Los Angeles Times.* Their reportage out of Washington was particularly strident. Robert E. Stripling, the Dies Committee's chief investigator, and J. B. Mathews, committee counsel, fed a steady stream of charges to Ray Richards, Hearst correspondent, and Warren B. Frances of the *Times'* Washington bureau, and their editors published the stories without verifying the allegations. For example, the *Times* should have known better than to use a story saying the Dies Committee was checking the possibility that *Pacific Citizen* was a Communist front. The *Times* quoted Stripling as saying the tone of the editorials in the Japanese American press "is very much like the line followed by the Communists." The Hearst papers said Stripling had found expressions like "not men of good will," and "filled with animal hates and tribal fears" in a column titled "Martin Dies, Demagogue," written by Tajiri.

According to reporter Richards, Stripling charged that these phrases represented "Communist terminology."

It soon became apparent, however, that in hearings scheduled in Washington the Dies Committee intended to discredit WRA with the aid of the papers seized in the raid on Kanazawa's apartment. Stripling's strategy was to depict JACL as a dangerous, un-American organization, and then to show that JACL through Masaoka wielded undue influence over WRA. But the strategy failed because he couldn't prove his thesis. Even before the hearings opened Stripling told the press he had JACL records showing a "secret meeting" was held in Washington on May 22, 1943, and "secret" government documents had been uncovered in JACL files. As it turned out the sinister "secret meeting" had been a public gathering for JACL members and friends. A detailed account of what had transpired—it was only a little less dull than most JACL meetings—had been published in *Pacific Citizen.* And most of the "secret documents" turned out to be policy directives WRA had circulated widely.

Despite the publicity, only a handful of spectators showed up when the hearings were opened. Masaoka and Kanazawa were summoned from Camp Shelby, where they were undergoing basic training, to be quizzed about their allegedly subversive activities. The most potentially damaging charge, if it could be proved, was that Masaoka was "dictating" WRA policy. The fact was that in his reports to JACL headquarters Masaoka had written that Dillon Myer "and his staff deal with me on the same basis of confidence and mutual trust as they do among themselves," and "I have been permitted to sit down and discuss every major policy before it was finally passed on." When Myer was called to the stand, he denied Masaoka wielded the kind of influence indicated by the quoted passages. Masaoka did indeed have a close working relationship with WRA officials and both sides floated many trial balloons in their discussions. It was ridiculous to read sinister motives into these discussions and to contend that Masaoka was dominating WRA policy. When asked about his activities, Masaoka declared that he did indeed represent JACL in Washington, and that as a citizen in a democracy it was his right and privilege to contact public officials about policy concerning his constituents. "We are living in a democracy," he asserted. "This isn't Japan."

The most telling testimony was presented by Myer, who charged that the Dies Committee for eight weeks had conducted its investigation

> in such a manner as to achieve publicity by sensational statements based on half-truths, exaggerations and falsehoods; statements of witnesses were released to the public without verification of their accuracy, thus giving nation-wide publicity to many distortions and downright untruths. This practice fostered public feeling of mistrust, suspicion and hatred that has had the effect of providing the enemy with material which can be used to convince the Orient's peoples that the United States is undemocratic and fighting a racial war.
>
> The Dies Committee's procedure is undermining the unity of the American people and betraying the democratic objectives which this nation and her allies are fighting to preserve. The grave international implications of WRA's program demand that it be approached thoughtfully and soberly and with maturity, and public statements concerning it should be made only after thorough understanding of the facts.

Point by point Myer challenged the Dies Committee to prove the loose charges it had circulated, and portions of which the press had printed. No, he said, "known saboteurs" were not being released from WRA camps. No, WRA wasn't providing the evacuees with liquor or overwhelming them with rationed luxuries. No, WRA had not given JACL "confidential" information not available to others. Finally, Myer complained that his agency's offer to cooperate with Dies Committee investigators in uncovering the facts had never been acknowledged. After three days subcommittee chairman Costello suddenly called off the investigation.

Larry Tajiri, who was in Washington on the possibility of testifying about *Pacific Citizen*'s activities, wrote: "Despite sensational advance publicity, the hearings failed to produce any evidence to substantiate charges made publicly of mass disloyalty, rampant subversiveness, coddling and pampering of evacuees in relocation centers, and JACL domination of WRA policy."

Kido commented: "This investigation, and its sudden abandonment, is tantamount to complete exoneration of our organization, but unfortunately that fact will not be publicized as widely as the wild stories from Dies Committee sources that were splashed on the front pages of the more sensational newspapers in various parts of the country."

In retrospect, it is apparent that the Dies hearings fiasco confirmed the turning of the tide for Japanese Americans which began with the reopening of military service six months earlier. The Dies Committee had promised so much that would discredit the Japanese Americans; when it failed to do so the hearings provided Myer with a forum in which he could refute distortions and plead for understanding and justice. Further, in attesting to the loyalty of the vast majority of Japanese Americans, Myer also acknowledged the presence of disruptive elements which, he said, would be segregated from the loyal. Only an overwhelming sense of compassion had prevented Myer from taking the step earlier. No one knew better than he that evacuee loyalty could not be measured in terms of simple black and white. But it was obvious that some sort of segregation policy had to be undertaken. In fact, the government's alleged inability to separate the sheep from the goats had been cited as one of the reasons that made evacuation necessary. *Pacific Citizen* observed editorially:

> The policy of segregating the bad apples from the good within the WRA's 10 barrels of humanity is in accord with a principle advocated for some time previously by the Pacific Citizen. There can be no doubt of the feasibility or the necessity of the program since there has been ample evidence of hindrance to good project administration and advancement of WRA policy through proselytizing, coercion, intimidation and even violence instigated by small groups wielding influence far out of proportion to their number.
>
> The manner in which the individuals to be segregated will be determined has not been revealed. With some persons there will be no question whatsoever, for long prior to announcement of this policy the WRA has been placing chronic troublemakers in isolation centers. With others who have for various personal and valid reasons asked for repatriation to Japan, there is no issue. In fact, this class of people may well welcome an opportunity to mingle with those of similar sentiments where they will not be subjected to the constant and, to them, objectionable demonstrations of Americanism which have been made a part of center life by the pro-American majority.
>
> It remains to be seen what course of action will be taken with what might be called the borderline cases where there is reasonable doubt. Contrary to the glib assertions of partisan sideliners, the problem is tangled with many ramifications which become

> increasingly obvious the closer one approaches. It may be expected that the WRA's liberal, understanding and American outlook—not to be confused with the "coddling" and "social theorist" tactics of which the agency wrongfully has been accused—will prevail to provide the maximum of justice compatible with the national welfare. . . .
>
> In short, it means that removal of the disloyal from the centers indicates automatically that those remaining are loyal, and deserving therefore of restoration of their abridged rights. Logically, if we are to maintain American principles, segregation means that those given a clean bill of health must be accepted as loyal Americans, unstigmatized by any previous state of being. The very fact that they have undergone, and passed, a test of loyalty should give them a distinction over other Americans who have not been questioned. . . .

The troubles of Japanese Americans were far from over. But the outlook was far brighter than it had been just months earlier. Without delay the Women's Army Corps was opened to Nisei girls, and shortly afterward Selective Service responsibility was restored.

Meanwhile, a WRA program under the direction of Thomas W. Holland redoubled its efforts to find employment in interior America for the evacuees. Holland had joined WRA while Eisenhower was director and his report about miserable camp conditions had persuaded Myer that resettlement back into normal life must be pushed with all possible dispatch. Holland had been the chief architect of a curious program under which, in the fall of 1942, ten thousand men who had just been confined in the camps were released in the Intermountain area to help farmers willing to swallow their prejudices if only they could get the sugar beets harvested. The harvest hands left the camps on temporary permits requiring them to return when the harvest was completed. There were virtually no incidents and the volunteers were enormously successful in proving to residents of rural areas that they weren't spies and saboteurs.

One of Holland's problems was that Japanese American farmers, who had been criticized on the West Coast for living in substandard housing and working for substandard wages, were accustomed to better pay and living quarters than hired hands were getting in other parts of the country. Secretary of the Interior Harold L. Ickes hired two Nisei from the Poston camp, Fred and Roy Kobayashi, to work on his Maryland farm but found to his astonishment they expected one hundred dollars a month plus room and board. The going wage in the area was fifty dollars a month with neither room nor board. Fred Kobayashi left after a few months to become a physical education instructor at the University of Maryland; in instance after instance employers found the Nisei were overqualified for the work for which they were hired. Holland himself had a happier experience. One day while visiting Manzanar he saw Jack Hirose painting signs. Holland's wife was a display artist and he figured she could help both herself and the relocation program by hiring Hirose. He was given a room in the Holland home, was soon accepted as one of the family and settled permanently in the Washington area.

JACL also diverted much of its meager resources into assisting the relocatees. Teiko Ishida moved from Salt Lake City to open a New York office and conduct a public-relations campaign to break down barriers in the way of jobs and housing. She was responsible for a five-thousand-dollar grant from the Carnegie Endowment to finance two speaking tours by Dr. Yatabe. Accompanied by Ruby Yoshino, now Ruby Schaar, a contralto of note, Yatabe spoke in dozens of cities between Boston and Washington. He visited churches, schools, service clubs and community groups, speaking before hundreds of persons who had never seen a Japanese American before. The two appeared before as many as five audiences in one day in Philadelphia, with Ruby's vocal performances preceding Yatabe's moving account of the frustrations, sacrifices, hopes and aspirations of America's Japanese minority. The other tour took Yatabe through the Midwest, this time accompanied by his young son Dudley, who was an accomplished pianist and boy soprano.

Joe Grant Masaoka, a tenacious bulldog of a fighter, worked the mountain states out of his Denver JACL office. One of his targets was Dr. John R. Lechner, a California free-lance demagogue who had become a highly vocal foe of the Japanese Americans after they rejected his proposal, immediately after Pearl Harbor, that he work for them for a fee. When Lechner came to Colorado to ply his trade, Joe Masaoka trailed him to his speaking engagements, asking pointed questions and challenging him to debate. Masaoka rounded up enough support to block an anti-alien land-law bill in the state legislature.

The public-relations effort was helped along immensely by the formation of a committee of prominent Americans called National JACL Sponsors. Some seventy distinguished business, labor, religious and educational leaders endorsed JACL and thereby attested to their faith in the loyalty of Nisei. Members of the committee that lined up the sponsors were Annie Clo Watson, executive secretary of the International Institute in San Francisco; Reed Lewis, director of the Common Council for American Unity; Clarence E. Pickett of the American Friends Service Committee; and Roger Baldwin, national director of the American Civil Liberties Union. Teiko Ishida, T. Scott Miyakawa, Peter Aoki and others worked with the committee. Miyakawa said not long before his death: "I still remember working with such friends as Pearl Buck, John Thomas of the Baptist Home Mission Society, Bishop Henry St. George Tucker and Roger Baldwin in trying to list people whom we in JACL wanted to ask to serve as sponsors." A longtime member of the Boston University sociology faculty, Dr. Miyakawa was the first director of JACL's Japanese American Research (Issei history) Project at the University of California at Los Angeles.

Among the better-known sponsors, who were from twenty-five states, were: Eugene E. Barnett, general secretary of the International YMCA; Dr. David De Sola Pool of the Spanish and Portuguese Synagogue, New York; Dr. Monroe Deutsch, provost at the University of California; Dorothy Canfield Fisher, author; Dr. Harry Emerson Fosdick, pastor of Riverside Church, New York; Arthur Gaeth, vice-president of the Intermountain Radio Network, Salt Lake City; Benjamin H. Kizer, chairman of the Washington State Planning Commission; Dr. Reinhold Niebuhr of Union Theological Seminary; James G. Patton, president of the National Farmers Union; Dr. Homer P. Rainey, president of the University of Texas; Charles S. Sprague, former governor of Oregon and editor of the *Oregon Statesman;* Monroe Sweetland of the American Red Cross; Norman Thomas of the Postwar World Council; Richard J. Walsh, president of the John Day Publishing Company; Dr. Ray Lyman Wilbur of Stanford University. Such sponsors gave JACL a credibility that was badly needed and helped open doors to many important offices.

On a different level, JACL about this time launched another program that proved extremely valuable in helping the Nisei to re-establish their economic base. It was the National JACL Credit Union, the idea for which was born as a result of a drive Hito

Okada made to an isolated little valley fifty or sixty miles east of Salt Lake City. Just ahead of the Evacuation, Fred Wada, a Southern Californian, had moved into the area called Keatley with about a dozen families. They rented land from a rancher named George Fisher and planned to raise vegetables in what they called the Food for Freedom project. The welcome they received wasn't exactly warm. A town meeting was called to determine whether "the Japs" would be allowed to stay. Wada made an impassioned plea for justice and fair play that swayed the ranchers in his favor and his colony settled down and produced a vast amount of food in an area that had been little more than hay and grazing land. Okada had visited Wada and on his way home he saw a small sawmill. Okada had been in the lumber-exporting business in Portland and was struck by the possibility of starting his own sawmill. He wrote to the U.S. Forest Service for booklets on lumbering which he received in due time along with a catalogue of other free booklets. It soon became apparent that the forests in that part of Utah were too limited for a profitable sawmill, but while perusing the catalogue one day, Okada found a booklet on what then was called cooperative banking. It turned out to be about credit unions—how people could band together and deposit their savings in a common pool from which members could borrow at low rates of interest. Okada reasoned that many members of JACL needed a few hundred dollars to re-establish themselves when they left the WRA camps, cash to buy clothing or household goods until paychecks began coming in regularly. Others would need money to set up businesses. But some banks wouldn't even accept deposits from Japanese Americans and getting credit was almost impossible. Why not start a JACL credit union? In his efforts to get a state charter Okada received encouragement and guidance from Carl S. Little, a leader in the Utah credit union movement who worked as a railroad ticket agent. To see Little during business hours, Okada would get into the line at his ticket window, wait his turn, and ask the necessary questions when he finally reached the head of the queue. After six months of preparatory work the Utah banking commission approved the JACL credit union's bylaws and issued a charter in September of 1943. Bill Yamauchi was named president, Shake Ushio vice-president and Okada general manager. Directors were Tatsuo Koga, Jun Kurumada and Yukio Inouye, all Intermountain JACL leaders. Members of the credit committee were Kay Terashima, Jim Ushio and Frank Tashima. Supervisory committee members were Toysie Kato, James Yamamoto and Constance Yamada. The membership fee was twenty-five cents, and one dollar was the minimum deposit. Saburo Kido, who was supplementing his income by teaching Japanese to military officers at Fort Douglas, took out the first loan to demonstrate how the system worked. Okada ran the credit union for many years without compensation until it grew large enough to pay him a small salary. The JACL credit union now has more than two thousand members and assets in excess of four million dollars.

It is not possible to say which of JACL's services was most valuable, for they served different functions. But for sustained and widespread impact nothing matched *Pacific Citizen,* the weekly publication. Tajiri, a thoroughly professional newspaperman, made *Pacific Citizen* a thoroughly professional newspaper that became an invaluable source of information, morale builder, purveyor of thought and opinion molder, and a public-relations vehicle both within and outside the organization. The widely scattered Japanese American community looked to *Pacific Citizen* each week for news about themselves and of importance to them from Washington, from the hate mongers on the West Coast, from distant war fronts. They pored over the vital-statistics columns to learn which of their friends had been married, celebrated a birth or mourned a death. They read the front page to get the details about the latest government directive. When Nisei troops reached the front, *Pacific Citizen* recounted their triumphs in battle in places with names like Livorno and Bruyères, Myitkyina and Mindanao. And week after week *Pacific Citizen* recorded the grim, lengthening toll of the dead, wounded and missing. *Pacific Citizen* reflected the times and perforce most of the news was bad. One subscriber said he looked forward to *Pacific Citizen's* arrival with great anticipation, but he waited until after supper to read it so it wouldn't make him lose his appetite.

A prodigious worker, Tajiri performed the bulk of the writing and editing, helped by his wife, Guyo, with assistance from time to time by friends with newspaper experience like Bob Tsuda, Dyke Miyagawa and others. With a limited staff and limited budget, Tajiri had to depend on secondary sources for much of his news. *Pacific Citizen* subscribed to newspapers from the larger

West Coast cities, New York, Washington, Chicago, Denver and elsewhere. Some JACL chapters underwrote subscriptions to hometown papers. Each day the mailman would bring in a huge bundle of newspapers and Tajiri would skim them all for news of interest to Japanese Americans. Guyo recalls:

> The amount of paper that crossed Larry's desk every day was enormous, and his desk was topheavy with newspapers, publicity handouts, magazines, letters. The fire department was impressed enough to come and check. Our private joke was that Larry, who smoked a pipe, was a fire hazard all by himself. He early developed the ability to put his hand into a towering pile of stuff to retrieve that one bit of paper with that one bit of information he wanted. "It's right here," he liked to say as his hand came up.
>
> People everywhere were marvelous about sending in clippings from their local papers about events that involved the Nisei and Issei. All the JACL chapters had their own correspondents, and they, too, were faithful about sending in news. There was also a good deal of material from WRA, the War Department and other government agencies. Since there was little advertising and almost no money for photo engravings, an unusual amount of news was packed into eight tabloid pages.

In time the linotype operator at the Century Printing Company learned to cope with the long lists of Japanese names. At first the printers were a bit uneasy about *Pacific Citizen* but they soon became emotionally involved with the stories they handled. Once, Guyo noticed the typesetter weeping as he worked on a particularly emotional story, and as the tales of outrages against the Nisei grew, the printers became as angry as the editors.

In addition to the news there were Tajiri's editorials—powerful, well reasoned, persuasive, sometimes angry but never embittered. He was, one observer said, an editorial David shouting defiance at the Goliaths of the newspaper world, challenging them to tell the truth, to cease their distortions and live up to the canons of responsible journalism. The editorials were backed up by regular columns like Tajiri's "Nisei USA," Kido's "Timely Topics," Bill Hosokawa's "From the Frying Pan," plus sporadic essays from a variety of Nisei writers, a column of whimsy gleaned from the camp newspapers, and "Ann Nisei's" (Guyo's) column for women with tips about decorating a barracks room or adjusting to life on the outside. Another well-received *Pacific Citizen* feature was a series of cartoons by Taro Yashima attacking Japanese militarism. Yashima had been an outstanding political cartoonist in his native country before seeking refuge in the United States.

Pacific Citizen under Tajiri's editorship was a remarkably effective organ for maintaining the morale of Japanese Americans. But equally important, it was a newspaper of record for a people buffeted by forces beyond their control. It told of the meanness of the weekly *Sumner* (Washington) *Standard* whose masthead said: "Our Objective: Banish Japs Forever from the U.S.A.," while on page 8 it listed the names of local servicemen including Sadao Jim Ikoma, Dale Mochizuki and Jim Mochizuki. *Pacific Citizen* recorded General DeWitt's charge that "a Jap is a Jap" on the same page reporting Nisei war service, and Governor Earl Warren's demand that no Japanese Americans be allowed to return to California. It told the story of a fifteen-year-old Nisei who refused to accompany his parents to the segregation camp at Tule Lake. It recorded the whole sad segregation story in which hundreds of angry, confused, frustrated evacuees turned their backs on America and agreed to go to Tule Lake in hopes of finding a better life. It told stories of courage, nobility and sacrifice and left an eloquent, indelible record of America in action in some of its best and worst moments.

Dr. Randolph Sakada, right, national president 1950–52, passes the gavel to George Inagaki, national president 1952–56.

The brilliant war record of the Nisei helped immeasurably in the postwar acceptance of Japanese Americans. Sergeant Pat Hagiwara leads the Nisei contingent in a Seattle July Fourth parade in 1956. *(Photo: Elmer Ogawa)*

As economic and political problems eased, JACL began to focus more on social diversions. Mr. and Mrs. Mas Ozaki of Chicago, about 1963. *(Photo: James S. Ogata)*

A mock fashion show at a JACL function in Chicago. From left to right: Mike Hagiwara, Lincoln Shimidzu, Smoky Sakurada, Harry Sabusawa, Joe Maruyama and Abe Hagiwara *(Photo: Edgar F. Zobel)*

A major task of the headquarters staff was transcribing, mimeographing and collating convention minutes. Mrs. Hana Okada, far left, two volunteers and Mas Satow.

A light moment during a district council meeting in 1959. From left to right: singer Pat Suzuki, Pat Okura, Joe Kadowaki, Mas Satow and Lily Okura.

Japanese American Creed

I am proud that I am an American Citizen of Japanese ancestry, for my very background makes me appreciate more fully the wonderful advantages of this Nation. I believe in her institutions, ideals and traditions; I glory in her heritage; I boast of her history; I trust in her future. She has granted me liberties and opportunities such as no individual enjoys in this world today. She has given me an education befitting kings. She has entrusted me with the responsibilities of the franchise. She has permitted me to build a home, to earn a livelihood, to worship, think, speak, and act as I please - as a free man equal to every other man.

Although some individuals may discriminate against me I shall never become bitter or lose faith, for I know such persons are not representative of the majority of the American people. True, I shall the American way: above board, in the open, through courts of law, by education, by proving myself to be worthy of equal treatment and consideration. I am firm in my belief that American sportsmanship and attitude of fair play will judge citizenship and patriotism on the basis of action and achievement, and not on the basis of physical characteristics.

Because I believe in America, and I trust she believes in me, and because I have received innumerable benefits from her I pledge myself to do honor to her at all times and in all places, to support her Constitution, to obey her laws, to respect her Flag, to defend her against all enemies, foreign or domestic, to actively assume my duties and obligations as a citizen, cheerfully and without any reservations whatsoever, in the hope that I may become a better American in a greater America.

Mike M. Masaoka

First read before the United States Senate, and printed in the Congressional Record, May 9, 1941

Hand Lettered by MASAO W. SATOW

In his spare time Mas Satow hand-lettered citations awarded by JACL. The Japanese American Creed, written by Mike Masaoka in 1941, was one of Satow's projects.

JACL committees spent long hours on their assignments. This is a Japanese American Research Project (history) committee meeting in Los Angeles. From left to right: Jerry Enomoto, William Marutani, Sim Togasaki, Mike Masaoka, Bill Hosokawa, Chairman Shig Wakamatsu, Mas Satow, Akiji Yoshimura and Yone Satoda.

Copies of the book *Nisei,* recording the one-hundred-year history of the Japanese in the United States, were presented at the White House by Mike Masaoka in 1969 to Japan's Prime Minister Eisaku Sato, to President Nixon and to Foreign Minister Kiichi Aichi (on the left). *Nisei* was the first publication of the JARP committee.

George Inagaki as "Callahan," chairman of JACL's fund-raising, fun-seeking arm, the Thousand Club *(Photo: Roy Hoshizaki)*

Dr. Thomas T. Yatabe, "granddaddy of JACL," not long before his death in 1977

In the face of internal opposition in the 1960's, JACL became more active in national human rights movements. Key Kobayashi (left), Pat Okura and Mike Masaoka march in a 1961 rally in Washington.

A JACL National Board meeting in San Diego in 1962. At the head table, from left to right, are Mas Satow, President Kumeo Yoshinari, future President Jerry Enomoto and Mike Masaoka

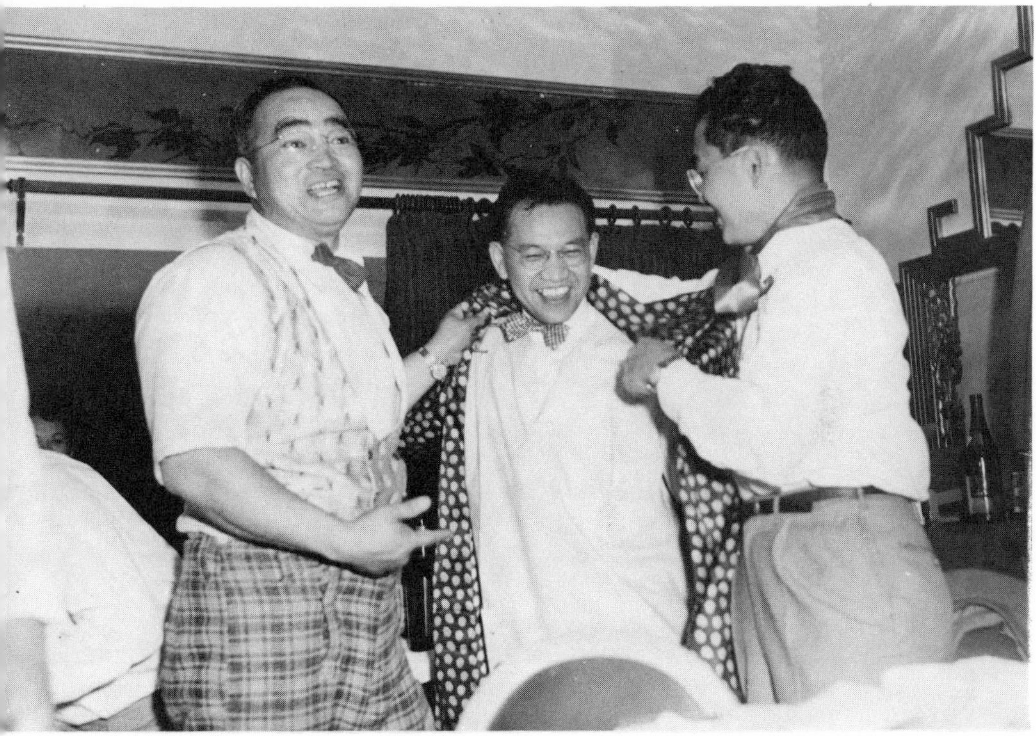

Thousand Club fun. From left to right: George Inagaki, Mas Satow and Roy Nishikawa

A growing interest in ethnic origins led to JACL group tours of Japan.

By the late 1960's, Sansei were taking a role in JACL affairs. These girls are promoting the 1970 convention in the "Windy City." *(Photo: Alvin Hayashi)*

On the eve of his retirement as national director, Mas Satow and his wife, Chiz, were honored at a testimonial during the 1972 convention in Washington, D.C. Dr. Roy Nishikawa presents them with a gift.

Mas Satow was succeeded amid controversy by David Ushio, who brought modern organizational techniques to JACL. Ushio is shown here with the 1973 Reno chapter cabinet. From left to right: Oscar Fujii, Jane Yamamoto, Ushio, President Wilson Makabe, Tom Oki and Bill Spahr

Warren Furutani, a charismatic Sansei leader, was among the members of JACL's Southern California staff who resigned when David Ushio was hired. *(Photo: Toyo Miyatake Studio)*

Shigeki Sugiyama, JACL president 1974–76, defeated an impeachment attempt.

JACL persuaded President Jerry Ford to rescind Executive Order 9066, which he did in this White House ceremony in 1976. Standing immediately behind the President is Senator Spark Matsunaga. Between the flags is Representative Norman Mineta and on his right are Representative Patsy Mink, Senator Daniel Inouye, Helen Kawagoe, David Ushio and Wayne Horiuchi. *(Official White House Photo)*

The half-million-dollar JACL headquarters at 1765 Sutter Street, San Francisco, was dedicated in 1976 and named in honor of Mas Satow.

A meeting in the boardroom of the national headquarters. Dr. Clifford Uyeda presides with National Director Karl Nobuyuki and his assistant, J. D. Hokoyama, on his left.

Planning redress campaign strategy. From left to right: J. D. Hokoyama, Dr. Clifford Uyeda and Karl Nobuyuki

At the San Francisco convention in 1980, Dr. Clifford Uyeda, left, turns over the presidency to Dr. James Tsujimura.

February 19, the anniversary of the signing of Executive Order 9066, which led to the Evacuation, is observed by some JACLers as a "Day of Remembrance." Speaking at a Portland observance is Minoru Yasui, who challenged the legality of the federal orders. *(Photo: Gary Akiyama)*

Among the witnesses at the redress hearings was Professor Gordon Hirabayashi, who in 1942 violated the curfew and Evacuation orders as a matter of principle.

Spectators at a Senate hearing on JACL's redress bill. From right to left: Mike Masaoka, Jerry Enomoto, Mrs. Lily Okura, Dr. Clifford Uyeda, Cherry Tsutsumida and Karl Nobuyuki

Witness Mike Masaoka recalled the events of early 1942 and the JACL decision, in which he had been deeply involved.

Past presidents of JACL at a reunion in 1980. Seated, from left to right: Kumeo Yoshinari, 1964–66; Pat Okura, 1962–64; Dr. Terry Hayashi, 1933–34. Standing: James Murakami, 1976–78; Frank Chuman, 1960–62; Henry Tanaka, 1972–74; Shigeo Wakamatsu, 1958–60; Shigeki Sugiyama, 1974–76; Jerry Enomoto, 1966–70; Judge Ravmond Uno, 1970–72; Dr. Roy Nishikawa, 1956–58; Dr. Clifford Uyeda, 1978–80 *(Photo: Wes Doi)*

XVII

The Way Back

In April of 1944 Mayor Fiorello LaGuardia of New York City called on Secretary of the Interior Ickes to discuss resettlement of Japanese Americans from the WRA camps. WRA, which had been an independent agency, had come under Interior's wing several months earlier in a move calculated to increase its clout in Washington. LaGuardia said he had no objection to receiving more evacuees in New York provided they were permitted to return to the Pacific Coast as well.

Ickes made a notation in his diary that LaGuardia's position "certainly has merit." There is no doubt that it did. The tide of war had turned in the Pacific. The Japanese were pulling back in the Southwest Pacific. General MacArthur was preparing to return to the Philippines. If there had ever been any remote possibility of the Japanese attacking the American Pacific Coast, by spring of 1944 there was none at all. If there had ever been any national security justification for evacuating Japanese Americans, now there was none at all. Ickes told LaGuardia he was trying to get the Army to lift its Evacuation order, which with the evacuees' departure had become in effect an exclusion order preventing their return.

The validity of continued exclusion was concerning many persons. The matter came up in a cabinet meeting on May 28. Secretary of War Stimson agreed with Ickes that there was no reason why the ban shouldn't be lifted. But it is revealing that more than concern for justice influenced Ickes' thinking. He was very much aware that lawsuits testing the constitutionality of the Evacuation were grinding their ponderous way toward the Supreme Court and this might pose problems. He noted in his diary on May 28, 1944: ". . . Before election [in November], the Supreme Court of the United States is very likely to uphold the petition for a writ of habeas corpus that is on its way up in favor of the petitioner. That would leave us on the eve of election in the position of having committed an illegal act."

On June 2 Ickes wrote to President Roosevelt urging an end to the exlcusion order. It said in part:

> I again call your attention to the urgent necessity of arriving at a determination with respect to revocation of the orders excluding Japanese Americans from the West Coast. It is my understanding that Secretary Stimson believes that there is no longer any military necessity for excluding these persons from the State of California and portions of the States of Washington, Oregon and Arizona. Accordingly, there is no basis in law or in equity for the perpetuation of the ban.
>
> The reasons for removing the exclusion orders may be briefly stated as follows:
>
> 1. I have been informally advised by officials of the War Department who are in charge of this problem that there is no substantial justification for continuation of the ban from the standpoint of military security.
>
> 2. The continued exclusion of American citizens of Japanese ancestry from the affected areas is clearly unconstitutional in the present circumstances. I expect a case squarely raising this issue will reach the Supreme Court at its next term. I understand that the Department of Justice agrees that there is little doubt as to the decision which the Supreme Court will reach in a case squarely presenting the issue.
>
> 3. The continuation of the exclusion orders in the West Coast areas is adversely affecting our efforts to relocate Japanese Americans elsewhere in the country. State and local officials are saying, with some justification, that if these people are too dangerous for the West Coast, they do not want them to resettle in their localities.
>
> 4. The psychology of the Japanese Americans in the relocation centers becomes progressively worse. The difficulty which will confront these people in readjusting to ordinary life becomes greater as they spend more time in the centers.
>
> 5. The children in the centers are exposed solely to the influence of persons of Japanese ancestry. They are becoming a hopelessly

maladjusted generation, apprehensive of the outside world and divorced from the possibility of association—or even seeing to any considerable extent—Americans of other races. . . .

I will not comment at this time on the justification or lack thereof for the original evacuation order. But I do say that the continued retention of these innocent people in the relocation centers would be a blot upon the history of this country. I hope that you will decide that the exclusion orders should be revoked. . . .

Franklin Delano Roosevelt chose not to act. Some weeks later Ickes wrote in his diary: "It is the President himself who has insisted that the ban not be lifted until after the election and in the meantime we are having the devil's own time trying to persuade people in the Middle West and in the East that the Japanese are perfectly safe in those areas when they cannot be trusted in California."

WRA itself had been troubled by the constitutional aspects of the Evacuation and continued confinement. As director, Milton Eisenhower had asked WRA's solicitor, Philip Glick, for a legal opinion. Glick's opinion, expressed in thirty typewritten pages, reached a conclusion remarkably similar to that of the Supreme Court two and a half years later. Some of Glick's salient points follow:

Japanese aliens are alien enemies and enjoy no civil rights, and the President has absolute control over the manner and degree of their detention.

Citizen Japanese may be detained or otherwise restrained to the extent reasonably necessary for the national safety, and other classes of citizens need not be affected by such restraints if the discrimination can be shown to be related to a genuine war need and does not, under the guise of national defense, discriminate for a purpose unrelated to the national war effort.

The chances are good that the courts will sustain the detention of Japanese at relocation centers. This judgment is based partially on the facts indicating that unrestricted movement of Japanese may interfere with the war effort and partially on the fact that the judgment of the military as to steps needed to protect the national security will not be lightly set aside by the courts in time of war. . . .

We are engaged in total warfare. The stakes are more than mere trade and empire; they involve the survival of our liberties and our form of government. If our democracy is to survive, our Constitution must prove adaptable to the needs of the times. It has met that test in the past and there is no reason to believe it will not do so today. Standard concepts of Constitutional law will therefore undoubtedly be applied in the light of current war needs. That such application must always be made is itself one of the most fundamental of our constitutional doctrines. . . .

It is very difficult to pick out the dangerous minority of the Japanese population and isolate them, if not impossible; due to the inability of most Americans to immediately recognize differences in features between members of the Japanese race to the same extent that they can do this with respect to other persons, the presence of any appreciable number of Japanese anywhere facilitates the infiltration of other Japanese who may be members of the Japanese armed forces, for the purpose of performing special tasks of sabotage and even for the purpose of laying the ground work for an actual invasion. . . .

We believe that the evacuation was within the constitutional power of the National Government.

An impartial student of the issue would find Glick's argument plausible if controversial, but aside from legal points on which the courts would have to rule, it is possible to challenge his logic on one important matter. Glick argued that since most Americans found it difficult to recognize differences in the features of individual Japanese, enemy infiltration was a great danger. The opposite was true. What Glick failed to note was that the features of Japanese Americans set them apart from Americans of other races and so any one engaged in hostile activity would be quickly detected. Glick said nothing about German or Italian enemy agents who would be indistinguishable from other whites who made up 80 percent of the American population.

What many Nisei in their inexperience had failed to comprehend, or only vaguely understood, is that under the American system of justice it is to the courts that an aggrieved citizen must appeal for redress. The courts had the power to pass on the legality of the actions of civilian government agencies or the military's relations with civilians. This accounts for the references by Glick and Ickes to the way the courts might view the Evacuation. As we have seen, Kido, Masaoka and other JACL leaders had given serious consideration early on to the wisdom of seeking a court test of General DeWitt's orders. In the end and after much anguish, they decided against it, partly because of the urgency of the times, partly because of the public temper, partly because of lack of funds, partly because they knew court determination might take years. If there had been greater Nisei understanding of the legal system, there might have been—and this is purely conjecture—demands that in the absence of martial law JACL at least seek an injunction to block DeWitt's orders.

As it was, four cases involving some aspect of the Evacuation reached the United States Supreme Court. They were *Fred Toyosaburo Korematsu* v. *United States of America,* Ex parte *Endo, Gordon K. Hirabayashi* v. *United States of America* and *Minoru Yasui* v. *United States of America.*

All made history, and victory in the Endo case gave legal standing to the Army's frantic decision to allow the evacuees to return to the Pacific Coast. But it is instructional to review the motives behind each of the lawsuits.

Little ideology or search for judicial review was involved in Fred Korematsu's case. He was a high school graduate who simply didn't want to be evacuated from his home in the Oakland area for good and sufficient personal reasons. So he refused to report for evacuation, was arrested and was charged. Only then did the American Civil Liberties Union of Northern California in the person of Wayne Collins, a militant San Francisco attorney, become involved.

For Gordon Hirabayashi, passive resistance to DeWitt's curfew and Evacuation orders was, at the beginning, a matter of conscience, a personal matter. He had no hesitation about helping others to prepare to be evacuated, but he himself could not comply on principle. It was only later that friends rallied around him to make his trial a test case.

But Minoru Yasui, the attorney, set out deliberately to test the legality of the curfew. Yasui, also on his own, contended the military had no jurisdiction over him as a civilian and invited arrest so that he could challenge the curfew order in court.

Mitsuye Endo, a California state employee and the only one to win her case, complied with the curfew and Evacuation orders. She was in the Tanforan assembly center when she agreed to have another San Francisco attorney, James Purcell, file a writ of *habeas corpus* demanding that she be released or that the government show cause why she should be kept in custody. In the beginning, Purcell had been asked by his friend Saburo Kido to seek a legal means of preventing the state government from discharging its Nisei employees. When the Evacuation became a fact Purcell, appalled and angered, went to work to win freedom for the Nisei.

Thus, JACL was peripherally involved in just one of these four court cases at the start. A committee supporting Hirabayashi paid most of his legal costs. Friends in the Minidoka and Topaz camps contributed a total of $3,000 to help Yasui. He spent $5,000 of his own funds, and his family paid the balance of his costs, which totaled about $10,000. Neither Purcell nor Collins was paid for his legal services. Purcell told the author he spent about $5,000 of his own money for printing, travel, stenographic and other costs. Collins put up more than $2,000 of his own, with other expenses being met by the ACLU of Northern California.

Once the urgent pressures of the Evacuation itself abated, the JACL leadership was able to take a longer view of problems and ultimately the organization's contribution in these cases was not insignificant. Walter Tsukamoto had resigned as special JACL counsel when he was inducted and A. L. Wirin, a well-known Los Angeles ACLU attorney, took over the responsibilities. Largely through his efforts, but with the assistance of Kido and others, JACL filed important *amicus curiae* (friend of the court) briefs to argue the case for the Nisei. In the Korematsu case the brief argued that there was no reasonable basis for the military's Evacuation order. The brief reviewed in detail such questions as dual citizenship, the concentration of persons of Japanese ancestry in certain population centers, the Japanese-language schools, religious views of Japanese Americans and the Kibei question. The brief also pointed out the admitted race prejudice of General DeWitt. Explaining JACL's interest, the brief said the organization cooperated in the Evacuation "at the request of the military" without conceding its constitutionality. JACL's investment in these briefs was approximately fifteen hundred dollars.

Yasui, after his arrest, had been charged with curfew violation and released on bond. In November of 1942 Yasui was escorted back to Portland from the Minidoka WRA camp and tried before Judge James Alger Fee in federal district court. Fee reached a curious decision. He agreed with Yasui that the military could not issue orders binding on citizen civilians in the absence of martial law, but then he ruled that since Yasui had been employed by the Japanese consulate in Chicago, he had forfeited his citizenship. Judge Fee found Yasui guilty, fined him five thousand dollars and sentenced him to one year's imprisonment. Yasui promptly appealed to the circuit court of appeals in San Francisco, which decided it would be wiser for the Supreme Court to take jurisdiction. Yasui spent the next nine months in solitary confinement in Multnomah County jail in Portland, denied a haircut, a razor or even a typewriter.

Hirabayashi's confinement was less grim. In fact, there were some comic-opera aspects to an admittedly serious case. After he was charged, Hirabayashi was lodged in King County jail. One of his regular visitors was an Army captain overseeing the evacuation of Seattle, who complained that only Hirabayashi stood in the way of 100-percent compliance and offered to send him to the Puyallup assembly center in a chauffeur-driven military limousine. In time Hirabayashi had enough seniority in his cell block to become the unofficial "mayor" in charge of keeping internal order.

Five months after Hirabayashi was booked, his case was heard by Judge Lloyd L. Black. The prosecution had only to prove that Hirabayashi was of Japanese ancestry and had refused to comply with both the curfew and the Evacuation orders. There was no question about any of this, but for legal reasons it was necessary to go through the motions. Gordon's parents were returned to Seattle from the Tule Lake camp as witnesses. Although friends offered to house them, the judge ordered the Hirabayashis to be held in jail. Gordon's father joined him in his cell and his mother was sent to the female wing where prostitutes and petty criminals quickly befriended her. One of them gave her the first professional hairdo she had ever had, and the Issei lady played the piano for them.

Only Gordon's father was called as a witness. He understood English adequately but in the unfamiliar surroundings he became somewhat confused so that an interpreter was called for. No one was available so Gordon, the defendant, was pressed into service to translate his father's statement that he was indeed Japanese, and his son was in the room.

The jury took only a few minutes to decide that Hirabayashi was a Japanese who came under the Army's orders and he had failed to comply with them. Noting that the maximum penalty was twelve months' imprisonment and that Hirabayashi had been confined five months already, Black sentenced the Nisei to thirty days for curfew violation and thirty days for failure to report for evacuation. The sentences were to be served consecutively for a total of sixty days.

Hirabayashi was anxious to get out of jail. He had heard that prisoners serving ninety days or longer could be assigned to a road camp, so he asked for a longer sentence.

Judge Black laughed and said he would be happy to add fifteen days to each of the sentences for a total of ninety days. Then he said something to the effect that it would be simpler to sentence Hirabayashi to ninety days for each violation, to be served concurrently. Although no one realized the significance at the time, this change in the sentence was to have an important part in the way the Supreme Court heard Hirabayashi's appeal.

Hirabayashi's attorney, Arthur Barnett, filed an appeal with the circuit court of appeals which, as in the Yasui case, bucked it up to the Supreme Court. Hirabayashi was returned to his cell and spent another four months there before the authorities agreed in February, 1943, to let him go to Spokane in Washington's eastern "free" zone to await the Supreme Court's decision.

The Supreme Court ruled on both the Hirabayashi and the Yasui cases on June 21, 1943. The Court chose to rule first on the curfew issue. It found unanimously that the Army acted lawfully when it suspended the rights of Japanese Americans through the curfew. Then, noting that Hirabayashi was under concurrent sentences which he would be serving automatically if found guilty on the first charge, it declined to consider the knotty matter of whether DeWitt's Evacuation order was a legal exercise of his powers. That issue was left in abeyance until the Supreme Court heard the Korematsu case some eighteen months later. One can only wonder what would have happened if the Court had chosen to rule on the Evacuation portion of Hirabayashi's suit.

Hirabayashi was now required to serve the balance of his ninety-day term in a road camp. The district attorney in Spokane couldn't send him back to the nearest federal camp, which was near Tacoma, but agreed to let him report to a camp in Tucson, Arizona. Since there were no funds to send Hirabayashi to the camp with an escort, he was allowed to hitchhike by himself. Hirabayashi made a leisurely trip, visiting his parents in Weiser, Idaho, and dropping in to see Larry Tajiri at JACL headquarters in Salt Lake City. In Tucson, the district attorney couldn't find

Hirabayashi's documents. He was told to go see a movie and come back later in the day. By then the paperwork was completed and the Nisei found himself in a camp in the Santa Catalina Mountains with some friendly Hopi Indians who had been picked up for refusing military service. Only later did anyone realize that Tucson was also in DeWitt's forbidden military zone.

In Yasui's appeal, the Court found him guilty of curfew violations for the same reasons applying to Hirabayashi. But the justices overruled the finding that Yasui had lost his American citizenship. Yasui's five-thousand-dollar fine was suspended, and he was given his freedom on the ground that he had served nine months in prison while waiting for his appeal to be heard.

In the absence of a Supreme Court determination of the Evacuation issue, several Nisei sought individual tests of the exclusion order. A suit was filed in July, 1944, in a California court on behalf of Mrs. Shizuko Shiramizu, widow of Sergeant Kiyoshi Shiramizu of Salinas, California, who died of wounds received in combat with the 100th Infantry Battalion in Italy; Masaru Baba, honorably discharged from the Army in 1942; and Dr. George Ochikubo, an Oakland dentist. Mrs. Shiramizu was being held in the Poston camp, Ochikubo was at Topaz and Baba was living in Reno, Nevada. The suit was filed under sponsorship of the American Civil Liberties Union with JACL cooperation. Wirin represented the ACLU and Saburo Kido was among the attorneys who signed the complaint asking why military authorities should not be enjoined from interfering with the return of the plaintiffs to their homes in California. A *Pacific Citizen* editorial put the suit in perspective:

> Court action to regain the rights which were restricted by the decrees issued by Lieut. Gen. John L. DeWitt, then commanding the Western Defense Command in the hysteria-ridden months following the outbreak of war, has been under consideration for the past 18 months or more. The fact that such action was not initiated until this week bespeaks the willingness of Japanese Americans to wait on the integrity of the military authorities involved, since the evacuation was ordered in the name of military necessity. During two years since the mass evacuation from the West Coast our Pacific military strategy has changed from the defensive to an offensive. Whatever military necessity which may have existed at the time of the evacuation order certainly does not exist today.

The injunction suit sponsored by the American Civil Liberties Union is the latest link in a chain of legal action forged to protect and to implement the Constitutional rights of the Japanese American group. The Korematsu and Endo cases which will be argued in October before the United States Supreme Court test the right of the military to evacuate a group of citizens without individual hearing or trial and to detain them in assembly centers and war relocation camps. It is expected that such judicial reviews of wartime restrictions to which Americans of Japanese ancestry have been subjected will do much to clarify the civil rights of the group under consideration.

It is a notable fact that the evacuated Japanese Americans have cooperated fully with the military orders on evacuation and exclusion, though questioning the validity of some of those orders. Such cooperation was given in the interests of national security and toward the full prosecution of the war effort, as Secretary of War Stimson has acknowledged in his statement: "Great credit is due our Japanese population for the manner in which they responded and complied with the orders of exclusion."

The fact that the promised restoration of war-shorn rights has not kept pace with the changing military situation on the West Coast and in the Pacific, and with the contributions of Japanese Americans to the general war effort, lends weight to the necessity of restitution by court action, the step which was taken this week in Los Angeles.

It is unfortunate that the fact of evacuation is now being interpreted in many quarters of the Pacific Coast as evidence of the disloyalty of the whole group. Rather than silencing the racists, the evacuation has been followed by an orgy of race mongering, using the time-worn slogans of the "yellow peril" which has been unequaled in a generation on the West Coast.

Americans of Japanese ancestry have not lost their faith in the ultimate justice. Their concern is only that any tendency on the part of the military authorities to appease the coastal hate mongers by continued exclusion will only make more difficult the reacceptance of the evacuees in the areas from which they were evacuated. The words of Gladstone, "Justice delayed is justice denied," which is quoted by a West Coast group which is working for the reintegration of the Japanese Americans into West Coast life, are certainly applicable here.

The Army soon made it clear it was not anxious to face a court test of its exclusion policy. In response to Judge F. J. T. O'Connor's order to show cause why it should not be enjoined from enforcing its exclusion order, the Western Defense Command in September issued "certificates of exemption" to Mrs. Shiramizu and Baba. In a curiously worded explanation the Army said:

> The pending civil action recently commenced in your behalf to enjoin the military authorities from interfering with any effort you may wish to make to return to California has resulted in an investigation and an examination of your case. As a result of this inquiry it appears that if you had made a written application to this headquarters for permission to return to California, it would have been granted. Accordingly, there is enclosed herewith a certificate of exemption from the exclusion order.

This was the first indication that written applications would be entertained, that applications for return to the coastal areas would be studied on an individual basis, and that at least some would be granted. The court order was lifted. Thus was the first crack made in what had been the military's intransigent refusal to rescind its exclusion orders.

But Dr. Ochikubo for undisclosed reasons was refused an automatic certificate. Accompanied by Kido as his attorney, Dr. Ochikubo then appeared before a three-officer military board in Los Angeles to make his case. Pending a decision, ACLU and JACL filed further test cases on behalf of six citizens confined in the Poston camp: Elmer S. Yamamoto, a Hawaiian-born Los Angeles attorney; Tadayuki Todah, Japanese-born veteran of service with the U.S. Army in World War I, naturalized citizen and restaurant operator; Kiyoshi Shigekawa, Terminal Island fisherman and union leader with two brothers in military service; Yoshio Ekimoto, farmer; Mary Duco, a native of Terminal Island. Meanwhile, one by one, Nisei were being permitted to go home. Kaoru Ichihara, who had been living in Spokane, was allowed to return to her job as a secretary with the Seattle Council of Churches. Esther Takei, formerly of Venice, California, left the Granada camp to enroll at Pasadena Junior College. Chitake Yamagiwa, who had spent the war years in Ann Arbor, Michigan, where his brother had been teaching Japanese to naval officers, was allowed to return to Kent in the White River valley south of Seattle to farm. Mine Hasegawa went back to her job at Firland Sanatorium near Seattle where large numbers of Japanese Americans had been treated for tuberculosis.

Ultimately the military board denied Dr. Ochikubo a certificate with the curt statement that his presence on the coast "would constitute a potential danger to military security and military necessity requires the continuance of his exclusion." JACL had been anxious to discover the Army's criteria for potential security risks—what the Army considered to be evidence of possible disloyalty—but the military board refused to be specific. A federal court then upheld the Army's action and denied Ochikubo's petition for an injunction. Military board hearings later were offered the six Poston petitioners, but they rejected them on the grounds that the Army had no jurisdiction over them since they were civilians.

An interesting evaluation of JACL's activities at this time was offered by California Assemblyman Chester H. Gannon, a Sacramento Republican and chairman of an interim committee on Japanese problems. He warned that JACL was a pressure group "fighting to return the Japs to California—not after the war but right now when we are about to put all our effort behind the gigantic task of whipping Japan." Gannon was quoted in an International News Service dispatch as saying: "This group was brought to my attention by another state legislator who himself had been solicited to make a donation to the League fund. The prime purpose of this League is to return the Japanese to California right now, restore all their rights and it is an organization whose membership is made up mainly of Easterners who know nothing of the Japanese problem in California." It was never explained where he got that impression.

But the JACL leadership would have no quarrel with Gannon about their goals. In fact, it might have helped them if Japanese Americans all over the country could appreciate what enemies like Gannon thought about the organization. By this time JACL's paid-up membership had plunged from some twenty thousand just before the Evacuation to seventeen hundred, about half of whom were associate members not affiliated with a chapter. The number of chapters had dwindled from sixty-six to sixteen, only ten of which were active. The reasons for this decline were several. Chapters had been dissolved after the Evacuation, many local leaders had joined the Army and there was no one to come knocking at doors to solicit membership. People working for twelve, sixteen or nineteen dollars a month in the camps were hardly inclined to send in dues payments voluntarily. Those who had relocated to the Midwest and East were intensely involved in the daily routine of life and found themselves drifting away from JACL and their ethnic ties. But perhaps the most important single reason for the drop in JACL membership was disillusionment with what appeared to be its losing struggle, and even an unfair resentment that it had not been able to accomplish more.

Even the Japanese-language newspapers—two were being published in Denver and one in Salt Lake City—were hostile to JACL. Because JACL and much of what it stood for were unpopular with the Japanese-reading public, the newspapers chose to ignore or downplay news pertaining to JACL's activities. It took a long time to win editorial support.

JACL's most effective means of keeping Japanese Americans informed was *Pacific Citizen,* but wartime newsprint shortages limited its circulation to eight thousand. Lacking advertising, it had to depend on subscription fees—three dollars a year for nonmembers and two dollars for members—to remain afloat. William C. Carr, a Pasadena real estate broker and head of an organization called Friends of the American Way, had this to say about *Pacific Citizen:*

> We have worked quietly for more national recognition of the work being done by the Pacific Citizen. To us on the outside away from the personal shocks that you [the evacuees] encounter, it is a marvel in its poise, its lack of bigotry, its lack of malice, its balance in reporting well. We hope it will secure national recognition. We feel that if it does secure that national recognition it will do a great deal in the camps to make the various folks there who do not see eye to eye with you, feel that, after all, the JACL is doing a fine job in making for more understanding and acceptance.

Despite the widespread apathy and antipathy toward JACL outside the Intermountain district, a faithful nucleus of about a hundred members signed up for the Buck a Month Club and sent what they could—sometimes as little as twenty-five cents—to help support the organization. Many of these contributors were servicemen. Income from Buck a Month paid the rent and telephone bill many months at headquarters. In February of 1944, with JACL trying to maintain four offices, there was only $1,000 in the bank and staff salaries were a month in arrears. After Teiko Ishida in the New York office sent out 18,000 letters to Caucasians describing JACL's work, contributions of $4,200 helped tide over the organization. Various foundations—among them the William

Paley Foundation, the Field Foundation, the Carnegie Endowment and others—made grants totaling $7,000 for specific projects such as printing and distributing pamphlets about the Japanese American struggle. JACL mailings during this period totaled some 150,000 pieces.

The Supreme Court finally got around to hearing oral arguments in the Korematsu and Endo cases on October 11 and 12, 1944. Korematsu was heard first, with Wayne Collins and Charles Horsky of Washington, D.C., appearing for him. Mitsuye Endo was represented by Purcell. Charles Fahy, the solicitor general, appeared for the government. Kido wrote of the hearings in *Pacific Citizen:*

> The nine justices heard the case with great interest. Very pointed questions were asked. This was particularly true in the Endo case as far as the government's position was concerned. But a certain amount of uncertainty was created because of the fact that Miss Endo is now in the Topaz Relocation Center and is outside of the jurisdiction of the district court of San Francisco where the original petition for writ of habeas corpus had been filed. Mr. Fahy argued that this may have mooted the case in that the decision would be of no effect if the court could not order any person to free Miss Endo. Chief Justice Stone replied that for that very reason it may be necessary for the Supreme Court to act.
>
> As to the Korematsu case, there were two points: one pertained to the constitutionality of the evacuation and the other was the claim that the exclusion order may be illegal in that it actually meant detention without due process of law. The attorneys for Korematsu claimed that Lieut. Gen. John L. DeWitt had exceeded his authority.
>
> Mr. Fahy argued that the government would like to have a clear cut decision on the evacuation orders and not on a technicality such as to declare that General DeWitt exceeded his authority. Otherwise the most important question of whether only citizens of Japanese ancestry can be evacuated would still remain unsettled.
>
> The courtroom was packed on both days with attorneys, tourists, and interested spectators, including Nisei. The Nisei who were in court for the first time were impressed with the fact that the constitutional question pertaining to evacuation was not as simple as they had thought before they heard the arguments. The fundamental principle which would be decided in the test case would be the wartime power of a commanding general in

an emergency. As in the Hirabayashi-Yasui cases, the justices seemed to be troubled with the question as to how far the courts can interfere with the military decisions of a general who is entrusted with the vital duty of national defense in an area where invasion was imminent. . . .

The question which many Caucasian friends have asked is: Are the Nisei financing these test cases? They are surprised when they are informed that the American Civil Liberties Union and the attorneys interested in the cases have carried the brunt of the cost. Even in the Yasui case, excepting for some help the Minidoka relocation center people gave, there was no contribution. This does not speak too well for persons of Japanese ancestry whose fundamental rights are involved. It is a source of considerable embarrassment because some government officials pointedly asked: Don't the Nisei expect to fight for their rights? Don't they realize that it costs money to carry on test cases?

Early in December, 1944, JACL met again in national convention at Salt Lake City. The theme was the future: "Your Place in America Will Be What You Make It Today." Doc Yatabe from the Chicago JACL office and Joe Grant Masaoka from the Denver office and Teiko Ishida from New York came to report on their activities. Other speakers included Masao Satow, YMCA national-board field representative based in Milwaukee, Togo Tanaka representing the American Friends Service Committee in Chicago, Mrs. Ruth Kingman of the American Committee on American Principles and Fair Play and A. L. Wirin of the ACLU. The news they brought was both encouraging and depressing. For every story of acceptance and adjustment among those who had relocated outside the camps, there was a story of public hostility. But there was much to be encouraged about. Joe Masaoka told of escorting Private First Class Thomas Higa, a combat veteran, for two months of a three-month speaking tour sponsored by JACL during which he made seventy-three appearances before Caucasian, Nisei and Issei groups and visited more than eighty newspapers. William Carr related how his organization erected an honor roll in Pasadena bearing the names of 112 Nisei from the community—one a WAC—serving in the Army. Leading Pasadena ministers took part in the dedication, and the salute to the flag was led by Lieutenant Jack Robinson, who went on to break the color barrier against blacks in professional baseball. The Reverend Clare Blauvelt, dedicating the honor roll, said:

"From the American Japanese families who once lived among us in this community 112 of their members have entered the armed forces of the United States. As an expression of the high regard and esteem in which we hold these comrades in a common cause we have inscribed their names upon this Roll of Honor and, beside one of them, have placed a Gold Star as the symbol of his supreme sacrifice."

Looking to war's end, the approximately one hundred delegates approved a 1945 budget of $39,866, then passed a resolution asking the federal government to recognize Issei contributions to the war effort by permitting them to be naturalized. They also asked for:

—Opening of all branches of the military to Americans irrespective of race.

—Automatic clearance for return to the West Coast for the families of Nisei servicemen.

—A statement from the Western Defense Command declaring that disloyalty was not the reason for the Evacuation.

The convention also recommended that the JACL constitution be amended to allow all citizens regardless of race to become members. Wirin told the delegates:

> The briefs which have been filed by the JACL in both cases, Korematsu and Endo, make clear that the reason for the opposition to race discrimination by the JACL is not merely because the immediate victims of such discrimination are present of Japanese descent, but because of the long history that persecution of one group is bound to result in the persecution of other groups. Unless one group is protected, no group will be free.
>
> As a non-Japanese, as a Caucasian, as an American with full rights, it seems timely to emphasize that the fight for the restoration of your rights is a fight you are also carrying on for the Chinese in the United States, the Negroes in the United States, for the Jews in the United States, and for all minority groups. The challenge which is ahead of us is a challenging fight for the preservation of such rights and not only yourself.

Tajiri commented in *Pacific Citizen:*

> The League will not depart from its present main task, which is the furthering of the welfare of persons of Japanese ancestry. . . . But it does, by this act, recognize that Americans of Japanese ancestry cannot limit and isolate themselves in activities in behalf of their group. The boundaries holding in racial minorities of this

> country must be broken down. . . . How far the JACL has gone in its realization of this fact was made evident in another resolution which called for consideration of a national conference to be called among all the minority groups in the country, an interracial American conference to discuss common problems.

This was the first definite move to broaden JACL's horizons beyond its strictly ethnic limits. But it was to be years before the policy was implemented. There was a lot left to be done about what Tajiri called "its present main task." (Actually, JACL had not been an ethnically pure organization since the mid-1930's when Dr. John Rademaker, then a graduate sociology student at the University of Washington, attended a Seattle JACL meeting, rose when new members were called and took the oath of membership with the Nisei in the group.)

The Supreme Court had until the end of its term in June of 1945 to return its decision on Korematsu and Endo. It ruled on December 18, 1944, three years and eleven days after the attack on Pearl Harbor.

In the Korematsu case the high court held, 6 to 3, that the Army's exclusion order was a valid exercise of its powers "as of the time it was made and when the petitioner violated it." In the Endo case the Court ruled unanimously that once the loyalty of an evacuee had been established, that person could not be kept subject to the authority of the WRA and the government had no authority to impose conditions on his freedom of movement.

While the Endo decision had the effect of reopening the coastal states to Japanese Americans, in the light of history the dissenting opinions of the three justices in the Korematsu decision may have been the most significant utterances. Tajiri noted in an editorial:

> The three dissenting justices have written vigorous opinions which strike at the racist implications of the evacuation and exclusion orders. Justice [Frank] Murphy, whose concurring opinion in the Yasui and Hirabayashi cases warned that the curfew order approached "the very brink of constitutional power," charged in the Korematsu case that such exclusion "goes over the very brink of constitutional power and falls into the ugly abyss of racism." Justice [Robert H.] Jackson also warned: "Once a judicial opinion rationalizes such a [military] order to show that it conforms to the Constitution, or rather rationalizes the Constitution to show that the Constitution sanctions an order, the court for all time has validated the principle of racial discrimination in criminal proce-

> dure and of transplanting American citizens. The principle lies about like a loaded weapon ready for the hand of any authority that can bring forward a plausible claim of an urgent need."

In several respects the Supreme Court decisions were something of an anticlimax. The legality of the curfew and Evacuation orders had been upheld previously in the Hirabayashi and Yasui cases. The Army had begun to permit evacuees to return to the West Coast on an individual basis. Almost from the very beginning, much of WRA's manpower and budget had been directed to getting the evacuees out of the camps. And finally, on the day before the Supreme Court announced its Endo decision, the Army lifted its exclusion order and restored the right of Japanese Americans to return to their West Coast homes.

The long trek back was about to begin.

XVIII

Denver, 1946

When the Supreme Court in December of 1944 ruled in the Mitsuye Endo case that evacuees could not be held against their will in the WRA camps, some thirty thousand had already moved out to work at jobs and make homes in interior areas. Almost all of them were young, educated Nisei with occupational skills. That left about eighty thousand still in the camps, including the very young and the elderly, but that figure is misleading. Nearly nineteen thousand of this number were in the Tule Lake segregation center and not immediately eligible for release. They included those who were segregated there because they had asked to go to Japan for any of a variety of reasons, as well as some of the original inmates of Tule Lake who were tired of being pushed around by the government and decided to stay in that camp for reasons unrelated to political loyalty even after it became a segregation center, plus all their dependents. As a consequence of the high court's decision WRA redoubled its efforts to get the remaining sixty thousand out of the camps.

As its first step WRA established a schedule of camp closings and announced all would be emptied before the end of 1945 regardless of the progress of the war. Then it set about preparing the evacuees, and the West Coast, for return to the homes they had vacated under duress three years earlier. In both objectives WRA had full JACL cooperation.

Both organizations set up offices in the coastal states to line up jobs, housing and public support. WRA opened seventeen offices,

JACL three. Joe Grant Masaoka left the Denver office in the care of Michi Ando, Min Yasui's sister, and moved out to San Francisco. George Minato, a onetime union organizer for Alaskan salmon-cannery workers, opened an office in Seattle. Scotty Tsuchiya, who had worked with JACL for a brief time in the early days of the Evacuation, took over in Los Angeles.

There was an enormous amount of work to be done. Anti-Japanese sentiment had to be overcome with appeals to reason. The military record of Nisei in uniform proved to be one of the most persuasive arguments for fair play. Nisei veterans as well as Caucasians who had served in combat with Nisei visited scores of communities and helped to break down hostility. Threats of economic boycott had to be dealt with. Local law enforcement officials had to be prodded to protect the returnees from vandalism, arson and trigger-happy nightriders.

The evacuees' humble quarters in the prewar Oriental ghettos had been taken over by black- and brown-skinned war industry workers; since there was no place to live, hostels had to be set up in churches and schools. Dillon Myer reported that by the end of 1945, after all the WRA camps had been vacated, 110 hostels were operating in California alone. Ironically, after war's end in August of 1945, the very military installations that the Evacuation was intended to safeguard were pressed into use as temporary homes for the returnees. Santa Ana Air Base in Orange County, Camp Kohler near Sacramento, Fort Funston in San Francisco were among the bases that housed the Japanese Americans.

Re-establishing the returnees proved to be infinitely more difficult than uprooting them had been; the process might be compared to trying to reassemble a broken egg. Many older Issei, primarily unattached bachelors, were reluctant to leave the shelter of the camps and at Granada and Minidoka a few had to be boosted physically onto trains that were to take them back to the Coast—to what, they did not know. Dr. Clifford Uyeda, a onetime JACL president, has charged that WRA "seemed totally insensitive to the plight of the Issei who had everything they worked for taken away from them and were then asked to go out into the hostile, uncertain and unknown society outside the camp."

But readjustment was difficult even for Nisei. Each individual has a story to tell. Let us look at the experiences of a few who had been dynamic leaders and towers of strength in the early years of JACL. Because JACL needed him as director of the Chicago office, Dr. Tom Yatabe had put off his return to dentistry. At war's end, when he was nearing fifty years of age, Yatabe decided against returning to Fresno and opened a practice in Chicago. On the other hand Dr. Terry Hayashi, a contemporary of Yatabe's, returned to San Francisco to rebuild his practice. Sim Togasaki's importing business had been destroyed by the war. He realized it would take some time before Japan could resume exports. While waiting, Togasaki volunteered to accompany a shipment of goats being sent to Okinawa by a mission group to start a milk and meat project. Kay Sugahara of Los Angeles had been a customs broker specializing in shipments from Japan. His business also was destroyed. He served during the war with the Office of Strategic Services, the predecessor of the Central Intelligence Agency. He realized early on that it was in America's interest to help rebuild Japan as a bulwark against communism in East Asia and carried the message to highly placed American officials. In time he went into the shipping business and acquired his own fleet of oil tankers, refrigerated transports and other vessels.

Jimmie Sakamoto, the blind Seattle publisher, lost his weekly *Japanese American Courier* in the Evacuation. Camp life had been particularly difficult for him. Many who resented the positions JACL had taken blamed Sakamoto personally. There had been rumors of plots to kill him. The hum of conversation would stop when Sakamoto's wife, Misao, entered the camp laundry room. Misao took her two older daughters to Notre Dame, Indiana, where she worked as a cleaning woman at St. Mary's College while Jimmie remained in camp with his aged parents and youngest daughter. After the war Sakamoto took his parents and daughter back to Seattle to await Misao's return. Sakamoto lacked the resources to start up his newspaper again. For a time his family lived in rented quarters on government assistance—his parents' old-age pensions and Jimmie's aid to the blind. Misao took care of the family and hired out as a domestic and hospital cleaning lady. One day they received a check in the mail from California JACL friends. Sim Togasaki and other old friends had contributed to buy Jimmie a guide dog. The Sakamotos wept together, not so much for the money but in realization that they hadn't been forgotten. Jimmie felt there were blinded veterans who needed a guide dog more than he did and decided against applying for one. He used some of the money to get badly needed surgery. Father Leopold Tibesar, who had converted the Sakamotos to Catholicism, took Sakamoto one day to the St. Vincent de Paul workshop where discarded items were rebuilt for sale in the thrift store and persuaded the manager that Jimmie could run the telephone soliciting campaign. He took on the job with characteristic enthusiasm and notable success, until one morning ten years after war's end he was hit and killed by a car on his way to work.

Clarence Arai had suffered from hypertension before the Evacuation. Despite a slight stroke while in Minidoka he managed to work part-time in the camp legal department. Three months after the Arais returned to Seattle in 1945 their only son, Ken, died at age nine of a malignancy. Clarence was shattered by the loss and his own health deteriorated. Unable to resume his law practice, he took up photography as a hobby and became widely recognized as an artist with the camera. To meet their bills his wife, Yone, went to night school and learned the art of coloring photographs with oils. She trained others and opened her own shop with five employees. At night she supervised a crew of waitresses at a leading restaurant. Yone also took care of her husband, who had his ups and downs, and her ailing mother-in-law, who also lived with them. For a dozen years until Arai died in 1964, Yone survived on an average of five hours of sleep a night.

Meanwhile, Kido was busily planning JACL's future. One idea dominated his thinking: the wartime sacrifice of Japanese Americans—the evacuees, the men who had fought and died for their country, the civilians whose lives had been disrupted—must not have been in vain. By the time Mike Masaoka returned to Salt Lake from Europe, Kido had a program well formulated in his mind. But first he had to get a mandate from the organization. And he needed Masaoka's talents. Masaoka had come home with vague but promising job offers from several large Eastern newspapers. "You can't abandon JACL now," Kido argued. "Our work is just starting." Masaoka was moved by both Kido's eloquence and his own sense of duty. He abandoned plans, at least temporarily, for a newspaper career and set about preparing for JACL's first postwar convention. It was held in Denver from February 28 to March 4, 1946, only six and a half months after the end of the fighting in the Pacific, with Min Yasui and his brother-in-law,

Toshio Ando, working furiously to nail down program details.

Even before the formal convention opened, the anger of JACLers who had been taunted, ridiculed, criticized and threatened by some of their peers for their unwavering loyalty burst through the surface of festive good cheer. In an informal afternoon meeting which went on far past the dinner hour, JACLers heatedly debated organizational policy toward Nisei draft-dodgers and those who had renounced allegiance to the United States only to seek desperately to avoid being sent to Japan from the Tule Lake segregation camp after the surrender.

Some of the delegates charged that many of the renunciants were troublemakers who had disrupted the camps, condemned JACL stalwarts as WRA stooges, ridiculed volunteers for military service as "suckers" and opted to go to Tule Lake because they either hated America or wished to escape military service. These individuals, one delegate asserted, would be a constant reminder that there were Nisei who wavered in their loyalty to the United States and they would always be a disruptive element in Japanese American communities. JACL was urged to go on record as demanding the immediate deportation of those who failed to express loyalty, and that Tuleans allowed to remain in the United States be required to carry special identification cards. Others expressed anger that if no distinction was made between those who stood on principle and those who wavered, the disloyal Tuleans would reap the benefits won through Nisei military sacrifice.

JACL had in fact made considerable efforts to help some of the draft resisters. Joe Grant Masaoka and Min Yasui first met with Nisei from the Amache camp at Granada being held at the Federal Correctional Institution outside Denver. Yasui, who had gone to jail to challenge the curfew order as discriminatory, endorsed restoration of Selective Service because it ended discrimination. Next they visited Amache to talk with confused young men being pressured by activists to resist military service. Then they traveled to Cheyenne, Wyoming, to talk with some fifty imprisoned draft violators from the Heart Mountain camp. (To put the number of resisters in perspective, it is necessary to note that more than seven hundred men from Heart Mountain signed up for the draft and took their physical examinations.) Some time later the pair visited the Gila and Poston camps and patiently listened to the protests of those opposing the draft. Their complaints had to do mostly with bitterness over evacuation on the basis of race; understandably they refused to serve in the uniform of a country that had mistreated them.

Yasui and Masaoka agreed that the Evacuation was unjust, but they also argued that the Nisei would be in a much stronger position to demand justice if they demonstrated their loyalty by complying with the draft law like all other citizens. By violating the law, the two declared, the resisters were not only establishing a criminal record for themselves, but taking an action that reflected on the loyalty of all Japanese Americans.

It is not likely that the counseling did much good. The issue had become too polarized for easy solution. Masaoka and Yasui wrote in their report: "Competent and sympathetic legal advice would have prevented some of the Nisei from violating the draft law."

Pacific Citizen and A. L. Wirin were also targets of the anger of some delegates. The newspaper was criticized for publicizing the efforts of some Tuleans to remain in the United States and the publicity was interpreted as sympathy for their plight. Wirin had served privately as counsel for some Tuleans as well as a group of Heart Mountain youths who had refused to register for military service.

Ultimately, cooler heads prevailed. It was pointed out that if Tuleans were required to carry special identification, all Japanese Americans could be embarrassed by being asked to show they were not from Tule Lake. JACL, it was decided, would not seek to influence the Justice Department in its determination as to which of the Tuleans would be permitted to rescind their decision to abandon America; JACL would enter test cases only if it appeared the rights of all Japanese Americans were being jeopardized. *Pacific Citizen,* it was pointed out, had an obligation to print the news. And Wirin, while serving as unpaid JACL counsel, was entitled to and often did serve private clients whose interests may have run counter to the League's position.

Debate over another issue revealed that some members had failed to learn from the lesson of the Evacuation. They questioned the wisdom of working with the American Civil Liberties Union because it had intervened in behalf of Communists, the German-American Bund and Gerald L. K. Smith, a notorious Fascist. JACL association with other minority groups was also questioned because "to cooperate with them would serve to compound our difficulties with those of others whereas we ought to concentrate on the problems of the Japanese alone."

The minutes of the meeting carry these passages:

> JACL on specific programs, such as testing the constitutionality of evacuation and the curfew orders, has cooperated with the ACLU because it is the best equipped organization to deal with such matters. It is recognized by the government itself as a defender of civil rights and liberties for all, regardless of race, color, or ancestry. It is America's watchdog on such matters. . . . The general consensus was that the problems of one minority were inextricably tied up with the problems of other minorities, that the welfare of one affected the welfare of others, and what is bad for one group is bad for others.

Next day, at the convention's formal opening, delegates answered the roll call from Boise Valley, Idaho; Chicago; Denver; Idaho Falls, Idaho; Magic Valley, Idaho; Milwaukee; Mount Olympus, Utah; New York; North Platte, Nebraska; Pocatello, Idaho; Salt Lake City; San Francisco; San Jose; Snake River, Idaho; and Yellowstone, Idaho. The Arizona; Davis County, Utah; Greeley, Colorado; Ogden, Utah; and Pueblo, Colorado chapters were missing at the start but most of them showed up later. Only San Francisco and San Jose were from the former prohibited zone. The delegates, their anger spent, heard Kido report on his six-year stewardship of JACL. Speaking of the organization's most difficult days, he said:

> It is the irony of fate that I was the president when the organization with 66 chapters and close to 20,000 members dwindled down to only ten active chapters and about 1,700 members. I went through the years when it no longer was a matter of pride to belong to JACL, but rather a thing to be shunned. Only those brave in heart and determined in purpose, with the utmost confidence in the good that organized effort can accomplish, remained with JACL. . . .
>
> The marvel to me is that JACL is still functioning and virile enough to have a national convention. No one can deny that the ideals for which JACL stands are sound. Otherwise, it could not have survived the trials and tribulations of wartime conditions. It should be a matter of pride to every JACLer that he was part of an organization which served its people and carried out its missions unwaveringly. Despite all the criticisms and hatred vented, one cannot overlook the contribution that JACL made by continuing its work for the general welfare.

Kido paid tribute to the sacrifices of Nisei servicemen, to JACL's overworked and underpaid staff and to Larry Tajiri's efforts as editor of *Pacific Citizen,* and then admitted that "our most difficult and unexpected task has been the educational campaign to make the Japanese Americans understand the position and role of the JACL. We did not realize that we would have to spend so much time in this field. Without the backing of our own group, we could not call ourselves representative."

Then, before an intent audience, Kido sketched the objectives for JACL which he had discussed at length in Salt Lake City with Hito Okada, Masaoka, George Inagaki and others. Even before the applause died down, the program and activities committee chaired by Dr. Randolph M. Sakada of Chicago went to work to shape the proposals into specific recommendations. In outline, they were:

1—Naturalization and citizenship rights for all persons of demonstrated loyalty to the United States without regard to national origin, race or creed, on the same basis for all immigrants. Enactment of this legislation would strike at the heart of most discriminatory acts against persons of Japanese descent. Such discrimination was based on the fact that by law Japanese nationals were "inadmissable to American citizenship."

2—Reparations—the word appears on pages 44 and 51 of the minutes—for losses caused by discriminatory treatment during the war. Congress should be urged to enact legislation creating a claims commission to pass on the legitimacy of losses and to compensate legitimate claimants.

3—Stay of deportation for "hardship cases" involving Japanese nationals, primarily international traders, and their families subject to deportation under existing laws.

4—JACL should take the initiative in calling a national conference of all minority groups to discuss mutual problems and ways to deal with them. The President should create a Department of Human Relations and Minority Problems.

5—The federal government should continue to discharge its obligations to the evacuees. No racial or ethnic discrimination should be tolerated in employment, housing or issuance of business and professional licenses.

6—The constitutionality of alien land laws and methods conceived by states to escheat lands held by Japanese Americans should be challenged in the courts.

7—The constitutionality of the Evacuation, specifically the basis for arbitrary discrimination against one group of American citizens, should be re-examined in the light of known facts and without the pressure of wartime hysteria.

8—JACL should create a special committee or commission to gather all surveys, documents and published material on various phases of the Evacuation and relocation and a library should be established to preserve this material.

9—All facilities of JACL should be extended to Nisei veterans to help them readjust to civilian life.

10—Every effort should be made to keep the subject of Japanese Americans in the public eye until their problems are resolved. Useful contacts developed during the war should be maintained and strengthened.

11—JACL should carry out a long-range Americanization program to help Japanese Americans individually and as a group to become "better Americans in a greater America."

12—A national JACL planning commission should be established.

13—A national scholarship and loan fund should be established to help deserving Japanese American students, and a similar fund should be established to help talented Nisei artists, musicians, dancers, etc., continue their studies.

14—To honor the American who has contributed most to better human relationships and who has thereby contributed to a better understanding of the Japanese in our country, every national convention should present a special distinguished-service award. A similar award should be made to honor the Japanese American who has contributed most to the welfare of the Japanese in the United States during each biennium. (A list of Japanese Americans who have since received this award appears in Appendix C.)

These broad, far-reaching and remarkably farsighted goals became the blueprint for JACL endeavors for the next three and a half decades. They were the product of the thinking of many JACL leaders but were reduced to acceptable form by Dr. Sakada and his committee including Peter Aoki, George Minato and George Fujii. JACL has never fully acknowledged its debt to these individuals. These sweeping goals were further refined into a series of resolutions by a committee chaired by Joe Grant Masaoka and including Alice Kasai, Yurino Takayoshi and Yukio

Inouye. The resolutions committee added one more point. It asked Congress to authorize admission of alien spouses of service-connected personnel into the United States from all countries irrespective of present immigration quotas and restrictions. This was particularly significant in the case of Japanese women marrying American servicemen, for it would breach the ban against Japanese embodied in the Immigration Act of 1924.

The delegates also approved budgets for 1946, 1947 and 1948 with little discussion. The 1946 budget called for spending $68,064 and was adopted without change. It included appropriations for offices in New York, San Francisco, Chicago, Denver, Los Angeles and Seattle in addition to $24,094 for national headquarters in Salt Lake City. (The delegates agreed to keep national headquarters in Salt Lake City for at least two more years.) In the two subsequent years, some of the regional offices were to be closed down or taken over by local chapters. Thus the budget dropped to $37,300 for 1947 and $26,100 for 1948. While many delegates expressed doubt that enough money could be raised to meet expenses, others insisted it was necessary to set goals and then go out and get the money. For the first time Japanese Americans in Hawaii were seen as potential donors. The budget committee, headed by Kay Terashima, also urged that JACL offer "living wages" to its employees. "Paid personnel of JACL should not be asked to sacrifice further; the war period is over, the emergency is passed," the committee's report said. Then it proposed an annual salary of $3,600 for regional representatives—sufficient for modest living in those times, but far from generous.

Several significant changes were written into the constitution and bylaws. Perhaps the most important was a provision for the popular election of national officers by the membership rather than having each chapter cast one ballot. The proposal called for a nominations committee to submit a slate of candidates at least four months before the national convention. The National Board would certify the candidates within one month and the national secretary would mail ballots to all members. Members would be given three weeks to return the ballots. The national secretary would tabulate the ballots "but shall not announce the results of the elections until the next national convention shall have convened."

Controversy centered on the manner of counting the ballots.

Some suggested an impartial board should be given the responsibility as protection for both members and the national secretary. Another proposal was to have at least three chapter presidents sit as the tallying committee, while still others urged that certified public accountants supervise the counting. Ultimately it was agreed unanimously that the proposal of the constitution committee (Mits Kaneko, chairman; Etsu Masaoka; Yuri Yamashita) that the national secretary do the counting be tried for the next convention and then reviewed.

The bylaws incorporated a pledge of membership to be signed, notarized or witnessed and then recorded before membership cards would be issued. The pledge read:

> I, the undersigned, do solemnly swear (or affirm) that I will support and defend the Constitution of the United States of America against all enemies, foreign and domestic; that I will bear true faith and allegiance to the same; that I do hereby forswear and repudiate any other allegiance which I knowingly or unknowingly may have held heretofore; and that I have taken these obligations freely, without any mental reservation whatsoever or purpose of evasion. So help me God.

The bylaws also adopted the Japanese American Creed, written by Mike Masaoka and read into the *Congressional Record* on May 9, 1941, as JACL's "official creed." Here is the text:

> I am proud that I am an American citizen of Japanese ancestry, for my very background makes me appreciate more fully the wonderful advantages of this nation. I believe in her institutions, ideals, and traditions; I glory in her heritage; I boast of her history; I trust in her future. She has granted me liberties and opportunities such as no individual enjoys in this world today. She has given me an education befitting kings. She has entrusted me with the responsibilities of the franchise. She has permitted me to build a home, to earn a livelihood, to worship, think, speak, and act as I please—as a free man equal to every other man.
>
> Although some individuals may discriminate against me, I shall never become bitter or lose faith, for I know that such persons are not representative of the majority of the American people. True, I shall do all in my power to discourage such practices, but I shall do it in the American way: above-board, in the open, through courts of law, by education, by proving myself to be worthy of equal treatment and consideration. I am firm in my belief that American sportsmanship and attitude of fair play will judge citi-

> zenship and patriotism on the basis of action and achievement, and not on the basis of physical characteristics.
>
> Because I believe in America, and I trust she believes in me, and because I have received innumerable benefits from her, I pledge myself to do honor to her at all times and in all places; to support her Constitution; to obey her laws, to respect her flag; to defend her against all enemies, foreign or domestic; to assume actively my duties and obligations as a citizen, cheerfully and without any reservations whatsoever, in the hope that I may become a better American in a greater America.

The creed has been quoted and reprinted widely but it came into being as something of an accident. The Salt Lake City chapter was printing a program for one of its functions and had been unable to sell an advertising space on the back page. Groping for something to use there, Masaoka sat down and quickly composed the creed. The actual writing took only a few minutes, but obviously he had been thinking about its content for a long time.

Two other convention decisions should be noted. The first was more an effort than a decision. The delegates agreed that the term "Japanese American" was awkward and something more suitable should be sought. But no one could think of a better term, so it was decided to keep "Japanese American" while a search continued. (More than a third of a century later, the search is still fruitless.) However, the delegates accepted a recommendation that JACL launch an educational campaign to eliminate the hyphen between the words "Japanese" and "American" and also to drop the hyphen in all similar descriptive names such as "Italian-American" and "German-American."

The convention was much more positive about a policy of "non-participation or intervention in the affairs of other nations unless the rights of Japanese Americans as citizens of the United States are directly involved." The policy statement contained in the minutes reads:

> The plight of the Canadian, Mexican, Brazilian and even of the Japanese in Japan itself is not the primary concern of JACL. Our first obligation is to the Japanese people here in the United States and the national board does not believe that we should divide our efforts by delving into international relations as a general principle. Rather, the board believes that we should concentrate every effort to wipe out discrimination and prejudice in the United States first before looking for new fields for operations. This means

> that JACL should not sponsor or take part in such projects as relief for Japan, or for any other country. But this prohibition does not enjoin individual members from participating in such campaigns as individuals; in fact, members are encouraged to participate in any and all worthy drives and campaigns of a civic character. At the same time the national board made it clear that when the rights as American citizens of Japanese Americans are involved, such as discriminatory treatment at international frontiers as in reported cases at the Canadian and Mexican borders, it becomes the duty of JACL to make strong representations and to use their every office to discourage such prejudiced and prejudicial treatment. Study of the status of Nisei stranded in Japan because of the war was ordered and national headquarters instructed to report its findings on this matter.

In retrospect, it may appear that JACL was overly ethnocentric and even timid about concerns beyond its own tiny group. But it is necessary to recall that JACL was organized to promote the welfare of that particular group, and to understand the uncertainty its members felt after the trauma of the Evacuation when demands to "deport" Nisei were being voiced by supposedly responsible persons. Still unsure of their status as Americans, they hesitated to take actions that might reflect adversely on their loyalty. The year 1946 was a time when the melting pot was still held up as the American ideal; pride in ethnic background was not to become popular and acceptable until several more decades had passed.

However, family ties could not be denied. As soon as Nisei stranded in Japan during the war were able to make contact with their families in the United States, strenuous efforts were made to bring them back home. Scores of private bills were introduced in Congress through the efforts of JACL at the behest of Japanese Americans to permit the return of those stranded.

In one of its final acts, the convention elected Hito Okada president in recognition of his dedicated service as treasurer during the war years. His cabinet was made up of George Inagaki of Venice, California, first vice-president; Masao Satow of Milwaukee, second vice-president; Bill Yamauchi of Pocatello, third vice-president; Dr. Takashi Mayeda of Denver, secretary to the Board; and Kay Terashima of Salt Lake City, treasurer. Mike Masaoka was retained as national secretary, but that was an unnecessary gesture.

Some time before the convention Kido had persuaded Masaoka to go to Washington to lobby for those parts of JACL's program that required congressional action. These included citizenship for the Issei, compensation for wartime losses, and stay of deportation for hardship cases. No one could say how long the assignment would take, nor how it would be accomplished. But Masaoka was anxious to give it a try. His funds would be extremely limited, but he had justice and the splendid cooperative wartime record of the Japanese Americans on his side.

To fill in for Masaoka, JACL's National Council asked Masao Satow to join the headquarters staff for one year. Satow was not anxious to leave the YMCA, but JACL's summons was difficult to turn down. Satow's one year stretched out into a quarter century of faithful service, and Masaoka became a permanent resident of Washington.

XIX

The Golden Era

The decade following war's end was JACL's golden era. The organization in its 1946 Denver convention had set urgent, deeply significant and sometimes seemingly impossible goals. In achieving them one by one, it demonstrated itself to be a mature, influential and respected organization with access to and influence on the nation's power centers. Tested and tempered in the crucible of war and the Evacuation, it now displayed the capacity to rise above Li'l Tokyo pettiness to become a national force. It knew what it wanted and it learned how to find satisfaction. The JACL of this period held little resemblance to the insecure, inexperienced, ineffective—if well-intentioned—organization of just two decades earlier.

Yet, strangely, every step was a struggle. The undeserved hostility JACL had experienced from Nisei during the war years persisted. Money was a perpetual problem. Membership remained but a fraction of the post–Pearl Harbor peak of some twenty thousand. Oddly enough, much of the financial support for JACL's legislative campaigns came from the Issei who, while ineligible for membership, understood the value of JACL's goals and responded generously to its appeals.

The League could not have achieved its objectives without an amazing amount of tireless work by two remarkable husband-and-wife teams—Mike and Etsu Masaoka in Washington, and Masao and Chizuko Satow back at headquarters, first in Salt Lake City and later in San Francisco. Most of the men who believed in and dedicated themselves to JACL were blessed with wives who supported their efforts and never resented the League as a rival for their husbands' time and attention. Harry Honda, who succeeded Larry Tajiri as editor of *Pacific Citizen,* observes: "National JACL presidents needed the understanding, help and encouragement of their families during their time-consuming administrations. At the chapter volunteer level, in many cases the wife of the elected president would serve as secretary, elected or otherwise. This all says something about belief in a cause." Perhaps the one notable exception is Hito Okada, who admits that JACL's demands were a factor in the breakup of his marriage to his first wife, Hana. But the pain of that experience was assuaged years later in a conversation with his daughter Carolyn. They were talking about what JACL had done for Japanese Americans and she commented that it had been able to eliminate racial discrimination against her. "There is still discrimination," Okada said, "it's just that you haven't felt it." Okada has never forgotten her reply: "That's because you did a good job, Dad."

Etsu Masaoka and Chiz Satow waded into the battles alongside their men. For years, Masaoka worked out of a tiny rented apartment in Washington with his typewriter on the dresser and Etsu was secretary, girl Friday, confidante and consultant as well as wife. Both Satow and Chiz had learned frugality during humble childhoods and they counted the organization's pennies as carefully as though they were their own.

In 1950, about the time JACL was experiencing some of its greatest legislative triumphs, there wasn't enough money in the treasury to pay the staff. Paychecks hadn't been issued for three months. It was at a district convention in Pocatello that Hito Okada, by then national president, and George Inagaki, soon to be a national president, came up with the idea for what was to become the Thousand Club. The objective was to persuade each of 1,000 members to contribute $25 annually, providing the national organization with a dependable $25,000 a year for operating expenses. After ten years the contributors would become "life members." In addition to the satisfaction donors would find in supporting JACL, they sponsored the Thousand Club Whing Ding at national conventions, where members set aside their serious concerns for at least one night of good food and levity.

Inagaki as "Callahan," sporting a derby and arm garters, presided over a Thousand Club column.

A series of dedicated JACLers followed in the club chairmanship and perhaps the most notable was Harold Gordon, who is credited with naming the party the Whing Ding. During the war Gordon had been a Naval Intelligence officer in the Pacific. After the war he happened to meet one of his Japanese-language instructors, Byron Honda, in Chicago. Honda invited him to a JACL meeting at which Mike Masaoka was to explain the goals adopted at the Denver convention. Gordon (who was nicknamed Tokuzo by Mas Satow) immediately threw himself into the JACL program, volunteered his services in many of the organization's legislative battles and as an attorney provided legal assistance to Nisei who were trying to get relatives stranded by the war in Japan back home. His banjo playing was a feature of the Whing Dings. Gordon's friend Shig Wakamatsu says: "I don't know of any Nisei who worked harder for JACL, or who so selflessly crossed ethnic lines to help his friends."

Like almost everything else JACL attempted, the Thousand Club had a difficult beginning. At first it was a struggle to sign up a hundred members. It took nearly ten years—Wakamatsu was chairman at the time—to reach the goal of a thousand members, whose contributions provided 40 percent of JACL's operating budget. By 1981 there were more than two thousand members and inflation had boosted the lowest category of membership dues to fifty dollars a year.

Masaoka's father had been a farmer turned grocer. Satow came from similarly modest origins. He was born in San Mateo, California, to Shuzo and Kiyose Satow. When Mas was still a toddler the Satows moved to Los Angeles where Shuzo supported his family much of the time as a "day worker," meaning he hired out by the day as a domestic, washing windows and cleaning the homes of the well-to-do. Both Masaoka and Satow scraped to get an education. After graduation from the University of California at Los Angeles in 1929, Satow went on to earn his Bachelor of Theology degree at Princeton Theological Seminary in 1932. Instead of going into the ministry he joined the staff of the Los Angeles YMCA as secretary of the Japantown office. There was no YMCA building in Li'l Tokyo and one of Satow's more difficult duties was to explain to his boys why his organization, dedicated to Christian ideals, denied them use of the downtown Y swimming pool. Satow ran his program out of a fourth-floor office in the heart of Li'l Tokyo. At the lunch counter of the Iwaki Drugstore on the ground floor, there was an attractive girl named Chiz Uyeda concocting sodas and serving blue plate specials. She and Mas were married just before the Evacuation in 1942 and set up housekeeping at the Santa Anita assembly center.

Satow enjoyed the YMCA and working with youngsters. But three weeks after he was elected a JACL vice-president at the Denver convention Satow took a year's leave of absence from his Y job in Milwaukee, resigned his League office and signed on as its Eastern-Midwest district representative to organize chapters, drum up membership and help with resettlement problems. Before the year ended it became evident Masaoka would be in Washington for a while. Masaoka took the title of Washington representative, heading the Anti-Discrimination Committee, JACL's lobbying arm which was supported by small contributions from as many as ten thousand Issei. Without their backing the Washington operation would have been in desperate straits. Satow was named acting national secretary (a title soon to be changed to "national director") and moved to the Salt Lake City headquarters where he could keep the League going and provide the organizational support that Masaoka needed.

Masaoka had headed for Washington with no firm idea as to how he would attain JACL's goals, or whether they could be achieved at all. But he was not one to be dismayed at the prospect of tilting at windmills. To understand the enormity of Masaoka's task, it is necessary to remember that Nisei were still virtually unknown in the nation's capital. There were no Nisei members of Congress to open doors and arrange introductions. Old friend Elbert Thomas, in the twilight of his long and distinguished Senate career, was anxious to help but now his greatest value lay in assisting Masaoka in meeting other members of Congress. Much of the time Masaoka was on his own, and for a chronicle of his activities we turn to the book *Nisei:*

> A professional lobbyist might have launched his campaign with a 10,000-dollar cocktail party in a downtown hotel. Masaoka began by calling on key members of Congress, members of important

committees who might be able to help him. Everyone who was acquainted with the Masaokas during this period emphasizes that Mike and Etsu worked as a team, she providing the quiet logistical support in the background while he trudged from office to office, testified at committee hearings, and put over his arguments in behind-scenes meetings. Many doors were closed to him at first, but he found help in unexpected places. A member of the Capitol guard, who had turned Masaoka away when he first came to Washington during the war, remembered him and proved extremely cooperative. Secretaries who saw Masaoka cooling his heels in outer offices day after day began to feel sorry for him, engaged him in conversation, and eventually they would put in a good word for him with their bosses. In time Masaoka became a familiar sight in the halls of the Senate and House office buildings. Lawmakers who never had occasion to talk to him knew him by name. Congressman Walter Judd of Minnesota, a onetime medical missionary in China, took an interest in Masaoka. Congressman Ed Gossett of Texas agreed to talk with Masaoka because he had heard of the 442nd's rescue of the Lost Battalion, and he became a strong advocate of liberalizing the immigration laws. Sheer persistence paid off in some cases. Masaoka had tried unsuccessfully for weeks to get an appointment with Congressman John Robison of Kentucky, a ranking member of the House Judiciary Committee which was involved with proposed bills for naturalization of *Issei* and evacuation claims. One day Masaoka saw Robison heading for the men's room. Masaoka quickly followed him, moved alongside and engaged him in conversation when he couldn't conveniently get away. Apparently he made an impression, for Robison invited Masaoka to go back to the office with him. In time he became a staunch supporter for the causes Masaoka was pushing.

There were many factors working for the *Nisei.* One was a growing realization that the evacuation had been a ghastly error, and some officials and prominent citizens were anxious to make amends. The pendulum, which had overreacted in one direction, was now swinging in the opposite direction. Another was the *Nisei* war record, a demonstration of loyalty that could not be ignored. One of Masaoka's close associates during this period was [Robert] Cullum, the former WRA aide, who had joined the staff of [JACL's] Committee for Equality in Naturalization. "Mike had a remarkable way of giving members of Congress the impression that he was on hand just to help them do the right thing," Cullum says. "He was able never to appear to be forcing anybody or anything. Mike was a prodigious worker, and he had a real talent for accepting advice without losing command of a situation. He soon gained a reputation for complete integrity. When you are playing on the side of the angels, you don't use a marked deck. All Mike had to do was tell the truth. But he told it well."

Masaoka's first success was passage of an amendment to the Soldier Brides Act in 1947. The amendment allowed American servicemen to bring Japanese wives and their children into the United States without regard to the exclusionary provisions of the 1924 immigration law. Although later successes, notably the Evacuation Claims Act a year later, were more widely acclaimed, the Soldier Brides Act was more significant in the long view. The key words in the Brides Act, says the book *East to America,* were "irrespective of race." The book observes: "They signaled significant progress in Congress and the nation at large on racial attitudes. The changing attitudes were further underscored by the report of Truman's Presidential Committee on Civil Rights, released October 20, 1947. One part of the report dealt with Japanese Americans and recommended passage of 'evacuation claims and naturalization legislation' and urged the various states 'to repeal discriminatory laws.' Masaoka, a consultant to the committee, obviously had some input. The report became the basis of President Truman's civil rights program recommended to Congress in 1948."

The year 1948 saw a series of heady victories for Masaoka, who was prodding Congress through the Anti-Discrimination Committee. On June 1 the President signed a bill offering citizenship "irrespective of race" to aliens who had served with the United States armed forces in World Wars I and II. This measure recognized Issei who had volunteered for specialized duty against Japan in World War II, and reopened naturalization to veterans of the previous war who had not taken advantage of the law that Tokie Slocum's efforts had made possible. On July 1, Truman signed another JACL-backed bill blocking the deportation of Japanese "treaty merchants" who had lost the right to live in the United States with the outbreak of war. Many had married American citizens and fathered American-citizen children, and their arbitrary expulsion would have imposed a great hardship on their citizen families. A day later, July 2, Truman signed the Japanese American Evacuation Claims Act, which Congress had passed without dissent. *Nisei* observes:

It is characteristic of Congress, perhaps, that it was able to agree on compensation for the evacuees before it did anything about their human rights. . . . The evacuees were given until January 3, 1950, to file claims against the government. By that deadline they filed 23,689 claims asking a total of $131,949,176—one-third of the sum the Federal Reserve Bank had estimated they had lost. The amount asked for broke down this way:

2,413 claims asked for sums of less than $500.
3,385 claims asked for sums between $501 and $1,000.
8,409 claims asked for sums between $1,001 and $2,500.
4,066 claims asked for sums between $2,501 and $5,000.
4,630 claims asked for sums between $5,001 and $100,000.
77 claims were for amounts in excess of $100,000.

The number of claims does not quite total 23,689, but federal records do not explain the discrepancy. At any rate, 60 percent of the claims were for less than $2,500—"pots and pans" claims for loss of household items—and 73 percent were under $5,000.

Predictably, the government was unable to find an easy way to settle these claims. In all of 1950 the Department of Justice heard only 211 claims—an average of $450 per claim.

Most appalling of all, it was costing the government about $1,400 per case to decide that a payment of $450 was equitable compensation!

Congress then approved a procedure [at Masaoka's urging] whereby a "compromise" settlement could be made without lengthy investigation. The Attorney General was permitted to pay three-fourths of the amount of a compensable claim, or $2,500, whichever was the less.

In 1952, 15,354 claims were compromised and settled for a total amount of $18,255,768. The original amount claimed was $46,664,332. By this time it took only $43.37 in administrative costs to settle an average claim for $773.65.

The final claim was paid late in 1965—more than twenty-three years after the evacuation. It was a compromise payment to Ed Koda, son of Keisaburo Koda, and to Mrs. Jean Koda, widow of Ed's brother, William. Their original claim was for $1,210,000. They were paid $362,500, and the Kodas had spent almost that much in litigation.

(The Koda family was in the business of growing rice on four thousand acres in the San Joaquin Valley, milling it and marketing it.)

It is essential to put these payments into proper perspective. Although some $38,000,000 was distributed, it amounted to only 10 cents on the dollar for losses as calculated by the Federal Reserve Bank. Many families did not file claims because they lacked the necessary documentary evidence of loss. The payments were by no means intended as reparations for wrongs which had been committed, recompense for injustice and humiliation or compensation for loss of time and earning power. The payments were little more than token reimbursement in the overwhelming majority of cases for literally the pots and pans and other household items that had been lost as a consequence of the Evacuation. It was a far from generous program. But it was a significant one inasmuch as Congress by acknowledging the justice of the claims also recognized the error of the Evacuation.

Meanwhile, California by greedily pursuing a series of escheat actions inadvertently forced a test of the constitutionality of its alien land laws, a test JACL welcomed. The state legislature voted $200,000 to prosecute violations of the alien land law. If the state could prove that land held in the names of Nisei had been purchased illegally for them by Issei, the property could be seized by the government without compensation and sold. To encourage counties to press such cases, the state offered to split the proceeds from the sale of such sequestered property. But by paying the state half the appraised value of the contested land, the owners could "compromise" the suit and retain their land. The state filed some eighty escheat cases between 1944 and 1948, seizing seven pieces of property and compromising eight others. Incensed by such outrageous blackmail, some of the victims with JACL's encouragement chose to fight. The Oyama case, which went to the U.S. Supreme Court after the California Supreme Court ruled in favor of the state, was a classic.

The circumstances were these: In 1934 Kajiro Oyama, an alien, bought six acres of land and recorded the deed in the name of his six-year-old son, Fred. Kajiro Oyama then went to court and was appointed as Fred's legal guardian. Kajiro Oyama later bought two additional acres for his son adjoining the first property. In 1944, when Fred was sixteen and his family was unable to return to defend his rights, the California attorney general filed escheat action charging the land had been bought "with intent to violate and evade the alien land law."

What followed is related in *East to America:*

> While the Oyama case was making its way through the California court system, hostile old-line California elements introduced a proposal to make existing alien land laws a part of the state constitution. It was called Proposition 15 and titled "Validation of Legislative Amendments to Alien Land Law." Proposition 15 was pushed by powerful, well-financed interests. The opposition was led by a still financially shaky JACL. With a war chest of only slightly more than $100,000, JACL sought to convince California voters of the injustice of Proposition 15 through the newspapers, an informational pamphlet, and frequent public appearances.
>
> Just five days before the election on November 5, 1946, the California Supreme Court upheld the state's seizure of Oyama's land. The outlook for defeating Proposition 15 appeared dark, but fortunately the California of 1946 was not the California of 1920. New generations had reached voting age. Veterans of World War II brought to the election their own point of view. The influx of tens of thousands of war workers unindoctrinated in California's anti-Orientalism introduced a strong new element to the electorate. To all of these elements the JACL argument was persuasive and together with reasonable members of the old California population, they defeated Proposition 15 by a margin of 1,143,780 to 797,067.
>
> The Oyama decision was appealed to the U.S. Supreme Court with JACL and other organizations filing *amicus curiae* briefs. Finally, on January 19, 1948, another long step toward equal treatment under the laws was achieved when the California verdict was reversed. Unfortunately, instead of attacking the alien land law head on, the high tribunal focused on Fred Oyama's rights as an American citizen. It found that California's alien land law clearly discriminated against Fred in that obstacles, which would not apply to minors of other ethnic origins, were placed in the way of Fred's right to receive property from his parents. The decision had the effect of making the alien land law unenforceable as it related to ownership by citizen-minors of Japanese ancestry, and eventually the pending escheat cases were dropped.

Following this decision JACL lobbyists persuaded the California legislature to reimburse those whose land had been escheated or who had paid to effect a compromise. Sam Ishikawa and Tats Kushida represented JACL in Sacramento together with Joe Grant Masaoka and June Fugita. They also succeeded in getting bills passed to grant state old-age pensions to Issei, to reduce sport fishing licenses for Issei from twenty-five dollars to the ten dollars charged all others and to restore liquor licenses formerly held by Japanese Americans.

It took three additional actions endorsed or instigated by JACL to lay California's alien land law, for so long a discriminatory deterrant to Japanese American assimilation, finally to rest. In the first case, Sei Fujii, feisty publisher of a Los Angeles Japanese newspaper, bought an unimproved city lot which the state subsequently sought to escheat. A district court cited the United Nations Charter, which specified that everyone is entitled to own property "without distinction of any kind such as race, color, sex, language, religious, political or other opinion, national or social origin, property, birth or other status," and ruled the California alien land law "untenable and unenforceable."

The second case involved the Masaoka family. Ike Masaoka and his wife, Sumiko, deeded a lot in Pasadena to his mother, Haruye. Ike and his brothers Henry, Tad, Mike and Joe Grant proposed to build a home on the property for her use during her lifetime, after which it would revert to the sons. This charitable and commendable action was illegal under the alien land law. Since Haruye Masaoka was an alien ineligible to citizenship the property was subject to escheat action and her sons would be guilty of a felony for trying to provide for her security. The brothers asked the court: "Can the state of California by statute relegate citizens of the United States to a position inferior to that of other citizens and, in some cases, inferior to aliens, merely because of their racial origin, in the matter of the right to make and enforce contracts; in the matter of providing for the security of persons and property; in the matter of the right to purchase land, sell, hold and convey real or personal property, and in the personal relationship of those citizens to their own parents. . . ."

This was a question the court found impossible to answer affirmatively, particularly in view of the fact that one of Mrs. Masaoka's sons had died in the service of his country, while four of the sons bringing the suit were veterans and three of them had been wounded in action. The court ruled the alien land law violated the equal protection clause of the Fourteenth Amendment "both as to the alien mother and citizen-sons" and was therefore unconstitutional.

About subsequent action, *East to America* notes:

> The alien land law had been ruled unenforceable and illegal, but it remained in the statute books. In 1956 JACL launched a campaign to repeal the law by the most impressive route possible—a direct vote of the people in a general election. The repeal measure was titled Proposition 13. Thanks to the almost total reversal in public opinion, victory was relatively easy. The newspapers, city and county governing bodies, political leaders, community organizations, labor unions, veterans groups—all of them had endorsed the alien land law when it was first proposed in 1913 and again in 1920—now joined in what amounted to a virtual crusade to wipe the slate clean. JACL leaders campaigned with characteristic zeal but the changing tide of public opinion made their work easy. More than 2.5 million Californians voted for repeal, winning by a two to one margin. Now there remained no legal barriers in the Golden State to prevent Orientals from buying farmland, homes, business buildings, or other real property on the same basis as anyone else.
>
> California had been the bellwether of legalized discrimination by state governments. The changes taking place in California soon were reflected elsewhere; one by one other states took the steps necessary to rid themselves of the taint. But the last of the alien land laws was not eliminated until 1966 when voters of the state of Washington, on the third effort spearheaded by JACL, finally removed this racist legislation from the law books.

Victory in the long struggle to eliminate discriminatory statutes was satisfying, but in reality the alien land laws had been rendered toothless fourteen years earlier by what certainly must be JACL's greatest legislative triumph. That was the landmark Walter-McCarran Act of 1952, which eliminated race as a consideration in immigration to the United States and naturalization. The alien land laws, and scores of other racially discriminatory measures, had been based on laws making Asian aliens ineligible for citizenship; the act of opening naturalization to them destroyed the peg on which the land laws had hung. Moreover, the Walter-McCarran Act eliminated the division of the world's peoples under American immigration statutes into desirable and undesirable, a categorization that deeply offended Asia's emerging nations and no doubt had much to do with the rise of militarism in Japan which led inevitably to the extension of World War II into the Pacific. For JACL, citizenship rights for the Issei and equality under immigration laws for the Japanese represented ultimate realization of the objectives that had gone into the formation of the League more than two decades earlier. But that victory was not won without some dramatic cliff-hanging and political heroics.

Mike Masaoka's original strategy had been to seek a congressional resolution eliminating race as a factor in naturalization. But that proved to be too simplistic an approach. Some of Masaoka's friends and advisers felt it was too soon after the war to seek legislation favorable to Japan. Some wanted to link naturalization with a thorough overhaul of immigration and naturalization laws. Others would put their first priority on European refugees. Still others suggested citizenship for only parents of Nisei soldiers killed in action. Another proposal was to provide naturalization only for Japanese already living in the United States. Masaoka explained his position:

> We were willing to accept almost any cooperation with the liberal elements, but we were most concerned that naturalization be granted our parents as early as possible since so many were in the twilight of their lives. Furthermore, if we could secure the repeal of the Japanese exclusion act of 1924, so much the better, for that would be Congressional recognition that the Japanese were "good enough" to be admitted into our country and, subsequently, to become citizens. It was obvious that if postwar Japan was to emerge as a democratic state, its nationals could not be treated less worthily than the nationals of other countries. So our task was to try to gain our minimum goals while not alienating either the liberals or conservatives to the extent that no legislation would result.

Congressman Judd in 1947 introduced a measure removing racially discriminatory provisions from immigration and naturalization laws. The House approved the bill but the Senate sat on it. Two years later, with Masaoka's encouragement, he introduced a similar bill. It passed the House again but this time the Senate made some extensive changes including limiting naturalization of Japanese to those already in the United States. The two versions went to a conference committee which restored the House provisions applying to the Japanese, but added rigid internal security measures in keeping with the then current political climate.

To understand how an immigration and naturalization bill became entangled in internal security matters, it is necessary to understand the state of the nation's mind. Late in 1948 a former high State Department official, Alger Hiss, was indicted for perjury after he denied charges that he gave secret government documents to Whittaker Chambers, a Communist agent and onetime *Time* magazine editor. In September of 1949 the Soviet Union exploded its first atomic bomb and a few weeks later eleven leaders of the United States Communist party were convicted of advocating the violent overthrow of the United States government. Many Americans were seeing Reds under every bed and Senator Joseph McCarthy, a Wisconsin Republican, fanned public fears with unfounded but plausible charges that Communists were widely entrenched in the federal government. Many members of Congress harbored an overwhelming fear of Communist infiltration and were willing to jeopardize some basic human rights to control it.

In 1950 Congress passed the Internal Security Act, also called the McCarran concentration camp measure after its sponsor, Senator Pat McCarran, a Nevada Democrat. Its Title II authorized the President, in case of invasion, insurrection or declaration of war, to order detention without trial of persons suspected of being spies or saboteurs. In effect, Title II codified the imprisonment of Japanese Americans during World War II and made the same kind of treatment a possibility for all citizens in a future emergency. President Truman vetoed the measure as "a long step toward totalitarianism." But McCarthy had stirred congressional fears enough to override the veto and the Internal Security Act of 1950 became law.

In the first weeks of the Eighty-second Congress, convened in January of 1951, Congressmen Judd, Francis E. Walter (Democrat, Pennsylvania), George P. Miller (Democrat, California) and Sidney R. Yates (Democrat, Illinois) again sponsored bills providing citizenship for Asian aliens. McCarran introduced an omnibus immigration and naturalization bill in the Senate shortly afterward. About this time Judd, who had been working so persistently for immigration and naturalization reform, ran into a bit of partisanship. Several years ago he recalled for Harry Takagi that he was approached one day by Democratic Speaker Sam Rayburn. According to Judd, Rayburn realized the Judd bill would pass but he wanted the Democrats to get credit for it. So he persuaded Judd to let Congressman Walter, also a friend of JACL, to introduce the House counterpart to McCarran's Senate bill. Favorable public hearings were held in April of 1951 and the Departments of State and Justice gave their blessings.

Among those endorsing the measure were the American Legion, Veterans of Foreign Wars, American Federation of Labor and National Grange, all of which reversed the positions they had taken in favor of the racially discriminatory Immigration Act of 1924.

But many liberals had strong reservations about some provisions of the omnibus bill which they feared would implant more firmly the security features of the concentration camp law. Some two hundred amendments were proposed in an effort to defeat the law. But both House and Senate passed their versions of the omnibus bill by substantial margins, minor differences were ironed out by a conference committee and it was sent to the White House on June 13, 1952.

President Truman was under enormous pressure from both sides. He approved of the changes in the immigration and naturalization laws but his liberal instincts recoiled at the security measures. Once again desirable reforms fell victim to a veto directed against unrelated provisions.

JACL was holding its twelfth biennial national convention in San Francisco with Dr. Randolph M. Sakada of Chicago as president when word of Truman's veto was received. Masaoka was still in Washington waiting for the verdict. He knew that Congress was itching for a fight and it well might override the veto. He also realized that while the Walter-McCarran measure had shortcomings, it should be passed because it might be a long wait for something that everyone could agree was ideal. When the House voted 278 to 113 to override, Masaoka knew it was now or never. At 10:30 on the night of June 26, Sakada called a special meeting of JACL delegates to announce that the Senate was scheduled to vote the next day and it was JACL's last chance to fight for immigration and naturalization reform. Richard Akagi, Masaoka's assistant in the Washington office, reviewed the day's events for the delegates and announced the National Board had decided to ask them to send telegrams to their senators urging them to override the veto. Telegram blanks were passed out. Mas Satow collected the handwritten messages and took them to a Western Union office for transmission.

At 11:30 next morning (2:30 P.M. Washington time) a convention session on increasing membership was interrupted and Haruo Ishimaru, at the time Northern California regional director, announced that the Senate was about to begin voting on overriding Truman's veto. JACL's decades-old hopes hung in the balance. So solemn was the moment that JACL for one of the few times in its history invoked the aid of the Deity. Ishimaru led the assembly—Christians, Buddhists, agnostics—in a moment of silent prayer for the success of their efforts.

The meeting was still in session when it was interrupted once more. Someone had just heard on a noon news broadcast that the Senate had passed the Walter-McCarran omnibus bill over the presidential veto, 57 to 26. Moments later a telephone call from Masaoka confirmed the news. The convention minutes report in deadpan fashion: "The delegates cheered and shed tears of joy in the realization that our major legislative goal of equality in naturalization had been achieved at last." In reality, pandemonium had broken loose. When Mike and Etsu Masaoka arrived in San Francisco next morning after an overnight propeller-plane flight, they were met at the airport by a large crowd of jubilant delegates.

In his report to the convention Masaoka was generous in recognizing those who had played key roles in making passage of the bill possible. A JACL task force composed of Tats Kushida, Sam Ishikawa and Joe Grant Masaoka had gone to Nevada to urge McCarran's supporters to let the senator know of their interest in the immigration-naturalization bill. John Tadano of the Arizona chapter had reached Senate Majority Leader Ernest W. McFarland, persuaded him the bill was important enough to enter on the Senate calendar and to vote for the override. Harold Gordon had risked his reputation as a Jewish liberal by speaking out forcefully in favor of the omnibus bill. There were many others. Masaoka had carried the ball, but it was a victory for the organization.

In recent years some observers have downplayed the importance of JACL's efforts to override the veto, asserting that rebellious Democrats were ready to join Republicans in frustrating Truman as they had in the past. Be that as it may, JACL had been the primary force in bringing immigration and naturalization policy reform to congressional attention. The same observers charge JACL took an extremely parochial position in judging the immigration and naturalization provisions affecting their own group to be more important than the repressive internal security portions of the measure. When asked about this point, Judd told Takagi: "In politics, you cannot draw up a bill that pleases everybody. You ought to go ahead and get the best you can. JACL, I think, wisely agreed to support the Walter-McCarran Bill. I've never had a qualm about this. There has never been one incident to indicate the un-wisdom of the decision. Most progress in government comes from minorities who have a cause, who are dedicated to it and are convinced it is right, and will work at it—which was JACL's role."

Masaoka, of course, points out that even more repressive legislation was already on the statute books.

East to America evaluates this historic episode in this manner:

> It did not take long for the Issei to avail themselves of the privilege of joining their children in American citizenship. By 1965, about 46,000 of them had become citizens of a country in which they had labored hard and to which they had contributed much. Overall, JACL, through the skill of its representative, Masaoka, probably gained much more influence in Washington than it enjoyed with the Japanese American community at large. Its record is an interesting example of the way in which a relatively small but well-organized group can achieve results when it focuses upon clear but limited objectives, particularly when those objectives right basic wrongs.
>
> However, not even Masaoka's skills and JACL's earnest concerns could have brought about the important legislative measures . . . if the behavior of the Japanese Americans themselves had not been exemplary. In later years when revolt became a popular credo, activists among the younger generation of Japanese Americans condemned the Issei and Nisei for having accepted the government's Evacuation order. They criticized Nisei men for stepping out of the concentration camps to offer their lives in the service of the nation that had betrayed them. JACL and Masaoka had urged Japanese Americans to cooperate with their government, unjust though its demands seemed at the time, as a patriotic duty in the clearly expressed hope that their sacrifice in the name of loyalty would lead to the righting of wrongs when the emergency was ended. That hope bore fruit as Masaoka seized every

opportunity to tell the story of the loyalty of Japanese Americans, dramatically demonstrated by their record on both the military and home fronts. That record proved to be a telling argument for righting historic wrongs.

There is one small postscript that illustrates JACL's adherence to principle. The next order of convention business after receiving word of the veto override was a report from the public-relations committee chaired by Pat Okura. One of its recommendations was that Masaoka be sent to Japan as a representative of the JACL "to make government, parliamentary and private contacts which would prove invaluable to JACL in securing accurate and official information regarding Japan and its policies generally." Okura declared it was essential for JACL to get firsthand information and Masaoka was the logical person to obtain it. George Inagaki added that since Masaoka was being asked about Japan by officials and others in Washington, he would be in a better position to comment on problems affecting the two countries if he had visited Japan. Since there had been talk among the delegates of doing something substantial for Masaoka as a gesture of appreciation for his labors, it would be logical to vote him a combination business and pleasure trip. But Sab Kido spoke up in virtually single-handed opposition. He reminded the delegates that at the 1946 convention JACL had determined to stay clear of international affairs, that there was the possibility JACL might be used as a tool by Japan and that contrary to Inagaki's argument, if Masaoka could plead ignorance about Japan it would be better for JACL in Washington. Ultimately the proposal was tabled. But times change. In 1968 Masaoka was summoned to Tokyo by the then Prime Minister, Eisaku Sato, to receive one of the highest decorations Japan can bestow upon a foreigner, the Order of the Rising Sun, Third Class, for his contributions to Japanese American amity and understanding. And when Masaoka resigned his Washington duties, JACL contributors gave him and his family a trip around the world.

XX

Pacific Citizen

During the war years when *Pacific Citizen* was performing such yeoman service its circulation was limited to less than nine thousand copies a week by newsprint restrictions. There is no doubt that many more copies could have been sold if they were available. The West Coast's Japanese-language papers along with their English sections had been forced to suspend publication and *Pacific Citizen* was the only national journal for Japanese Americans. Readers might be strongly opposed to JACL itself, but they had a need to know what was going on. So they subscribed to *Pacific Citizen* for themselves and sent gift subscriptions to Caucasian friends. For a time during the war years it is likely *Pacific Citizen* was the only part of JACL's program that had widespread acceptance among Japanese Americans.

But with war's end the situation changed abruptly. Newsprint became available, but *PC*'s circulation dropped alarmingly. At the time of the Denver convention early in 1946, *PC* had 7,500 subscribers and $6,500 in the bank. Two years later its circulation had slipped to 5,400 and there was only $2,900 in its cash reserve. There were many reasons for this change. The Japanese-language dailies had resumed publication with expanded English sections to provide the reborn communities on the West Coast with local news. The people of Los Angeles or San Francisco were no longer scattered throughout the country; it was no longer necessary to read *Pacific Citizen* to learn about friends. Gift subscriptions were not renewed. Although the battle was not over, many subscribers no longer felt the need to support a militant editorial voice such as Tajiri's *PC* had been in a time of peril. Since *PC* reflected the Nisei plight during the desperate struggle, it is likely that unconsciously many wanted to put it aside and forget about it. And while *PC*'s income was dropping, publication costs soared as prices and wages were freed from wartime controls. At the 1948 national convention in Salt Lake City the *Pacific Citizen* committee headed by Togo Tanaka felt the need to ask for a $2,500 subsidy from JACL and a similar sum from the Anti-Discrimination Committee, which was making extensive use of *PC*'s columns to carry news of its activities.

Editor Larry Tajiri was cast in an anomalous position. JACL owned the newspaper which was the voice of the organization. *PC* was obligated in one sense to cover JACL activities as a house organ, but particularly during the war years it also had to cover the wide range of events affecting all Japanese Americans. While a creature of JACL, *PC* had received no monetary support from it aside from staff salaries. *PC* met its bills from what little advertising had been available and the $2 annual subscription fee (non-JACLers were charged $2.50). However, only about one third of the membership subscribed. Finally, as an organizational organ, *PC* could not go out and compete vigorously head on for advertising and circulation with privately operated newspapers. *PC*'s status within JACL was complicated even more by publication of the monthly *JACL Reporter,* a true house organ with Mas Horiuchi, national headquarters office manager, as editor. The *Reporter* made no pretense toward editorial excellence. It simply recorded JACL housekeeping items and chapter activities; one of its mandates was to list the names of all members as they paid their dues. The *Reporter* was justified on the curious ground that since members weren't subscribing to *Pacific Citizen* in sufficient numbers, another publication was necessary to give them contact with the national organization. To finance the *Reporter,* fifty cents of the one-dollar individual annual membership fee sent to headquarters by the chapters was earmarked for the publication. Actually, it did not cost five thousand dollars per year (based on ten thousand members at fifty cents each) to print the *Reporter,* but after a half dozen years the national organization, unable to determine nonduplicating roles for its two publications, dropped the *Reporter.*

By the time JACL met in San Francisco in 1952, *PC*'s financial situation hadn't improved appreciably despite efforts to get the chapters to sell both advertising and subscriptions. The newspaper's problem was complicated by the impending transfer of JACL headquarters to the West Coast where the bulk of the Japanese American population had returned. The leadership was leaning toward a San Francisco location since it was the League's original home. Kinmon Gakuen, where a Japanese-language school had been run, had rented space to JACL's Northern California regional office for forty-five dollars a month and offered quarters on the third floor for a combined national-regional office for one hundred dollars. That seemed to be a reasonable rent and the National Council would have approved the transfer immediately except that bids from San Francisco shops for printing *Pacific Citizen* were at least fifty dollars a week higher than in Salt Lake City. On the other hand bids from Los Angeles shops were comparable to what *PC* had been paying, but no suitable space had been found in the area for national headquarters.

The question, then, was whether it would be wise to separate *Pacific Citizen* from national headquarters for a saving of fifty dollars per week. Intense discussion over this point extended over portions of two convention sessions. Tajiri argued that it was essential to keep the newspaper together with headquarters of the organization it served. Saburo Kido, by then practicing law in Los Angeles, took the other view, contending *PC*'s location should be decided on its own merits without regard to where national headquarters would go. Kido favored Los Angeles, citing the Japanese American population in Southern California, which was substantially larger than that of the Bay area, and the concentration of businesses which were potential advertisers. But Kido was thus laying himself open to charges of conflict of interest. He was in the process of satisfying a lifelong ambition to run his own newspaper by buying control of the bilingual *Shin Nichibei* (New Japanese American), the smallest and weakest of three bilingual dailies that had sprung up in Los Angeles. Since *Shin Nichibei*'s plant was idle much of the time, Kido would be in a position to offer to print *Pacific Citizen*.

The convention at first tabled a motion to move *PC* to either Los Angeles or San Francisco depending on where headquarters would go. But in the second discussion session the motion was amended to transfer the newspaper to Los Angeles. The minutes show Tajiri again voiced strong opposition to an isolated *PC* in

Los Angeles, citing problems for both the editor and headquarters. However, only one vote was cast against the move. Kenji Fujii of the Eden Township, California, chapter said he favored keeping *Pacific Citizen* in Salt Lake City until the issue had quieted down and insisted that his ballot be so recorded.

Understandably, Tajiri felt completely let down that his wishes had been ignored. He was also disappointed about inadequate financial support, and unhappy that the convention went on to authorize an "operating committee" to "aid the PC in its operation." The newspaper had been under the general supervision of a *Pacific Citizen* Board that concerned itself largely with business matters, leaving editorial and news policy to Tajiri. The operating committee, proposed by Sim Togasaki, presumably would take a greater interest in news operations although it was never specified how this would be done. Tajiri patiently explained that the *PC* staff consisted of only two and a half positions, that he had never had an operating board looking over his shoulder during ten years of his stewardship when his product was highly acclaimed, and expressed doubt that such supervision would work or was necessary. The combination of events caused Tajiri to decide it was time to move on. He had no desire to work in Los Angeles and submitted his resignation effective in September. Perhaps the crowning indignity in a situation handled with something less than grace despite the accolades showered on Larry and Guyo for a decade of distinguished service was a request that Tajiri not start a rival newspaper, which, of course, he had no intention of doing. Tajiri joined the *Colorado Springs Free Press* briefly before being hired by the *Denver Post* where he became widely recognized as a distinguished drama critic until his death in 1965.

Tajiri had made *Pacific Citizen* a superb newspaper when the Japanese American community needed it most. It sustained JACL as a credible organization during its roughest times. Perhaps the only serious complaint against *PC* was that it told more of the truth than some readers were comfortable with. Unfortunately it was never in a position to make money, a problem that always has plagued much of the press, and this was important when JACL itself was struggling financially. It was regrettable that in the end *PC* became a pawn in a power struggle between Northern and Southern California elements of JACL.

Kido was given the responsibility of establishing *PC* in Los

Angeles. It made economic sense for both JACL and Kido to move *PC* into his *Shin Nichibei* plant. Harry Honda, then on *Shin Nichibei*'s English staff, was named editor. A Los Angeles native, Honda had worked since 1936 on Japanese American journals in Los Angeles and San Francisco, with interruptions for military service and college on the GI Bill. The first *PC* issue under his editorship was that of October 4, 1952.

Honda was given two charges when he took over: maintain the high tone of the Tajiri years, and put *PC* on a self-supporting basis. Both were extremely difficult goals. Two years later *PC* Board Chairman Sim Togasaki said the move to Los Angeles had been wise in that no JACL subsidy was now needed, but circulation was still only sixty-three hundred whereas membership had climbed to twelve thousand. Proposals to provide *PC* to every JACL household by adding a dollar to the membership fee were heard from time to time and finally one was adopted in January of 1961. This meant inclusion of more organizational news plus columns, usually of dubious interest, from elected JACL officials. Tajiri, however, continued to write his column for the paper even after he moved to Denver. But the argument over whether *PC* should seek to be a newspaper of general interest to Japanese Americans or a house organ continues at each national convention and at each meeting of the *Pacific Citizen* Board. It is likely to be a controversy that will go on as long as there is a *PC.* Honda explains his editorial policy this way: "To represent JACL as a public relations medium, and to serve as an educational resource by reporting the achievements, contributions, problems and issues affecting persons of Japanese ancestry. That policy is broad enough to include both JACL-oriented and general news. Space is provided for divergent views to help guide public policy."

That is not the kind of policy likely to stir up much excitement, but Honda has been so generous about providing space for dissent that occasionally he has upset older JACL stalwarts. It is a well-known fact, of course, that dissenters are more energetic and usually more articulate writers of letters to the editor than those who endorse a position.

Only once has *PC* been sued for libel. In 1961 John Lechner charged he had been libeled by one of Tajiri's columns. Lechner somehow had managed to persuade the California state legislature to consider a resolution commending him for his "Americanism" and JACL had been instrumental in blocking the resolution.

The then national president, Frank Chuman, in testimony before an Assembly committee had described Lechner as "one of the most bigoted, racist, rabble-rousing individuals in the state of California against loyal citizens and residents of Japanese ancestry." Tajiri had made reference to this testimony in his column. *Pacific Citizen* refused to make a retraction and Lechner, reminded that truth is the best defense against charges of libel, abandoned his suit.

Shin Nichibei did not prove to be a good investment for Kido. He had neglected to audit its books thoroughly before buying the paper and presently he found that some of the so-called accounts receivable had already been paid and friends of the previous management had been presented with lifetime subscriptions. Eventually its losses became more than he could take and he had to give up the venture. His successors, who renamed the paper *Nichibei Mainichi,* were no more able to keep it going; Southern California's Japanese American community simply couldn't support three daily ethnic newspapers. One day in 1967 the Internal Revenue Service padlocked the *Nichibei Mainichi* for nonpayment of taxes. *Pacific Citizen,* an innocent bystander, was in danger of missing its deadline until circulation manager Yuki Kamayatsu explained the problem to an IRS agent who agreed to let Honda move out his type. *Pacific Citizen*'s next printshop home was at *Crossroads,* a Nisei weekly best known for editor Wimp Hiroto's irreverent columns. When *Crossroads* expired in 1971, Honda had his type set at John Yamamoto's shop next door. Yamamoto retired in 1976 and Honda persuaded JACL to let him spend fifteen thousand dollars for a used phototypesetting machine to speed up operations at less cost.

Honda has spent some three decades getting *Pacific Citizen* out each week. It is largely a labor of love which he once described in these words: "As part of the multi-ethnic press in America, *Pacific Citizen* stays abreast of major issues facing Japanese Americans. We are still a minority among minorities and we do not forget them. While much has been accomplished by JACL, the purpose for founding it in 1930 is still valid—that persons of Japanese ancestry shall not be denied their freedom and rights because of race, creed or color."

Has Honda as editor carried out the charge he received from Kido? That is hard to say. Times change. Since every family now receives a copy of *PC* with membership in JACL, its circulation fluctuates around the twenty-three thousand level. The subscription price is built into the dues structure, so there is no similarity between the current situation and the financial problems Tajiri faced. Nor is there much resemblance in the nature of the news in the two eras. Tajiri edited the paper in a desperate time of conflict, tension, anger, savage rhetoric and battlefield death—all elements of dramatic reporting and grist for powerful and trenchant editorial comment. The news today may be significant but it is rarely of the same robust quality. If the times are relatively dull, it is difficult for the journal that chronicles them to remain consistently lively.

XXI

Years of Change

After JACL's golden era the years sped by swiftly, while Nisei as a group simultaneously struggled to make up for the economic setback of the war years and took advantage of the improving social and political climate. A series of earnest, dedicated men took office as presidents of JACL, all of them much more attracted by the opportunity to serve than by whatever personal glory the unpaid, time-consuming job promised. Some were fortunate enough to seize upon significant and important issues that stirred and united the membership as before. But compared to the critical goals achieved in the first decade after the war, many of the projects were somewhat short of earthshaking. It was less the fault of the leadership than of the changing times.

Hito Okada, elected president in 1946, was returned to office in 1948 as the first JACL leader chosen by the general membership. But the system proved to have major shortcomings. First, the nominating committee, made up of seventeen representatives from all parts of the country, had no way of meeting together to discuss possible candidates and their merits. Second, by mail it was almost impossible to persuade a possible candidate to run, which was a necessity in a volunteer organization. And third, while sixty-four hundred ballots were mailed to the members, only 30 percent were returned. The response was as low as 8 percent from one chapter; the best showing was 52 percent from Sacramento. Finally, while the constitution called for election by majority vote, none of the three candidates for each of the three vice-presidencies won a majority. When headquarters polled the chapters to ascertain their wishes, only forty-six of the sixty-three chapters bothered to return their votes. Despite this dismal showing the convention decided to give popular balloting another try. At the 1950 convention in Chicago, Dr. Randolph Mas Sakada, who had lost to Okada two years earlier, was elected president, but the system didn't work a great deal better. Out of slightly more than ten thousand ballots sent to the membership, only about thirty-eight hundred were returned; more than six thousand members had not participated in what was intended to be a democratic election. After that the organization went back to the old system of having the National Council, made up of representatives from each chapter, elect the national officers.

Okada's two administrations, 1946–48 and 1948–50, had seen the start of JACL's Washington office and the launching of the Anti-Discrimination Committee's efforts to win justice through legislation. In November, 1946, JACL helped defeat California's Proposition 15. The Soldier Brides Act was amended in 1947. That same year the Supreme Court found for Fred Oyama, nullifying California's alien land law, and for Torao Takahashi, giving Issei equal rights as commercial fishermen. In 1948, a bill blocking deportation of treaty merchants, and the Evacuation Claims Act were passed. And in 1950 JACL was successful in a campaign that was particularly close to Mas Satow's heart; under pressure from JACL the American Bowling Congress allowed nonwhites to join.

Dr. Sakada was a thirty-eight-year-old optometrist practicing in Chicago when he became JACL's ninth president in 1950. It was his good fortune to be in office when Congress passed the Walter-McCarran Act, eliminating race as a qualification for citizenship and immigration. Earlier in his administration Congress had approved the JACL-initiated proposal to expedite Evacuation claims payments by automatic compromise. A new goal of a million dollars was set for the JACL Endowment Fund, that sum to be built up by urging those who received payments for Evacuation losses to contribute 10 percent of their checks. Not many years after he stepped down, Sakada's career was ended by cancer.

George Inagaki, who succeeded Sakada, perhaps was JACL's most reluctant president, although he had no reason to be. Inagaki had demonstrated his leadership qualities in various local and regional JACL offices and was elected Okada's first vice-president in 1946. But he resisted nomination for the presidency in 1948 and 1950, pleading the pressure of business—he was general manager of a large floral nursery and later the first Nisei president of the Los Angeles flower market. In reality the close relationship he had developed with Mike Masaoka when they were in Washington—both told friends they were closer than brothers—had him believing that his lack of a college degree was an insurmountable handicap. Of course it wasn't. Inagaki had been the first Nisei high school valedictorian in Northern California and was an honor student in junior college before the Depression forced him to drop out to help support the family. In addition to a genuine admiration for Masaoka's other talents, Inagaki regarded with awe his friend's ability to speak extemporaneously on almost any subject with fluency and persuasiveness. By comparison, Inagaki felt inarticulate. Inagaki was no orator, but actually he spoke well. As a student he had placed second in a Nisei student oratorical contest. His subject had been the alien land law. It was Masaoka himself who persuaded Inagaki to seek the presidency. Prior to the 1952 convention in San Francisco Masaoka told his friend it appeared likely President Truman would veto the Walter-McCarran Act, that it would take money to start a new lobbying campaign and that Inagaki, who was fluent in Japanese, would be needed as JACL president to seek contributions from the Issei.

(Inagaki, who was stationed by the Army at Pearl Harbor for much of the war, served for a time as Admiral Chester W. Nimitz' personal interpreter. After the war Joe Grant Masaoka wrote to Nimitz asking why the Navy continued to refuse to accept Nisei. Nimitz responded that as far as he was concerned he would be proud to have Nisei serving under him. Shortly afterward the Navy began to accept Japanese Americans.)

As it turned out, the Truman veto was overridden but Inagaki became president nonetheless. He served two terms, 1952–54 and 1954–56. During his administration JACL chapters sponsored Americanization classes for Issei so they could qualify for naturalization. JACL headquarters were moved from Salt Lake City to San Francisco on July 15, 1953. In 1955, under a bill pushed by JACL, Issei aliens became eligible for California old-age assistance.

It was also under Inagaki's leadership, at the 1956 convention in San Francisco, that JACL first took a position on the plight of Iva Toguri, a Nisei who had been convicted of treason for broadcasts she allegedly had made on Radio Tokyo during World War II. She had been found guilty in a San Francisco courtroom under conditions smacking of lynch-mob justice, with much of the testimony later proving perjurious. The trial, which lasted fifty-six days, created a great deal of interest but JACL as an organization failed to provide her with support. JACL's National Committee for Iva Toguri noted in a booklet published in 1975: "While Japanese Americans may have sympathized with her predicament, there was very little they could effectively do to help while their own position in American society was under attack." She was released in January, 1956, after serving six years and two months of a ten-year term, only to face an Immigration Service effort to deport her. This would have amounted to exile of a citizen and the JACL convention passed a resolution condemning the proceedings. The deportation was blocked, but another twenty years were to pass before JACL won a pardon for her. That campaign will be described in the next chapter.

In his later years a chronic heart ailment restricted Inagaki's activities. In April of 1977 Saburo Kido died in San Francisco after many years of failing health. Inagaki attended the funeral, but that night was stricken with a severe heart attack in his hotel room. Confined to his home most of the time thereafter, Inagaki died June 14, 1978.

Dr. Roy N. Nishikawa, a Los Angeles optometrist, was president for the 1956–58 term. In the fall of 1956 California voters laid to rest the infamous 1913 alien land law which had been designed specifically to deprive Japanese farmers of the right to own the soil they tilled. The two-to-one margin at the polls was a heady victory for JACL. In the state of Washington JACL began what was to become a ten-year campaign to repeal a similar law. JACL under Dr. Nishikawa also began a campaign to eliminate use of the derogatory term "Jap" as a shortened form of "Japanese." Many Americans had used "Jap" innocently as the convenient equivalent of "Swede" or "Turk" without being aware of the long, bitter history of hostility during which it had become a cruel epithet. Some Nisei were inclined to respond to "Jap" with anger; JACL wisely chose to launch a low-key educational campaign. It centered on widespread distribution of a pamphlet titled *Please Don't* that explained why Nisei resented use of the word. Most dictionaries today note that "Jap" is a derogatory term used disparagingly. Dr. Nishikawa, like virtually all former national JACL presidents, has continued to be active in the organization at lower levels.

Shigeo Wakamatsu, a Chicago chemist, was JACL's president for the 1958–60 term. In that biennium the last Evacuation claim was settled and, as a sign of changing times, the man who as head of the Native Sons of the Golden West had spearheaded that organization's wartime anti-Nisei campaign admitted the policy had been a mistake. In Idaho, JACL chapters persuaded the legislature to repeal its ninety-two-year-old antimiscegenation statute. But another decade was to pass before the Supreme Court of the United States recognized the validity of interracial marriages, in a case in which William M. Marutani of Philadelphia, onetime national JACL legal counsel, participated. That was the case in which Richard P. Loving, a white, challenged the laws of Virginia, which refused to recognize his marriage to a woman of Indian and black descent. Marutani was the only attorney aside from the counsel for the principals who was invited to speak. The high court agreed unanimously that states cannot outlaw marriages between whites and nonwhites. Also during Wakamatsu's administration JACL made subscription to *Pacific Citizen* part of its dues structure.

Another high point of Wakamatsu's term was the admission of Hawaii into the Union as the fiftieth state on August 21, 1954. Hawaii's desire for statehood had been stymied for years by those who feared its high percentage of citizens of Asian ancestry, particularly the Japanese. Any doubt of their loyalty should have been wiped out by the exemplary performance of Japanese Americans, civilians and servicemen, during World War II. JACL —and Masaoka in Washington particularly—had worked closely with the Hawaiian Nisei, and statehood at long last was a particularly satisfying victory over racial prejudice. War hero Daniel K. Inouye became Hawaii's first representative and the first Nisei in Congress and, later, the first Nisei in the U.S. Senate. He was succeeded in the House by another war hero, Spark M. Matsunaga, who also went on to the Senate. Patsy Takemoto Mink also represented Hawaii in the House and, after leaving office, served briefly as a high State Department official before resigning to take the presidency of the liberal Americans for Democratic Action for three terms.

However, Wakamatsu's greatest service to JACL was performed after he completed his term. As president he had pushed hard for a project to record the history of Japanese Americans. At the 1960 convention in Sacramento the idea was approved and the new president, Frank Chuman, a Los Angeles attorney, named Wakamatsu to head the effort. For the next two decades and more, Wakamatsu devoted most of his spare time to what was first called the Issei History Project and later renamed the Japanese American Research Project (JARP). The community took enthusiastically to the idea. The story of the Japanese in the United States certainly deserved recording, but since it didn't seem anyone was going to write such a history, why not commission one? As a matter of fact, JACL had been considering such a project informally for some time. Togo Tanaka, Larry Tajiri and Bill Hosokawa were asked to look into the possibilities. Tajiri and Hosokawa were in Denver. Tanaka was flying frequently on business between Chicago and Los Angeles and several times he stopped in Denver for discussions with the other two. The consensus was that a book ought to be written, but it would take about five thousand dollars to get someone to research and write it. And where would JACL find that kind of money?

Once the project was announced the money became available with surprising ease. Each chapter named a history-project chairman to help raise funds and collect information. Many individuals made contributions in memory of their parents. Before long more than $200,000 was collected. Wakamatsu's committee included Mike Masaoka; Yone Satoda and Sim Togasaki of San Francisco; Akiji Yoshimura of Colusa, California; Katsuma Mukaeda and Gongoro Nakamura, Los Angeles Issei leaders; Bill Hosokawa; and Masao Satow. The committee met for the first time in 1962 at the Seattle convention, drafted a budget and roughed out plans.

The key problem was unanticipated. No one had a firm idea of what the project should accomplish, nor did JACL's mandate make it clear. Togo Tanaka's informal committee had been thinking of a one-volume narrative history. Others saw the history in terms of the yearbooks published in some communities in which everyone who ordered a copy was assured that a picture of his family would be included together with a write-up of its activities. Still others weren't quite sure of the difference between a factual history and a novel. In his foreword to the book *East to America,* one of JARP's products, Wakamatsu wrote:

> The committee was agreed that it should chronicle the story of the Japanese Americans, but among those who had supported us there was no consensus about what that story was and how it should be told. My original concept was simply to commission a qualified writer to research the subject and produce a readable volume focusing on the drama, the struggles, and the tears and laughter in the experiences of a little-known American minority. Our friends in the academic community had in mind a vastly more ambitious program. They argued for a systematic study which would produce, in addition to the human materials we sought, the "hard" sociological and economic data necessary to measure progress and put old myths to rest.

Ultimately the goal turned out to be far more comprehensive and complex—and more valuable—than had been anticipated. Asked to draw up an outline for the project, Dr. T. Scott Miyakawa came up with three primary objectives: to conduct an in-depth sociological survey of Issei and Nisei, to publish a definitive and scholarly history of Japanese Americans and to assemble a documentary collection including oral histories. These goals were accepted. However, most Nisei were unfamiliar with the glacial pace of academia; when they became restless that nothing seemed to be resulting from the history project, a fourth goal was added. That was publication of a "popular" history as contrasted with the "scholarly" volume promised for some future time.

As the first step toward achieving the original goals, an academic home for the project was established at the University of California at Los Angeles through the good offices of alumnus Frank Chuman. JACL made a grant of $100,000 to UCLA, which became JARP's cosponsor in what Wakamatsu has called "a partnership between a major university and an ethnic group seeking to learn more about itself and to share that knowledge with others." Dr. Miyakawa took leave from Boston University to become project director and Dr. Robert A. Wilson, a Japan scholar in the UCLA history department, was named to administer the fund. Dr. Gregg Stone of the University of Minnesota and his wife, Dr. Gladys Ishida Stone, designed a seventy-three-page questionnaire to probe into the lives and times of more than a thousand Issei and over three thousand of their children and grandchildren. Most of the Issei interviews had to be administered bilingually by local JACL volunteers and took as long as nine hours each to complete. The UCLA study was bolstered by a $140,000 grant from the Carnegie Corporation, and $400,000 from the National Institute of Mental Health. When the project threatened to bog down of its own weight, JACL hired Joe Grant Masaoka as expediter and he and Dr. Wilson traveled widely to collect documentary material and conduct oral interviews. The project, as well as the Nisei world, suffered a serious loss when Masaoka died in 1970. Miyakawa had to return to Boston University in 1966 and Dr. Gene N. Levine took over the sociological study.

The popular history was JARP's first product. Even before its publication in 1969 it spawned a controversy that presaged a growing rift within the organization between the conservative older members who had experienced the bitter war years and the rough times before then, and younger members who had been caught up in the rhetoric and rebellion that were sweeping the land. The book was titled *Nisei,* with a subtitle, *The Quiet Americans; The Story of a People.* No one aside from the publishers and the JARP committee had seen the manuscript, which ran to some one hundred and sixty thousand words. But when the title was announced, the National JACL Ethnic Concern Committee headed by Dr. David Miura, a Long Beach dentist, objected that the word "quiet" perpetuated "a negative racial stereotype" of Japanese Americans and was "noxious to the New Nisei and Sansei." When Miura suggested in the press that unless the title were changed "we may be compelled to initiate, or join with others in a general effort to boycott the purchase of the book," the public witnessed the spectacle of one JACL committee threatening to torpedo the efforts of another.

The author, who had accepted JARP's commission on the condition that he would be free to set down the facts as he saw them, insisted the adjective was not offensive, but rather, accurate and appropriate, and any other interpretation of the facts would be revisionist history. His resistance to what he considered to be censorship was supported by Wakamatsu and his committee and the title was retained. The controversy raged for weeks as Harry Honda devoted generous amounts of *Pacific Citizen* space to arguments pro and con from the membership. It is quite possible that the Ethnic Concern Committee's efforts backfired, for many

Nisei who might not have bought the book purchased it to see what the fuss was all about. If any found it offensive, they remained silent. To the contrary, they found the book something they could identify with, for it was their story. Wakamatsu says: "*Nisei* enjoyed remarkable success. It became assigned reading in college ethnic history classes, and countless term papers were composed with *Nisei* as the primary source of information. In that it circulated the story of Japanese Americans, the book admirably met JARP's goal. But additionally, it served two unanticipated purposes. As a commercial success it helped to replenish JARP's treasury so other projects could be assisted, and it made publishers aware of Japanese American history while encouraging Japanese Americans themselves to write for publication."

In retrospect, there would seem to be an inconsistency on the part of those who sought to force a title change. They were JACL's most liberal elements, intensely dedicated to liberal principles. Any sort of censorship should have been anathema to them. Yet, anomalously, they could argue that their action did not constitute an attempt to censor a work they disagreed with. In an earlier time, when JACL's senior leadership was more naïve, it got involved in a vaguely similar situation involving the right of two Nisei to make a living. Their profession was wrestling. In the vaudeville world of pro wrestling they performed as The Great Togo and Mr. Moto, two villains to be booed and hissed at by the spectators. Television then was in its infant years and pro wrestling films were standard viewing fare. Some Nisei were mortified by the frequent appearance of Mr. Moto and The Great Togo on the "boob tube" and demanded that something be done about this affront to Japanese American dignity. In 1950 JACL's National Committee Against Discrimination in Entertainment and Allied Fields contacted the Federal Communications Commission, the National Association of Radio and Television Broadcasters, five broadcasting networks and more than a hundred TV stations to request that wartime hate movies and films featuring Togo and Moto not be shown. The first request is understandable but the second is less defensible. Generally, the response was to the effect that they would ban hate movies produced as part of the wartime propaganda campaign, but they didn't see any particular harm in Nisei playing the roles of the bad guys in a wrestling film.

JARP's three original goals have been met. The sociological survey produced a wealth of material which resulted in a book, *The Japanese American Community: A Three-Generation Study,* coauthored by Dr. Levine and Dr. Robert Colbert Rhodes. Levine also directed a companion study, *The Economic Basis of Ethnic Solidarity: A Study of the Japanese Americans,* by Dr. Edna Bonacich and Dr. John Modell. JARP also commissioned Frank Chuman's *The Bamboo People,* a detailed study of the tangled legal history of Japanese Americans, and Dr. Masakazu Iwata's unpublished manuscript *Planted in Good Soil: Issei Contributions to U.S. Agriculture,* a review of the Issei farming experience. A listing of other publications stemming from JARP appears in the Notes and Sources at the back of this volume.

The mass of material collected by JARP, including many hours of tapes, has now been classified and catalogued at the UCLA Research Library. And the scholarly history has been published, although it may not be quite as "scholarly" as some academicians would have wished. This is the result of a compromise for the sake of readability; a truly scholarly treatise is not likely to have commanded any substantial readership among the rank and file of Japanese Americans who had anticipated it for so long. The book, titled *East to America,* was coauthored by Dr. Wilson and Bill Hosokawa and published in 1980. In a very real sense, the truly scholarly products of JARP are the studies produced by scholars like Levine, Modell, Bonacich, Dr. Darrel Montero and others of their ilk.

Chuman served as president during the 1960–62 term, when JACL initiated a program for the aging and recognized the Junior JACL program. The biennium also saw the resignation of Mike Masaoka as Washington representative. For some time there had been discussion about JACL's proper stance in Washington now that its major goals had been achieved. Ever present was the knowledge of JACL's limited funds. The consensus was in favor of a limited watchdog presence, ready to sound the alarm if trouble should arise. Masaoka opened a consulting office, primarily for Japanese companies, and took on JACL as one of his clients. Masaoka was aware of the danger of confusion. He was being retained on the one hand to promote the interests of Japanese firms whose objectives might or might not be compatible with those of JACL, and on the other by an American organization with whom he had been identified from the beginning and whose members frequently were mistaken for Japanese. But he managed to walk the tightrope with remarkable facility. As for Chuman, like Wakamatsu he is likely to be better remembered for his later role with JARP than for his presidential term. Chuman's *Bamboo People* is an authoritative legal history.

K. Patrick Okura, president from 1962 through 1964, had become interested in JACL through his UCLA classmate Kay Sugahara, who was Los Angeles chapter president at the time. Sugahara persuaded Okura in 1935 to become the chapter's full-time executive secretary. An office was opened in the California Bank building on San Pedro Street in Li'l Tokyo where Sugahara had his customs brokerage. The pay was one hundred dollars a month, with Okura responsible for raising much of the money. Many Issei businessmen aided JACL with contributions and by supporting various functions sponsored by the chapter. One of the projects was Nisei Week, a commercial and cultural promotion and community extravaganza that is still a Li'l Tokyo summer attraction. Okura held the JACL position for two years. After being evacuated to a Santa Anita stable stall, Okura took a position as a psychologist at Boys Town, Nebraska. He and his wife Lily helped organize the Omaha chapter in 1947 and Okura became its first president.

Much to the consternation of some old conservatives, the national JACL under Okura's leadership moved sharply from the middle road on civil rights issues to a strong advocacy role. In the summer of 1963 Martin Luther King, Jr., was organizing his Washington demonstration for black rights. Masaoka in Washington, Mas Satow in San Francisco and Okura in Omaha agreed JACL should participate. But they also knew there would be opposition from the membership.

"There were a number of older Nisei who were fairly well established in business and who were proud that we had pulled ourselves up by our bootstraps following the Evacuation," Okura said recently. "In that short period we were able to gain social and economic status far beyond what we had prior to the Evacuation. It was the feeling of the great majority of our chapter leaders that what the blacks did was their business, their problem, and that they should improve their lot in the same way we had, and we shouldn't get involved in the civil rights movement. I was convinced that after the way we had been discriminated against we should take a leadership role in the whole area of civil rights."

Okura called an emergency meeting of the National Board to establish a position. Because Omaha was central and Okura's home, it was a logical site for the meeting. But he had another reason. He says: "We wanted to be isolated from any large Japanese American community where some of our members would have been under pressure to oppose involvement." This was simple recognition of the fact that the outlook of Nisei in the Japanese American communities on the West Coast was somewhat more insular than that in other parts of the country.

The Board had little difficulty in hammering out a strong civil rights statement and it authorized JACL participation in the Martin Luther King demonstration. Okura flew to Washington where he was joined by some thirty JACLers from New York, Philadelphia and other Eastern communities, who marched together under a JACL banner. More than two hundred thousand Americans gathered on the Mall to join in expressing their support of black demands for equal rights. The rally was capped by King's memorable speech in which he declared: "I have a dream that this nation will rise up and live out the true meaning of its creed, 'We hold these truths to be self-evident; that all men are created equal.' " There were seats on the platform reserved that day for Okura and Masaoka, but the crush of the throng prevented them from making it up there. Okura later came under strong criticism from some elements of the membership. Today he says: "History shows that we did the right thing. What we did was the only action we could take as Americans."

As a matter of fact, although many members were unaware of it, JACL had been an early member of the burgeoning civil rights movement. In 1947 it joined the Civil Liberties Clearing House in Washington. The following year it was among the founding members of the National Leadership Conference on Civil Rights.

In 1964 Okura decided to seek a second term against the advice of friends. He felt there was work that had been left undone, particularly steering JACL toward more active participation in Japanese-American relations. A substantial portion of the membership wanted JACL to remain a purely Japanese American organization that would have nothing to do with Japan itself. (Yet, most of them found nothing inconsistent about inviting the local Japanese consul to sit at the head table at chapter functions.) Others, like Masaoka and Okura, contended Americans of Japanese ancestry had an obligation to do all they could to develop good relations between the two countries. The National Council stuck with the policy of passing the presidency around and elected Kumeo Yoshinari, an Oregon farm boy who had become a chemist in Chicago.

It was during Yoshinari's administration that true equity was built into the immigration laws. The Walter-McCarran Act of 1952, which removed racial bars from the immigration and naturalization laws, had been a giant step forward, a necessary liberalization of earlier measures. But its quotas were still weighted heavily in favor of north European nations under the so-called national origins system. It restricted immigration from south and central Europe, Asia and Africa. Only token quotas were provided for peoples of the Asia-Pacific Triangle, which included Japan. A cabinet-level committee named to study revisions was focusing on the national origins system until Masaoka directed its attention to the Asia-Pacific Triangle, asserting that Asians deserved equal consideration. By an odd quirk Masaoka lobbied all three Kennedy brothers—President John F. Kennedy, Attorney General Robert Kennedy and Senator Edward Kennedy, who was chairman of the subcommittee on immigration. Congress finally approved the desired changes in 1965. President Lyndon B. Johnson signed the new law in ceremonies at Ellis Island, the onetime immigration station in New York harbor, with Masaoka as one of the honored witnesses. The new law provided for admission of immigrants on the basis of their skills and relationship to those already in the country, and not on the basis of race or nationality. JACL under Yoshinari also stepped up pressure for enforcing fair housing statutes, and expanding its public-relations program.

Although JACL's operating budget topped $100,000 for the first time in a nonemergency year in Yoshinari's administration, JACL continued to be pressed for funds. Only Mas Satow's ultraconservative husbanding of resources enabled the dollars to go as far as they did. During much of this time JACL headquarters were housed on the third floor of the dingy clapboard building at 1634 Post, across the street from what is now the Miyako Hotel in San Francisco's Japantown. The pungent aroma of cooking from an adjacent Korean restaurant often was wafted up into JACL offices where walls were painted an institutional buff and the furniture was mostly contributed hand-me-downs. Faithful, efficient Daisy Uyeda was administrative assistant in charge of operations. Yone Satoda, who was courting Daisy, remembers urging Satow to spruce up the offices but he always pleaded insufficient funds. Mas and Chiz were also frugal in their own living. Often their lunch was a bowl of instant noodles prepared in a back room. Since they had no children, JACL was their family. The organization was small enough and informal enough so that the Satows could run it like a mom-and-pop operation. When Daisy left to marry Satoda, Chiz took over her duties. An enormous amount of mail moved through the offices and Chiz enjoyed linking names with faces when she and Mas went to the national conventions. Mas' responsibility of keeping in touch with the chapters necessitated a heavy travel schedule. In one stretch he visited twenty-seven chapters in twenty-seven days. Asked why he kept up such a pace, Satow replied: "They needed me to help pull together the various groups and to maintain peace in the family. You know, I love those folks. They're crazy sometimes, but they're the best in the world." Friendly, outgoing, patient, he had a knack for remembering faces and names, and it is likely that he knew as many Nisei as anyone. When there was more work than they could fit into an eight-hour day, Mas and Chiz would take papers home and work on the dining room table. Satow would spend endless after-work hours in a labor of love—hand-lettering the literally hundreds of citations and awards that JACL presented to individuals who had served the organization.

A generation of JACL volunteers who were summoned to National Board or high-level committee meetings wryly remembers Satow's frugality with JACL funds. Invariably he booked them into small San Francisco or Los Angeles Japantown hotels, two to a room, and he was equally conservative about meals. Pat Okura says: "There were other hotels that were not that much more expensive, but Mas' position was that we were spending the membership's money and we mustn't give the impression of splurging. He took a very firm stand on that. But if we didn't have that kind of person running JACL affairs, we would have put ourselves in a deep financial hole."

XXII

The New Generation

Jerry Jiro Enomoto, a California penologist who later headed the state prison system, was elected JACL's sixteenth national president in 1966 at the San Diego convention. He was the first of a new generation of JACL leaders—Nisei who had yet to reach adulthood at the time of Pearl Harbor. He was a fifteen-year-old in San Francisco when war disrupted the Japanese American community. In later years he recalled that the outbreak of hostilities was just another incident in his busy young life. He regarded the curfew regulations as simply an inconvenience, and the experience of the Evacuation and camp life was just another adventure as it was to other teen-agers. Inevitably, this background resulted in subtle differences between his adult outlook on Japanese American issues and that of his predecessors in JACL, who had been in decision-making roles through the prewar and Evacuation years. But if he had not been sharply aware personally of the humiliation and injustice of the Evacuation, its implications did not escape him in maturity. He developed a compassion for the underdog to go with a strong activist will. As JACL president his background and relative youth—he was forty at the time of his election—gave him a special rapport with the many younger Nisei and Sansei (the "third generation") swept up in the restlessness of the times, which manifested itself in campus revolts, antiwar demonstrations, black anger and violence in the cities. Enomoto could listen patiently to their protest and understand.

But his administration also saw a widening generation gap in

JACL. The fervor of Sansei activism, which extended into and grew in intensity during the term of his successor, Raymond Uno, puzzled and repelled many of the older, "quiet" Nisei members, particularly when the activists sought to change JACL's stance and thrust. The flap involving Dr. S. I. Hayakawa, the Canadian-born semanticist and educator, is illuminating. Hayakawa, named acting president of San Francisco State College in 1968, vigorously put down student anarchism on the campus and won the admiration of most Americans and older Nisei. They agreed with Hayakawa's view that radical Sansei were foolish to ape the noisy protest of radical blacks against capitalism and "American imperialism." On the other hand Sansei activists rejected vehemently the image of Japanese Americans as quiet, conforming and eager to adapt to the majority's culture. When the San Francisco JACL chapter booked Hayakawa as a dinner speaker, younger members forced the board to withdraw the invitation. In Los Angeles, Sansei activists picketed an appearance by Hayakawa.

In the 1968–69 holiday issue of *Pacific Citizen,* a few months after he had been elected to a second term, Enomoto wrote:

> JACL is becoming a little more "relevant" as a human relations type organization. The 20th Biennial Convention in San Jose sounded a louder than usual note for involvement and progress in the civil rights area. It marked the first time that an open forum on civil rights was held, substituting for the usual reports and repetitious discussion in this area. . . . Some of the youth [Junior JACLers] are found in the most militant factions of college dissidents. Whether we agree with their views or not, it may pay off to remember that, in a very real sense, we are paying the price for years of failing to care enough to set certain wrongs right in America. Youth is impatient and will often sneer at our insistence upon respect for law and order when they see evidence that a similar insistence upon justice is missing. . . . In this, as in all conflict, the failure of the moderate to speak and act may leave the field to the extremist. Those Sansei students on any campus who feel inside that they must be militant will do what they feel they have to do. I would hope that those Sansei who consider themselves moderates will feel inclined to add their voices to the debate. Neutrality here is an impossible stance.

The stance of most JACLers was, of course, in favor of a strong national human rights program, but they were uneasy about being pushed too far too fast. Rocking the boat, which Sansei militants insisted was the only acceptable tactic in propelling society toward their goals, frightened many of their elders. The schism within JACL reflected the age and ideological division that also divided the broader American community. It was Enomoto's lot, and later Uno's, to keep the organization from breaking up over these differences. They did it mostly by listening to all sides and, in the vernacular of the day, keeping their cool.

At the convention in San Jose that re-elected Enomoto in 1968, JACL took on as its next major project repeal of Title II of the Internal Security Act of 1950 which, as noted earlier, codified the imprisonment of Japanese Americans in 1942. It provided a legal basis for imprisonment without trial of suspected security risks in time of war, insurrection or invasion. At a time when many Americans were extremely nervous about Communist subversion and disturbed by campus unrest, repeal of a harsh internal-security measure seemed to be an impossibility. The timid failed to count on the audacity and dedication of some young boat-rockers. Raymond Okamura and Paul Yamamoto were named cochairmen of the Committee to Repeal the Emergency Act—Edison Uno joined its leadership later—and they pushed a vigorous campaign to get rid of the concentration camp law. With enthusiastic chapter assistance they drummed up editorial and popular support. Senator Dan Inouye of Hawaii introduced a repeal bill which the upper house approved unanimously in December of 1969. Democratic Congressmen Spark Matsunaga and Chet Holifield of California, cosponsors of a House version, ran into trouble in the Internal Security Committee, where Republicans Richard Ichord of Missouri and John Ashbrook of Ohio backed an ineffective substitute bill. After lengthy maneuvering the Ichord-Ashbrook proposal was defeated by the full House. The Matsunaga-Holifield measure, which by then had acquired other cosponsors, was accepted on September 14, 1971, by a vote of 356 to 49. Majority Leader Mike Mansfield, later to become an outstanding ambassador to Japan, arranged to have the Senate consider the House measure almost immediately and it was accepted without opposition. On September 25, in Portland, President Nixon announced he had signed the repeal bill. Nixon was on his way to greet Emperor Hirohito, who was scheduled to stop in Anchorage, Alaska—his first time ever on American soil—en route to Europe. If the timing of the announcement was an attempt to link the Nisei-supported repeal with Hirohito's visit, it was a misguided move. The Nisei through JACL had struck a blow for democracy that benefited all Americans; their experience had made them particularly sensitive to the injustice of Title II and, contrary to what White House staffers may have thought, any connection with the Japanese themselves was only peripheral.

Enomoto's term ended on a tragic note at the convention in Chicago in the summer of 1970. Evelynn Okubo, a Sansei Junior JACLer, was found knifed to death in her convention hotel room and her roommate Carol Ranko Yamada was severely slashed. The slaying was never solved. The death, understandably, cast a pall over the convention. Charging the hotel with negligence, JACL assisted the Okubo family's efforts to seek recompense. When the Hilton hotels failed to respond satisfactorily, JACL instituted a short-lived boycott against the chain.

Raymond Uno, a Salt Lake City attorney, was elected JACL's seventeenth president in Chicago, with Henry Tanaka of Cleveland named president-elect to succeed Uno in two years. Born in Ogden, Uno was the first second-generation JACLer to head the League. Raymond's father, Clarence, was an Issei who had served in the U.S. Army in World War I and acquired citizenship under legislation which JACL lobbied for through Tokie Slocum. Clarence Uno was secretary of the Japanese Association in El Monte, California, and joined the JACL there in the late thirties. When Selective Service was instituted Clarence was named to the local draft board. But that kind of record didn't deter the FBI from searching the Uno home after Pearl Harbor and seizing, among other things, Raymond's BB gun. Raymond was eleven years old at the time. The Uno family was evacuated to Heart Mountain. Clarence ran the camp Selective Service office. One night, after attending a draft board meeting, he died of a heart attack. The family relocated in Ogden where Raymond completed high school, enlisted in the Army in 1948 at age seventeen and was sent to Japan as an interpreter and translator in counterintelligence. He served in the Korean War, returned to the United States in 1952 and got his law degree from the University of Utah in 1958. Uno served as a juvenile court referee, became deputy county attorney and then moved into the state attorney general's office for three and a half years before going into private practice. He currently is a state circuit court judge. A Salt Lake City JACLer named Sue Kaneko persuaded Uno and some of his friends—Tats Misaka, Tubber Okuda, Jimmy Mitsunaga—to join JACL and all of them went on to become League leaders. In 1968, with no previous political experience, Uno ran for the state senate on the Democratic ticket against a strong Republican incumbent. Uno and Tub Okuda and Ted Nagata signed notes for one thousand dollars each at a bank, printed some fliers and conducted a strong door-to-door campaign. Uno lost, 10,105 to 9,958, a difference of just 147 votes; a switch of only 75 votes would have won it for the Nisei.

Uno's special interest was young people, a key reason being that he has five sons. He became chapter president and then youth commissioner for the Intermountain District Council. From JACL's point of view, he came along at an opportune time. Militant Sansei were groping in search of their identity, but few had expressed any great interest in JACL, which they saw as irrelevant to the social and political issues of the day. On the other hand, thoughtful Nisei were searching for ways to get younger people involved, fearing JACL would die a natural death if it failed to attract Sansei membership. But they weren't sure how it could be done, for activist Sansei and their Nisei elders saw eye to eye on almost nothing. Uno seemed to have some answers. His predecessor, Enomoto, was among those urging Uno to run for JACL's presidency. He won handily but soon encountered a series of problems that shook the organization to its foundations.

The first involved the Pacific Southwest district office in Los Angeles run by Jeffrey Matsui and Warren Furutani, an eloquent, charismatic activist Sansei with a strong following. It was for these talents that he had been hired. One day a Nisei member dropped into the JACL office and noticed some posters on the wall. They were of Ho Chi Minh, Che Guevara, Cesar Chavez and a Black Panther leader or two, all idolized by radical youth. The United States, of course, was at war with Ho's North Vietnam and many Sansei were serving in Indochina. But the greatest outrage was expressed by JACLers in the Central California District Council, many of whose members were small farmers who felt their livelihoods were being threatened by Chavez' union-organizing campaign.

Uno went to Fresno to try to put out the fire, meeting with

local leaders like Fred Hirasuna and Harry Kubo as well as the rank and file of the membership. Recently Uno recalled: "I tried to pacify them by telling them that the young people are learning about life and we have to help them, that they live in the big city where they feel the influence of radical elements." He pacified them somewhat by sending Furutani into Central California where he was shown how Chavez was targeting his efforts against vulnerable Nisei farmers and forcing some of them out of business. Then Uno went on to Los Angeles where members of the JACL staff took him to meet black and Chicano leaders and learn of their aspirations. Somehow, Uno knew, he had to steer JACL on a middle course that would win the backing of the conservative and moderate backbone of the organization as well as the young activists who shared a deep empathy for the downtrodden and underprivileged. "I don't think I was entirely successful," Uno says now. "Neither side was willing to give. The posters didn't come down, at least not immediately, although I told the staff I didn't think they had a place in a JACL office. Later on, some of the Central California chapters threatened to secede from the national organization, but we managed to keep the organization together."

What this episode revealed was that the Los Angeles office was operating semi-autonomously with little or no accountability to the national director in San Francisco. In fact, it was discovered later that the policy-setting National Board had set down no hard and fast guidelines for the Southern California activists who had been given a virtually free hand to do what they judged to be best for JACL.

The crisis was not solved to anyone's satisfaction; it merely simmered down and was succeeded by a new issue resulting from Mike Masaoka's decision to end his professional connections with JACL. Masaoka had represented JACL full-time, then part-time in Washington for a quarter century. His consulting business for Japanese firms was going well but JACL was taking an inordinately large part of his energies. He felt it was time for a change. Under ordinary circumstances hiring a successor would have been no more than routine, but Masaoka had made the Washington position an extremely powerful one. In many instances, he, rather than the elected president, was looked upon as JACL's spokesman. Many regarded him as the man behind the scenes who made JACL function. He had a large part in setting JACL policy. His opinions were gospel to old-time JACLers; younger members, particularly the Southern California activists, felt Masaoka's thinking was outdated and were anxious to put a progressive of their choice in Washington.

Several Sansei applied for the job. One of them was David Ushio of Salt Lake City, who had virtually grown up with JACL. His father, Shake Ushio, a Utah native, had been a League stalwart during the difficult war years. David had spent two and a half years in Japan as a Mormon missionary, returned to Brigham Young University for a degree in political science, and was looking for a job when Raymond Uno called one day in 1971 to invite him to apply for a position as Masaoka's assistant. After Masaoka's resignation took effect, Ushio would be in line to take over the Washington office. All the candidates were interviewed by the personnel committee, but Masaoka had the final word. He picked Ushio.

Thus Ushio became Masaoka's hand-picked successor, which meant he automatically had the blessings of Masaoka supporters and the hostility of detractors. Even before Ushio reported for work he came under fire on a number of counts: He was from an area with few Japanese Americans and was unfamiliar with West Coast problems; he was a Mormon which made him insensitive to civil rights; his wife Judy was a Caucasian which meant he had no pride in his race. (She can trace her ancestors on both sides to the Mayflower.) It didn't seem to occur to his detractors that much of their criticism was applicable to the Mike Masaoka of 1941. Some even suggested the "Utah Mafia" was taking over JACL—Uno as president and Masaoka and Ushio in Washington.

As Masaoka's assistant Ushio proved an apt student. Moreover, he was a take-charge type, a self-starter who needed no prodding. He moved unbidden into any vacuum that needed filling. The campaign to repeal Title II was nearing a climax and Ushio had a part in the lobbying—transforming the grass-roots support being generated by the chapters into commitments in Congress. Ushio also undertook much of the preparatory work for the 1972 national JACL convention in Washington, D.C.

Then, unexpectedly, it was announced Mas Satow would retire on his sixty-fifth birthday on February 14, 1973, and a new national director would be sought. That news posed a dilemma for Ushio. He explains it this way:

> I had to make a decision as to whether I wanted to stay on as Washington representative with relative autonomy, or go after the national director's job which at the time was pretty much a caretaker situation. If I opted to stay in Washington, I was taking a chance on the way the national directorship would evolve. I had no objection to working under the right kind of boss. It became clear to me that we were going to get one of two types of national directors. One would be a radical activist, a "power to the people" type. I couldn't live with that. The other possibility would be a director who would sit back and be just another caretaker. I needed as my boss somebody who I could be totally compatible with, being the aggressive advocacy type that I am, but no one like that was on the scene. That left one other possibility if I were to remain with JACL. I could go after the job myself.

As Ushio floated the idea, he received conflicting advice. Some urged him to take over the organization to revive it and keep it out of the hands of the radicals. Others urged him to remain in Washington; they would take care of the problem in San Francisco. Ushio decided to seek the directorship.

Mike Masaoka complains that Ushio made the decision without ever consulting him. Masaoka naturally felt slighted. He felt his protégé still had much to learn. When they finally got around to talking about it, Masaoka urged Ushio to stay in Washington. This is the way Ushio remembers the conversation: "He told me it would take five years to get the situation in San Francisco straightened out. He said that in Washington I could get involved in lots of interesting things, and after a couple of years I could move into some important government job if that's what I wanted. He said I would get cut up in JACL politics on the West Coast and he didn't want to see that happen to me." It was a prophetic observation but, unmoved by Masaoka's fatherly advice, Ushio in the spring of 1972 flew to San Francisco to meet with JACL's personnel committee. Ushio was told the proceedings would be confidential and he was urged to be totally candid. Nonetheless, the meeting was taped. Soon afterward Los Angeles JACLers heard that Ushio had told the personnel committee he would fire the entire Pacific Southwest district office staff if he was chosen national director.

This was a distortion of what Ushio had said. He had been expressing his views on the need for staff professionalism, the need for members of the national staff to concentrate on policies laid down by the national organization, leaving local community issues to local chapters. The entire staff would have to be members of his team carrying out national policy under his direction, he said. Then Ushio was asked what he would do if the staff wasn't performing. "I'd fire them," Ushio replied. The Los Angeles staff had not been mentioned in this part of the discussion. The question was meant only to probe Ushio's management philosophy. But the rumors proved damaging.

The leaked implication that the Los Angeles office lacked professionalism was deeply resented by the staff. Furutani retorted that Ushio's knowledge of the Japanese American community, its problems, its experiences and its youth had been acquired by picking the brains "of the JACL unskilled staff" prior to going to Washington, whereas his people had been working for years with young Japanese Americans.

The personnel committee, after eight hours of discussion, voted four to three to recommend Ushio over the other leading candidate, Alan Nishio, student counselor at California State University at Long Beach, with excellent professional and community credentials. What tipped the balance in Ushio's favor was his Washington experience. In a year of aggressive activity he had performed well and learned a great deal about JACL. Nishio's acquaintance with the League was limited. But there is no reason to believe he would not have served JACL well. In fact, there were many who said the ideal setup would have Nishio as director in San Francisco with Ushio running the Washington office. The final decision was to be made by the National Council at the convention in Washington in late June. Nishio did not attend but his cause was championed vigorously by the paid Pacific Southwest district office staff, the propriety of which was questioned by some, and most of the Southern California delegates, who had been persuaded that Ushio was determined to fire their people without giving them a chance.

In heated debate on the National Council floor, the past president Enomoto, the retiring president Uno and the future presidents Henry Tanaka, Shig Sugiyama and Jim Murakami all spoke up for Ushio. But Robert Takasugi, a Los Angeles attorney who was to become the first Nisei federal judge on the mainland, contended that Nishio was "five times better" than Ushio. Furutani got up to say that the JACL staff had to work with blacks, Chicanos and whites and "Dave does not have this experience." Pacific Southwest staff members Ron Hirano, Victor Shibata, Ron Wakabayashi and Furutani all endorsed the statement of Jeffrey Matsui, district director, that his faith in the JACL leadership had evaporated and he could not work under Ushio.

Murray Sprung, a Caucasian member of the New York City chapter, put the issue in perspective: "A motion was made to accept the recommendation of the personnel committee. A 'No' vote is a vote of no confidence in the personnel committee and Executive Board. I am sorry to hear a threat from the younger members that says in effect, 'If you don't think the way we do, we quit.' "

At one point several delegates asked that the personnel committee's tapes be made public. This led to another long discussion over the ethics of revealing confidential proceedings. When Ushio said he had no objection, the tapes were played. Later, Furutani said: "The staff had heard second-hand about the goings-on of the personnel committee. What we heard astonished us and shook some foundations of friendship and trust. At the convention things became clarified and some things we heard were taken out of context, but the bulk of the nonsense was verified when the staff heard the tapes."

But not all agreed it was nonsense. The vote to support the personnel committee's report—to hire Ushio—was 56½ for, 26½ against. Matsui, Furutani, Wakabayashi, Shibata and Hirano had taken their positions; now there was nothing to do but resign, leaving the Southern California operation in charge of Drew Tamaki, the office manager. Uno was deeply saddened. "It was a real loss for JACL," he observed later. "Those young men had leadership qualities, they were bright and articulate and could relate to other young people. But the backbone of JACL, the ones who were going to sustain JACL come hell or high water, were moderates who couldn't be pushed too fast."

But it is likely that north-south rivalries rooted in JACL's earliest years had at least a part in the controversy. More than a year earlier the National Board had made a tentative commitment to move national headquarters from San Francisco to the Japanese Cultural Center scheduled to be built in Los Angeles as part of the Li'l Tokyo urban renewal project. Since the final decision to move headquarters would have to be made by the National Council, Shigeki Sugiyama, governor of the Northern California–Western Nevada District Council, launched a move to keep the offices in San Francisco. The San Francisco chapter had a ten thousand dollar surplus from the 1956 convention set aside to build a national headquarters building, and with this nest egg it was easy to persuade the northern chapters to back the project. At the 1972 convention the Northern California–Western Nevada district presented the idea of launching a national drive to raise up to a half-million dollars to build a headquarters in San Francisco. Caught off guard, Southern California didn't oppose the idea. But to lose the opportunities both to capture headquarters and to put their own man in it was not easy to take for many from the south.

The controversy left scars that were to plague Ushio throughout his tenure. It was understood Ushio would move to San Francisco in December and spend some time learning about headquarters operations in a gradual transfer of authority before Satow stepped down officially on February 14, 1973. But there were some who interpreted Ushio's early arrival as unseemly impatience to seize the reins. This kind of sniping continued throughout Ushio's stormy administration despite his impressively productive efforts to modernize the organization and bring vitality and relevance to its program.

One of the few 1972 convention events not marked by contention was a testimonial luncheon honoring Satow's quarter century of selfless service to JACL. Some of his friends and associates who were too busy to attend the entire convention flew to Washington for the day to take part in the tribute. When Satow joined the staff in 1947 JACL was made up of twenty-five chapters, only two of which were on the West Coast, and approximately thirty-one hundred members. In the ensuing years it had grown to ninety-four chapters spread out coast to coast with upward of twenty-seven thousand members, making JACL the largest Japanese American organization. The accolades showered on him that day were warm, lavish and sincere.

The convention also saw Raymond Uno, with no little relief, turn over the presidency to Henry Tanaka, a soft-spoken, thoughtful forty-nine-year-old former Oregonian who had become a social worker in Cleveland. Tanaka called the first meeting of his National Board in San Francisco in September. Ushio was on hand to outline his proposals for staff functions. Ushio took on himself overall responsibility for all JACL programs, fiscal affairs and staff, public relations, financial development and high-level liaison with government and other organizations. In addition Ushio was to serve as JACL's spokesman. As chief executive officer he would direct a volunteer organization with an annual budget approaching $300,000. This was a weighty responsibility for someone still in his mid-twenties with little practical experience in the Japanese American community. But Ushio did not lack for either confidence or ambition and Tanaka's Board expressed no hesitation about approving his ideas.

After his retirement Satow moved smoothly into a new career as senior adviser to the president of the Sumitomo Bank of California. Chiz stayed on with JACL and indirectly this created one of Ushio's first major problems as director. What Ushio found as he got deeper into the directorship was the sort of incomplete and confusing records that could be expected of any organization that for decades had been run by two people like a family operation. In some cases important information existed only in memory or penciled notes. Chiz Satow could make the system work. She knew where to locate documents or find a letter, and that had been adequate over the years. But it would not work in the kind of fast-moving JACL that Ushio had in mind. He needed efficiency and systematic office management. Chiz treated Ushio like a son, but he was convinced she had to be replaced regardless of the consequences.

After consulting with Tanaka, Uno, Enomoto and others, Ushio took a deep breath and sat down with Chiz one day. He expressed appreciation for all that she and her husband had done for JACL and told her the organization well might have failed to survive without them. And then, as gently as he could, he told her that as the new director he needed his own team, that he would have to make changes that she would find unpleasant. As Ushio recalls it, her response was: "I understand, David."

But many old-time JACLers didn't. They were uncomfortable with change and resented Ushio for being its agent. They felt the removal of Chiz Satow before she wanted to step down symbolized the ruthlessness of the new administration. The generation gap also showed. Old-timers would have been more tolerant of change if Ushio had taken more pains to cultivate them, consult them, stroke them. He thought he was showing the proper deference for his elders, but in their estimation it wasn't enough.

Ushio was on the telephone frequently with Tanaka in Cleveland during this period, seeking his counsel while steering JACL in a new direction. During the later Satow years, after most of the great postwar battles had been won, JACL had focused increasingly on membership services—a health insurance program, the credit union, group travel to Japan, bowling tournaments, national and district conventions, testimonial banquets. This kind of activity brought in memberships. It was what was wanted by the members, whose median age advanced each year, and it is what they got. (Even Saburo Kido, it will be recalled, sought to leaven the prewar JACL's political thrust with an extensive fraternal program.)

While recognizing the need for membership services, Ushio was more interested in making JACL a nationally important force operating on the cutting edge of social and political change, taking a strong advocacy position on all human rights issues while looking after the interests of Japanese Americans. To this end he became visible at conferences and meetings outside the Japanese American community. He cultivated the media, issued press releases and called press conferences, and soon found himself being sought out for comment on various issues of the day as the spokesman of the Japanese American minority. Ushio's reaction to President Gerald Ford's pardon in 1974 of Richard Nixon for his part in the Watergate scandal offers an example. Ushio issued a strong statement charging Ford had erred. Some JACLers protested that their organization had no business speaking out on such a subject. Ushio replied that a basic national issue was involved affecting all Americans, that the pardon denied the people the opportunity to let due process judge Nixon's actions and that Japanese Americans had an obligation to speak out. The explanation did not satisfy members who felt JACL should address itself primarily to local and narrow ethnic issues. Tanaka supported Ushio's action, but it left President-elect Shigeki Sugiyama uneasy. Speaking broadly, Sugiyama explained:

> My feeling was that JACL should concentrate on developing more cohesion among Japanese Americans, developing pride in their heritage, seeking out those things that would serve community needs. On some issues I got the feeling JACL was following other minorities just because they were mouthing the ideology of the times regardless of whether it was relevant to, or served the direct interests of, Japanese Americans. Certainly JACL needed to work with other organizations, but I felt its primary concern was its own constituency and its own community.

In a sense, Ushio was steering JACL on an activist course that paralleled Warren Furutani's despite differences in their styles. Ushio worked through the system; he wore tie and jacket and eschewed street vulgarities that some activists delighted in using for shock effect. Who, then, was Ushio representing? Was Ushio reflecting the views of JACL's rank and file? Or was he leading and shaping opinion? He knew, of course, that the elected leadership set League policy and the paid staff implemented it. But sometimes he walked a tightrope. He was too aggressive to wait long for direction, impatient with the slow process of the leadership seeking a consensus. He was by nature inclined to want to show the way and expect the League to follow, growing exasperated if it failed to do so. To the above questions Ushio responded in these words:

> A lot of the way in which the national organization functioned was a direct reflection of the personality and the interests of the director. I can't get around that. But I did take pains at board meetings, at conventions, to lay out what I thought was the direction the organization ought to go. And hearing no objection, I assumed silence to mean consent. A person will take as much latitude as he is allowed to take. I made a lot of judgment calls on my own and, to Hank Tanaka's credit, he backed me completely.

All this activity gave Ushio the kind of high visibility that did not sit well with some of the membership. Trouble was building up and the situation didn't improve when Shigeki Sugiyama took over the presidency at the 1974 convention in Portland, where a record $562,900 budget was adopted.

Sugiyama, born in Alameda, California, in 1927, had just entered high school when his family was evacuated in 1942. His father had been a gardener. In 1944 Shig left the family at the Topaz, Utah, WRA camp and went to Ann Arbor, Michigan, where he completed high school. He was a freshman at the University of Michigan in 1946 when he was drafted. Sugiyama applied for Officer Candidate School and was commissioned as a second lieutenant in the infantry. He served in Japan, Korea, Germany and Vietnam as well as at various United States posts and retired in 1966 with the rank of lieutenant colonel. He returned to the San Francisco Bay area and earned his bachelor's degree in political science and master's in public administration while employed by the U.S. Civil Service Commission.

Sugiyama's entry into JACL coincided with the rise of student activism. He feels that his military background, particularly his service in Vietnam, was at the root of much opposition that followed him up the ladder of the national JACL hierarchy.

Dissatisfaction with the Sugiyama-Ushio administration erupted at the quarterly meeting of the Pacific Southwest District Council in February of 1975. There was a long discussion of Ushio's performance—errors of both commission and omission. Most of the charges were vague. District Governor Masamori Kojima tried vainly to pin down what the complainants meant by "misfeasance, malfeasance or non-feasance in office," the constitutional grounds for impeaching officers. Clearly, however, the hostility was directed at Ushio, who could be fired but not impeached. Criticizing the roundabout effort to oust Ushio by attacking Sugiyama, Dr. Roy Nishikawa, a former national president, declared: "Here we're saying he's guilty and if not fired, let's impeach the National Board." The upshot was approval of a resolution to impeach Sugiyama. Fourteen chapters voted for the resolution, five abstained, one chapter split its vote and seven chapters were absent. The resolution listed nine counts in a "bill of particulars" but they were so vague and sketchy that there was a demand, after the vote, that they be written more specifically.

The Pacific Southwest District Council meeting was held February 9, 1975. *Pacific Citizen* reported the impeachment demand in its issue dated February 21. Sugiyama, who lived in Washington, D.C., got the first details about the movement to unseat him when the mailman delivered the newspaper. On February 23 he sent a memo to members of the National Board, chapter presidents and staff saying he had just learned of the accusations of misconduct through *Pacific Citizen,* had seen no specifics that he could respond to and intended to continue to direct and support the work of the staff who "I believe have worked most conscientiously and faithfully" during the past two years.

Then Sugiyama and Ushio hurried out to Los Angeles to meet with the district council, which was convened on March 9 to prepare a bill of particulars to support the impeachment motion. But first the delegates voted 13 to 9 to rescind the motion to impeach and replace it with a request to the National Board to investigate the Southwest district's concerns. That opened the way for a six-hour session at which various grievances were aired with Sugiyama and Ushio responding. It would require too much space to recount here all the details, many of them picayunish.

Citing two of the charges will suffice to illustrate the nature of some of the lesser complaints. Ushio thought the logotype JACL displayed on its stationery, featuring a shield and an eagle, was a bit dated. On his own, he asked artist Hats Aizawa to come up with a more modern design. Some members demanded to know by what authority Ushio had acted. He replied that he felt this was an administrative detail within his authority. Under pressure Ushio agreed to go back to the old design after the new stationery was used up. But when membership cards went out imprinted with the new design, Ushio was accused of insubordination. Ushio also was criticized for failing to produce transcripts of the 1974 convention minutes. Satow had made it a practice to transcribe the tapes himself, typing away night after night as he listened to the tapes. Ushio was aware of the importance of the minutes, but other projects higher on his priority list kept getting in the way.

District Governor Kojima put the controversy in perspective in a *Pacific Citizen* column. He wrote in part:

> Today we are a different organization from that run by Mike Masaoka, Mas Satow and other old-timers. . . . Mas kept the administration to a minimum of paperwork, records and directives. His administration was mainly through personal contacts with key JACL leaders throughout the country. A phone call to his office always seemed to reach him; it didn't go through layers of secretaries and administrative assistants. A problem from a distant chapter reached his ears and back came the suggested solution.
>
> JACL replaced him with a modern, PR-oriented, urbane and corporate-chic national director. Directives, memos, stats, copies, and other impersonal missives poured out from the national staff in line with the new mode of administration. A new breed of administrator—put it on paper, confirm phone calls with memoranda of understanding or else "it's no go," all information to flow upward to headquarters and all decision to flow downward, national director to relate to chapters through district governors and regional staff, all communications to officers and members in corporate-correct warm words with no real personal feeling, *interface* rather than personal communications.
>
> JACL had updated its national staff with a much-needed modern administrator able to deal with complexities of taxes, state and federal regulations, modern accounting, real estate, a million dol-

> lar budget, etc., that were not present or ignored in the past. JACL, however, neglected to update its membership or its structure.
>
> What works in a modern impersonal bureaucracy didn't in our unsophisticated chapter, district and national structure based upon a combination of personal commitments, feeling of ethnic affinity and volunteerism.
>
> The present administration is impersonal and members had no shared basic assumptions on which to interpret its words and actions. Lacking such elements the members could not relate to the national director and his massive outflow of communications, except in the familiar terms of "personal power play."
>
> Though the debate in the special district meeting of March 9 was couched in terms of issues . . . members felt the national president was defaulting on most major issues by the policy of "benign neglect." In his absence the national director was reaching important policy decision through administrative directives. . . . In essence, the Pacific Southwest District Council members are demanding grassroots and participatory democracy in JACL.

In reality, this perceptive analysis was as much a criticism of the membership's inability to adapt to the requirements of the times as it was an indictment of Ushio's insensitivity to the human needs of the organization and the inability of the president, isolated in Washington, to maintain closer touch with the staff on the other side of the continent.

Briefly, the controversy threatened to become a regional issue, with the Northern California–Western Nevada and the Central California district councils condemning the attack on the administration, and the Midwest District Council endorsing Pacific Southwest's efforts. But by the time the National Board met in San Francisco in June to consider the charges, much of the heat had dissipated. Since he was a "defendant," Sugiyama turned the chair over to former president Jerry Enomoto, and Raymond Uno was named parliamentarian. Also on hand as participants without vote were the past presidents Henry Tanaka and Dr. Roy Nishikawa. In a fifteen-hour session the Board considered a hundred-page transcript of proceedings in the first Pacific Southwest district session, and fifty questions posed by the Midwest district. Then it adopted a resolution by 14 votes to 2, saying, "there is insufficient cause to recommend the resignation or termination" of Ushio. But the resolution went on to say that "certain shortcomings and deficiencies of the national director had been revealed" and that the National Board was partly responsible for not being more definitive in setting policies for Ushio's guidance, and urged that steps be taken to correct the problems.

A month and a half later JACL celebrated one of its happiest milestones—dedication of its half-million-dollar national headquarters building at 1765 Sutter Street in San Francisco. The bitterness of the Sugiyama-Ushio hearing, the first event held in the then undedicated building, was all but forgotten as new and old-time JACLers gathered. The three-story neo-Victorian building, designed by San Francisco architect Noboru Nakamura, remarkably was virtually debt-free. A committee headed by Steve Doi, Tad Hirota and Mas Satow had headed the fund drive, in which 5,500 contributors gave some $450,000—an average of about $80 per donor. In addition there were many gifts of furnishings and decorations. Despite the tragedy of the Evacuation, the Nisei and Sansei generally speaking had made an astounding economic comeback.

JACL's third national president, Dr. Terry Hayashi, a spry octogenarian, and Jack Kusaba were cochairmen for the fete. Mike Masaoka came out from Washington to deliver one of his red-blooded, flag-waving speeches. Sab Kido was too ill to attend but former presidents like George Inagaki, Frank Chuman, Jerry Enomoto and Hito Okada came to celebrate with Mas and Chiz Satow and remember the hard old days. Dave Ushio, showing no scars from his recent ordeal, managed to pick up the inevitable loose ends and coordinate all the activity. But for some the occasion was a last hurrah. Less than eight months later, Satow was dead at age sixty-eight; he was born on Valentine's Day and died on March 3, the Japanese-Girls' Day festival. More than a hundred of his thousands of friends were named honorary pallbearers.

Six months after the dedication Ushio submitted his resignation to Sugiyama. Ushio's letter said all the proper things and Sugiyama responded similarly. Noting that Ushio has been a controversial figure, Sugiyama wrote: "During a period of change and turmoil within our nation and within JACL, we can be proud —David's positive leadership has resulted in new opportunities being opened for JACL programming at national and international areas heretofore untapped."

Ushio's resignation was to become effective at the end of the fiscal year on September 30, 1976. He would handle the national convention in Sacramento in July and give the League an opportunity to find a successor. There were many reasons for Ushio's decision. He and his policies had been vindicated by the National Board hearing. But the demands of the job kept him away from his family. He was now thirty years old and had to decide whether he wanted to remain a big fish in a little pond—"If I stayed another five years I probably would remain the rest of my life"—or go out and try to be a big fish in a big pond. When an opportunity came to join Jimmy Carter's presidential campaign staff, Ushio left two weeks before the scheduled departure date but returned for a month after the election to help the acting director, Don Hayashi.

Two weeks after announcing his resignation, a public-relations ploy launched months earlier bore fruit. The Seattle chapter had discovered that Executive Order 9066, which President Roosevelt had signed on Feburary 19, 1942, to authorize the Evacuation, had never been rescinded. Legally, it had died along with other wartime measures when war was formally proclaimed ended on December 31, 1946. But E.O. 9066 had not been specifically laid to rest. Although there was no legal need to do so, it seemed like a good idea to get that done. The Seattle chapter got Governor Daniel J. Evans of Washington to bring the situation to White House attention. Meanwhile, Wayne K. Horiuchi, who by then was JACL's Washington representative, started a campaign to get various citizens to write to the White House expressing astonishment that E.O. 9066 still existed and urging President Ford to expunge it from the books. The target date was February 19, 1976, the thirty-fourth anniversary of the bill's signing.

Weeks passed, and nothing happened. What took place next was an object lesson in the way things are accomplished in Washington. Horiuchi stirred up interest among members of Congress and kept in touch almost daily with the White House staff. Ushio telephoned other Washington friends. George Wakiji, a VISTA public information officer, learned that Dr. Myron B. Kuropas, whom he had known in Chicago, had recently joined the White House staff to look after ethnic matters. Wakiji got him interested in E.O. 9066. Eventually, all this pressure converging from many directions began to have an effect. On Tuesday, February 17, Horiuchi was told by Kuropas to stand by. Ushio, in San Francisco, caught a late-night plane to Washington. About noon on the eighteenth, word came from the White House that President Ford would sign a proclamation rescinding E.O. 9066 at 11:30 A.M. the next day. The White House asked Senators Dan Inouye and Hiram Fong and Congressmen Spark Matsunaga, Patsy Takemoto Mink and Norman Mineta to be present. Ushio and Horiuchi were given the responsibility of inviting other Japanese American guests to the ceremony. They had only a few hours to make up a list, extend the invitation by telephone and arrange for security clearance. When someone couldn't be reached on the first call, chances were that there wasn't time to call back. There were a good many bruised egos over the invitation list. Many JACL leaders were left out. Some who may or may not have been deserving were invited.

It would have been easy for Ushio to plead confusion due to pressure. But when asked later about the invitation list, he replied forthrightly: "Those people were there because they had been strong supporters of JACL and they had been strong supporters of mine. We were in position to make choices between people who were stabbing me in the back and people who were bending over backwards to help me."

Most of the West Coast delegates flew the "red-eye specials," the planes that leave San Francisco and Los Angeles late at night and reach Washington just in time to disgorge their passengers into the morning traffic jam. They and the other Japanese Americans, some twenty-five in all, were escorted into the Cabinet Room. Before television and press cameras President Ford made a brief statement, then signed the proclamation titled "An American Promise." It read:

> In this Bicentennial Year, we are commemorating the anniversary dates of many of the great events in American history. An honest reckoning, however, must include a recognition of our national mistakes as well as our national achievements. Learning from our mistakes is not pleasant, but as a great philosopher once admonished, we must do so if we want to avoid repeating them.
>
> February 19th is the anniversary of a sad day in American history. It was on that date in 1942, in the midst of the response to the hostilities that began on December 7, 1941, that Executive Order No. 9066 was issued, subsequently enforced by the criminal penalties of a statute enacted March 21, 1942, resulting in the uprooting of loyal Americans. Over one hundred thousand persons of Japanese ancestry were removed from their homes, de-

tained in special camps, and eventually relocated.

The tremendous effort by the War Relocation Authority and concerned Americans for the welfare of these Japanese Americans may add perspective to that story, but it does not erase the setback to fundamental American principles. Fortunately, the Japanese American community in Hawaii was spared the indignities suffered by those on our mainland.

We now know what we should have known then—not only was that evacuation wrong, but Japanese Americans were and are loyal Americans. On the battlefield and at home, Japanese Americans—names like Hamada, Mitsumori, Marumoto, Noguchi, Yamasaki, Kido, Munemori and Miyamura—have been and continue to be written in our history for the sacrifices and the contributions they have made to the wellbeing and security of this, our common Nation.

The Executive Order that was issued on February 19, 1942, was for the sole purpose of prosecuting the war with the Axis Powers, and ceased to be effective with the end of those hostilities. Because there was no formal statement of its termination, however, there is concern among many Japanese Americans that there may yet be some life in that obsolete document. I think it appropriate, in this our Bicentennial Year, to remove all doubt on that matter, and to make clear our commitment in the future.

Now, therefore, I, Gerald R. Ford, President of the United States of America, do hereby proclaim that all the authority conferred by Executive Order No. 9066 terminated upon the issuance of Proclamation No. 2714, which formally proclaimed the cessation of the hostilities of World War II on December 31, 1946.

I call upon the American people to affirm with me this American Promise—that we have learned from the tragedy of that long-ago experience forever to treasure liberty and justice for each individual American, and resolve that this kind of action shall never again be repeated.

President Ford had a key role in another event pushed by JACL to right an injustice. For years, some JACLers had been bothered that their organization had done nothing to support Iva Toguri, who had been convicted of treason in 1949 for allegedly making propaganda broadcasts for Japan in World War II. Much evidence had surfaced since her trial to indicate that she had been convicted unjustly. But the League did nothing about it until 1969 when it passed a resolution in her support. No action was specified and nothing further happened until the convention in 1974 at Portland. Edison Uno, long a determined knight jousting on behalf of unpopular causes (he wrote a *Pacific Citizen* column titled "Minority of One") introduced a resolution that extended JACL's apology to her "for long silence and inaction," offered the League's services in seeking to correct the miscarriage of justice and instructed the organization to ascertain whether she would accept JACL's help. In anticipation of Uno's resolution, Ushio had gone to see Toguri's San Francisco attorney, Wayne Collins, Sr., who never hesitated to refer to JACLers as "a bunch of jackals" for having cooperated in the Evacuation. Collins would have nothing to do with Ushio until he shouted: "Don't hold it against me. I was just a kid when you had your trial and if you had presented a better case Iva wouldn't need a pardon now." After that Collins agreed to let Ushio talk with Iva.

JACL organized a National Committee for Iva Toguri headed by Dr. Clifford Uyeda and including many of the younger members who had pushed for repeal of Title II. They published a booklet titled *Iva Toguri: Victim of a Legend,* shedding new light on the case, and were successful in drumming up widespread editorial and popular support for a presidential pardon. A major boost came from Senator-elect S. I. Hayakawa, far from popular with many of the younger JACLers working hardest for Iva Toguri, who urged President Ford to grant the pardon. In the final crunch, JACL called on White House friends for help once more. In one of his last acts as President, Ford granted Iva Toguri a full and unconditional pardon.

Now, JACL was ready to take on still another major challenge.

XXIII

Search for Redress

The two-year term of James F. Murakami, inaugurated as twentieth JACL president at Sacramento in 1976, was dominated by a single issue that came to be called redress. That was the idea that the federal government should be made to compensate Japanese Americans in some unspecified manner for the injustice of the Evacuation. Murakami was the last president-elect to take over the top job after a two-year "apprenticeship." This procedure having proved unwieldy, the organization went back to letting chapter delegates to the biennial national convention choose a leader who would assume the presidency immediately. Like the four men who preceded him in office, Murakami was a member of the postwar generation. He had been graduated from high school at the Amache WRA camp in Colorado, going on to win a degree in engineering at the University of California at Berkeley. He operated his own electrical and mechanical engineering and consulting firm in Santa Rosa, California.

Redress was an issue that had been simmering under the surface of JACL for years. Even while the Evacuation was under way in 1942 there had been talk of seeking compensation for material losses from the federal government after the emergency ended. "Reparations" had been discussed in the first postwar JACL convention in 1946, and the subject kept cropping up sporadically after that. But for the most part, until more than a quarter century after the Evacuation, the Nisei were too preoccupied with the routine matters of establishing families and careers to do much about demanding recompense for their distressing experience. In a sense, the conditions that led to revival of the reparations issue within JACL were not unlike the situation that led to strong anti-JACL feeling within the WRA camps; in both instances, once the urgency and demands of daily life slackened, there was time to ponder and brood about injustices. But years after war's end, many found that time had eased the pain and healed the scars, and the prospect of reopening old wounds was not inviting. There was a substantial element within the JACL membership that was willing to let the past rest in peace.

But many younger members, who had no firsthand knowledge of the Evacuation, were convinced the chapter could not be closed until the United States government had been made to pay —money, they contended, was the American way of compensating victims of a wrong—for inflicting an injustice on an entire people. In 1970 they persuaded the national convention to approve a resolution calling for legislation to rectify "the worst mistake of World War II." Similar resolutions were passed in 1972 and 1974, and Ed Yamamoto of Moses Lake, Washington, worked hard to stir up interest. But nothing substantial came of them, causing Edison Uno, a lecturer at San Francisco State University, to complain that the JACL leadership was only lukewarm on the issue. Uno was the most active advocate during this period, traveling widely to argue before JACL chapters that the organization should make the federal government admit responsibility for false imprisonment, wrongful detention and denial of civil and constitutional rights, and that it should assume legal liability. Such action, Uno contended, would clear Nisei as a group of any question of loyalty, educate the general public about a historical episode that had been largely ignored, possibly prevent a repetition in some future emergency and provide money that would help fund community needs.

There were equally persuasive arguments against the program. It was contended that since so many members were hostile or at least indifferent to the idea, an all-out JACL push would divide the organization. A demand for monetary compensation would not only cheapen the sacrifice Japanese Americans had made in response to their government's wartime mandate, but well might provoke such a widespread public backlash that the educational objective would be negated. The Japanese American

Evacuation Claims Act of 1948, although providing woefully inadequate compensation for Evacuation losses, was a government admission that a wrong had been done, and a new campaign was likely to take so long and be so costly that other urgent JACL programs would suffer. It would be more meaningful if, instead of seeking compensation, JACL sought reversal of the Supreme Court decision in the Korematsu and Endo cases, which put the stamp of legality on the Evacuation.

The word "reparations" repelled many Nisei. It carried the connotation of payment extracted by victors in war from a defeated nation. Ironically, it was John Dean, the Nixon White House counsel disgraced in the Watergate scandal, who proposed a more suitable word. Addressing a JACL district convention in Los Angeles, Dean endorsed the movement and suggested the term "redress," which appears in the Constitution's First Amendment guarantee to citizens of the right "to petition the government for a redress of grievances."

When Uno died at age forty-seven just before Christmas in 1977, Dr. Clifford Uyeda, a retired San Francisco pediatrician, took up the campaign. As chairman of the JACL National Committee for Redress, Dr. Uyeda wrote thirty-five articles that were published in *Pacific Citizen* in an effort to create a consensus. His committee unveiled its redress proposal at the national convention in Salt Lake City in the summer of 1978. In essence, it called for payment of $25,000, tax-free, to each Japanese American forced out of General DeWitt's exclusion areas or to his survivors. Another hundred million dollars would be set aside in a trust fund to be administered for the benefit of Japanese Americans by a commission of Japanese Americans nominated by Japanese Americans. Persons of Japanese ancestry uprooted from Central and South America and incarcerated in the United States also would be eligible for payment.

The sum of $25,000 seemed modest enough as compensation for false imprisonment, but since some 120,000 individuals were involved, the total amounted to approximately three billion dollars. Such a staggering figure did not deter the delegates. Members of the National Council, representing all the chapters, voted unanimously to adopt the proposal as JACL's goal. But some individuals were disturbed by the emphasis on financial compensation. *Pacific Citizen*'s headline over the redress story read:

CONVENTION MULLS OVER REDRESS PROPOSAL: $25,000 PER DETAINEE

The committee's proposal, in addition to spelling out the monetary demand and the way it would be distributed, had mentioned that redress was being sought "to remind our nation of the need for continued vigilance and to render less likely the recurrence of similar injustice." But *Pacific Citizen*'s front-page story focused entirely on the monetary angle and made no mention of other objectives. Furthermore, despite Dr. Uyeda's warning that JACL's proposal was just a wish list that now would have to be presented to Congress and no one could tell what its reaction would be, many read the headline with visions of sugarplums dancing in their heads and precipitously assumed they were about to get a $25,000 handout from Uncle Sam.

Even before the convention ended there was evidence the redress program was in for a difficult time. At the last business session someone thrust an editorial from that afternoon's *Deseret News* in President Jim Murakami's hands and asked him to read it aloud. The *Deseret News,* usually reflecting the views of the Mormon Church, which had been friendly toward the Nisei, questioned the wisdom of seeking individual cash indemnities. Then it said: "One of the objectives of the action, says a JACL spokesman, is to attempt to deter future imprisonment of U.S. residents who have not been charged with any crime other than ancestry. But would such a deterrent really work in case of another surprise attack? Aren't there better resources, such as building solid relationships among Americans regardless of race? Certainly Japanese Americans have done remarkably well in this regard."

The delegates were jolted again a few hours later at the Sayonara Banquet. S. I. Hayakawa, junior United States senator from California, sat quietly at the head table as the prestigious Japanese American of the Biennium award was presented to Patrick Okura, a tireless veteran of many human rights campaigns. He was a worthy choice, yet there were some in the audience who wondered why Hayakawa was not receiving the award instead of waiting to be called to make the main address. During the preceding biennium more than three million Californians had cast their ballots for him. California, for more than a century the fountainhead of the nation's anti-Orientalism, had chosen this son of Japanese immigrants to represent it in the U.S. Senate. For pure impact on the national scene no other Japanese American had come close. Why hadn't he been chosen for JACL's gold medal? The answer became apparent when Hayakawa rose to speak. He launched into a lecture admonishing Japanese Americans to stop looking back and concern themselves with the problems ahead. Although he did not say it in so many words, he was telling the Nisei to forget about collecting compensation for past wrongs and devote JACL's energies to contemporary problems threatening the relations between the United States and Japan.

Newspapermen caught the incongruity of Hayakawa's remarks and questioned him after the speech. Next morning the *Salt Lake City Tribune* published a story, distributed nationwide by the wire services, that began: "The Japanese American Citizens League has no right to ask the U.S. government for reparations for Japanese American citizens placed in relocation camps during World War II, according to Sen. S.I. Hayakawa. . . . 'Everybody lost out during the war, not just Japanese Americans,' and the JACL asking for $25,000 in redress for each Japanese American placed in relocation camps was 'ridiculous'. "

JACL spokesmen quickly responded, quoting from the redress committee's booklet explaining their case: "Redress for the injustices of 1942–1946 is not just an isolated Japanese American issue; it is an issue of concern for all Americans. Restitution does not put a price tag on freedom or justice. The issue is not to recover what cannot be recovered. The issue is to acknowledge the mistake by providing proper redress for the victims of the injustice, and thereby make such injustices less likely to recur."

Murakami's administration was notable for two other developments. First was the search for a successor to David Ushio, who had announced his resignation on February 5, 1976. More than thirteen months later Karl Nobuyuki, then thirty-one years old, was selected from among sixteen applicants. Born at the Gila River WRA camp, Nobuyuki grew up in East Los Angeles and graduated from the University of Southern California. He was an administrator for the city of Gardena, California, specializing in writing grants applications, when he applied for the JACL post.

Nobuyuki and Ronald K. Wakabayashi, who succeeded him as national director, were associated in a drug abuse treatment program in which JACL had a strong role. While Wakabayashi was

JACL youth director in the Pacific Southwest district office, he and Nobuyuki made contact with young Sansei who were involved in drug abuse. The two organized the youths and their parents into a self-help program called Go for Broke, operating out of a storefront in East Los Angeles. Utilizing the efforts of this group as a vehicle, JACL was able to receive funding for a training program in drug-abuse work. Among the trainees were Nobuyuki, Wakabayashi, J. D. Hokoyama (who became Nobuyuki's assistant at JACL headquarters), John Hatakeyama (who became director of the Asian Pacific Mental Health Clinic for Los Angeles County), Craig Shimabukuro (later JACL's Pacific Southwest regional director) and Gary Uyekawa (now a physician's assistant). Out of this training course evolved the Asian American Drug Abuse Program, where Wakabayashi served for eight years before moving on to JACL headquarters. Pat Okura, who was a top-echelon National Institute of Mental Health official, was instrumental in getting federal funding for the drug program. Go for Broke's advisers included a number of individuals who were, or became involved in, JACL. Among them were John Sato (later Pacific Southwest regional director), Jerry Enomoto (former national president), Robert Takasugi, Alan Kumamoto (former JACL youth director) and June Okita.

The second event was the rededication on March 5, 1977, of the year-old national headquarters as the Masao W. Satow Memorial Building and the launching of a program to publish a history of JACL as a memorial to Satow. But even this well-deserved tribute became controversial when Sakuro Kido died a month later. There were many who contended Kido was "more deserving," although of course there is no way to quantify depth of dedication and service.

In view of the job ahead after adopting the redress proposal, the delegates in Salt Lake City in 1978 chose Dr. Uyeda to succeed Murakami. Among JACL presidents Dr. Uyeda was unique in that he had never headed a chapter or held district office. However, he had been named JACLer of the Biennium in 1976 in recognition of his efforts to win a presidential pardon for Iva Toguri, and for his chairmanship of a committee concerned with halting the slaughter of whales, an issue that stirred hostility against Japan which reflected on Japanese Americans. (See Appendix D for a list of JACLers of the Biennium.)

As political realities began to sink in, Dr. Uyeda presided over a gradual shift in the thrust of the redress proposal from a demand for three billion dollars from Congress to a request for a fact-finding commission to investigate the circumstances surrounding the Evacuation. The change did not come about without considerable acrimony, particularly on the part of those who continued to contend that money was the essence of redress.

John Tateishi, a teacher at San Francisco State College, was chairman of the Redress Committee when it came up with the new position. The committee's position was that the proposal voted in Salt Lake City constituted "guidelines" rather than a "mandate." In its new guidelines the committee dropped mention of any specific sum for redress. It endorsed the commission idea. It took the position that persons who had been subjected to the Evacuation should be compensated, but it was unable to suggest what would be an equitable amount for each individual. The committee also recommended that a substantial amount of money be made available to a foundation or trust. It would be controlled by a board dominated by Japanese Americans. Individuals could apply to the foundation for aid. It would also award grants to help retirement homes, provide scholarships for the study of constitutional issues and support worthy Japanese American community projects. JACL's inability to come up with a recommendation for specific monetary amounts only underscored the difficulty the commission would face in determining the form and amount of reasonable and equitable redress.

On August 2, 1979, a year after the action at the Salt Lake City convention, six senators jointly introduced a bill, S. 1647, whose short title was Commission on Wartime Relocation and Internment of Civilians Act. The sponsors were Democrats Dan Inouye and Spark Matsunaga of Hawaii, Alan Cranston of California and Frank Church of Idaho, and Republicans S. I. Hayakawa of California and James A. McClure of Idaho. Later they were joined as cosponsors by Democrats Bill Bradley of New Jersey, Mike Gravel of Alaska, Henry M. Jackson and Warren G. Magnuson of Washington, Patrick J. Leahy of Vermont and John Melcher of Montana, and Republicans Barry Goldwater of Arizona and David Durenberger of Minnesota. The bill's purpose was to establish a commission to review the facts surrounding the Evacuation and "recommend appropriate remedies."

Senator Hayakawa, who scorned JACL's original money-centered goal, could embrace S. 1647, telling the Senate: "My colleagues and I are calling for the establishment of a fact-finding commission in order to carefully investigate the question of wrong-doing by the federal government, and to make recommendations on the possible need for remedies. Nearly 40 years have passed since Executive Order 9066 was issued and a thorough look at the facts is long overdue."

A companion bill, H.R. 5499, was introduced in the House on September 28 sponsored by nine Democrats: Majority Leader Jim Wright of Texas, Majority Whip John Brademas of Indiana, Norman Mineta, Bob Matsui, Phil Burton and Glenn Anderson of California, Peter Rodino of New Jersey and Sidney Yates and Paul Simon of Illinois. More than 110 other congressmen, including 39 of the 43 from California, were listed as cosponsors. The bill was assigned to the Subcommittee on Administrative Law and Government Relations of the Committee on the Judiciary. It was chaired by George E. Danielson, who represented the Monterey Park area of Los Angeles County, which had a large Japanese American constituency.

JACL's position on these bills was formalized in San Francisco on November 10, 1979. First, the JACL Political Education Committee met to draw up recommendations to be presented to the Executive Committee. The Political Education Committee was chaired by Cherry Tsutsumida of Washington, D.C., governor of the Eastern District Council and top-level civil service administrator. Also at the meeting were Mike Masaoka; Kaz Oshiki, veteran administrative assistant to Congressman Robert W. Kastenmeier, a Wisconsin Democrat; Bob Kiyota, administrative assistant to Congressman Phil Burton; Ron Ikejiri, JACL's Washington representative; Dr. Jim Tsujimura, national JACL vice-president; Karl Nobuyuki; and two other members of the JACL staff. It was evident to them that a demand from a small and relatively unknown organization for three billion dollars was likely to be no more than a gallant but futile gesture regardless of its merit. It was a much more realistic strategy to ask Congress to authorize a presidential commission to review the entire history of the Evacuation, to determine whether a wrong had been done and, if it had, to propose an equitable form of redress. This recommendation was presented to the Executive Committee chaired by President Uyeda, and accepted unanimously.

Among the rank and file of the membership, as well as among outsiders, there were some who scoffed that it was obvious that a wrong had been committed, and saw the commission as a meaningless attempt to avoid the issue. But there was undeniable logic in getting Congress involved since it would be up to Congress to determine the form of redress.

John Tateishi said JACL would not inject discussion of compensation into the debate over the bills "because of an inconsistency of views among the JACL membership." In other words, the manner of redress would be left to the commission's recommendation since JACL wasn't sure about what it should ask for. Here again Hayakawa agreed with JACL, when he told the Senate: "The fact that there is controversy on this point [redress payments] explains why such a commission is necessary." Declaring JACL's new position was consistent with the Salt Lake City convention decision, Tateishi went on to explain: "It was felt the primary objective is to seek establishment of the commission and that the commission in turn would recommend compensation."

S. 1647 sailed through the Senate on May 22, 1980, after picking up a significant amendment in the Senate Committee on Government Affairs. It was brought out that approximately a thousand Aleut Native Americans had been evacuated from villages in the Aleutian Islands during the war and interned in makeshift quarters in southeastern Alaska, even though they had no ethnic or blood link with Japan, and they were included in the commission's study.

Congressman Danielson held hearings on June 2 at which, in addition to the original House bill, a second proposal (H.R. 5977) was considered. It had been introduced by Congressman Mike Lowry, a Washington Democrat, at the request of some Seattle Nisei including JACLers and provided for payment of fifteen thousand dollars to each evacuee plus fifteen dollars for each day he or she had spent in a camp. William Hohri of Chicago, representing an organization he called the National Council for Japanese American Redress, spoke for the Lowry bill, charging the study commission proposal was a "charade." Tateishi and Mike Masaoka presented lengthy testimony on behalf of H.R. 5499. The House approved H.R. 5499 on July 21, 1980, with 297 yeas, 109 nays and 45 not voting. There had been little doubt that the bill would pass, but some JACLers expressed dismay that as many as 109 members of Congress would vote against a simple proposal to examine history. On July 24 the Senate and House reached agreement on minor differences in their bills and sent the Senate version, which had been introduced first, to the White House. President Jimmy Carter signed it in a ceremony on July 31. Dr. Uyeda, Tateishi, William J. Yoshino and John Saito left the national convention then in session in San Francisco to fly overnight to Washington and attend the signing. Carter commented:

> It is with a great deal of pleasure I sign this legislation into law. The commission study is adequately funded. It is not designed as a witch hunt. It is designed to expose clearly what has happened in that period of war in our nation when many loyal American citizens of Japanese descent were embarrassed during a crucial time in our nation's history. I don't believe anyone would doubt that injustices were done and I don't think anyone would doubt that it is advisable now for us to have a clear understanding as Americans of this episode in the history of our country. . . . We also want to make sure their [the Commission's] efforts will prevent any recurrence of this abuse of the basic human rights of American citizens and also resident aliens who enjoy the privileges and protection of not only American law but of American principles and ideals.

But the preliminaries weren't over. There was the matter of naming the seven commissioners provided for by the law—three to be selected by the President and two each by the House and Senate. To accommodate various political interests, the law was amended to expand the commission to nine members, allowing the House and Senate to appoint three each.

President Carter named Dr. Arthur S. Flemming, chairman of the U.S. Commission on Civil Rights and Secretary of Health, Education and Welfare in President Eisenhower's cabinet; Joan Bernstein, former general counsel of the Department of Health and Human Services; and Judge William Marutani of the Philadelphia court of common pleas. The Senate picked Edward W. Brooke, former United States senator from Massachusetts, a Republican and a black; Hugh B. Mitchell of Seattle, who had been appointed to fill a vacancy in the Senate (1945–1946) and was later elected to two terms in the House (1949–1953); and Father Ishmail Vincent Gromoff, a Russian Orthodox priest who was one of the evacuated Aleuts. The House appointees were Arthur J. Goldberg, former ambassador to the United Nations and U.S. Supreme Court justice; Congressman Daniel Lungren of Long Beach, California, a Republican; and the Reverend Robert F.

Drinan, a Jesuit priest who was a five-term Democratic congressman from Massachusetts.

The distinguished makeup of the panel served as assurance that the commission would be taken seriously. For Japanese Americans the appointment of Judge Marutani was of particular significance. JACL had debated whether it would be wise to ask President Carter to name a Japanese American to the commission. It was argued that a Nisei would find it almost impossible to be objective. On the other hand someone who had experienced the Evacuation would be able to provide the commission with a special understanding of the subject. Ultimately JACL submitted five nominees, including Marutani, then fifty-four years old, a Nisei born in the little farming community of Kent just south of Seattle. He and his family had been evacuated to Tule Lake. Refused enrollment at the University of Colorado because of a Navy research project on campus, Marutani left camp to attend a small Methodist college in South Dakota. When he volunteered for naval pilot training he was turned down because of his ancestry. He joined the Army, was commissioned and saw service in occupied Japan. Marutani was graduated in law from the University of Chicago in 1953, joined the firm of MacCoy, Evans and Lewis in Philadelphia, served as national JACL legal counsel from 1962 to 1970 and was named JACLer of the Biennium in 1966 for his volunteer work with black civil rights activists. In 1975 he was appointed to the bench by Governor Milton Shapp. When Marutani stood for election in 1977 he led a field of twelve candidates with 194,615 votes.

The commission elected Joan Bernstein its chair and named Paul Bannai, the first Nisei to be elected to the California state legislature, as executive director. It opened hearings in Washington, D.C., on July 14, 1981. Bernstein set the parameters for the commission's inquiry: "The commission is not conducting an inquisition or a trial. Our intent is to seek to understand what happened, how and why. We need to understand how it was that the nation's military and civilian leaders decided to evacuate and confine approximately 120,000 people for no other reason than their ancestry. We need to examine what protections the law offered, and whether those protections need to be expanded. And finally, the commission must come to grips with the difficult, but crucial, question of redress."

A stream of former government and military officials, attorneys, sociologists and other academicians, religious and community leaders and Japanese Americans themselves—more than seven hundred in all—appeared before the commission as its hearings moved from Washington to Los Angeles, San Francisco, Seattle, Anchorage and Unalaska in Alaska, Chicago, back to Washington, then to New York and finally to Boston. The "what" of the Evacuation story was told in vivid, intimate and often moving detail by Japanese Americans who remembered the experience with excruciating pain. Many had refused to talk about their anger and frustration and humiliation for decades, had kept it all pent up until this opportunity arrived to speak to those who wished to hear, and now their stories gushed forth in an emotional flood of recollection that brought tears to the eyes of narrators and spectators alike. They spoke of rejection, of broken hearts and health, of precious possessions and opportunities lost, of friends and kin who had cracked under the pressure of the times. There was no doubt at all that great damage had been done.

The "how" and the "why" were more difficult to arrive at, but gradually understanding emerged. The tragedy of the Evacuation, it became apparent, took shape less from racially inspired malice—although there was plenty of that—than from ignorance, fear, timidity, insensitivity and the zeal of patriots who in rushing to defend their country forgot what America stands for. The racists were largely silent as the push for the Evacuation picked up momentum. They had crawled out from under the rocks only after the Japanese Americans were behind barbed wire, to clamor that they were being pampered in the camps, to demand that they be banished from the West Coast forever and stripped of their citizenship.

There was ignorance: no one in authority in Washington was knowledgeable about the Japanese American minority. Some of them were aware of their ignorance and sought the facts before war came. Curtis B. Munson of the State Department was assigned to learn what he could about Japanese Americans. Lieutenant Commander Kenneth Duvall Ringle was dispatched on a similar mission by Naval Intelligence. His son, Ken Ringle, has written that one of his father's most fiercely held beliefs was that "the overwhelming majority of Japanese Americans would prove loyal American citizens in any war with Japan—loyal despite racial discrimination against them as cruel as any this nation has produced." Few others held that opinion then, and not many were willing to listen. Munson's reports to Washington were in a similar vein. James Rowe, the Justice Department official most closely involved in the Evacuation, told the commission he never saw the Munson report. Nor was Ringle ever consulted by the Army before it ordered the Evacuation.

There was near hysterical fear: American forces had been caught asleep at Pearl Harbor and military commanders on the West Coast were determined to take any measure necessary to avoid a repetition of that debacle. Colonel Bendetsen, former assistant chief of staff of the Western Defense Command, told the commission there was a "very real and present danger" of a Japanese invasion of the West Coast. "If we had not turned back the forces [at Midway] there would no doubt have been an invasion of the West Coast because there was nothing to stop it," he said. Actually, the tide had begun to turn in April, 1942, when Colonel James H. Doolittle's planes took off from the carrier Hornet and bombed Tokyo. The Evacuation had just barely begun by that time. The Battle of Midway, in which Japan's naval forces were irreparably damaged, marked the beginning of the end. It was fought June 3–6, 1942. The Evacuation was not completed until October.

There was timidity: Attorney General Biddle had grave doubts about the legality of suspending the civil rights of Nisei and the necessity of the Evacuation. FBI Director J. Edgar Hoover had assured him Japanese Americans posed no security problem. Yet Biddle timidly deferred to Secretary of War Stimson, who was listening to his generals. Biddle wrote in his memoirs: "But I was new to the cabinet, and disinclined to insist on my view to an elder statesman whose wisdom and integrity I greatly respected."

There was insensitivity: no indiscriminate action was taken against German or Italian aliens or Americans of German and Italian extraction. When asked by Senator Brooke why the distinction between the Japanese enemy and Japanese Americans had been ignored by those considering the Evacuation, Bendetsen replied that "it was human nature." Even President Roosevelt, despite his record as a humanitarian and democrat, was culpable. Rowe told the commission what had been apparent to earlier students of the period: "I don't really think he spent much time on [the Evacuation issue]. It's a serious thing to say, but I think it was a minor thing to him." Former Assistant Secretary of War McCloy suggested that what was done to Japanese Americans was "retribution" for Pearl Harbor before he was challenged by Commissioner Marutani and withdrew the word in some confusion.

The defense presented by the officials most responsible for the Evacuation decision was predictable and, no doubt, sincere. They did what they as patriotic Americans thought was necessary to protect their country in a time of great peril. McCloy told the commission he believed the Evacuation was "reasonably undertaken and thoughtfully and humanely conducted." At another point he said the program had been "carried out in accordance with the best interests of the country considering the conditions, exigencies and considerations which then faced the nation."

If there had been serious consideration of the implications of the due process and equal protection clauses of the Constitution for the Evacuation, it was not brought out. Both clauses, obviously, were violated by the Evacuation.

A curious sidelight of the hearings was an attempt by a few to put Masaoka and JACL on trial. One witness, Frank Chin, charged JACL "created" the loyalty oath which WRA used to separate the "loyal" from the "disloyal." He told the commission: "They campaigned for the loyalty oath and a segregation camp for those who flunked it. The Army and the WRA administered it. And the FBI enforced it. . . . The JACL had no power over Japanese America before camp. No power of its own. The JACL became the Nikkei leadership at the government's pleasure, not by any form of popular Japanese American approval. The rift between the Japanese Americans was created by the government when they imposed JACL leadership and Mike Masaoka on the Nikkei."

The record, of course, supports little of this. When Masaoka sought to answer some of the charges, Chairman Bernstein assured him that neither JACL nor any other organization was on trial. The charges appear to have been made without, to borrow McCloy's language, "considering the conditions, exigencies and considerations" of the times.

Pondering the unremitting hostility JACL has faced from a small minority over the years, Judge Marutani in his *Pacific Citizen* column decried the "vicious and, at times, irresponsible and reckless attacks upon one's [fellow] ethnic member[s]" that he called "ethnic hara-kiri." Marutani observed that these "ethnic assassins" almost blindly attack their own "while they remain, or at least seem to remain, oblivious to those major forces in our society which currently seek to degrade an American because of race, religion, national origin and such other irrelevant factors." Marutani went on: "What is further troubling to us is that very often these ethnic assassins are tainted by the very same negative factors that they purport to condemn, namely clothing themselves with the aura of self-righteousness as they relentlessly pursue their nefarious destructive activities. . . . Can it be self-insecurity that can only be assuaged by sacrificing another of their own?"

As this is written, the commission is busily sorting through a vast mass of testimony in its search for conclusions. It could well find that despite the good intentions, the decisions made "in the best interests of the country" caused grievous harm to the principles that make that country uniquely great. But, as someone observed, determining the form that redress should take for the immediate victims will require a Solomon's wisdom.

JACL's long future will be profoundly affected by the commission's report and what Congress does with it. In a time of wholesale slashes in federal spending, any sizable monetary appropriation seems unlikely. Commissioner Dan Lungren in one of the earliest hearings warned that there is "not a body of support in Congress for financial redress." Senator Inouye has insisted that while he is not opposed to financial redress, the primary objective is to establish a historical and official record of what happened as a warning about what could happen again in times of stress.

Whatever the commission recommends, it is likely that Congress will be influenced in large measure by current factors unrelated to the Evacuation—inflation, for example, Reaganomics, federal budget deficits, trade disputes with Japan and the balance of payments, even the distress of the Detroit automobile industry. Redress is, of course, a matter that should be considered strictly on the issues: Was an injustice done to an American minority on a racial basis? If so, should the victims be compensated? And what form should redress take?

JACL has spent an inordinate amount of time, effort and capital on this program and a perception of victory is essential to make it all seem worthwhile. Two of JACL's three objectives—to educate the public and to help prevent any recurrence of such injustice—appear to have been achieved. Newspapers, news magazines and television gave extensive coverage to the redress hearings, recalling for the mass of Americans the tragedy of a long-ago chapter of history. Authors of future textbooks will have no excuse for ignoring or glossing over the Evacuation. There is no assurance, of course, that the United States will never again be guilty of a similar outrage, but at least the national consciousness has been raised. However, the third goal, monetary redress, is in doubt. And because of the emphasis JACL and others have placed on money, it is not likely the campaign will be seen as successful without substantial payment.

And after redress, what?

This is a question that the president elected in 1980, Dr. James Tsujimura, a Portland ophthalmologist, and the national director since 1981, Ronald K. Wakabayashi, must help answer for the future. There are many problems needing to be addressed. Numerous Nisei have retired or are approaching retirement. For better or worse, third- and fourth-generation Japanese Americans are drifting away from the ethnic community. What, if anything, is to be done about this development? And what sort of role should JACL seek within the growing Asian American population where a swiftly rising tide of Korean, Chinese, Filipino, Indo-Chinese and Pacific Islander immigrants has lifted their numbers far above that of Japanese Americans? Each of these ethnic groups has interests and problems unfamiliar to Japanese Americans, and pride that tends to keep each group independent. These are all significant issues, even though they lack the excitement of redress or the bitter urgency of the Evacuation.

In the last few years JACL has widened its horizons. A chapter has been formed in Honolulu and one in Tokyo among Nisei and Sansei living in Japan. Social contact has been made with the descendants of Japanese immigrants in Canada, Mexico and South America. In the summer of 1981 Charles Kubokawa, chairman of the JACL International Relations Committee, led a delegation to Mexico City for the first Pan-American Nisei Conference. This promises to become a useful forum at which descendants of Japanese immigrants in various Western Hemisphere nations can talk about their problems and successes.

The national budget is creeping toward the million-dollar mark. There is serious talk of a new course for JACL. Masaoka has suggested that JACL should move its headquarters to Washington, D.C., to maintain a watchdog role over government, while developing regional and local programs through the chapters to satisfy the diverse interests and needs of a membership that is no longer homogeneous. This idea is supported by others, among them the former JACL president Henry Tanaka.

JACL's first half century was eventful, significant, often confused but certainly far more productive than its founders ever dreamed possible. The only thing sure about the organization's next fifty years is that they will be totally unlike the first fifty. The nation itself has changed, but the change that has come over its Japanese American minority is far more profound. Fifty years from now, it will take an objective observer such as *Rashomon* lacked, quietly watching the drama unfold, to tell us what happened and what it all means.

Appendix A

Mike M. Masaoka's Statement Before the Tolan Committee, San Francisco, February 21, 1942

On behalf of the 20,000 American citizen members of the 62 chapters of the Japanese American Citizens League in some 300 communities throughout the United States, I wish to thank the Tolan committee for the opportunity given me to appear at this hearing. The fair and impartial presentation of all aspects of a problem is a democratic procedure which we deeply appreciate. That this procedure is being followed in the present matter, which is of particularly vital significance to us, we look upon as a heartening demonstration of the American tradition of fair play.

We have been invited by you to make clear our stand regarding the proposed evacuation of all Japanese from the West Coast. When the President's recent Executive order was issued, we welcomed it as definitely centralizing and coordinating defense efforts relative to the evacuation problem. Later interpretations of the order, however, seem to indicate that it is aimed primarily at the Japanese American citizens as well as alien nationals. As your committee continues its investigations in this and subsequent hearings, we hope and trust that you will recommend to the proper authorities that no undue discrimination be shown to American citizens of Japanese descent.

Our frank and reasoned opinion on the matter of evacuation revolves around certain considerations of which we feel both your committee and the general public should be apprised. With any policy of evacuation definitely arising from reasons of military necessity and national safety, we are in complete agreement. As American citizens, we cannot and should not take any other stand. But, also, as American citizens believing in the integrity of our citizenship, we feel that any evacuation enforced on grounds violating that integrity should be opposed.

If, in the judgment of military and Federal authorities, evacuation of Japanese residents from the West Coast is a primary step toward assuring the safety of this nation, we will have no hesitation in complying with the necessities implicit in that judgment. But, if, on the other hand, such evacuation is primarily a measure whose surface urgency cloaks the desires of political or other pressure groups who want us to leave merely from motives of self-interest, we feel that we have every right to protest and to demand equitable judgment on our merits as American citizens.

In any case, we feel that the whole problem of evacuation, once its necessity is militarily established, should be met strictly according to that need. Only these areas, in which strategic and military considerations make the removal of Japanese residents necessary, should be evacuated. Regarding policy and procedure in such areas, we submit the following recommendations:

1. That the actual evacuation from designated areas be conducted by military authorities in a manner which is consistent with the requirements of national defense, human welfare, and constructive community relations in the future;

2. That, in view of the alarming developments in Tulare County and other communities against incoming Japanese evacuees all plans for voluntary evacuations be discouraged;

3. That transportation, food, and shelter be provided for all evacuees from prohibited areas, as provided in the Presidential order;

4. That thoroughly competent, responsible and bonded property custodians be appointed and their services made available immediately to all Japanese whose business and property interests are affected by orders and regulations;

5. That all problems incidental to resettlement be administered by a special board created for this purpose under the direction of the Federal Security Agencies;

6. That the resettlement of evacuees from prohibited areas should be within the State in which they now reside;

7. That ample protection against mob violence be given to the evacuees both in transit and in the new communities to which they are assigned;

8. That effort be made to provide suitable and productive work for all evacuees;

9. That resettlement aims be directed toward the restoration, as far as possible, of normal community life in the future when we have won the war;

10. That competent tribunals be created to deal with the so-called hardship cases and that flexible policies be applicable to such cases.

Although these suggestions seem to include only the Japanese, may I urge that these same recommendations be adapted to the needs of other nationals and citizens who may be similarly affected.

I now make an earnest plea that you seriously consider and recognize our American citizenship status which we have been taught to cherish as our most priceless heritage.

At this hearing, we Americans of Japanese descent have been accused of being disloyal to these United States. As an American citizen I resent these accusations and deny their validity.

We American-born Japanese are fighting militarist Japan today with our total energies. Four thousand of us are with the armed forces of the United States, the remainder on the home front in the battle of production. We ask a chance to prove to the rest of the American people what we ourselves already know: That we are loyal to the country of our birth and that we will fight to the death to defend it against any and all aggressors.

We think, feel, act like Americans. We, too, remember Pearl Harbor and know that our right to live as free men in a free nation is in peril as long as the brutal forces of enslavement walk the earth. We know that the Axis aggressors must be crushed and we are anxious to participate fully in that struggle.

The history of our group speaks for itself. It stands favorable comparison with that of any other group of second generation Americans. There is reliable authority to show that the proportion of delinquency and crime within our ranks is negligible. Throughout the long years of the depression, we have been able to stay off the relief rolls better, by far, than any other group. These are but two of the many examples which might be cited as proof of our civic responsibility and pride.

In this emergency, as in the past, we are not asking for special privileges or concessions. We ask only for the opportunity and the right of sharing the common lot of all Americans, whether it be in peace or in war.

This is the American way for which our boys are fighting.

Appendix B

Saburo Kido's Address at the Emergency JACL Meeting, San Francisco, March 8, 1942

Fellow Members:

This most likely may be the last National Council meeting we shall be able to hold for a long time to come. In a sense, this is a farewell gathering for most of us since we shall not know where we will be scattered, nor for how long. It is with a heavy heart that I say these words.

Events have transpired in rapid succession since we last met at Portland, Oregon, in 1940. Soon after we returned to our respective homes from that memorable convention, Japan definitely announced her military alliance with the Axis powers. Then in July, 1941, after Japan invaded Indo-China, our government took a positive stand by placing embargoes against that country and by freezing Japanese assets in the United States on July 28, 1941.

An Emergency National Board meeting was held in San Francisco on August 10, 1941. At that time a recommendation was made to secure the services of a full-time secretary. We fully realized the gravity of the situation arising from international tension and we thus took the step which necessitated the raising of $5,000 for the office of National Secretary and Field Executive. We were fortunate that Mr. Mike Masaoka, who was then chairman of the Intermountain District Council, was available for this newly created office. I am sure you all agree with me that we made an excellent appointment, and that we have attained excellent results with the meager funds at our disposal.

I shudder to think how helpless we would have been if we did not have the services of a full-time secretary. Mr. Masaoka has been working day and night, traveling wherever he is needed most, in all sections of the Pacific Coast. His contacts with the various governmental agencies have been most valuable. He has relayed important information to the chapters, and his efforts at coordinating their activities have helped to maintain the morale of the Japanese communities. Through his efforts and through the splendid operation on the part of you officers and leaders of the chapters, our organization has come to be recognized as the representative body of the Nisei in this country.

When the first ominous signs pointed to possible Japanese-American hostilities, we began to make preparations to mitigate the blows which may be directed against us because of our Japanese extraction. All our chapters swung into public relations work. It is a fact that everyone worked hard to meet the emergency, although many of us were lulled into overconfidence because of the friendly expressions extended us by our American friends.

It has been our constant fear that race prejudice would be fanned by the various elements which have been constantly watching for an opening to destroy us. They included many of our economic competitors and those who believe this country belongs to the "whites." Many of them wanted to indulge in the unpatriotic pastime of using us as a political football in this hour of America's greatest peril.

We had expected some form of persecutions in the various sections of the country. The experience of the first World War made us anticipate such a course of events. On the other hand, we were counting on the better understanding we thought we had created. We all had expected that the public officials, at least, would serve as a buffer against possible mass hysteria. We never dreamed that such a large number of them would ride on the band wagon, to reap political benefit out of this abnormal condition. We hoped that such a thing could not happen in America again. We know now that disillusionment was in store for us.

Today we are preparing to go into temporary exile from the homes in which we were born and raised, or which we have purchased through the small income we have saved. The very foundations which have taken years to build up are being torn from under us. Many of you are wondering where our constitutional rights have flown to. Most of us still cannot believe that we, citizens of this country, have been placed ahead of "alien enemies" for evacuation from military areas.

When we hear our erstwhile friends of peaceful days, those who praised us to the skies as model citizens, brand us more dangerous than the so-called "enemy aliens," we cannot help but wonder if this is all but a bad dream.

The past few weeks have been a regular field day for those who have awaited for the day to "clean up the Japs." When many of our friends of long years standing begin to entertain doubts about us, it is a bitter pill to swallow. One cannot help but realize how lonesome we are today.

Certain fundamental rights are guaranteed to all persons, but especially to citizens, in both our State and Federal Constitutions. We are today witnessing the spectacle of some state agencies trampling upon these rights in utter disregard of these laws. I am confident that the day is coming when those who are responsible for these outrageous violations of our rights will be ashamed of their conduct. We hope the thinking citizens will appreciate the principles which are at stake with us American citizens in this crucial test.

Even in our darkest hour, we are grateful to find that we still have friends who have faith in our loyalty, who believe that we are sincere when we say America is our country and we shall be glad to serve her in any capacity to win this war. Our friends are under pressure themselves, but they have remained true to us when we needed them most. They have furnished us the courage and strength to retain our self-respect and to continue to have faith in the noble ideals upon which this country has been founded.

When President Roosevelt was compelled to issue his orders whereby the military commanders were authorized and directed to prescribe military areas from which any or all persons may be excluded, and with respect to which the right of any person to enter, remain in, or leave shall be subject to whatever restrictions the Secretary of War or the appropriate military commander may impose in his discretion, it was a confession on the part of the state and local governments that they were unable to enforce the law to protect and assure us personal safety.

It seems to me that the Federal Government and the military authorities are ordering evacuation in order to prevent mob violence from running rampant, thereby interfering with the successful operation of the war. I have implicit confidence that we are being asked to go into exile not because we are dangerous as potential "fifth columnists" or "saboteurs," but because of the prospects of lawlessness of certain segments of citizenry.

Ever since the declaration of war, we have been grateful to our Federal Goverment for the fairness with which our case has been handled. We are glad that we can become the wards of our government for the duration of war. We already have been assured of humane treatment and full protection of our property rights.

In all our judgments and decisions, we have adopted the policy of selecting the course which will produce the most good for the largest number. In view of the existing threats of vigilantism and lawlessness, we have decided that evacuation under military supervision is the wisest course. Those of you who can afford to take independent action by going to new lands should do so. But we believe that you should not enter into the neighboring states in any large numbers. What is dangerous for California, Oregon, or Washington is dangerous for Idaho, Colorado, Utah, Arizona, and other neighboring states. Furthermore, we should not jeopardize the welfare of those who already have settled in that area and who are enjoying amicable relationships.

No matter where you go, unless it is in small numbers, you will be in constant danger of arousing unfavorable reactions. This is the reason why we are urging one and all to wait for the military authorities to make the necessary preparations. We still have hopes that areas will be created in each state so that aliens and citizens forced to evacuate will be resettled within the state where they have been residing and to whose wealth they have contributed by long toil and efforts.

As patriotic citizens and law-abiding residents, we should be willing to place our future into the hands of the Federal government. Both the Presidential order and the statements from Gen. De Witt, who is the military Commander of this area, have made it clear that everything possible will be done for our welfare.

This matter of evacuating at least 120,000 residents under non-violent conditions is unprecedented. Germany and other nations under dictatorship have ruthlessly uprooted peoples from their homes and transplanted them to new lands. But as far as America is concerned, we hope this will be the first and last such mass evacuation.

There are numerous complicated problems which must be solved if a humane and just evacuation is to be carried out. We should do our utmost to help the authorities. Undoubtedly many phases of the difficulties to be met will not come to their attention, as a measure to avoid confusion.

Many of you are worried about the care of expectant mothers; also those who are bedridden or who are afflicted with infections or contagious diseases; and those who are in hospitals at the present time. Many of us are wondering whether we can use our own cars to the reception centers, such as Owens Valley, and then have the government help us dispose of the car. We are wondering what we should do with our household furniture; what means of transportation will be provided, and a host of other similar questions.

Most of us will be able to live a few months on our own means, but the large marjority will have to become the wards of the government if this war and our exile is to last for any length of time. It is necessary to ascertain whether any person will be permitted to go to the interior area created for the Japanese regardless of their means. After all, money is not of much concern when our personal safety is at stake.

During the course of your deliberations on matters pertaining to this vital question of evacuation, we must give some time to the future of our organization. Out of the little infant organization brought into this world in 1930 at Seattle, Washington, we have our full-grown JACL, flowering to maturity in a sudden spurt in this hour of emergency. The leadership of the Japanese communities was expected to fall into our hands within the next five or ten years, but the sudden turn of world events has placed that full responsibility upon our shoulders almost overnight.

We must now answer some pertinent questions. Should we continue to function despite the fact that a large number of us may become the wards of the Federal Government? If so, where will our headquarters be located? How will we finance our organization? Should we keep on publishing our official organ, The Pacific Citizen?

I may say here that the individual chapters most likely will disintegrate unless each community is permitted to resettle as an entity.

My personal opinion is that we should continue to function because there are important missions to be carried out. Our people are going to be scattered to the four corners of this nation. We should serve as a clearing house in order that we may be able to keep in touch with one another.

As the only non-denominational organization now existing in the Japanese communities and on a national scale, the JACL will not fail to get recognition by the government, especially for its role in keeping up the morale of the Japanese people.

We must send speakers to the Middle West, the South, the Atlantic seaboard, and other parts of the country to regain our good name and reputation. If nothing is done to counteract the impression which is being created by many of these public officials who are enjoying the grand picnic of trampling upon the weak and defenseless, we shall remain forever a despised group.

Never in the thousands of years of human history has a group of citizens been branded on so wholesale a scale as being treacherous to their own native land, regardless of racial descent. We question the motives and patriotism of such men and leaders who intentionally fan racial animosity and hatred.

It is possible that those of the Atlantic seaboard and in Washington, D.C., are wondering what specimen of human deviltry we are, considering the amount and persistence of falsehoods being circulated against us. It would be important for several of our leaders to visit our President, his Cabinet members and the law-makers, and thus serve as an exhibit of the quality of our Nisei citizenry.

Fellow members, no matter whatever we may do, wherever we may go, always retain your faith in our government and maintain your self-respect. Let us keep our chins up despite all the travesty being committed upon our good name and rights. We are going into exile as our duty to our country because the President and the military commander of this area have deemed it a necessity. We are gladly cooperating because this is one way of showing that our protestations of loyalty are sincere.

We have pledged our full support to President Roosevelt and to the Nation. This is a sacred promise which we shall keep as good patriotic citizens.

The sacrifice which we have been called to make is just as great as that which our selectees have been called to make, for ours is the call to quietly uproot ourselves from all that we know and hold dear and to make our way into a wilderness of which we know not. Ours is not a spectacular front-page type of duty to country, but rather a kind of "behind the lines" service which we have borne: "WE ALSO SERVE" must be our badge of courage in these trying days, for we also serve, each in his own way, this country of which we are so fond. What greater love, what greater testimony of one's loyalty could anyone ask than this: leave your homes, your businesses, and your friends in order that your country may better fight a war?

When we leave let us leave with a smiling face and courageous mien. Let us look upon ourselves as the pioneers of a new era looking forward to the greatest adventure of our times. Let us conquer whatever frontiers may await us with the same fortitude and patience as did our fathers and mothers who contributed more to the development of the west than most of us realize. Let us serve our country in the hardest way possible for us to serve, keeping in mind that we have the same objective in mind as a hundred and thirty million other Americans, the ultimate and complete victory of democracy's forces.

Appendix C

Japanese Americans of the Biennium, honored by JACL for their contributions to the prestige of the Nisei in America and their influence on an area of American life

1950—Mike M. Masaoka, Washington, D.C., JACL's Washington representative

1952—Minoru Yasui, Denver, attorney and human rights activist

1954—Hiroshi Miyamura, Gallup, N.M., winner of the Congressional Medal of Honor in Korea

1956—George Inagaki, Los Angeles, floral industry leader

1958—Bill Hosokawa, Denver, newspaperman

1960—Representative Daniel K. Inouye, Honolulu, first Nisei to be elected to Congress

1962—Minoru Yamasaki, Detroit, architect

1964—Henry K. Kasai, Salt Lake City, a naturalized Issei, civic leader

1966—Representative Patsy Takemoto Mink, Honolulu, first Nisei woman to be elected to Congress

1968—Norman Y. Mineta, mayor of San Jose, Calif.

1970—Dr. Paul I. Terasaki, Los Angeles, medical scientist

1972—Congressman Spark M. Matsunaga, Honolulu, for his role in repeal of the Emergency Detention Act of 1950

1974—Raymond S. Uno, Salt Lake City, civic leader

1976—Michi Weglyn, New York City, author of *Years of Infamy*

1978—Patrick K. Okura, Washington, D.C., federal mental health official

1980—Dr. Harvey A. Itano, San Diego, Calif., in the field of medicine and science for his discovery of the causes of sickle cell anemia; George Nakashima, New Hope, Pa., in the fields of arts, literature and communication for his work as a furniture designer; Dr. Minoru Masuda, Seattle, in the fields of education and humanities for his work in community mental health

Appendix D

JACLers of the Biennium, selected in recognition of contributions to the strength and growth of the Japanese American Citizens League

1956—Abe Hagiwara, Chicago, and Jerry Enomoto, San Francisco
1958—Mrs. Sue Joe, Long Beach, Calif., and Kumeo Yoshinari, Chicago
1960—Joe Kadowaki, Cleveland
1962—Frank Oda, Sonoma County, Calif.
1964—Fr. Clement, Downtown Los Angeles
1966—William Marutani, Philadelphia
1968—Takeshi Kubota, Seattle
1970—Dr. Roy Nishikawa, Wilshire, Los Angeles
1972—Helen Kawagoe, Gardena Valley, Calif.
1974—Dr. James Tsujimura, Portland
1976—Dr. Clifford Uyeda, San Francisco
1978—Ed Yamamoto, Moses Lake, Wash.
1980—John Tateishi, San Francisco

Notes and Sources

Chapter I—Much of the material about the earliest Nisei is from the book *Nisei,* also by the author. Dr. Tom Yatabe, George Kiyoshi Togasaki, Dr. Kazue Togasaki, Jimmie Sakamoto and others were interviewed at length. Yatabe's recollections published in the December 23, 1955, issue of *Pacific Citizen* were helpful. The files of Sakamoto's newspaper, the *Japanese American Courier,* preserved at the University of Washington library in Seattle, were consulted. Surviving issues of *Nikkei Shimin,* the publication of the San Francisco New American Citizens League, were also consulted.

Chapter II—In 1980 the author interviewed Masao Igasaki in a Los Angeles nursing home and Miya Sannomiya in a retirement home, in the company of Charles Kamayatsu and Harry Honda, and also talked with Bob Okazaki and Suma Sugi Yokotake in Los Angeles. The files of the *Courier* provided many details about the convention. In the 1960's JACL's official newspaper, *Pacific Citizen,* published Saburo Kido's memoirs serially, and they provided many details which were supplemented by conversations with Kido and his wife, Mine.

Chapter III—Suma Sugi Yokotake supplemented the stories about her mission carried in *Pacific Citizen,* written by Kido and Mary Oyama Mittwer. Kido had a large file of letters from Tokie Slocum which he used in writing of Slocum's efforts.

Chapter IV—Kido's memoirs, Jimmie Sakamoto's *Courier,* and a lengthy interview with Toshio Hoshide all contributed to this chapter.

Chapter V—Copies of the few remaining issues of *Nikkei Shimin* provided details. The author was a member of the *Courier* staff that put out *Pacific Citizen* in Seattle in the 1930's.

Chapter VI—Files of the *Courier* and *Pacific Citizen,* as well as newspaper clippings in the scrapbook kept by Clarence Arai's widow, Yone Arai Bartholomew, provided details.

Chapter VII—The author attended the 1936 convention in Seattle, meeting people like Kido, Walter Tsukamoto, Mas Satow, Tamotsu Murayama and Sim Togasaki for the first time. Kido's memoirs and the files of the *Courier* backstopped personal recollections.

Chapter VIII—The *Courier*'s files were supplemented by recollections of Mike Masaoka, Sim Togasaki and numerous others.

Chapter IX—Saburo Kido was interviewed extensively in the late 1960's to supplement his memoirs. After his death, his widow provided human insights into Kido's life. All the JACL leaders mentioned in the latter part of this chapter were interviewed at the time *Nisei* was written.

Chapter X—In a taped interview in 1978 George Roth related details of the Anti-Defamation League's activities. The Tolan Committee report provides a complete transcript of its hearings. The *Seattle Times* and the *Post-Intelligencer* carried details of the unhappy school-secretary episode.

Chapter XI—Detailed minutes of the 1942 emergency meeting were kept, and these were consulted. Eke Inouye, shortly before his death, and other Nisei in the Idaho Falls area told the author of their experiences. Masao Satow recalled inviting John J. McCloy to dinner during many reminiscing sessions with the author.

Chapter XII—General DeWitt's *Final Report,* a 618-page book published in 1943 by the U.S. Government Printing Office, provides many details about the Evacuation. Vicky Mikesell, George Inagaki, Minoru Yasui and Gordon Hirabayashi were interviewed about their experiences. Guyo Tajiri, Takayoshi Okamoto and others corresponded with the author about their recollections.

Chapter XIII—Ben Yoshioka's impressions of Li'l Tokyo were carried in *Pacific Citizen.* Hito Okada provided details of JACL's financial problems in a long interview. Milton Eisenhower was interviewed at length for this book by Harry Takagi.

Chapter XIV—The author was among those attending the emergency conference in Salt Lake City. His recollections supplement the detailed information available in the convention minutes—120 legal-size pages, single-spaced.

Chapter XV—Etsu Masaoka, Neil Fujita and Martha Kaihatsu told their stories in the course of long interviews. The furor created by Questions 27 and 28 is covered in almost every publication about the Evacuation.

Chapter XVI—*Pacific Citizen* carried detailed accounts of the sordid Dies Committee activities as well as the story of JACL's efforts to help in the relocation program. Guyo Tajiri provided insights into her husband's editorship, and Hito Okada offered details about formation of the JACL Credit Union.

Chapter XVII—Harold Ickes kept a detailed diary which is preserved in the National Archives. Professor Yukio Morita of Aichi Prefectural University in Nagoya, Japan, published a booklet of portions pertinent to the Japanese American experience. Philip Glick, WRA solicitor, produced a series of memoranda discussing the constitutional basis of the WRA program; these also are preserved in the National Archives. Gordon Hirabayashi and Minoru Yasui provided personal recollections. *Pacific Citizen* is the source of material about the other test cases leading to reopening of the West Coast, and the 1944 JACL conference.

Chapter XVIII—The 1946 convention minutes, supplemented by recollections of various individuals, are the source of most of the material in this chapter. Misao Sakamoto and Yone Arai Bartholomew related their postwar experiences.

Chapter XIX—Many sources, all acknowledged in the text, went into the writing of this chapter. Harry Honda was particularly helpful in providing information about his longtime friends, Mas and Chiz Satow.

Chapter XX—The author has been associated with *Pacific Citizen,* off and on and in one capacity or another, since it was edited in Jimmie Sakamoto's *Courier* office in Seattle. The author served for a time on the *Pacific Citizen* Board, and his Frying Pan column has been a *Pacific Citizen* fixture since 1942. Harry Honda and Guyo Tajiri also provided details.

Chapter XXI—An impressive number of publications have resulted from the JARP program. In addition to those listed in this chapter, some of the more ambitious ones are *East Across the Pacific: Historical and Sociological Studies of Japanese Immigration and Assimilation,* edited by Hilary Conroy and T. Scott Miyakawa; *The Economics and Politics of Racial Accommodation: The Japanese of Los Angeles, 1900–1942,* by Dr. John Modell; *The Japanese American Community: A Study of Generational Changes in Ethnic Affiliation,* by Professor Darrel M. Montero. Scores of scholarly papers and Ph.D. dissertations have been based on JARP research. George Inagaki, Pat Okura and Yone Satoda were the subjects of lengthy interviews. The author also was associated many years with Shig Wakamatsu in the Japanese American Research Project.

Chapter XXII—Raymond Uno, David Ushio, Shig Sugiyama and others were the subject of long taped interviews from which much of the material in this chapter was developed. *Pacific Citizen* carried detailed accounts of the "impeachment" episode.

Chapter XXIII—The author was present at both the 1978 and the 1980 conventions, when much of the activity covered in this chapter took place. *Pacific Citizen*'s thorough accounts of the redress commission's hearings supplemented documents and other reports.

Index